CITIZENSHIP BETWEEN ELECTIONS

CITIZENSHIP BETWEEN ELECTIONS

An Inquiry Into
The Mobilizable American

JAMES N. ROSENAU

THE FREE PRESS
A Division of Macmillan Publishing Co., Inc.
NEW YORK

Collier Macmillan Publishers
LONDON

The Free Press
A Division of Macmillan Publishing Co., Inc.
866 Third Avenue, New York, N.Y. 10022

Collier-Macmillan Canada Ltd.

Library of Congress Catalog Card Number: 73–16907

Printed in the United States of America

printing number
1   2   3   4   5   6   7   8   9   10

Library of Congress Cataloging in Publication Data

Rosenau, James N
  Citizenship between elections.

  Includes bibliographical references.
  1. Political participation--United States.
2. Political psychology. I. Title.
JK1118.R67 1974   320'.01'9   73-16907
ISBN 0-02-926970-9

In memory of WNR
always attentive, never mobilized

CONTENTS

Chapter 8
THE BALANCING OF ATTITUDES   321

Chapter 9
THE STRUCTURE OF PERCEPTIONS   341

Chapter 10
THE INFLUENCE OF PRESENT RESPONSIBILITIES   387

LIST OF FIGURES

LIST OF TABLES

PREFACE

If it seems contradictory to describe a volume as large as this one as exploratory, it is nonetheless accurate. The focus is on a dimension of political participation that has not been previously examined, either theoretically or empirically, and I have thus had to start fresh, both in the conceptual organization of the subject and in the analysis of the unique data I was fortunate to acquire. The book is lengthy, not because it provides a definitive discussion of a complex subject, but because it takes a first look at a neglected set of phenomena that are so extraordinarily complex that it seemed advisable to range freely over the theoretical and empirical terrain. I have spared the reader most of the twists and turns in my thinking and have skipped over innumerable possibilities for additional analysis of the data. So little is known about the dimension of citizen behavior examined here, however, that parsimony proved unattainable.

The importance and neglect of the subject also serves to justify the analytic procedures employed. My treatment of the empirical materials is likely to cause methodological purists to wince. The analysis relies heavily, though not exclusively, on data derived from a mail questionnaire that was administered in 1964. The purist will surely question—as do I—the reliability of such data, and even more the use of simple statistical tests, the interpretation of very low but significant correlations, and the utility of findings about citizen behavior that occurred a decade ago, before Vietnam, Kent State, Watergate, and all the other events that have since rocked American society. I do not deny the legitimacy of these questions. On the contrary, I believe that an interview survey is likely to be more reliable than a mail questionnaire, that complex data reduction techniques might have been used instead of cruder correlational methods, that low correlations are not especially informative even when statistically significant, that I might have interpreted the data without using tests of significance as guides, and that it would be useful to compare the findings with those from other data sets and other points in time. Yet, one has to begin somewhere and proceed in some fashion. Having lucked into some unique data on an important and neglected topic via a 73 percent response to a 10-page, 246-variable mail questionnaire, I chose not to cling to methodological purism. Given the paucity of our knowledge about citizenship between elections, I saw the empirical materials as a marvelous opportunity, although others might see them as a methodological nightmare.

So I make neither extravagant claims nor apologies for the data and the way they have been treated. From the start I eschewed the use of data reduction techniques and opted for a more extended analysis because it seemed to me that too little was known about these phenomena to risk losing important and unanticipated information. The data are so voluminous, however, that some uniform basis for distinguishing between more meaningful and less meaningful findings seemed necessary, and the .001 level of statistical probability was chosen for this purpose. Similarly, while I recognize that many things have changed in American life and politics since the data were gathered, I have not been deterred by the argument that the data may be obsolete. My concern here is with the recurring and not the deviant patterns of politics and, as a result, I have tried to examine these data at a level of generality that is not bound to narrow periods of time.

The reader, of course, may not consider this aspect of participation as important or neglected enough to justify my procedures. I hope, however, that this exploratory inquiry will foster further, and more methodologically tight, inquiries into the topic, perhaps pursuing some of the findings uncovered here.

The dimension of political participation that I see as having been neglected is rooted in the fact that citizen participation in public affairs often, or always, occurs in an interactive situation. For most active citizens there is an activator—another citizen, an organization, or a public official who evokes the behavior that we call participation through an appeal for support. The bulk of the growing literature on participation neglects this interactive characteristic and considers attentive and active citizens to be those who follow the course of public affairs, discern a need for action, and then voluntarily undertake to establish first-hand contact with public affairs through various forms of behavior. To be sure, such citizens are not necessarily treated as rational actors who are free to act or not to act, depending on the costs and benefits they calculate to flow from their action or inaction. Most inquiries recognize that participation emanates from sources which may render it non-rational. The social background of the participator, his sense of efficacy, his level of information, his degree of satisfaction with the political system, his personality, his organizational memberships, his attitudes toward issues, his community's norms with respect to the appropriateness of being politically active, his rights and privileges as a citizen and the structural features of his polity that encourage or inhibit participation—these are only a few of the more salient variables that have been examined as sources of attentive and active citizenship. Whatever the sources that may be identified, however, the resulting behavior tends to be seen as self-initiated. It is widely assumed that once a citizen becomes attentive to public affairs, he will subsequently participate in them on his own. But attentiveness does not necessarily lead to action. Any leader of any organization, even one comprised of highly concerned citizens, will affirm that most of the membership cannot be counted on to respond to calls for action at any given time.

In short, to view citizens as responsive to antecedent conditions is not to treat them as responsive to specific stimuli. To see them as provoked to action by their socio-economic status and other environmental circumstances is not to posit them as reacting to specific appeals for support. To trace the interaction of variables is not to analyze the interaction between mobilized citizens and those who mobilize them. And it is these specific stimuli from mobilizers appealing for support that we have in mind when we refer to a neglected dimension of participation.

Upon reflection, the fact that participation tends to be treated as self-initiated rather than as responsive behavior and/or interaction is somewhat startling. The political process is generally seen as sustained by the aggregation of support, and while some of this support may be self-initiated, most of it is generated through the efforts of mobilizers, be they spirited citizens, organizational leaders, politicians, and/or public officials. Or, if this is an overstatement, it is at least an open question whether most participation is self-initiated or evoked. Equally commonplace is the notion that politics involves "the production of intended effects," but again this basic orientation remains unexplored. Or at least it is the rare inquiry that examines the participatory acts of citizenship with a view to determining the extent to which they are the products of what another actor intended.

Admittedly I may have exaggerated somewhat the neglect of the interactive dimension of political participation. As will be seen in Chapter 2, a few studies that view participation as mobilized behavior do exist, the best known probably being those that focus on the role of candidates, parties, and mass media in mobilizing people to vote. But aside from studies of voters and elections, the foregoing characterization of the literature is not much exaggerated. The number of investigations, empirical or theoretical, that view participation between elections as responsive or interactive behavior is miniscule in comparison to those that presume self-initiation. Stated more precisely, studies that examine *both* the stimuli of mobilizers and the responses of mobilizees (i.e., the participating citizens) in nonvoting situations are virtually nonexistent.

Some of the reasons for the neglect of the interactive context of participation are not difficult to discern. In the first place, the long-range factors that shape the behavior of citizens are complex, numerous, and difficult enough to comprehend without the additional task of probing the immediate stimuli to action. Second, and perhaps more important, tracing the production of intended effects empirically is extraordinarily difficult (as one can never be sure that they would not have occurred in the absence of the stimuli considered to evoke them), and constructing a research design that allows for the observation of such interactions is hard to achieve other than in a simulation laboratory and may require a great deal of luck. Third, our democratic beliefs lead us to value the volunteered, self-initiated acts of citizens more than those that are mobilized. Discussions of the impact of public opinion on governmental policies, for example, usually differentiate between the number of individually prepared letters or telegrams and the number of signed petitions or printed forms received by officialdom —the former figure somehow being seen as representing purer, and more genuinely participatory, acts than the latter.

While the neglect of mobilized participation can thus be explained, it is clearly time to build this dimension into models of active citizenship. Recent progress in unraveling the dynamics of attentiveness now makes it possible to introduce the nuances and modifications of an interactive perspective. Such is the purpose of this book: to outline a model and explore some preliminary data that bear on the question of why some attentive citizens can be mobilized to engage in a participatory act under certain conditions and others cannot.

The modern computer notwithstanding, great quantities of data are not generated, processed, and analyzed easily. I am thus indebted to many persons and institutions. To name them and express appreciation for their contributions may seem like a formality, but it is far from perfunctory. Without these contributions the book could not have been completed. Indeed, it could not have even been started. So it is with heartfelt warmth that I record here my gratitude to the Center of International Studies at Princeton

University and its then Director, Klaus Knorr, for the support necessary to prepare and distribute the questionnaire and for permission to reprint here as part of Chapter 2 a greatly revised version of my *The Attentive Public and Foreign Policy: A Theory of Growth and Some New Evidence* (Center Monograph 31, dated March 1968); to Jay P. Boris for his creativity in designing a special computer program that rendered the data manageable and interpretable; to Linda Alphonso, Marilyn Ayres, Judith Benn, Elizabeth Boris, Marilyn Falik, Joyce Fishbane, Paulette Kellner, Jane Lindsay, Bette Misdom, Margot Reiner, Linda Robinson, Esti Rosenblum, and Dorothy Stefanik for their help in coding and organizing the original data output; to the Research Council of Rutgers University for its support that enabled so many assistants to prepare the initial data; to the Department of Political Science, the Polimetrics Laboratory, and the Mershon Center of Ohio State University for their support in later stages of the data analysis; to Dennis Gombert, Richard Haller, James Ludwig, Edwin P. McClain, Jr., and George R. Ramsey, Jr. of Ohio State for their programming and research assistance in the final phases of the project; to my Ohio State colleague C. Richard Hofstetter for his substantive advice and programming assistance at several crucial stages; to Herbert B. Asher, G. R. Boynton, Samuel P. Hayes, Bernard C. Hennessy, Robert M. Krauss, Alan Rosenthal, William A. Scott, Roberta Segal, and Sidney Verba for their critical reactions to various sections of the manuscript; and to Janet Miller and Kay Neves for typing the manuscript. Norah Rosenau put up with, and gave enormously to, this project for one-fourth of her lifetime and no words can even begin to reflect my gratitude for her substantive suggestions, her editorial improvements, and her endless patience with my endless requests for criticism and support.

None of these persons or institutions, of course, is in any way responsible for the form or content of this product. They contributed to bringing it into being and to whatever credit it deserves, but I alone should be held to account for the rest.

James N. Rosenau

Los Angeles, California
March 6, 1974

It would clear the air of a good deal of cant if instead of assuming that politics is a normal and natural concern of human beings, one were to make the contrary assumption that whatever lip service citizens may pay to conventional attitudes, politics is a remote, alien, and unrewarding activity. Instead of seeking to explain why citizens are not interested, concerned, and active, the task is to explain why a few citizens *are*.

—Robert A. Dahl

. . . We lack adequate data on the characteristics and behavior of that thin layer of persons highly active in politics. From our daily impressions of politics we feel that persons who have opinions of high intensity are likely to seek energetically to achieve the ends in which they believe. These blocs of intense opinion combined with frenetic activity slip through the tines of national sampling procedure. Yet the endeavors of these small blocs of opinion-holders often energize—or brake—the machinery of state. Little bands of dedicated souls leave their imprint on public policy.

—V. O. Key

. . . In the fifties, how many saw the ferment and turmoil of the sixties? It is dangerous to conclude too much precisely because we know so little about what moves people to social action.

—Charles V. Hamilton

CHAPTER 1

CITIZENSHIP BETWEEN ELECTIONS

As money is to an economic system, so is support to a political system. Mobilized or latent, voluntary or coerced, support is the currency of democratic and authoritarian polities alike. Without support, officials cannot be elected, dictators cannot dictate, opponents cannot oppose, revolutionaries cannot revolt, policies cannot be implemented, goals cannot be achieved.

Like money, moreover, support is a currency that circulates in every stratum of society and through every medium of communication. It is sought or acquired through the mails and over the air. It is exchanged in face-to-face situations and at large gatherings. The marketplaces of support are everywhere: in voting booths and on street corners, in smoke-filled rooms and at mass rallies, in the halls of legislatures and at the meetings of bureaucrats, in diplomatic conferences and on battlefields, in leadership echelons and at the grass roots.

Unlike money, however, support is a currency that lacks definite form. Sometimes it is tangible and countable.[1] Often it is difficult to perceive and measure. Those in the polity who specialize in generating and allocating support are thus unable to emulate their counterparts in the economy and keep abreast of their progress by recording transactions in black or red on either side of a ledger. Politicians are never sure of their holdings, as the amount of support available can fluctuate erratically and the forms that it takes can undergo frequent change. For this reason wherever support can be withheld, efforts are likely to be made to mobilize it.

Yet there is nothing mysterious about support. Intangible, elusive, and changeable as it may be, support is not a mystical entity. It is not a "thing" that is used by some persons and abused by others. It is not a possession that can be stored or an object that can be wielded. It is not a quality people acquire or a quantity they utilize. Rather, support exists exclusively in the actions and interactions of identifiable people. Its existence can be observed only when behavior is observed. Support occurs when one individual (on behalf of himself or others) offers or withholds from another individual (and any larger aggregate he may represent) either attitudinal agreement or tangible resources. The evidence of attitudinal agreement can take many forms—a vote, a written expression, attendance at a rally—but whatever its content, it consists of behavior that can be included in a count of behaviors like it, either by the actor for whom it is intended, by his opponents, or by disinterested observers. Similarly, while there are many kinds of tangible resources that can be proffered or withheld—such as time, labor, money, and supplies—these become aspects of support only when accompanied by behavior through which they are or are not transferred from the supporter to the supported.

Although support can consist of a single action in which an

---

[1] But, as one analyst who sought to compare the support present in two situations put it, *"It is clearly nonsense to designate the amount of 'support' for the war by a single number. . . . At any given point in time, support should be considered a chord, rather than a note."* John E. Mueller, "Trends in Popular Support for the Wars in Korea and Vietnam," *American Political Science Review*, Vol. 65 (June 1971), pp. 359, 361 (italics in the original).

individual offers or withholds evidence of agreement or tangible resources without the intended recipient acknowledging or even recognizing the transfer, it takes on political significance only when the action gives rise to a reaction in which the transfer is explicitly accepted, rejected, or otherwise acknowledged by the intended recipient, his opponents, or disinterested observers. In short, when the student of politics traces and analyzes support, he focuses on relationships among people. For him support comes into existence when human beings interact with one another—when they command and obey, protest and resist, plead and persuade, applaud and acquiesce. Potential support is thus human interaction that can occur; withheld support, interaction that did not occur; mobilized support, interaction that has occurred; loss of support, interaction that has diminished. If there is no interaction, there can be no support. There can be no mobilizers of support without mobilizees.

The human and relational nature of support, it should be added, makes it far more attractive for analyzing politics than the more widely used concept of power. Too often power tends to be treated as a possession or quality—such as the power of oil or the power of eloquence—but from the perspective of the political process, possessions or qualities are meaningful only in terms of the relationships they foster or preclude.

In many political systems the relational nature of support is especially evident during election campaigns. Indeed, at such times the mobilization of support achieves mass and nationwide proportions, as it is sought from every citizen eligible to give it, even from those who are not normally aware they have support to give or withhold. Support-building activities are conducted on an extraordinary scale during elections because these are the only moments in the life of such political systems when the opportunity to give or withhold support is distributed equally among the citizenry. At all other moments in the cycles of democratic life, the distribution of support is highly selective and unequal. During the long periods between elections the capacity to give or withhold support accrues only to those citizens who are sufficiently attentive to public affairs that their support is capable of mobilization. Those who lapse into apathy upon leaving the voting booth lose this capacity until the next election campaign, when their eligibility to vote again makes it worthwhile for mobilizers of support to expend energy to overcome the apathy.

In the United States most citizens turn to other matters and away from public affairs after casting their votes. Those who remain attentive—or, as we shall collectively refer to them, the Attentive Public—comprise but a small minority of the Mass Public (as we shall refer to the citizenry as whole). Even if extremely loose criteria of attentiveness are used, the ranks of the Attentive Public do not constitute anything like a majority of the electorate. In the words of one astute observer, "Surely the highly attentive and active public of which we have been speaking constitutes normally no more than 10 to 15 percent of the adult population. . . ." [2] Yet, despite its size, as the prime source of public support available between elections, the Attentive Public clearly plays a crucial role in the processes of democracy.

THREE POLICY-MAKING ROLES

Let us be careful, however, in delineating the place of the Attentive Public in the policy-making process. By concentrating on it we run the risk of exaggerating its role and dismissing as irrelevant the mass of apathetic citizens. For all practical purposes the Attentive Public *is* the public between elections. Yet it is also the case that officials and others who mobilize support are inclined to recollect the outcome of previous elections and disposed to anticipate the advent of future ones, and these recollections and anticipations can and do serve as determinants of the behavior of officialdom. Key dimensions of the policy-making process, therefore, unfold independently of what the Attentive Public thinks or is mobilized to do. Since the timetable of democracy always contains elections scheduled in the foreseeable future, the apathetic voter and the Mass Public to which he belongs can never become

---

[2] V. O. Key, Jr., *Public Opinion and American Democracy* (New York: Alfred A. Knopf, 1961), p. 546. For more extended data on the size of the Attentive Public, see Chapter 2.

entirely irrelevant to its policy-making processes. Indeed, a Washington lobbyist argues that the impact of voting during elections is nine times greater than that of citizenship between them:

> Ninety per cent of what goes on here during a session [of Congress] is decided on the previous election day. The main drift of legislation is decided then: it is out of our control. There is simply no substitute for electing the right folks and defeating the wrong folks.[3]

In a like manner the Attentive Public's role can be exaggerated by assuming that attentiveness necessarily leads to the provision of support. As will be seen, this is not always the case. It is perfectly possible, both psychologically and behaviorally, to follow the course of events closely without being responsive to the appeals of mobilizers. Citizens who are responsive constitute a group we shall refer to as the Mobilizable Public, while the Attentive Public is conceived to consist of those who are attentive but not mobilizable as well as those who are mobilizable.

There is still another danger inherent in attempts to analyze this mobilizable segment of the Attentive Public, that of misconstruing the mobilized activity as leadership and exaggerating its role accordingly. As will be seen, the Attentive Public consists, by definition, of followers. Elsewhere we have defined leaders as those individuals who can regularly circulate their opinions to persons unknown to them,[4] a capacity which members of the Attentive Public, for all their interest and activity, do not possess. Thus our emphasis upon the importance of the Attentive Public must be seen in relation to the far greater role being performed by the

---

[3] Quoted in Donald R. Matthews, *U.S. Senators and Their World* (Chapel Hill: University of North Carolina Press, 1960), p. 193. For a contrary view, in which the Attentive Public's inter-election activities are seen as more powerful determinants of the course of events than elections, see Garry Wills, "Elections Do not Change Much," *New York Times*, August 7, 1972, p. 27.

[4] James N. Rosenau, *National Leadership and Foreign Policy: A Case Study in the Mobilization of Public Support* (Princeton: Princeton University Press, 1963), pp. 6–7.

even smaller minority of the citizenry who occupy positions of governmental and nongovernmental leadership.

In delineating the boundaries of the Attentive Public's influence, we do not mean to minimize its contribution to either local or national policy-making processes. While it is not the primary source of public policy, it is a vital and necessary one. In particular, as a substitute for the electorate between campaigns, the Attentive Public would appear to perform three distinct roles, each of which has a critical bearing upon the policies that are adopted at both the local and national levels.[5] One of these roles is as a sounding board for policy debate. The Attentive Public serves as an unorganized audience before whom local and national leaders, both governmental and nongovernmental, carry on discussion and argumentation that eventuates in policy choices. The second role is a more active one and involves the actual provision of support. It is performed through the activities of those organized segments of the Attentive Public that have been mobilized into pressing their attitudes and demands upon local or national leaders. The third role combines the first two and is more directly that of a surrogate electorate: as a result of its concern for particular policies and situations, the Attentive Public, in both its unorganized and organized form, unintentionally provides continual evidence of what might occur at the next election. Let us take a closer look at each of these roles.

The Attentive Public as an Unorganized Audience

At any moment in time some citizens are, perhaps for a variety of unrelated reasons, all engaged in following the course of public affairs. They do this in one or all of a variety of ways: by scanning newspapers, attending lectures, questioning leaders, conversing with acquaintances, discussing with friends, writing letters,

---

[5] For empirical evidence that the combination of the three roles played by the Attentive Public has important consequences for the conduct of public affairs between elections, see Donald J. Devine, *The Attentive Public: Polyarchical Democracy* (Chicago: Rand McNally, 1970), Chapters V–VII.

reading books, watching television, joining organizations, perusing magazines—to mention only some of the more obvious forms of attentiveness. The sum of all these uncoordinated activities is a constant reminder to governmental and nongovernmental leaders that their activities are being observed and evaluated. As one observer puts it, "Much of what is perceived as 'public reaction' to political events depends upon public visibility, and visibility depends largely upon forms of political participation beyond the vote itself." [6]

This visibility also provides leaders with a never-ending set of clues as to the matters that are of concern to their "constituents," how the latter feel about various proposed solutions, what the limits of their tolerance are, and on which questions attentiveness can be translated into active support. Sometimes the clues are plainly manifest in letters-to-the-editor columns, in the mail that leaders receive, and in the questions and applause that their speeches evoke. Still other clues can often be inferred from the audience ratings for particular radio or television programs, from the size and enthusiasm of crowds at rallies and forums, from the kinds of books that make the best-seller lists, from the changing circulation figures of the news media, and from the increases or declines in the membership rolls of certain types of organizations. Furthermore, leaders acquire impressions and information about the unrelated activities of attentive citizens by observing the behavior of other leaders who seem to be responding to perceived drifts in public sentiment.

Exactly how different type of leaders evaluate and utilize the uncoordinated attentiveness they perceive is not of concern here. Suffice it to state that while it is not necessary for governmental or nongovernmental leaders to be slaves to the values and demands implicit in the attentiveness they perceive, they cannot totally ignore it or their support will diminish and they will not be able to lead for long. Since support can be mobilized only from among those who have not lapsed into post-election apathy, it

[6] Philip E. Converse, "The Nature of Belief Systems in Mass Publics," in David E. Apter, ed., *Ideology and Discontent* (New York: The Free Press, 1964), pp. 206–61.

seems clear that, even as an unorganized, inchoate, and widely scattered group, the Attentive Public inevitably enters into the calculations of leaders and thereby plays a significant role in the democratic process. Inchoate as it may be, the Attentive Public offers the spectacle of citizen concern. For leaders its many diverse and unrelated acts of attentiveness constitute the potential for organization, for mobilized support that can inhibit or facilitate the realization of leadership goals. Accordingly, the sum of the uncoordinated activities of attentive citizens serves as an empirical base on which leadership perceptions and actions are founded. As an unorganized audience, the Attentive Public thus contributes to the establishment of outer limits beyond which policy choices are not likely to be made. In its unorganized form the Attentive Public cannot give much direction to the performance of leaders, but it can and does restrain them from pursuing courses of action that are not rooted in the value system of the community. Like any audience, the Attentive Public can permit the show to go on or force a closing through its degree of attention to and appreciation of the performance.[7]

The Attentive Public as Organized Groups

The relationship between leaders and members of the Attentive Public is not confined to the former's perceptions of the latter's uncoordinated activities. Direct interaction occurs when

[7] One experienced journalist suggests that the impact of attentive citizens may be greater than they recognize: "The mail coming into the White House and the Congress is a major factor in all this—much more than the letter-writers realize. These letters are expressing the moral conscience of the nation. . . . Public opinion in this way still exercises great influence. It affects the decisions of the Executive and the legislature. It is for equality, peace, and freedom. It is more powerful than the lobbyists for special interests. And it is a much greater force for moderation in the White House and in the Congress than is generally realized." James Reston, "Washington: How Corrupt is America?" *The New York Times*, February 26, 1967. For a contrary view that stresses the ease with which the constraints imposed by public opinion can be exaggerated, see Bernard C. Cohen, *The Public's Impact on Foreign Policy* (Boston: Little, Brown, 1973), *passim*.

a governmental or nongovernmental leader at the local or national level seeks to mobilize support on behalf of his goals or in opposition to those of other leaders. Every leader derives his leadership from a followership, either because he occupies a position which entitles him to act on behalf of a particular group or because his achievements have attracted wide adherence. Thus whether he is a corporation executive, a city mayor, a college president, a legislator, a renowned artist, a minister, a bureaucrat, or a lobbyist,[8] he always has a group of attentive followers from whom he can seek to mobilize support in the event a need for it arises. As will be seen, only some of the support potentially available to a leader can be mobilized, and thus the life of democratic systems is marked by a direct and continual interaction between their leadership and attentive strata.

Obviously different leaders will engage in support-building activities at different times and on different issues. Only rarely is every segment of the Attentive Public subjected to mobilization efforts and even more rarely, if at all, are its ranks entirely activated. At any moment in time many members of the Attentive Public are likely to remain unorganized, either because mobilization efforts are not being directed at them or because they ignore those that are. The structure of the Attentive Public at any moment is thus a consequence of the number, identity, and organized activity of those of its segments who are mobilized by their respective leaderships. Taken as a whole, these organized segments constitute the Mobilizable Public.

As previously indicated, in other words, to be an attentive citizen is not necessarily to be mobilizable. Some persons are capable of sustaining a continued interest in public affairs even as they ignore, resist, or are otherwise unmoved by efforts to translate their interest into support-giving activity. In addition, some citizens can be mobilized on certain types of issues but not on others, with the result that their membership in the Mobilizable Public is variable while their membership in the Attentive Public remains constant.

[8] For a systematic delineation of leadership types, see Rosenau, *National Leadership and Foreign Policy*, pp. 5–16.

In short, mobilizable citizens are recruited from the ranks of the unorganized audience that constitutes the Attentive Public. Just as the latter is conceived to be a substratum of the Mass Public, so is the Mobilizable Public viewed as a substratum of the Attentive Public.[9] The relationship among these strata of the citizenry is set forth diagrammatically in Figure 1–1. Here the variability in the size and composition of the Attentive and Mobilizable Publics is also suggested. Both consist of a core of citizens who have a generalized and continuing concern about public affairs, but both also include an ever-changing cluster of persons who are attentive or mobilizable only with respect to highly selected aspects of public affairs and who return to being inattentive or unmobilizable whenever the particular issues or leaders that aroused them become quiescent.

The policy-making role played by the Attentive Public as organized groups is of considerable consequence. By concentrating support for or against particular policy alternatives, the Mobilizable Public helps set the agenda of issues considered by officials[10] and, in the process, reinforces or diminishes the tendency of officials to prefer some alternatives rather than others. If as an unorganized audience the Attentive Public sets outer limits to policy choices, in its organized form it performs the role of highlighting certain alternatives within these limits. As a result, irrespective of whether the highlighted alternatives are adopted as policies, the insistence of the Mobilizable Public serves to encourage greater precision in the specification of ends and means on the part of officialdom. Obviously government leaders cannot acquiesce to all or even most of the conflicting demands of every mobilizable group that is

---

[9] For an elaboration of the distinctions between the Mass and Attentive Publics, see James N. Rosenau, *Public Opinion and Foreign Policy: An Operational Formulation* (New York: Random House, 1961), Chap. 4. For an extended discussion of the distinctions between the Attentive and Mobilizable Publics, see Chapter 3.

[10] For a cogent analysis of the agenda-setting role of active citizens, see Roger W. Cobb and Charles D. Elder, *Participation in American Politics: The Dynamics of Agenda-Building* (Boston: Allyn and Bacon, 1972), Chapters 5–7, 10.

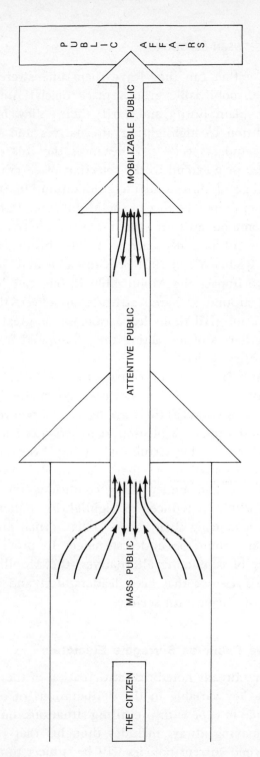

Figure 1–1
The Interaction of the Mass, Attentive, and Mobilizable Publics

active, but neither can they leave them unanswered. Hence, if nothing else, mobilizable groups place officials under constant pressure to explain, justify, and clarify their policy choices.

In addition to highlighting alternatives and forcing their clarification, under special circumstances the role of the Mobilizable Public may extend to the selection of certain alternatives from the range of those under consideration. In those rare instances when a preponderance of the Mobilizable Public is unified around a common attitude, the range of alternatives open to officialdom is substantially narrowed. The history and outcome of the Civil Rights Act of 1964 provides a clearcut illustration of the extensive impact the Mobilizable Public can have when it closes ranks around a shared attitude. In effect, the mobilized support for some civil rights legislation was so great at that time that the alternative of not acting was eliminated from the range of possible policy choices.

On most questions, of course, the Mobilizable Public is anything but uniform in its outlook. Normally its ranks are divided in as many ways as there are leaders who have a viewpoint to advance and a reservoir of support to activate. Each group that is mobilized tends, by virtue of having been mobilized, to encourage the formation of others that proffer support in contrary directions, and under these conditions the role of the Mobilizable Public is reduced to highlighting policy alternatives rather than narrowing their range. This normal and "reduced" role, however, cannot be underestimated. In providing support for a variety of conflicting alternatives, the Mobilizable Public supplies the pressures that keep leaders alert and facilitate the functioning of a democratic society.

The Attentive Public as Surrogate Electorate

We have already noted that anticipation of the next election constitutes a key variable in the deliberations of officials. Decisions are made to cope with prevailing situations, but the context of decision-making always includes thoughts that project ahead to the day when current policies will be subject to assessment in the voting booth by the Mass Public. Through both its unorganized and organized concern for particular policy proposals, the Attentive Public serves as a primary source for these projections. The daily reactions of attentive citizens and the actions of mobilized ones not only highlight current policy alternatives and place them within limits; they also expose officials to currents of thought that are strong among the citizenry and thus provide them with an on-going measure of their progress toward re-election. Explicit references to the next election may not be a part of the concern expressed by the Attentive Public, but the expression of concern can in itself yield clues about future voting behavior.

The role of surrogate electorate is, of course, not performed exclusively by the Attentive Public. Public opinion polls, conducted at frequent intervals by a variety of organizations, also tap the thinking of the citizenry and are thus closely followed by officialdom.[11] President Lyndon Johnson's habit of taking the latest poll results from his breast pocket and showing them to skeptical visitors was a vivid demonstration of the fact that the Attentive Public is not officialdom's only line of communication to the apathetic electorate. Yet polls are not without severe limitations. They measure general attitudes but not the intensity or stability with which attitudes are held, and are thus subject to wide fluctuations and often convey ambiguous meanings. Leaders know that, say, 63 percent approval today can easily become 49 percent approval tomorrow, either because a momentous event intervenes or the wording of the question is altered slightly.[12] The Attentive Public, on the other hand, contributes a more stable indication of the content and intensity of attitudes. The

---

[11] For cogent discussions of the role polls can play in the inter-election period, see Fred E. Katz and Fern V. Piret, "Circuitous Participation in Politics," *American Journal of Sociology*, Vol. 69 (January 1964), pp. 367–73; Launor F. Carter, "Survey Results and Public Policy Decisions," *Public Opinion Quarterly*, Vol. 27 (1963), pp. 549–57; and Adam Yarmolinsky, "Confessions of a Non-User," *Public Opinion Quarterly*, Vol. 27 (1963), pp. 543–48.

[12] For a striking illustration of how polls can measure transitory phenomena and fluctuate widely, see how the degree of approval "of the way [the] President is handling his job" varied between polls taken before and after crises, in Nelson W. Polsby, *Congress and the Presidency*

importance and long-range electoral consequences of an issue can be inferred from the degree to which attentiveness is sustained and the extent of the support that is mobilized. In some ways, therefore, the activities of the Attentive Public may be a more reliable predictor of how future elections might be resolved than are polls.[13]

An earlier caution, however, must be reiterated. The Attentive Public is not the electorate and leaders know that the values and attitude structures of its members are not necessarily representative of the broad mass of voters.[14] On what are called the "big" issues of an inter-election period the degree of representation is perhaps considerable,[15] but on lesser matters the meaning of attentiveness can, like polls, be quite ambiguous. Under certain circumstances, in fact, the activities of the Attentive Public can provide highly misleading clues to the trends in mass opinion. In particular, if only one kind of activity is used as a basis of assessment, the discrepancy between attentive and mass opinion can be extensive. For example, if letter-writing is taken out of the context of the full range of activities through which attentiveness is being expressed at any one time, the result can, in the words of one observer, give "sensationally false pictures of mass sentiment." [16] Recent electoral research has even uncovered "instances . . . where 'vocal' opinion as measured by public letter-writing may suggest a 60–40 division on an issue, whereas from the same sample treated at the same time in the head-count sense, the same

---

(Englewood Cliffs, N.J.: Prentice-Hall Inc., 1964), p. 26. In this connection also see Philip E. Converse and Howard Schuman, " 'Silent Majorities' and the Vietnam War," *Scientific American*, Vol. 222 (June 1970), pp. 17–25.

[13] For a succinct discussion of the potentialities and limitations of polls, see Leo Bogart, *Silent Politics: Polls and the Awareness of Public Opinion* (New York: Wiley, 1972).

[14] For an incisive discussion of this point, see Philip E. Converse, "The Nature of Belief Systems in Mass Publics," *op. cit.*

[15] Cf. Philip E. Converse, "Comments on 'Public Opinion and the Outbreak of War'," *Journal of Conflict Resolution*, Vol. IX (September, 1965), p. 332.

[16] Matthews, *U.S. Senators and Their World*, p. 222.

issue showed a 25–75 division, i.e., strongly in the opposite direction." [17] Indeed, there is even evidence to suggest that Senator Goldwater's defeat in the 1964 presidential election was due partly to his excessive reliance, as a basis for the themes of his campaign, on the letter opinion received in his headquarters.[18] Perhaps even more striking are the findings of an inquiry into the attitudes toward the war in Vietnam held by four different activist populations, those that had discussed the issue, those that had tried to change the opinions of others on it, those that had written letters about it, and those who participated in demonstrations with respect to it: the proportion of persons found to be "hawkish" on the issue increased substantially from the first through the third of these groups, while those in the fourth group were predominantly "dovish" in their attitudes. As the investigators put it, the differences among the various groups "illustrate most vividly how an official who 'reads' public preferences by looking at the poll results from a representative sample of the population would find something quite different from what an official observing the preferences of the activists would find; the latter official, moreover, would find something quite different depending on which activist group he observed." [19]

As in the case of polls, in short, there are limits to the reli-

---

[17] Philip E. Converse, "Comments on 'Public Opinion and the Outbreak of War'," p. 332. A striking example of this point is provided by a comparison of the results of a 1940 poll of mass opinion on the proposed selective service legislation and "a sample of 35,000 letters to fourteen Senators of differing views": while 70 percent of those polled approved the measure, 90 percent of the letter-writers opposed it. Cf. Robert A. Dahl, *Congress and Foreign Policy* (New York: Harcourt, Brace and Company, 1950), p. 34. Still another example along this line can be found in Raymond A. Bauer, Ithiel de Sola Pool, and Lewis A. Dexter, *American Business and Public Policy: The Politics of Foreign Trade* (New York: Atherton Press, 1963), p. 191.

[18] Philip E. Converse, Aage R. Clausen and Warren E. Miller, "Electoral Myth and Reality: The 1964 Election," *American Political Science Review*, Vol. LIX (June 1965), pp. 332–35.

[19] Sidney Verba and Richard A. Brody, "Participation, Policy Preferences, and the War in Vietnam," *Public Opinion Quarterly*, Vol. XXXIV (Fall, 1970), p. 330.

ability of the Attentive Public as an indicator of long-range electoral consequences. The role of the Attentive Public as a surrogate electorate can hardly be ignored, but so can it easily be exaggerated.

AN OVERVIEW

The way in which the Attentive Public performs its various roles at any moment in time obviously depends on a vast array of variables. Many of these involve the behavior of leaders, their interaction with each other, their attitudes toward the public, and their sensitivities to mobilized support. Others are to be found in the political system, the access to policy-making which its structure permits, and the degree of involvement on the part of the citizenry that is fostered by its processes. Still others arise out of the nature of the issues that provoke controversy and dominate the course of events. A final set of variables are inherent in the Attentive Public itself. Obviously the performance of its several roles will be partly a consequence of the many character-istics and orientations that determine the number and behavior of the individuals who become attentive to public affairs and responsive to the support-building efforts directed at them.

It would be pretentious to claim that this book thoroughly explores all these variables. Our concern is with the role of active citizenship between elections, but the subject is too vast to permit equally penetrating analysis of all its aspects.[20] We have been able to concentrate upon only certain variables and deal only cursorily with the remainder. More specifically, since our empirical data provide a unique opportunity to probe the sources of member-

---

[20] Indeed, even our conception of "citizenship" is a restricted one. As will be seen in Chapter 3, we use the term to mean only those activities through which persons relate themselves to public affairs, and we do not refer to any of the attitudes or other forms of behavior that have been ascribed to the citizenship role. For a useful discussion of the various dimensions of the role, see Robert E. Lane, "The Tense Citizen and the Casual Patriot: Role Confusion in American Politics," *Journal of Politics*, Vol. 27 (November 1965), pp. 735–60.

ship in the Mobilizable Public, it is this aspect of attentive citizenship that constitutes the central focus of the book. The ensuing chapters seek to uncover the dynamics whereby some members of the Attentive Public can be stimulated to respond to a support-building effort while others cannot. In order to gain insight into the dynamics of mobilizability—as we shall call the propensity to be responsive to mobilizers—we have undertaken an investigation of a particular segment of the Attentive and Mobilizable Publics. Our data allow us to contrast the social backgrounds, perceptions, attitudes, and political activities of 3,362 citizens who at two proximate yet different moments in American history were subjected to two specific mobilization attempts, but only about half of whom responded to the stimulus. Happily, moreover, one of the two mobilization attempts dealt with a foreign policy issue and the other focused on a domestic issue, thus permitting an assessment of the extent to which the differences between attentive and mobilizable citizens is a function of situational factors. Chapter 5 outlines the circumstances under which the two mobilization attempts were undertaken and describes how the data were derived from them. Chapters 6 through 12 systematically probe the data in an effort to delineate both the common and different experiential, attitudinal, perceptual, and behavioral sources of attentiveness and mobilizability.

Although the bulk of what follows is thus oriented toward empirical analysis of a single set of data, our main concern is to use these materials as a basis for enriching comprehension of the Attentive Public at a theoretical level. Admittedly, there are severe limits to a single data set as a basis for generalizations, but so little is known about the dynamics of mobilizability that we have not avoided theorizing about the more general meaning of the patterns depicted by the data. Indeed, in order to make maximum use of the data, we first devised a crude model consisting of thirty-eight major hypotheses about the patterns we expected the data to yield. In explicating our premises about attentive and mobilized behavior we relied on both the existing literature and our own intuitive feel for why some attentive citizens respond to mobilizers and others do not, a procedure which maximized use of the data in the sense that it explicitly organized our analysis and provided a means for subsequently offering conclusions based on tested hypotheses rather than unsystematic interpretation. These premises and the hypotheses derived from them are presented in the next three chapters. Subsequent to the analysis of the empirical materials we shall return, in Chapter 13, to the original model and revise it in the light of the findings.

Such a procedure has been followed because this is, in fact, the way systematic knowledge accumulates. "A useful model rarely presents itself in finished form and all at once to the investigator who needs it." [21] Rather, accretions to social scientific understanding normally occur through a never-ending interplay between theory and data. One starts with some theoretical notions and gathers empirical materials designed to test and amplify them. The latter in turn clarify the theory and identify points where new theorizing is required. Then, with the theory perfected, one turns again to the empirical world for further clarification. If this ragged process is repeated often enough, order and comprehension eventually emerge. So it is with this inquiry. Our present comprehension of the Attentive Public developed in stages and it would both mislead the reader and discourage further research to present the findings and interpretations as if they logically followed from an elegant model that had been developed at the outset.[22]

To be sure, the reader has not been subjected to many of the steps through which our data have been sifted and organized. Progress in research would never occur if the investigator took his

[21] Donald E. Stokes, "A Variance Components Model of Political Effects," in John M. Claunch, ed., *Mathematical Applications in Political Science* (Dallas: The Arnold Foundation, 1965), p. 81.

[22] Indeed, it is perhaps useful to record that the book evolved out of an initial interest in the limited question of whether an individual is more likely to provide support in response to the mobilization efforts of a friend or a politician. Data bearing on our original hypothesis that mobilizability potential increases the less the functional distance between mobilizer and mobilizee is presented in Chapter 11.

readers down all the dead ends and into all the pitfalls that preceded his arrival at clarifying conclusions. Nevertheless, the quickest way to cut off the interplay between theory and research is to render the latter so consistent with the former that no questions remain outstanding. The conclusions of one study are most valuable if they serve as hypotheses for the next and thus we have presented the main outline of our model of the Attentive Public in the next three chapters and postponed perfecting it until after the empirical data have been examined.

CHAPTER 2

CITIZENSHIP IN AN INTERDEPENDENT WORLD

Almost everywhere people are bored by foreign policy.

  The Economist
  Oct. 10, 1964, p. 117

[Norman R. Morrison], a Quaker official described by friends as upset over Administration policy in Vietnam, burned himself to death in front of the river entrance of the Pentagon late this afternoon.

  The New York Times
  Nov. 3, 1965, p. 1

Although its sponsors had hoped to attract as many as 75,000 people to a rally to urge President Nixon to free Lt. William L. Calley by Executive Order, only about 250 heeded the call.

  The New York Times
  May 29, 1972, p. 31

Kay Worden, a 47-year-old Boston sculptress and mother of five ... came to Columbus Monday and personally placed 12 full-page newspaper ads [costing $15,000] in "major Ohio cities" with this large-type plea: "OUR PRESIDENT NEEDS YOUR HELP [TO END THE WAR IN VIETNAM]"

  Columbus Citizen-Journal
  May 23, 1972, p. 6

Two of these four accounts of citizen behavior were published before the U.S.'s involvement in Vietnam reached monumental proportions. Two were published after the peak of this involvement and very near its end. Yet the discrepancy between those in each pair is the same. In both cases, the first account is of indifference and apathy and the second of deep concern, even tragic action. This difference vividly poses the problem examined in this chapter: what is happening to citizenship between elections? In this era when ideology is said to be ending and alienation mounting, is attentiveness to public affairs growing or is apathy deepening? Are more people more mobilizable or has affluence overwhelmed commitment? Were the turbulent protests of the Vietnam period the culmination of a long-term trend toward widespread public concern and involvement, or were they only the agonies of a small, vocal minority? Will the world's mounting interdependence, by bringing heretofore distant issues into the personal worlds of citizens, render them ever more attentive to public affairs between elections? Or will the very technological developments that place citizens closer to the course of events also render issues more complex and make attentiveness more difficult?

These questions are easier to raise than to answer. Most of the systematic evidence available points to a set of conclusions that is contrary to one's impressions of recent years. There is, on the one hand, an abundance of data showing that the number of persons in the United States who consistently keep abreast of public affairs is very small. On the other hand, the extremity of the act of taking one's convictions from Boston to the people of Ohio and the even more extreme act of self-immolation seem to indicate a growing involvement in the course of events between elections. To unravel these contradictory tendencies, our analysis will proceed in five steps. We shall first look at some of the findings bearing on the size of the Attentive and Mobilizable Publics. Next, we shall note several interpretations which treat these findings as evidence of a static situation. Third, we shall record the impressions that lead us to conclude that the findings convey a misleading picture of present and future trends. Fourth, we shall identify several characteristics of attentiveness and mobilizability that may foster a slow and continuous growth in the relative size of the Attentive and Mobilizable Publics. Finally, we shall present some systematic evidence of this growth.

AN ACTIVE MINORITY

Notwithstanding the importance of the roles played by the Attentive Public, it is small in size by almost any quantitative standard. The varied and intensive activities of attentive citizens tend to give a misleading picture of the number of persons involved. One group's intense activity will often capture headlines which will in turn provoke comparable behavior on the part of opposing groups, and, as this spiralling process continues, the extent to which concern is widely shared tends to be exaggerated. The vigorous demands and angry protests of the Attentive Public may command the respect of officials and attract the attention of news media, but its members constitute a distinct minority of the population as a whole.

It is difficult to describe the size of the Attentive Public in the United States with a precise figure or percentage, since much depends on the criteria used to classify persons in its ranks. Different observers use different definitions and measures of attentiveness, and the resulting estimates often vary considerably. Whatever the criteria that are used, however, the Attentive Public is rarely portrayed as a majority of the citizenry. Rather, the varying estimates usually fall well below 50 percent of the adult population.[1]

The fact that the Attentive Public emerges as an active

---

[1] For an exception in which 83 percent were classified as attentive by including those who said they followed public affairs "only now and then," as well as those who responded "most of the time" and "some of the time," see M. Kent Jennings and Harmon Zeigler, "The Salience of American State Politics," *American Political Science Review*, Vol. LXIV (June 1970), footnote 4, beginning on p. 524. For a more stringent set of criteria that avoids use of the lower end of the measurement scale, see pp. 174–75 below.

minority regardless of the criteria used to assess it can be readily illustrated. The circulation figures of newspapers and magazines that report and analyze public affairs in a serious and extended fashion, for example, contrast sharply with those of printed media that treat such matters in a cursory and simplified manner. Perhaps the most striking comparison in this regard is the oft-cited one between the readership of *The News* and *The New York Times* in the world's largest metropolitan area: in 1972 the daily circulation of the *News*, a tabloid that reports on scandal and sex far more vividly than on issues of public policy, was 2,125,181, whereas the corresponding figure for the *Times*, with its thorough treatment of public affairs, was 814,290.[2] A similar picture is conveyed by the difference between the circulations of such politically oriented publications as *The Atlantic, Harpers*, and *National Review* on the one hand, and those of such essentially unpolitical magazines as *Cosmopolitan, Redbook*, and *Sports Illustrated* on the other. None of the first three reported a 1972 circulation of more than 340,899, while none of the last three circulated fewer than 1,428,279.[3]

The picture remains unaltered by comparisons of the audience for public and nonpublic affairs programs presented by the electronic media. One elaborate analysis of the television viewing habits of 2,427 adults, for example, found that only 4 percent cited "regular news" first as their "favorite program," and only a slightly higher proportion (7 percent) specified "other information and public affairs" programs first. The average viewer prefers programs "that provide pleasant relaxation rather than serious stimulation," and "aside from the day's news and weather—which he watches regularly—he rarely uses the set as a deliberate source of information, and he is extremely unlikely to turn on serious and informative public affairs presentations even if he is watching while they are on the air." [4] Similar findings, based on the diaries

---

[2] *1972 Ayer Directory of Publications* (Ayer Press, 1972), pp. 596, 607.

[3] *Ibid.*, pp. 409, 581, 587, 596, 602, 606.

[4] Gary A. Steiner, *The People Look at Television: A Study of Audience Attitudes* (New York: Alfred A. Knopf, 1963), pp. 126, 127, 228–29.

kept by 6,834 viewers over various two-week periods, were uncovered by another study that focused not on preferred programs, but on actual viewing behavior: "On an average weekday in the fall of 1969, 25 percent of adult men and 22 percent of adult women reported watching the national programs. Perhaps the most striking statistic, however, is the 53 percent who did not watch a single evening news show over the two-week diary period."[5]

Innumerable anecdotes could be cited showing that most citizens resent the intrusion of public affairs into their viewing hours. Daytime coverage of Congressional hearings or emergency meetings of the United Nations Security Council invariably arouses criticism from soap opera viewers,[6] for example, and the ire of sports fans reached unprecedented peaks when the orbital flight of Gemini 5 was unexpectedly hampered by electrical power problems and the networks cancelled coverage of two exhibition football games until the problem was solved and the safety of the astronauts assured.[7] Similarly, when President Johnson scheduled a 9:00 P.M. appearance before a joint session of Congress to appeal for a law guaranteeing blacks the right to vote, the event was covered in New York by the three TV networks and, as a

---

[5] John P. Robinson, "The Audience for National TV News Programs," *Public Opinion Quarterly*, Vol. 35 (Fall 1971), pp. 404–05. See also John P. Robinson, "World Affairs Information and Mass Media Exposure," *Journalism Quarterly*, Vol. 44 (Spring 1967), pp. 23–30; and J. Robinson and J. Swinehart, "World Affairs and the TV Audience," *Television Quarterly*, Vol. 7 (1968), pp. 40–59.

[6] Among the letters Senator J. W. Fulbright received during heated hearings his Foreign Relations Committee held on the escalation of U.S. involvement in Vietnam, a recurring theme was expressed by a Cleveland woman who wrote, "Please conduct any further Vietnam inquiry in private, or between 4:30 P.M. and 7:30 P.M. Interference of regular daytime television programs is losing you the support of housewives." *The New York Times*, February 11, 1966.

[7] One network received 1,625 telephoned objections to the cancellation in New York, 1,800 in Los Angeles, 1,200 in Chicago, 1,400 in Washington, 300 in St. Louis and 100 in San Francisco. Cf. *The New York Times*, August 22, 1965, p. 73.

result, the independent stations in that city enjoyed "substantial increases" in the size of their audiences, winning viewers who usually watched network entertainment shows that had been cancelled.[8]

While the minority status of the Attentive Public can only be inferred from the data on mass media consumption, it is directly evident in the findings of researchers who have probed the practices of citizenship. Summarizing a number of studies pertaining to questions of foreign policy, for example, Hero observes that "possibly as many as 15 percent of American adults display a significant degree of interest in world affairs" and that "many of these interested citizens possess only rather trivial or peripheral information on international relations."[9] A dramatic illustration of this general point is provided by the finding that, in 1964, 28 percent of a representative sample of 1,501 adult Americans "were not aware that most of China is now ruled by a Communist government."[10]

The advent of heavy involvement in Vietnam and internal dissension over the issue does not appear to have had an impact on this pattern of information. A national survey of a representative sample of 1,499 citizens conducted in the spring of 1967, when the Vietnam issue seemed to reach unprecedented intensity on the domestic scene, found that 13 percent "had attempted to convince someone to change his views on Vietnam," 2 percent had written to officials about the issue, 1 percent had expressed themselves through letters to newspapers, and half of 1 percent had participated in marches or demonstrations.[11] Similarly, a survey of another national sample in 1966 found that "28 percent of the American public had a reasonably correct idea of the

---

[8] *The New York Times,* March 17, 1965, p. 91.

[9] Alfred O. Hero, *Americans in World Affairs* (Boston: The World Peace Foundation, 1959), p. 6.

[10] Martin Patchen, *The American Public's View of U.S. Policy Toward China* (New York: Council on Foreign Relations, 1964), p. 5.

[11] Sidney Verba and Richard A. Brody, "Participation, Policy Preferences, and the War in Vietnam," *Public Opinion Quarterly*, Vol. XXXIV (Fall 1970), p. 326.

number of American troops in Vietnam (another 29 percent were off by as much as 300,000 troops), 45 percent did not know any country which was giving refuge to Viet Cong and North Vietnamese troops, and 43 percent could not pick out the nearby country which permitted U.S. air bases within its borders." [12]

The findings for attentiveness to domestic affairs reveal slightly more activity and involvement, but again none of the figures even approach a majority of the citizenry. A national cross-section sample of 8,000 respondents, for example, was found to include 21 percent who reported discussing public issues with others "frequently" and 13 percent who said they had conveyed their opinions on a public issue to Congressmen or other public officials "one or more times in the past year." [13] Likewise, a nation-wide sample used to study the 1964 presidential election yielded the finding that "only about 15 percent of the adult population reports ever having written a letter to a public official, and of the total stream of such letters from the grassroots, two-thirds are composed by about 3 percent of the population." [14] Similarly, while many Americans are "joiners" and belong to a vast array of

---

[12] Don D. Smith, " 'Dark Areas of Ignorance' Revisited: Current Knowledge About Asia Affairs," *Social Science Quarterly*, Vol. 51 (December 1970), p. 669.

[13] Discussions with others or contacts with officials do not appear to be unrepresentative forms of attentiveness. When the same researchers compiled a "political activity index" out of the responses to twelve relevant items, they classified 10 percent of the respondents as "very active," 17 percent as "active," 35 percent as "inactive," and 38 percent as "very inactive." Julian L. Woodward and Elmo Roper, "Political Activity of American Citizens," *American Political Science Review*, Vol. XLIV (December 1950), pp. 874–76.

[14] Moreover, these figures apparently represent the maximum extent of letter-writing practice: "Where letters to newspapers or magazines are concerned, the constituency is even more restrictive still: only about 3 percent of the population recalls ever having written such a letter, and two-thirds of such letters are turned out by not more than half of one percent of the population." Philip E. Converse, Aage R. Clausen, and Warren E. Miller, "Electoral Myth and Reality: The 1964 Election," *American Political Science Review*, Vol. LIX (June 1965), p. 333.

formal organizations, it has been estimated that only 31 percent belong to organizations that "sometimes" take a stand on public issues.[15] Still another dimension of activity was probed in a nationwide sample of 970 American adults, only 27 percent of whom reported that they "regularly" follow "the accounts of political and governmental affairs," while 53 percent responded "from time to time" and 19 percent answered "never." [16]

With respect to local affairs, too, the percentages fall short of the halfway mark. In a sample of 525 registered voters in New Haven, for example, Dahl found that 47 percent discussed local affairs with friends, 27 percent communicated their views to local officials, 16 percent had had contact with New Haven officials, and only 13 percent had "done anything actively in connection with some local issue or local problem—political or nonpolitical." [17] Only 3 percent of Dahl's sample cited all four of these activities, and 40 percent did not cite any of them.[18] Even smaller rates of participation are reported by Presthus: using samples of 479 and 655 in two small communities of upstate New York, he found that no more than 1 percent discussed any of ten different issues with a friend, not more than 5 percent attended any public meeting connected with the processing of nine of the issues, and not more than 3 percent "contributed work or money" in connection with nine of the issues. (The tenth issue, raising funds for a hospital, elicited such activity from 38 percent of the sample.) [19]

There is no need to pile finding upon finding. The general pattern remains consistent through all the studies that touch upon

---

15 Robert E. Lane, *Political Life: Why People Get Involved in Politics,* (Glencoe, Ill.: The Free Press, 1959), p. 75.

16 Gabriel A. Almond and Sidney Verba, *The Civic Culture: Political Attitudes and Democracy in Five Nations* (Princeton: Princeton University Press, 1963), p. 89.

17 Robert A. Dahl, *Who Governs? Democracy and Power in American City* (New Haven: Yale University Press, 1961), p. 279.

18 *Ibid.,* pp. 277–79.

19 Robert Presthus, *Men at the Top: A Study in Community Power* (New York: Oxford University Press, 1964), pp. 259, 262.

citizenship between elections.[20] Indeed, it is even evident in the activity that occurs *during* elections. Of the nearly 1,800 citizens who made up a representative sample used to study the 1956 presidential election, 28 percent were found to have tried to convince others to vote in a particular way, 10 percent reported contributing financially to the campaign of a party or candidate, 7 percent said they attended "political meetings, rallies, dinners, or things like that," and 3 percent cited "other" types of work during the campaign.[21] In short, it does seem that "a really intense commitment to politics probably is limited in American society to a small fraction of political activists." [22] Moreover, viewing the electorate as a whole, one researcher concluded that

> About one-third ... can be characterized as politically apathetic or passive; in most cases, they are unaware, literally, of the political part of the world around them. Another 60 percent play largely spectator roles in the political process; they watch, they cheer, they vote, but they do not do battle. In the purest sense of the word, probably only 1 or 2 percent could be called gladiators.[23]

[20] For extended summaries of the available data on attentiveness to public affairs, see James C. Davies, *Human Nature in Politics* (New York: John Wiley & Sons, 1963); Robert E. Lane, *Political Life*; and Lester W. Milbrath, *Political Participation: How and Why Do People Get Involved in Politics?* (Chicago: Rand McNally and Co., 1965), p. 21. For data on "twelve different acts of political participation" that are also consistent with the patterns identified here, see Sidney Verba and Norman H. Nie, *Participation in America: Political Democracy and Social Equality* (New York: Harper & Row, 1972), p. 31.

[21] Angus Campbell, Philip E. Converse, Warren E. Miller, and Donald E. Stokes, *The American Voter* (New York: John Wiley & Sons, 1960), p. 91. For additional data on attentiveness during all the election campaigns between 1952 and 1964, see Donald J. Devine, *The Attentive Public: Polyarchical Democracy* (Chicago: Rand McNally, 1970), pp. 46–64.

[22] Campbell, Converse, Miller, and Stokes, *The American Voter,* p. 104.

[23] Milbrath, *Political Participation,* p. 21.

AN EVEN MORE ACTIVE AND STILL SMALLER MINORITY

If persons consistently attentive to public affairs constitute a small minority of the citizenry, those of this group who can be mobilized to give time, energy, money, or other forms of support with respect to a public issue are an infinitesimal segment of the population. The above estimate that the "gladiators" are "probably only 1 or 2 percent" of the citizenry may exaggerate the proportion of Mobilizables in the society. No doubt some of the foregoing data reflect mobilized activity, but none of them were collected in order to assess the size of the Mobilizable Public and thus they should not be treated as indicators of anything more than the degree to which attentive concern is prevalent among the general public.[24] To enter the Mobilizable Public is to be ready to put aside the obligations and worries of personal life in order to invest time and effort on behalf of distant problems when asked to do so by remote leaders whom one does not know. Obviously, few persons have the resources and inclinations to respond to such appeals for support. Most are too constrained by habit, inertia, family needs, occupational commitments, and a host of other aspects of their daily routines to be mobilizable—with the result that the task of political mobilizers is truly an awesome one. The problems faced by the advertiser who seeks to shape the preferences of consumers, by the employer who tries to direct the energies of employees, by the teacher who attempts to affect the response of students, by the parents who seek to alter the responses of children—or, indeed, by anyone outside the realm of politics who undertakes to modify the behavior of others—are nothing in comparison to the mobilizer who sets out to win support for public issues. Such a mobilizer must reach across all the cultural and socio-economic divisions of the society, and then somehow convince strangers that compliance with his appeals for support is justified.

Estimating the proportion of the citizenry that is susceptible to mobilization is an even more difficult task than calculating the

---

[24] The distinctions between attentiveness and mobilizability are elaborated below, pp. 98–109.

size of the Attentive Public. Precise data on the subject are virtually nonexistent. Even in the area of electoral behavior, where there has been considerable systematic research, "the hard knowledge about the interaction between campaigns and the voter is thin." [25] What evidence there is in this area suggests that the mobilization of support is difficult even under the best of circumstances: with all the norms pertinent to active citizenship aroused and emphasized by the drama of a contest for the White House, the predispositions of only 14 percent of the voters of Erie County, Ohio, were found to be activated by the presidential campaign of 1940 and only an additional 8 percent were mobilized to change their vote from how they had intended to cast it before the campaign began. The remainder of the eligible voters in the County would probably have behaved as they did even if the campaign had not preceded the election.[26]

A more recent indication of the limits of mobilization during electoral campaigns is provided by the data on the success of the efforts by presidential candidates to raise funds through direct mail pleas. In 1964 the Republican party sent out 15 million pieces of literature appealing for financial support for Barry Goldwater's candidacy. The result was 380,000 replies, or 2.5 percent of the original mailing.[27] Senator George McGovern was four times as successful in 1972 when he used a direct-mail appeal to finance his effort to win the Democratic presidential nomination —he received about 160,000 responses to more than 1,200,000 mailings—but the proportion mobilized was still not more than a small minority.[28] It is likely that the mobilizers were delighted

[25] V. O. Key, Jr., *Politics, Parties, and Pressure Groups,* 5th ed. (New York: Thomas Y. Crowell, 1964), p. 483.

[26] Paul F. Lazarfeld, Bernard Berelson, and Hazel Gaudet, *The People's Choice: How the Voter Makes Up His Mind in a Presidential Campaign* (New York: Duell, Sloan and Pearce, 1944), p. 103.

[27] *The New York Times,* February 20, 1966, p. 47.

[28] *The New York Times,* July 24, 1972, p. 14. It was subsequently reported that during the campaign itself McGovern's fund-raising efforts yielded small contributions totalling more than $14 million from more than 650,000 people. See *The New York Times,* November 26, 1972, p. 42.

with the results in both instances, inasmuch as the dollars supplied by these small percentages were sufficient to sustain the candidacies. That a small group can make a big political difference, however, does not negate the finding that only a small proportion of those reached by appeals for support are likely to respond. Later we argue that, given the size of the citizenry, even a miniscule rate of growth on the part of the Attentive Public can have profound consequences. But for the present we are concerned with identifying the parameters and not the consequences of mobilizability, and it seems clear that the ranks of the Mobilizable Public are not very great even during elections.

In the absence of systematic efforts to assess the size of the Mobilizable Public between elections, the best we can do is to search for a central tendency among what fragments of evidence there are.[29] One such fragment is provided by the account, noted at the outset of the chapter, of the effort to mobilize support on behalf of Lt. William L. Calley. Another can be found in an analysis of 2,930 letters protesting the Advertising Council's participation in a campaign urging public support for the United

[29] It should be noted that one thorough, systematic study of mobilized behavior directed at society-wide goals does exist, namely, the analysis that Merton and his colleagues did of Kate Smith's marathon broadcast on behalf of war bonds in September, 1943. In one day of reiterated emotional appeals this radio star sold some $39,000,000 in war bonds. Using a content analysis of Smith's appeals, an intensive "focused interview" with 100 donors, and a cross-sectional poll of nearly 1,000 persons, Merton probed the question of how so many persons were moved to respond to the appeal. The results of this inquiry, however, offer little guidance in our search for clues to the size of the Mobilizable Public. As Merton's study reveals, a major source of Smith's success was the wartime context in which she made the appeal, whereas we are concerned here with the dynamics of mobilizability involving the more normal circumstances of stimuli to respond to the day-to-day issues of public affairs in the postwar world. In short, Merton investigated essentially nonpolitical behavior in a unique setting and his findings are thus only peripherally relevant to our problem. Cf. Robert K. Merton, with Marjorie Fiske and Alberta Curtis, *Mass Persuasion: The Social Psychology of a War Bond Drive* (New York: Harper & Brothers, 1946).

Nations. The evidence is unmistakable that all these letters were provoked by the John Birch Society, which in July 1963, sought to mobilize its membership through a call for protesting letters in its monthly *Bulletin*. Estimates of the Society's membership at the time varied from 15,000 to 60,000, so that wherever the true figure fell between these two extremes, the 2,930 mobilized to write constituted a distinct, possibly even a small, minority of those who received the appeal.[30]

A more precise estimate of an association's mobilizable stratum can be derived from our own data, which were partly developed in order to obtain a specific measure of mobilizability within one segment of the Attentive Public. As will be seen, in this case only about 4 percent of those known to be members of the Attentive Public were mobilized by an identifiable stimulus.[31]

Still another bit of evidence is available in the account of what happened when Another Mother for Peace, a women's organization, spent several months of 1970 mobilizing its membership to write letters to consumer manufacturers who also made weapons for the Defense Department.[32] Some 200,000 pieces of literature, including 25,000 "Consumer Peace Action Kits," were mailed. They called on the members to write one or more heads of some twenty corporations asking that their firms cease working for the government. The Kits provided names and addresses to whom to write as well as suggestions as to what the letters should emphasize. When all the firms were subsequently contacted and asked how many letters they received protesting their production of war products, the investigator found that "probably not more than 5,000 messages traveled from this population [of 200,000] to

---

[30] For an account and analysis of this attempt at mobilization, see Hannah Wartenberg and Wagner Thielens, *Against the United Nations: A Letter-Writing Campaign by the Birch Movement* (New York: Bureau of Applied Social Research, 1964).

[31] See below, pp. 170 and 172.

[32] David M. Krieger, "The Another Mother for Peace Consumer Campaign—A Campaign That Failed," *Journal of Peace Research*, No. 2 (1971), pp. 163–66.

the various targets." [33] And the impact of the 2½ percent that were mobilized was even less than this proportion implies:

> Of the five firms listed only in the mailing of the 25,000 Consumer Peace Action Kits in August, the largest volume of mail opposing war production any had received was twenty letters. One firm indicated receiving only one letter, another only four. None of these firms indicated that they had received any contrary mail, and none indicated they planned any policy change on the basis of these few letters.[34]

Another fragment of evidence indicating that the Mobilizable Public is a small segment of a small minority of the citizenry is provided by an episode that started on December 4, 1953. On that day Senator Joseph R. McCarthy urged a nationwide television audience "to write or wire the President of the United States" their doubts about his Chinese trade policy and, as a result, some 9,500 letters and telegrams were received by the White House in the next twenty-four hours.[35] The Senator's appeal also evoked efforts by newspapers and other groups to get people to write Eisenhower in support of his policy, but when a final tally was announced several days later the number of messages received had risen to only about 50,000.[36] If the combined audience of the Senator and those who sought to mobilize opposition to him is conservatively estimated at a couple of million viewers and readers, it is clear once again that the extent of mobilized activity was very small.

Nor is the extent of mobilized activity significantly greater when the situation is reversed and the President appeals to a nationwide television audience to write letters to members of Congress on behalf of a particular viewpoint. On March 29, 1973, President Nixon urged viewers to write Congress in support of his efforts to limit federal spending and to exercise fiscal restraint.

---

[33] *Ibid,* p. 165.
[34] *Ibid.*
[35] *The New York Times,* December 6, 1953, p. 1.
[36] *The New York Times,* December 10, 1953, p. 29.

It was reported that in subsequent weeks Senator Adlai E. Stevenson of Illinois received some 3,200 letters (of which 307 endorsed the President's budget restraints) and that Senator John G. Tower of Texas received 7,351 letters (of which 580 applauded the President's efforts to hold down spending),[37] hardly impressive figures when the size of presidential television audiences in Illinois and Texas are taken into account.

The proportions are not any greater when the efforts to mobilize support rely on varied and repeated appeals rather than on a single broadcast or letter. For example, in 1962 the Institute for World Affairs Education (IWAE) of the University of Wisconsin, in cooperation with the Foreign Policy Association, "undertook the task of stimulating a large, heterogeneous, statewide audience to take part in an informed discussion of world problems." [38] The effort spanned eight weeks and the key to it was a "Fact Sheet kit" that participants purchased at a nominal fee. The kit, called "Great Decisions—1962," contained background materials on eight major foreign policy issues that enabled their buyers both to follow corresponding mass media presentations and to participate in a small group discussion of each issue. Both the program and the kits were widely publicized throughout the state:

> A series of half-hour films prepared by the National Educational Television and Radio Center was shown over WMVS-TV to a large potential audience in southeastern Wisconsin. Each of these films was followed by a half-hour locally produced television to TV panelists. The *Milwaukee Journal* radio station, WTMJ-AM, carried weekly a one-and-one-half-hour program dealing with Great Decisions. The *Journal* itself provided a substantial amount of pre-program space and carried a special article on a Great Decision's topic in the Sunday Editorial Section during each week of

[37] *The New York Times*, April 27, 1973, p. 9.
[38] Robert W. Hattery, *"Great Decisions: 1962"—A Survey of Kit Buyers in Two Wisconsin Communities* (Milwaukee: Institute for World Affairs Education. The University of Wisconsin-Milwaukee, n.d.), p. iii.

the program. Finally, numerous volunteer organizations in the Milwaukee and Racine areas worked closely with IWAE and FPA to assure maximum community participation in discussion groups. Among these organizations, the Milwaukee Council on World Affairs was especially active in all phases of the program. Many organizations and individuals likewise worked together to promote Great Decisions in other areas of the state.[39]

All this effort, however, resulted in the sale of only 1,060 kits in the state of Wisconsin.[40] Of the 448 kits distributed in Milwaukee and Racine Counties, moreover, 121 were purchased by high school and college students.[41] Since the population of these two counties exceeded 850,000 persons in the 1960 census, the fact of only 327 non-student buyers suggests the severe limits within which those who seek to mobilize activity pertaining to public affairs must operate.[42]

The last three fragments of evidence reflect efforts to mobilize an unorganized audience, but apparently Senator McCarthy, President Nixon, and the IWAE would not have been more successful if they had sought to activate an organized group. As the leaders of many organizations based on voluntary membership have doubtless discovered, the shared values that organizational affiliation implies do not necessarily enhance mobilizability. A variety of sociological inquiries into the structure and functioning of voluntary organizations indicate rather clearly that mobilization of their memberships is not easily accomplished. As one analyst who sought to summarize research in this area put it, "The general finding with respect to participation is that voluntary associations tend to be characterized by an active minority

39 *Ibid.*, pp. 3–4.
40 *Ibid.*, p. 9.
41 *Ibid.*, p. 8.
42 For some additional data along these lines, see Bernard C. Cohen, *Citizen Education in World Affairs* (Princeton: Center of International Studies, 1953), Chapters IV–V.

which actually controls the association's affairs and an inactive majority which participates only occasionally in the organization's activities and which in other ways expresses disinterest and apathy." [43]

Exceptions to the foregoing pattern sometimes occur, albeit these often prove to be more illusory than real. Perhaps the most conspicuous in this regard is the initial success of Common Cause, a grass roots, nonpartisan, and nationwide organization founded in 1970 through newspaper advertisements and a direct mail campaign. Designed as "a citizen's lobby" to force reforms of the political system, Common Cause sent letters to 200,000 citizens in August 1970, asking them to join for an annual fee of $15 and holding out the promise of information on issues and of stimuli to action (i.e., mobilization efforts indicating where, when, and how members could exert pressure on government officials).[44] Some thirteen months later it was reported that 215,000 dues-paying members had been recruited, that the organization had lobbied successfully on behalf of several causes (including the 18-year-old vote amendment), and that it consisted of "a hyper-active constituency" that "constantly worry the Common Cause staff for something to do." [45] Subsequently, however, it seemed that this would not be an exceptional case after all, despite initial

---

[43] David L. Sills, *The Volunteers: Means and Ends in a National Organization* (Glencoe, Ill.: The Free Press, 1957), p. 19. For other summarizing treatments of behavior in voluntary associations, see Alfred O. Hero, *Voluntary Organizations in World Affairs Communication* (Boston: World Peace Foundation, 1960); John C. Scott, Jr., "Membership and Participation in Voluntary Associations," *American Sociological Review*, Vol. 22 (June 1957), pp. 315–26; Herbert Maccoby, "The Differential Political Activity of Participants in a Voluntary Association," *American Sociological Review*, Vol. 23 (October 1958), pp. 524–32; and Herbert H. Hyman and Charles R. Wright, "Trends in Voluntary Association Memberships of American Adults: Replication Based on Secondary Analysis of National Sample Surveys," *American Sociological Review*, Vol. 36 (April 1971), pp. 191–206.

[44] *The New York Times*, August 18, 1970, p. 10.

[45] *The New York Times*, October 6, 1971, p. 30.

success. Three months later it was reported that Common Cause was reorganizing its personnel, experiencing budgetry problems, and shifting its thrust from lobbying in Washington to "grassroots activism on local issues." Apparently its membership renewals were occurring at a rate of only 60 percent, and its efforts to recruit new members seemed to show that they had exhausted the appropriate segment of the Mobilizable Public. A $10,000 advertisement placed in *The New York Times* in November 1971, "yielded only about 300 new memberships," or less than enough to pay the cost of the ad. "Based upon that," one of its top officials was quoted as saying, "we concluded that this was no longer the way, that most people who would join us because of such advertisements had already joined and that we would have a major shift in emphasis to the state [and local] groups." [46] Thus, whatever the future progress of Common Cause—and at the time of reorganization its leaders were projecting a 15-percent-a-year growth—its early history again demonstrates that mobilizability is not a pervasive characteristic among the citizenry.

A STATIC MINORITY?

Estimating the size of the Attentive Public is not of interest only to researchers. In May 1970, it became an intense political issue when the incursion into Cambodia produced heated controversy about the extent of popular support for the Nixon Administration's policies in Southeast Asia. Critics contended that the policies were widely rejected, while their defenders, including the President, claimed that they enjoyed the support of "a silent majority" and were rejected by only "a vocal minority." Each side sought to demonstrate the empirical validity of its claims through innovative mobilization techniques. The critics sought to swell the ranks of peace marchers and the defenders called on those who agreed with them to turn on their car headlights during daytime driving. Neither effort was conspicuously successful, but together they indicate that the researcher's concern for accurate

[46] *The New York Times,* December 24, 1971, p. 1.

empirical description of the Attentive Public is more than an academic question.[47]

Indeed, the politicization of the question suggests a widespread feeling that profound changes may be occurring in the structure of the public. Data gathered about single episodes do not show trends, and to conclude from the available evidence that attentiveness and mobilizability are not pervasive phenomena between elections is not to say anything about emerging patterns. There is no reason to presume that the size of the Attentive Public is constant in proportion to the population. On the contrary, there are reasons to speculate that in the long run its ranks will swell at a faster rate than those of the citizenry as a whole.

It should be noted that our speculations along these lines are discrepant with one important datum and contrary to several competing interpretations of what is happening to citizenship between elections. The datum is the long-term, nationwide trend uncovered by Walter Dean Burnham showing decreased participation in presidential elections.[48] His findings clearly indicate that, ever since the latter part of the 19th century, the rate of voter turnout every four years has in all parts of the country declined. A slight upsurge for the 1932–1960 period is discernible, but nevertheless "current turnout rates . . . remain substantially below 19th-century levels." [49] Burnham attributes this trend to a failure of the political system—and particularly the party system—to

---

47 For another illustration of this point, see Milton J. Rosenberg, Sidney Verba, and Philip E. Converse, *Vietnam and the Silent Majority: The Dove's Guide* (New York: Harper & Row, 1970).

48 "The Changing Shape of the American Political Universe," *American Political Science Review*, Vol. LIX (March, 1965), pp. 7–28.

49 *Ibid.*, p. 11. It may well be, moreover, that the mean turnout rate of 68 percent for the 1932–1960 period represents a temporary deviation and not a shift in the overall pattern of decline. Or at least the comparable figures for the 1964 and 1968 elections suggest such a conclusion: these were 62 and 60 percent respectively (cf. *The New York Times,* December 11, 1968). The figure of 55 percent for the 1972 election, which was based on an electorate expanded by 18-year-olds, further indicates that the 1932–1960 period is a deviation from rather than a reversal of the central tendency.

accord legitimacy to non-middle-class values and thus "to inte-grate the apolitical half of the American electorate" into it.[50] In addition, Burnham offers an interpretation of the impact of television and the other mass media exactly opposite to the one outlined below and suggests that some part of the discrepancy between the turnout for 19th-century and late 20th-century elections is explained by the fact that the former were "major sources of entertainment in an age unblessed by modern mass communications, so that it is more difficult for politicians to gain and keep public attention today than it was then." [51]

While Burnham's datum appears indisputable, it does not necessarily undermine our expectation of slow growth in the Attentive Public. Even if his interpretation of the long-term trend is accepted—and other interpretations also seem plausible[52]—there is no reason to assume that the diminution of the active voting population must be accompanied by a corresponding de-crease in the ranks of citizens active between elections. Our reasons for anticipating increased attentiveness seem as applicable to a period of declining voter participation as to one marked by an upswing in the turnout. If the size of the Attentive Public should ever approach that of the active electorate—and our spec-ulation does not foresee this occurring for several decades, if ever —then a continuation of the long-term voting trend might imply a decline in attentiveness. Otherwise, however, the widening of the eligible electorate that Burnham posits as underlying the proportionate decline in turnout has little bearing on the pro-

[50] *Ibid.,* p. 28.

[51] *Ibid.,* p. 12.

[52] Conceivably, for example, the decline in voter turnout stems not from an alienation of non-middle class groups, but from an apathy of those in the middle class. That is, perhaps the former are becoming active voters in an effort to obtain more from the political system, while some of the latter are becoming inactive voters because of satisfaction with its opera-tion. The analysis of the impact of affluence noted below is consistent with such an interpretation. For another, more elaborate analysis—and rejec-tion—of the Burnham interpretation, see Philip E. Converse, "Change in the American Electorate," in Angus Campbell and Philip E. Converse, eds., *The Human Meaning of Social Change* (New York: Russell Sage, 1972), pp. 266–98.

cesses identified below as likely to encourage greater numbers to be active between elections. At most, Burnham's interpretation indicates that excessive optimism about the evolution of a more politically mature public should be avoided and that any theory of growth along these lines should be limited to the proposition that only citizens holding middle class values are likely to enter the Attentive Public in increasing numbers.

Another interpretation contrary to the one advanced below is offered by John E. Mueller, who compared public support for the Korean and Vietnam wars and found them to be roughly the same, a conclusion which leads him to speculate that the intense opposition to the Vietnam conflict was mainly a consequence of changes in the "intellectual left." [53] Mueller argues that, contrary to widespead impressions, the turbulence of the mid-1960s stemmed less from a growing Attentive Public than from greater activity, "a new vocalism," by essentially the same small minority of intellectuals. He sees them as having "picked up and helped develop effective new techniques for political expression" from the civil rights movement in the early 1960s, and as then moving on to the Vietnam issue in 1965 when the war intensified and civil rights successes lessened the attractiveness of that issue.[54] While this interpretation of what happened to the intellectual left seems sound, and while the intensity of citizenship between the 1964 and 1972 elections probably did convey an exaggerated picture of its extent, Mueller's interpretation leaves too much unexplained. As noted below, there are too many indications that the new techniques of expression spread well beyond the ranks of the intellectuals and that more people are becoming more attentive to conclude that the practices of citizenship have undergone substantial change for only one group.[55]

[53] "Trends in Popular Support for the Wars in Korea and Vietnam," *American Political Science Review,* Vol. LXV (June 1971), pp. 358–75.

[54] *Ibid.,* p. 372.

[55] Actually, Mueller acknowledges that the Attentive Public may be growing (*ibid.,* p. 373), but the acknowledgment is quite peripheral and unnecessary to his central argument. For an extensive elaboration of his analysis of the structure of public support, see John E. Mueller, *War, Presidents and Public Opinion* (New York: John Wiley, 1973).

One other interpretation of the prevailing scene needs to be summarized before advancing our thesis that the Attentive Public is growing. It is a composite of several approaches, all of which focus on the impact of affluence and industrialization on the individual in modern America. Satiated by luxury, stultified by television, atomized by large organizations, de-personalized by computer accounting systems, deprived of complaints by the welfare state, isolated from the centers of political decision by the sheer magnitude and complexity of society, the individual is said to be turning away from public affairs rather than toward them. The old blueprints of order and life in community, society, and world no longer seem appropriate to the intricacies of life in the space age.[56] Science defies Marxism, guerrilla warfare confounds democratic liberalism, urban life overwhelms traditional conservatism. At the same time, the outmoded values have not been replaced by new ones that provide a means of comprehending and evaluating the new issues of our time and that thus give direction to political energies. Accordingly, it is alleged that people are either retreating to anomic forms of satisfaction or returning to the comforting folds of family and church. But whether the behavior is deviant or conventional, the result is said to be the same: the citizen seeking anomic pleasures and his church-going counterpart searching for fundamentals are both moved by intensely personal drives. They have in common an inward orientation and selfishness that, the argument concludes, preclude the concern for other people and the commitment to larger goals on

[56] Extended analyses of this point can be found in Edward Shils, "The End of Ideology?" *Encounter,* Vol. V (November 1955), pp. 52–58; Seymour Martin Lipset, *Political Man: Where, How and Why Democracy Works in the Modern World* (Garden City: Doubleday and Co., 1960), Chap. 13; Daniel Bell, *The End of Ideology: On the Exhaustion of Political Ideas in the Fifties* (Glencoe, Ill.: The Free Press, 1960), pp. 369–75; and Joseph La Palombara, "Decline of Ideology: A Dissent and an Interpretation," and Seymour Martin Lipset, "Some Further Comments on *The End of Ideology,*" *American Political Science Review,* Vol. LX (March 1966), pp. 5–18.

which involvement in politics is presumed to rest. The arena of public affairs offers little pleasure or excitement in comparison to the three-week tour of European capitals, the television spectacular, the family outing, or the narcotic dose.

There is much to be said for this line of reasoning. Wealth is widespread and a great many people now enjoy unprecedented luxury. Crime, drug addiction, juvenile delinquency, and other forms of anomie are national problems, and they seem to be linked to larger social trends. Statistics on family life and religious practice reflect the patterns described.[57] The television screen certainly commands the energies and dampens the imaginations of millions of citizens. And one need look back no further than to the 1950s to find a convergence of these tendencies and a resulting torpor pervading the national community.[58] Some might argue that a similar torpor set in as the Vietnam conflict waned in the early 1970s.

Furthermore, there are some systematic data indicating that the affluence in the economic realm has had an impact on some of the key attitudes that sustain the political system. A careful analysis of nationwide public opinion surveys from the 1940s through the mid-1960s yielded evidence that the period was marked by a diminution of a sense of partisanship and a declining sense of

[57] For example, a survey conducted in 1966 yielded the finding that about one of every three Protestants attends a religious service weekly, a rise of about 8 percent over the comparable figure for 1952, and that two out of every three Roman Catholics go to Mass every Sunday, or a 5 percent upswing over the 1952 figure. Cf. *The New York Times*, August 21, 1966, p. E13.

[58] For provocative analyses that posit the 1950s as an era of national torpor, see Robert L. Heilbroner, *The Future as History* (New York: Harper & Brothers, 1960); Emmet John Hughes, *America the Vincible* (Garden City: Doubleday & Co., 1959); Karl E. Meyer, *The New America: Politics and Society in the Age of the Smooth Deal* (New York: Basic Books, 1961); W. W. Rostow, *The United States in the World Arena: An Essay in Recent History* (New York: Harper & Brothers, 1960); and Meg Greenfield, "The Great American Morality Play," *The Reporter*, June 8, 1961, pp. 13–18.

urgency about electoral outcomes,[59] trends which were interpreted as suggesting that "there has been a growing state of confidence between men and government. . . . The headlines will not show this consensus, nor will the demonstrations at city hall or on the campus, but the ordinary man in the Age of Affluence is beginning to find some greater sense of hope and peace and self-assurance expressed in a less acrimonious political style." [60] While there is no basis for concluding that this new style will not change again or that it necessarily involves diminished involvement in politics, its character is certainly consistent with the interpretation that the torpor of natonal life has, except for the brief period of concern about Vietnam, extended into the political arena.[61]

A GROWING MINORITY?

Notwithstanding the tendencies that have accompanied affluence—and, in a curious way, partly because of them—it seems reasonable to speculate that contrary tendencies are also operative that, on balance, will foster a growth in the ranks of the Attentive Public. It must be emphasized that we are not positing a rapid and widespread increase in citizenship between elections. Sudden spurts of such activity seem highly unlikely in view of all the incentives to apathy that have kept down the ranks of the Attentive Public for so long. If a sudden and sharp rise in the attentiveness and mobilizability of the citizenry were to occur, it is more likely that it would reflect a temporary, impetuous, and impulsive expression of increasing malcontent than a structured and sustained concern about the course of events. From the perspective of political stability, it is quite appropriate

---

[59] Robert E. Lane, "The Politics of Consensus in an Age of Affluence," *American Political Science Review*, Vol. LIX (December 1965), pp. 874–95.

[60] *Ibid.*, p. 895.

[61] Actually, Lane takes no position on whether the practices of citizenship between elections are intensified or diminished by affluence. Some of his indicators suggest the likelihood of a decrease in political participation, but, as noted below, one of them points to an increase.

that travel, television, and family occupy the time of people.[62] Any quick and widespread turn away from such pursuits to public affairs would indicate the advent of disruptive politics, and that is not what we foresee when we predict the growth of the Attentive Public. Our speculation concerns a small but steady expansion of the number of citizens who develop and maintain a continuing interest in public affairs. Stated in crude quantitative terms, the tendencies we shall be discussing are not likely to accelerate the rate of growth of the Attentive Public by more than, say, one-tenth of one percent a year. Such a rate can have profound long-range consequences for the conduct of public affairs, but for the moment we are asserting only that it has started, and nothing in the ensuing analysis is intended to imply a larger scale of change.

The origin of such an assertion is, admittedly, a highly impressionistic interpretation of recent history. The 1960s and 1970s appear to be vastly different from the 1950s. Torpor seems to have given way to the protest march, the teach-in, the boycott, and the petition. The Mobilizable American appears to have supplemented the Satisfied American. Where the debilitating influences of material abundance once seemed to be the dominant concern of thoughtful observers, the limits of civil disobedience now appear to be at least an equally dominant preoccupation. Where people once seemed preoccupied with their pocketbooks, increasing numbers now appear even more concerned with their consciences. Where letters-to-the-editor columns once seemed short and filled with trivia, they now appear long and full of agitated reactions to public affairs. Where students once seemed lethargic and involved in conventional study, now they seem to

---

[62] Although intended as an empirical observation, obviously this statement of what is appropriate also has important normative implications. For extended discussions of the philosophical ramifications of equating political stability with private pursuits, see Carole Pateman, *Participation and Democratic Theory* (Cambridge: Cambridge University Press, 1970); and Dennis F. Thompson, *The Democratic Citizen: Social Science and Democratic Theory in the 20th Century* (Cambridge: Cambridge University Press, 1970).

perceive the rally and the picket line as legitimate settings for educational experience. Where the heroes of mass culture once adhered to an unwritten rule prohibiting political commitment, now the tensions of public affairs "seem to be inducing more and more Hollywood stars to take a stand on political issues." [63] Where the array of "soap operas" available on daytime television was once confined to such themes as the troubled marriage and the fortune-hunting male, now it includes a series in which the heroine is "a peace activist married into a wealthy conservative family." [64] Where the national scene once seemed to be dominated by modes of consumption, it now conveys the impression of being pervaded by acts of expression. Indeed, the instances of self-immolation, like the one cited at the outset of this chapter, become especially meaningful in the context of this surge toward expression. Whatever else they represent, such actions are an extreme form of expression, and it seems symbolic of the changes since the 1950s that even a few individuals have felt compelled to resort to expressions of this kind.

Some would argue that the tumult and change since the 1960s amounts not to an evolution of political involvement, but to a revolution in legitimacy, to a crisis of authority in every sphere of American life. Only a few years ago the rank and file of labor generally ratified the contracts negotiated by their leaders, students usually abided by the decisions of college faculties and university administrators, voters ordinarily nominated the primary candidates offered by party hierarchies, blacks typically acquiesced to the low status accorded them by whites, boys characteristically accepted the obligation to serve in the armed forces, tenants habitually paid their rents. Such givens of the recent past are today's uncertainties. Indeed, it has been argued that the challenges to authority are so pervasive that what used to be extreme political attitudes are now conventional bargaining positions, what were once stable groups are now hostile factions, and what once constituted administrative routines are now contested issues.

[63] *The New York Times,* August 5, 1965.
[64] *The New York Times,* December 11, 1969.

It is not difficult to develop a plausible explanation for such a breakdown in legitimacy. It can be argued that the ties that have bound Americans together in a national community have disintegrated as a cumulative result of the blacks' quest for equality, a war in Southeast Asia that proved terribly expensive and morally dubious, and mounting evidence that the fruits of an industrial civilization can be polluted to the point of being poisonous. Long-standing goals and cherished symbols are no longer satisfying. Individuals and groups are fearful for their safety and angered by their inability to improve their condition. Thus private demands have intensified and feelings of community have atrophied, giving rise to a crisis of authority in all the institutions of the society. The privatization of interests and the polarization of conflicts have, in turn, led the citizenry to resort to new citizenship practices to defend their needs and proclaim their wants. Frustrated and desperate, they regard the traditional practices as no longer adequate and feel that preferences must be publicly as well as privately communicated to government. With the broad ties of a national community being replaced by the narrow bonds of similar age, sex, color, or job, groups are emphasizing what divides them rather than what unites them. As a result, this argument concludes, confrontation is replacing accommodation as the means of resolving conflict.

While some aspects of this pessimistic explanation certainly seem accurate, a more positive interpretation of the tumult in public affairs also seems plausible. Blacks are pressing, Vietnam has had profound moral and social repercussions, and the quality of the environment has deteriorated; but to conclude that these realities have led to a breakdown of community and to the emergence of a politics of confrontation is to make an unjustified leap in social analysis. Such may well be the case and future generations may look back on the 1960s as the beginning of the end of a united United States. Nevertheless, it does not take a greater inductive leap to arrive at a very different interpretation of the signs of increased involvement in public affairs. This interpretation would argue that what we are witnessing is not the disintegration of communities but the fulfillment of individuals; not a crisis of authority but the emergence of a belief that authority can be shared; not a privatization of interests but a widening of public concerns; not a rising frustration over ineffectiveness in public affairs but a growing conviction that effectiveness is possible. The bases for such an interpretation are elaborated below and we contend that it accounts for the signs of change better than either the notion that affluence has caused people to retreat from the public arena or the contrary thesis that a breakdown in authority has caused them to enter it.

Appearances, of course, can be deceptive. It is conceivable that the signs of growing involvement in public affairs are only a temporary, impetuous and anomic spurt of activity over the war in Vietnam. The torpor of the 1950s may well return as that agonizing conflict recedes into history. Or perhaps the social processes it intensified will gain momentum and authority will deteriorate even further. Possibly, too, both processes are at work and destined to unfold side by side as an enlarged and more flexible definition of pluralism allows the affluent to retreat and encourages the underprivileged to heighten their demands. In either event, certainly it is possible that the appearance of growing involvement is, as Mueller stresses, nothing more than greater activity on the part of the same minority that has always comprised the Attentive Public. Perhaps we have mistaken qualitative innovations in the form of activity for quantitative changes in the amount of it. Teach-ins reflect attentiveness and protest marches reflect mobilizability, but do they also reflect a more widespread practice of citizenship between elections? Is the Attentive Public growing or is it merely becoming more visible? The foregoing analysis of the emerging scene provides no clear-cut answer, and unfortunately the available findings cannot be transformed into trend data that are adequate for a searching probe of the question.

Although it is possible that the greater intensity of citizenship in recent years may convey a misleading picture of its extent, direction, and durability, we are nonetheless inclined to reassert our original impressions and to interpret recent trends as signs of growth in structured and sustained attentiveness rather than as an impulsive and transitory surge of activity. We do so because such an interpretation seems more appropriate to explain recent trends in citizenship activity than any of the existing theories of anomic behavior in an affluent and industrial civilization. Theories of anomie and the breakdown of authority may be applicable to certain societies, but they leave too much unexplained about modern American society. Thus we have had to develop a theory of issue-area attentiveness that we shall henceforth refer to as our "growth hypothesis." To anticipate the ensuing analysis, we argue that a number of historic patterns conducive to active citizenship between elections converged during the 1960s and that the very forces which gave rise to an era of affluence also fostered attentiveness. Small but discernible accretions in the Attentive Public will therefore be revealed if appropriate trend data can be gathered.

CITIZENSHIP IN AN INTERDEPENDENT WORLD

Two long-term historical patterns, one immediate historical circumstance, and an assumption that attentiveness tends to become habitual, together underlie our conviction that the torpor of affluence and the crisis in authority mask an underlying trend toward a more active citizenry. The most important of these factors is probably the mounting interdependence of men and nations. As the pace of technological change quickens, the individual is drawn ever more deeply into the web of world affairs. This process might be called the "shrinkage" factor, since it encompasses all the ways in which the rapid and dynamic developments in communications and transportation have shrunk social and political distances within and between nations.[65] Comsat and

---

[65] Another, more elegant label for the shrinkage factor is provided by McDougal: "People on opposite sides of the globe who never confront each other nevertheless continuously affect each other in a process of interdetermination with respect to all values which for rough descriptive purposes may be termed a world social process." Myres S. McDougal and Associates, *Studies in World Public Order* (New Haven: Yale University Press, 1960), p. 165.

the jet are symbolic of changes that culminated in the 1960s and that have increased the interdependence of communities. Today an event in one part of the world can have repercussions in every other part. An assassination in Dallas is, within minutes, a searing experience in Buffalo and a painful one in Buenos Aires. An astronaut's blast-off into outer space is a moment of tension in millions of living rooms. A labor dispute in California poses a question in Trenton of whether to buy grapes or lettuce. A presidential dinner in Peking is a vicarious culinary experience, if not a welcome political event, in Tucson. A power failure in Toronto is a night of darkness in New York City. A distant political struggle, or a stranger's tormented psyche, results in a luggage search on boarding a plane in Minneapolis. A massacre in Mylai occasions feelings of shame or assertions of patriotism in Boston. A conflict in the Middle East precipitates murder at a sporting event in Munich and an oil shortage in Muncie. The international or national event, in short, *is* personal experience and daily life, making it increasingly difficult not to be aware of public affairs.

Mounting interdependence not only means that distant events impinge on daily life. The impact of technology has also had the consequence of widening the choices open to individuals. Compared to earlier generations, most Americans today have a much greater range of choice when deciding on a purchase, a marriage partner, an occupation, a place to live, or when forming attachments to friends and groups. The greater capacity for choice has in turn increased the sense of self-worth of the citizen, emboldening him to demand more of government. "This is probably the first age in history in which such high proportions of people have felt like individuals," one group of scholars concluded. "No 18th-century factory worker, so far as we know, had the sense of individual worth that underlies the demands on society of the average resident of the black urban ghetto today." [66]

[66] From the fourth annual report of the Harvard University Program on Technology and Society, as quoted in *The New York Times,* January 18, 1969, p. 1.

The second long-term pattern is equally significant and also derives from the pace of technological change. It is the continuing trend toward greater educational opportunity. Required by technology, facilitated by affluence, and demanded by the enlarged aspirations of an upwardly mobile people, the commitment to education and to the acquisition of training have steadily expanded until, in the last decade, more than half of each year's high school graduates go on to college. By 1966, for example, 4,673,026 students were enrolled in college, a figure that represents a 5.8 percent increase over the previous year, a 52 percent increase over 1961, and a 113 percent increase over 1956.[67] The 1970 census revealed such "an explosive growth in the amount of education obtained by young Americans . . . that what has been regarded as a generation gap is shown largely to be an education gap"—with the proportion of persons with college degrees having tripled since 1940 (from 6 to 16 percent), the proportion with one or more years of college having more than doubled (from 13 to 31 percent), and the proportion of high school graduates having risen from 38 to an unprecedented 75 percent.[68]

Nor is the educational trend confined to formal institutions of learning. A growing number of adult education programs relevant to public affairs are being conducted by many types of organizations and associations, by the mass media, and even by government officials. Where college reunions once consisted of wild parties, now they are also—or even wholly—the scene of serious discussions led by the faculty. Where trade unions once supplied members with newspapers containing social news and information on the bread-and-butter issues of labor-management relations, now they also offer summer school courses on world affairs[69] and educational materials on specific issues of foreign

---

[67] Garland G. Parker, "Statistics of Attendance in American Universities and Colleges, 1966–67," *School and Society*, Vol. XCV (January 7, 1967), p. 22.

[68] *The New York Times*, February 4, 1971, p. 1.

[69] See Alfred O. Hero, *The U.A.W. and World Affairs* (mimeographed, 1965).

policy.[70] Where business once equated their responsibilities with production and profit, now a "social responsibility theme seems suddenly to have gathered a steamroller momentum" and "in speech after speech in recent months executives have urged their colleagues to take a more active role in politics and civic affairs, to join the war against poverty, to improve relations with government, academic circles and students." [71] Where newspapers once stressed their entertainment features, now they also give prominent space to their public affairs columnists and advertise them in a "spectacular and expensive way." [72] Where local radio and television stations once left public affairs programming to the networks, now some 20 percent of such radio stations and some 30 percent of such television stations "have reached the point where they do more than give routine attention to news and show real responsibility and quality in their news services." [73] Where the television networks once confined public affairs programs to the least desirable viewing hours, now they are capable of devoting three and a half hours of prime evening time to a panoramic

[70] Delegates to the 1965 convention of the Building Trades Department of the AFL-CIO, for example, "approved an active program through 8,000 local unions and 525 state and local councils to bring a full understanding of the United States participation in Vietnam to each of the building trades' 3.5 million members." *The New York Times*, December 3, 1965, p. 9.

[71] Robert A. Wright, "Beyond the Profits: Business Reaches for a Social Role," *The New York Times*, July 3, 1966, Section 3, p. 1. Viewed from the perspective of facilitating citizenship activity between elections, perhaps the most important expression of social responsibility on the part of the business community was taken by the Western Union Telegraph Company when it established a special reduced rate for "personal opinion messages" from anyone anywhere in the country who wanted to send his views to the President, the Vice President, or any senator or representative. See *The New York Times*, January 22, 1962, p. 11.

[72] Ben H. Bagdikian, "A Golden Age of Oracles," *Columbia Journalism Review*, Vol. IV (Winter 1966), p. 11.

[73] William A. Wood, "The Sound of Maturity," *Columbia Journalism Review*, Vol. IV (Winter 1966), p. 7.

survey of U.S. foreign policy.[74] Where government officials once conducted their activities at their own convenience, they are now more inclined, for a variety of reasons, to adjust the form and timing of their deliberations to the habits of the Attentive Public: more than 400 members of Congress, for example, conduct regular interview programs for local radio and television stations[75] and, even more significantly, in 1965 the President for the first time delivered his State of the Union address to Congress at 9:00 P.M., thereby exposing a nationwide television audience to proceedings that previously had started at noon.

These trends in formal and adult education are bound to have enormous consequences for the expansion of the economy and the continuing pace of technological change,[76] and their political repercussions are also likely to be extensive. With more and more citizens receiving formal education or participating in adult education programs, and with the means of communicating information and ideas becoming ever more efficient, it seems unlikely that the degree of attentiveness to public affairs will not also increase. There is nothing magical about education, to be sure. Possession of a college degree or exposure to the State of the Union address is no guarantee that an individual will acquire sensitivity to politics. But for most individuals formal training does seem to make a difference. One of the most consistent findings of social science is that, in general, the more formal education a person has, the more likely he is to follow the course of events and engage in attentive citizenship. For example, we noted earlier that only 7 percent of the citizenry regard information and public affairs programs as their favorite television fare, but this is an

---

[74] Over the NBC network on September 7, 1965, before an audience estimated at more than 21 million people in 12 million homes. See the *Washington Post,* September 10, 1965, p. B15.

[75] *The New York Times,* August 1, 1965, p. 63.

[76] For an impressive survey of the motivational dynamics underlying recent trends in adult education, see John W. C. Johnstone and Ramon I. Rivera, *Volunteers for Learning: A Study of the Educational Pursuits of American Adults* (Chicago: Aldine Publishing Co., 1965).

overall figure that changes considerably when broken down in terms of seven different levels of educational accomplishment: 4 percent at the lowest level (six years of grade school or less) and 23 percent at the highest level (post-college) cited such programs, and the figures for the intervening levels increased progressively with the amount of education.[77] While this does not mean that the membership of the Attentive Public will grow in proportion to the increase in educational attainments of the citizenry, it does seem plausible that the increase will provide both the incentive and the capacities for an expanding membership.[78]

The culmination and success of the civil rights movement in the early 1960s constitutes the immediate historical circumstances that leads us to believe that a trend toward more active

[77] Steiner, *The People Look at Television*, p. 126. For more elaborate data showing the pervasiveness of the relationship between education and attentiveness, see below, pp. 291–96.

[78] An alternative, more long range explanation posits education as an intervening rather than an independent variable. That is, the rise in education is seen as a result of changes in the society's class structure and as, in turn, producing greater attentiveness. Comparative research into the patterns of political participation in five countries, including the United States, has shown clear-cut indications that high social status is one of two major routes to active citizenship between elections (organizational involvement is the other). It was found that in all five countries high status individuals acquired the skills and motives which facilitate sustained participation, thus leading to the conclusion that the "political life styles of citizens will not be markedly changed until extensive industrialization alters the status structure of society, and thereby increases the overall level of political information, attentiveness, efficacy, and so forth." (See Norman H. Nie, Bingham Powell, Jr., Kenneth Prewitt, "Social Structure and Political Participation: Developmental Relationships," *American Political Science Review*, Vol. 63 [June and September, 1969], pp. 361–78 and 808–32 [the quote is from p. 826].) While it is undoubtedly the case that the impact of educational changes on the growth rate of the Attentive Public merely reflects more basic changes occurring in American society, we have not attempted to cast our growth hypothesis at this more all-encompassing level. For our purposes it is sufficient to stress that, whether it is treated as an independent or intervening variable, education makes a significant contribution to the resources and predispositions that are necessary to active citizenship.

citizenship between elections has started. Education provided an increased capacity for attentiveness and mounting interdependence fostered greater motivation toward it, but still lacking was confidence that utilization of the new talents and expression of the new motives would justify the time and energy required. The civil rights episode supplied this in a vivid way. The relationship between citizenship activity and the new civil rights legislation in 1964 and 1965 was unmistakable to anyone who followed the course of public affairs. As a result, we would argue that "subjective political competence"—the belief that through active citizenship one can affect the course of events[79]—was given an enormous nationwide lift. The prolonged and widespread use of nonviolent techniques of protest not only produced a visible readiness on the part of federal officials to press for the adoption of remedial civil rights legislation, but it also legitimized the conviction that the individual citizen could contribute to the outcome of the policy-making process. At no other time in modern American history has active citizenship seemed so efficacious as it did when demonstrations in Birmingham served as the immediate impetus for President Kennedy's submission of a greatly broadened civil rights bill to Congress in June 1963; when the House Judiciary Committee approved the bill within two months after the "March on Washington" in August 1963; when a vast letter-writing campaign was followed by the defeat of a Senate filibuster and passage of the bill in May–June 1964; and when demonstrations in Selma preceded President Johnson's request for and Congress's acceptance of new voting rights legislation in the spring of 1965. Moreover, these developments were accompanied by a less spectacular but no less successful effort on the part of the peace movement to provide support for the nuclear test-ban treaty, which was ratified by more than two-thirds of the Senate in September 1963.[80]

---

[79] For an elaboration of the subjective competence concept, see below, pp. 147–48 and 356–57.

[80] This is not to imply that the rate of political participation remained constant in the United States for the 170 years prior to the 1960s. On the

Events seemed to say that officials are more accessible than ever, that communications do reach them and do produce reactions. As indicated by the quotation that opens Chapter 5, President Kennedy spoke explicitly of his accessibility and his receipt of the messages citizens sought to convey by marching around the White House. Both the civil rights and peace movements later came upon harder times, but the fact that officialdom can be responsive had nevertheless been established for the present generation.

The intensity of subsequent controversies and the techniques used to wage them are one form of evidence that the civil rights movement was a source of increased attentiveness to public affairs. Many of the issues that have arisen since the 1964–1965 successes of the civil rights movement appear to evoke the same intense involvement and the same forms of protest that were characteristic of the public's participation in the civil rights debate. It does not seem to be a coincidence, for example, that the debate on the Vietnam situation after 1965 involved numbers of people and reached peaks of intensity through picketing, rallying, moratoria, letter-writing, and other methods of communicating support or dissent that have no parallel in debates over American foreign policy. The ambiguous nature of that war and its escalation were no doubt especially conducive to controversy, but that is hardly a sufficient explanation for the breadth and depth of the debate. The Korean War was also undeclared and conducted in a distant Asian land for limited purposes and with modern weapons and pinpoint bombing, but it certainly was not marked by domestic controversy as heated and pervasive as that which

---

contrary, it has been demonstrated that a revolution in mass political letter-writing occurred in the 1930s. [See Leila A. Sussmann, *Dear FDR: A Study of Political Letter-Writing* (Totowa, N.J.: The Bedminster Press, 1963), p. 12.] Our argument is that the early 1960s marked a turning point in the extent of citizenship activity and that the forces involved are such that an enduring trend rather than a temporary fluctuation has been set in motion.

accompanied escalation of the Vietnam conflict.[81] Since the methods of protest and counterprotest used with regard to Vietnam were so similar to those introduced in the civil rights episode, it seems reasonable to attribute at least a part of the controversy over Vietnam to an expansion of subjective political competence among the citizenry.

The persistence of the Vietnam protests between 1965 and 1968 is itself an indication that the civil rights episode probably laid the basis for a high sense of political competence among a generation of citizens. At least it seems reasonable to suggest that the earlier successes in the civil rights area sustained widespread opposition to the war in the face of continued escalation and contrary to the historic pattern in which citizens, especially those in high socio economic statuses, rally to the support of beleaguered foreign policies.[82] Such a rallying did not occur. Nor did apathy or alienation set in among the ranks of concerned citizens. Members of the Attentive Public did not interpret the continued

[81] A good measure of the difference between the domestic controversies generated by the limited wars in Korea and Vietnam is provided by a comparison of the number of persons and organizations associated with policy-oriented advertisements placed in the "News of the Week in Review" section of the Sunday edition of *The New York Times* during the two periods. For the first year after the inception of American bombing raids on North Vietnam in February 1965, a total of 27 advertisements were placed in this medium by 25 different groups or organizations. Some of the advertisements indicated support of U.S. policy, but most opposed it. All together, the 27 advertisements contained the names of 9,476 individuals as sponsors of the positions advanced in their texts. On the other hand, similar expressions of opinion for the entire Korean War, from July 1, 1950, through August 1, 1953, totaled two advertisements, one without signatures placed by the American Friends Service Committee asking for contributions to send clothing to Korean children and one placed by Eugene Greenhut of 10 East 44th Street, New York, proposing a plan for ending the Korean conflict and "insuring democracy's survival in the Free World."

[82] William A. Gamson and Andre Modigliani, "Knowledge and Foreign Policy Opinions: Some Models for Consideration," *Public Opinion Quarterly*, Vol. XXX (Summer 1966), pp. 187–99.

escalation of the U.S.'s involvement in the conflict as evidence that officials were not receiving the public's message of concern and their sense of political competence did not drop. Instead they became more active than ever, exhibiting unshakable confidence that eventually their messages about the need for de-escalation in Vietnam would receive consideration in Washington. Fortified by the earlier successes of the civil rights movement and perhaps spurred on by the fact that President Johnson was known to read and attach great importance to public opinion polls, active citizens were able to sustain their belief in their own political competence and continue to openly assert their demands for a change in Vietnam policy even though in fact that policy was moving in the opposite direction throughout 1965, 1966, and 1967.

If the successes of the civil rights movement sustained the subjective competence of active citizens during the lean years of escalation in Vietnam, consider what the setback to President Johnson in the 1968 New Hampshire presidential primary, his subsequent decisions not to run for re-election and to cease the bombing of North Vietnam—not to mention the progressive de-escalation of American involvement subsequent to 1968—did for citizens' estimates of their capacity to affect the course of events. The early 1960s may have established high political competence for a generation, but the late 1960s and early 1970s probably raised it irreversibly to a new plateau of confidence and expectation.

A vivid demonstration of the resilience of subjective political competence was provided by the spurt of citizenship activity that followed the decision to send U.S. troops into Cambodia and the Kent State tragedy of May 1970. Disorder and violence on campuses commanded the headlines in the immediate aftermath of these events, but a closer reading of accounts of the Attentive Public's activities reveals that the unexpected events in Indochina did not evoke primarily malaise and disorder. For the most part active citizens were galvanized into creative, peaceful, and vigorous forms of political action. Faced with a major setback to their aspirations for Southeast Asia, they reacted, not with aimless despair, but with intense activity which seemed to rest on the conviction that it was possible to bring about a reversal of policy and to prevent future decisions of this kind. What stood out were not the few "crazies" who fomented riots and fire-bombed buildings, but the many citizens who turned to "leafleting," to calling on members of Congress, and to other constructive efforts to mobilize support for their aspirations. The Cambodian decision and the Kent State tragedy may have, at least temporarily, politicized the university and polarized the society, but they also lay bare a remarkable commitment to the democratic process.[83]

Reactions to the Cambodian and Kent State crises also made evident that, contrary to Mueller's interpretation, concern about Vietnam was not confined to left-wing intellectuals. Among other groups spawned by the events, for example, was the Corporate Executive Committee for Peace, which in six weeks was joined by "more than 350 executives in the top levels of business" and which then sent a delegation of "100 executives from as many corporations" to Washington to lobby against the war in Vietnam.[84] An additional indication that the increased sense of political competence spread well beyond the intelligentsia is provided by the role of the clergy in the Vietnam protests. Quite apart from the traditional pacifism that has always marked a small segment of the clergy, reaction to the conflict in Vietnam was manifest among thousands of clergymen throughout the country. The National Emergency Committee of Clergy Concerned About

---

[83] That extensive involvement in protests can reflect—at least for some citizens—a commitment to the democratic process is readily discernible in the data generated to test the hypothesis (p. 981) that "frequent participation in protest activities for instrumental purposes is likely to be associated with a commitment to the peaceful maintenance of the political order, likely to foster a sense of involvement in the society, and hence likely to create bonds of identification with the society, and engender a realization that 'private partialities' must often be compromised in the interests of social peace." See Peter K. Eisinger, "Protest Behavior and the Integration of Urban Political Systems," *Journal of Politics*, Vol. 33 (1971), pp. 960–1007.

[84] *The New York Times,* June 24, 1970, p. 10.

Vietnam had 145 local chapters within a month after it was organized. That this activation of the clergy arose out of an expanded subjective political competence that had been expanded earlier in the decade is readily apparent in at least one explanation of the changed behavior offered at the time:

> The most important immediate cause of the current wave of protests has been the civil rights movement. In the period following the Freedom Rides of 1961 large numbers of churchmen got their first taste of leadership in a major social movement. Their success, which surprised many, prompted radical rethinking of their role as clergymen and led to the present mood of 'stand up and be counted.'[85]

Nor, it must be stressed, was the contagion of the civil rights episode confined to the issue of Vietnam. In the New York area alone, for example, the months immediately following the enactment of civil rights legislation witnessed a march by 4,000 postal workers demanding pay increases,[86] a protest by 35 elderly women who demonstrated against the extension of Interstate Highway 287 through historic sites by ensconcing themselves in the bulldozer's shovel,[87] a threatened boycott of classes by City College students opposing a proposal to introduce tuition fees,[88] and a sit-in by 400 residents of Mount Vernon who objected to the rebuilding of the outmoded Cross County Parkway into a superhighway.[89]

One meaning of all these diverse activities seems clear: although ideologies may have provided guidance in the past, for active citizens the present is marked by attentiveness to specific issues and sensitivity to their boundaries. Technological advance, while rendering broad ideological frameworks obsolete for mem-

---

[85] Edward B. Fiske, "War and the Clergy," *The New York Times*, February 15, 1966, p. 2.

[86] *The New York Times*, July 24, 1965, p. 19.

[87] *Ibid.*, May 25, 1965, p. 43.

[88] *Ibid.*, November 14, 1965, p. 58.

[89] *Ibid.*, May 19, 1965, p. 1.

bers of the Attentive Public, has also equipped them with the capacity to discriminate and the motivation to follow events in the nuclear age. Thus overriding precepts have given way to issue boundaries as bases for approaching public affairs. Unable to fall back on grandiose value systems as the source of their judgments about any situation, but at the same time better able and more inclined to assess situations, attentive citizens are readier to seek comprehension and evaluation of issues in their own terms. Where an all-encompassing system of thought may have once served to guide them through the maze of never-ending problems that mark local, national, and international life, now they rely on several belief systems, each of which is internally consistent and independent of any other. Rather than adhering to a "conservative" or "liberal" philosophy, the attentive citizen has, among others, a civil rights philosophy, a war-peace philosophy, and a resource utilization philosophy. What a member of the literary fraternity has said about his colleagues can also readily be used to describe active persons in a variety of professions: "Not many writers are today really more interested in a worked-out political ideology or large-scale political involvement than they were, say, in 1960, yet on a series of specific political-moral issues, they do respond with vigor and sometimes passion." [90]

Today's member of the Attentive Public, in other words, neither clings to ideological blueprints nor moves erratically from issue to issue, searching for meaning in a complex world. Rather he makes his peace with complexity by accepting it and fragmenting it into manageable issue-areas. The quick shifts in attention that some view as disoriented and anomic[91] are thus, for members of the Attentive Public, pragmatic adjustments to the fast-moving pace of events. In the words of one member, "I am quite crisis- and issue-oriented." [92]

[90] Irving Howe, "The Writer Can't Keep to His Attic," *New York Times Magazine*, December 5, 1965, p. 44.

[91] For example, see William Kornhauser, *The Politics of Mass Society* (Glencoe, Ill.: The Free Press, 1959), p. 46.

[92] Sally Cook, an activist student at the University of Chicago, quoted in *The New York Times*, September 5, 1965, p. 45.

This is not to deny, of course, that some members of the Attentive Public possess such crude ideas about public affairs that they are unable to sustain their membership after an issue that engaged their simplistic value structure wanes. As will be elaborated in the next chapter, the Attentive Public is conceived to consist, at any moment in time, of a permanent core of multi-issue members and a number of single-issue persons whose identity is continuously changing as the rise of new issues and the attenuation of old ones activate and dissolve corresponding attention groups. Our growth hypothesis does not account for the temporary and fluctuating presence of the latter among the Attentive Public. The evidence that the less a person participates in public affairs the more his attitudes toward them are likely to be simplistic and unstable is too persuasive[93] for us to identify single-issue citizens as more than momentary members of the Attentive Public. What we have been discussing are the multi-issue citizens who are broadly and consistently concerned about public affairs. It is they whom we conceive as equipped with complex belief systems and as emerging in growing numbers from the educational upsurge, the shrinkage factor, and the experiences of the early 1960s.

One other main component of our growth hypothesis is an assumption about how the increased capacity for attentiveness acquired through education interacts with the greater subjective competence acquired through experience. Our analysis thus far has tended to imply that the former precedes and facilitates the latter. Now we need to make explicit our notion that the reverse process is also operative and that the interaction between education and experience is mutually reinforcing. It seems reasonable

---

[93] For incisive presentations and discussions of the evidence bearing on this correlation, see Philip E. Converse, "The Nature of Belief Systems in Mass Publics," in David E. Apter, ed., *Ideology and Discontent* (New York: The Free Press of Glencoe, 1964), pp. 206–61; and Herbert McClosky, "Consensus and Ideology in American Politics," *American Political Science Review*, Vol. LVIII (June 1964), p. 372.

to expect that for some persons the experience of developing a philosophy to cope with events in one issue-area heightens subjective politicial competence and encourages the further development and articulation of philosophies that are appropriate to other areas. Attentiveness thus tends to sustain itself. It becomes a habit —at least it becomes habitual for those whose objective and subjective competence have reached a point at which they are able to discriminate issue boundaries and to overcome the paralyzing temptations of simplistic generalizations.

The assumption that attentiveness may become habitual is central to our growth hypothesis because it implies that not every person who enters the Attentive Public on a single-issue and temporary basis will necessarily return to a condition of apathy as the problem that engaged his attention passes from the scene. It may well be that the vast majority of any single-issue group will return to apathy, but for a few citizens—those whose educational attainments and tolerance for complexity are sufficient to sustain a multi-issue concern about the course of events—the experience of a single issue may serve as the basis for new citizenship habits. In attentiveness and mobilizability, as in everything else, one has to begin somewhere, and for some individuals the initial impetus toward permanent membership in the Attentive Public may be provided by a "big" issue that momentarily breaks down the habits underlying apathy. Each major crisis of public affairs may thus leave in its wake a residue of new multi-issue recruits to the Attentive Public.

In other words, just as dynamic national leaders can bring about the politicization of citizens, so can momentous national issues. More specifically, just as the appeal and style of a Woodrow Wilson, a Franklin Roosevelt, an Adlai Stevenson, or a John Kennedy appear to have enlarged the Attentive Public by heightening the salience of public affairs, so may have the Cuban missile crisis, the Vietnam conflict, and the Watergate episode—to mention three of the more obvious examples—served to solidify the habit of attentiveness for many citizens. Indeed, as we have already suggested, the civil rights episode probably accomplished more in this regard than the combined efforts of all the national leaders and organizations who have sought to generate active citizenship between elections in the last fifty years.

THE LIMITS OF SPECULATION

Our growth hypothesis asserts, in sum, that a highly successful civil rights movement and increasing amounts of education have had such a significant impact upon both subjective and objective political competence in a shrinking world that more and more citizens can be expected to become and (because of the habit-forming nature of attentiveness) remain involved in the course of public affairs between elections. As such, of course, this reasoning is long on speculation and short on empirical evidence and conceptual distinctions. It rests on a delicate network of assumptions and hypotheses that need to be articulated and explored before precise expectations about the growth and future of the Attentive Public can be asserted with confidence. To perfect and test the hypothesis we need to examine the dynamics of attentiveness and mobilizability more closely. We have identified historical trends, but we have not linked them to the backgrounds, attitudes, and behavioral predispositions that underlie and sustain the habit of attentiveness and the propensity to be mobilized. We have assumed that citizenship between elections is marked by sensitivity to issue-area boundaries, but we have not specified the informational and attitudinal requirements of a capacity to discriminate one kind of issue from another. We have said that remote events are becoming increasingly proximate for concerned citizens, but we have not considered whether this is as true for foreign as for domestic policy issues. We have distinguished between the more and the less educated, but we have not differentiated other types of citizens or investigated whether different types engage in different degrees and forms of attentiveness. We have proceeded as if an expansion of subjective political competence leads to a corresponding increase in political activity, but we have not offered data that demonstrate such a relationship.

For all we know, in short, our prediction of slow growth in

the ranks of the Attentive Public may turn out to be untenable when its components are subjected to careful scrutiny and confronted by empirical data. Before proceeding to those tasks, however, an initial test of the validity of our growth hypothesis would seem to be mandatory. Further analysis might well be wasted effort if relevant data showed that the ranks of the Attentive Public had remained constant and had never grown at a faster rate than the population as a whole. Hence, after the formulation presented in the preceding pages was developed, we attempted to gather data that would reveal whether the trend line of attentiveness in postwar America should be drawn in an upward, downward, or horizontal direction. So as also to assess whether the shrinkage factor has led to a greater attentiveness to foreign policy issues, an effort was made to uncover data that reflected concern with international as well as national and local matters.

As previously indicated, such data are not readily available. Except for the voting studies, there are no comprehensive and systematic materials on citizenship activities, and of course the voting studies focus mainly on attitudes or activities occurring every fourth year and may thus have little relevance to what citizens think and do between elections.[94] The only data available for the interelection periods are survey data based on interviews and these suffer from two important weaknesses. One is that surveys with items that probe the extent and types of activities in

[94] Perhaps it is noteworthy that one set of data quite relevant to our growth thesis, compiled by Robert E. Lane from national surveys made during the 1952, 1956, and 1960 elections, also support the thesis. Using several questionnaire items designed to probe whether respondents felt they "ought to vote under various more or less discouraging circumstances," Lane constructed a "citizen duty" scale and found that through the eight-year period the data could be interpreted "as indicating a reinforced or growing belief that good citizenship means a politically more active citizen." See Lane's "The Politics of Consensus in an Age of Affluence," p. 894, 895. For another analysis in which data gathered during four presidential campaigns and two off-year elections between 1952 and 1964 are found to show a slight trend toward increased attentiveness (in every respect but "magazine attention"), see Donald J. Devine, *The Attentive Public: Polyarchical Democracy*, p. 55.

which citizens engage have not been made with sufficient regularity to provide clear-cut longitudinal trends. Two responses to the same item in surveys taken ten years apart, for example, are hardly enough to permit the observer to discern a trend. In the absence of comparable data on citizenship activity compiled on a regular basis, analysts have had to draw their longitudinal inferences from findings at widely scattered points in time.[95]

The second weakness of the available survey materials is

[95] One observer, for example, had to rely on surveys published in 1950 and 1961 to assess the trend of citizenship activity. He concluded that the trend was not upward since in the first survey 13 percent of the public reported having written a member of Congress "in the last year," while the comparable figure for the second survey was 9 percent. See Fred I. Greenstein, *The American Party System and the American People* (Englewood Cliffs: Prentice-Hall, Inc., 1963), p. 11. Two other observers, on the other hand, came to the contrary conclusion that writing letters to Congress was a "growing" practice on the basis of a contrast between a 1946 survey that yielded 15 per cent of the nationwide sample who reported having written or wired their representatives in Washington and a 1954 survey that uncovered 20 percent who said they had engaged in such behavior. See Malcolm E. Jewell and Samuel C. Patterson, *The Legislative Process in the United States* (New York: Random House, 1966), p. 343. Still another finding that supports our growth thesis—but that is based on only four points in time between 1953 and 1967—was developed by Hyman and Wright, who found a "small but noteworthy increase in the percentage of American adults who belong to voluntary associations." If it is assumed—as we do in subsequent chapters—that membership and activity in such associations is a form of attentiveness to public affairs, this conclusion is not only consistent with the thesis being advanced here, but it is also necessary (though not sufficient) to sustain it. Had a contrary trend on organizational activity been uncovered, the basic premise of this chapter would seem extremely questionable. For a full analysis of the data, see Charles R. Wright and Herbert H. Hyman, "Voluntary Association Memberships of American Adults: Evidence from National Sample Surveys," *American Sociological Review*, Vol. 23 (1958), pp. 284–94; and Herbert H. Hyman and Charles R. Wright, "Trends in Voluntary Association Memberships of American Adults: Replication Based on Secondary analysis of National Sample Surveys," *American Sociological Review*, Vol. 36 (1971), pp. 191–206.

that they inevitably reflect what citizens reported about their activity rather than what it actually was, and such self-reports are susceptible to considerable distortion. The societal norm that one ought to be active as a citizen can lead respondents to exaggerate the activities they say they undertook. Additional distortion can be introduced by the widespread tendency to want to please the interviewer by reporting what he presumably wants to hear. The absence of frequent surveys further compounds these problems inherent in data based on self-reports. If comparable inquiries into citizenship activity had been undertaken every six or twelve months during the postwar years, presumably the distortions arising out of the self-reporting problem would be randomly distributed and could thus be discounted. Since this is not the case, however, one can only conclude that, in the words of V. O. Key, Jr., "no trustworthy information exists on variations in the size of the politically active sector of the population through time." [96] New materials thus had to be gathered for the growth hypothesis to receive a preliminary test sufficient to justify further theoretical refinement.

SOME HARD DATA

The new data we have generated were uncovered in the records of letters received from the public by officials and newspapers. Although such records are kept by only a small proportion of those to whom citizens write about public issues,[97] we found enough to permit a reliable test of three crucial aspects

[96] *Politics, Parties, and Pressure Groups,* 5th ed. (New York: Thomas Y. Crowell Company, 1964), p. 594.

[97] A letter of inquiry sent to all 100 U.S. senators on April 22, 1966, yielded 65 respondents who said they did not keep tabulations of their incoming mail, 6 who reported some kind of record along these lines, and 29 who did not reply to the inquiry. On February 4, 1966, a similar letter was sent to the managing editors of 128 randomly selected daily newspapers with circulations over 50,000, and, of these, only 11 reported keeping systematic records of the letters they receive on public issues.

of our growth hypothesis. All told, we found four very different sources whose detailed records extend back into at least part of the 1950s and therefore allow us to test our hypothesis that the Attentive Public is slowly growing, that the early 1960s were a turning point in the extent of citizenship activity, and that this upward trend was not altered by the de-escalation of the United States' involvement in Vietnam.[98]

The records that extend farthest back in time are those kept by the White House. Beginning in the second Truman Administration, a weekly "report" has been made of all the mail received in the White House. Except for occasional periods for which the reports were either mislaid or not compiled, the presidential archives contain weekly tallies of mail received from 1949 to the present. Although it proved possible to acquire the weekly reports for only the 1949–1968 period, certain overall totals of mail received by the President during the 1969–1972 period were also obtained. The records of the other three sources, *The New York Times*, Senator Philip A. Hart of Michigan, and the *New York Post*, were also compiled on a weekly basis, but do not span as long a period of time. The first two of these records are virtually complete for the periods from 1958 and 1959 through 1972, while the records of the *New York Post* are somewhat scanty from 1955 through 1962 but are more complete thereafter until 1970, when the practice of keeping them was abandoned.[99]

---

[98] In addition, three other sources supplied less detailed records that have been used to supplement the findings developed out of the four primary sources. (See Table 2–2.)

[99] For their assistance in uncovering and supplying the particular data presented here, we are deeply grateful to John B. Oakes, Louise Polk Huger, Mildred Liebowitz, and Kalman Seigel of *The New York Times;* James A. Wechsler and Eve Berliner of the *New York Post;* Senator Philip A. Hart and his executive assistants, Lelia McKnight and Mildred Wade; Philip D. Lagerquist of the Harry S. Truman Library; W. D. Aeschbacher of the Dwight D. Eisenhower Library; Dan H. Fenn, Jr., and John F. Stewart of the John F. Kennedy Library; Harry J. Middleton and Charles W. Corkran of the Lyndon Baines Johnson Library;

Plainly these are hard data. They reflect citizenship behavior that actually occurred rather than behavior that was estimated to have occurred in the past or expected to occur in the future. Moreover, they reflect behavior that was recorded with sufficient frequency and detail to permit multidimensional analysis of longitudinal patterns. All four sources kept the records in terms of daily or weekly totals and also broke down these totals by issues. Hence we are not only in a position to discern the overall trends for the postwar period, but we can also identify the different trends in citizenship activities directed toward local, national, and international issues. In addition, these data are derived from a nationwide and heterogeneous segment of the Attentive Public. They encompass the intelligentsia and other elites throughout the nation who write to *The New York Times*, the less educated groups who pen letters to tabloids like the *Post*, the varied types of persons in all parts of the country who are inclined to write to the President, and the activist elements of a particular constituency who express their subjective competence through letters to their representatives in Congress.

These newly gathered materials are, of course, not entirely free of methodological limitations. There is the question of whether letter-writing is a sufficiently representative form of attentiveness to justify the assumption that these materials provide an adequate test of our growth hypothesis. In addition, the totals subsume letters written by children, cranks, and others whose activity does not stem strictly from attentiveness to public issues. Then there is the problem of whether the classifications used by the four sources were uniform throughout the period for which the records are available. The staffs of officials and newspapers change, and the criteria of classification may thus also change. Moreover, the White House and the modern daily newspaper are

---

Roland L. Elliott, Deputy Special Assistant to President Richard M. Nixon; Gordon Pates of the *San Francisco Chronicle*; Arthur P. Gallagher of the *Ann Arbor News* (Michigan); and C. E. Carpenter and Desmond Stone of the *Democrat and Chronicle* (Rochester, N.Y.).

large, complex organizations, and those who compiled the tabulations presented here did not necessarily see all of the incoming mail.[100]

Although important, neither these problems nor any of the more specific ones noted below appear to be sufficiently limiting as to negate the presumption that the ensuing materials are especially suitable for our purposes. If our growth hypothesis has any validity, then the trend should be upward for all four sources subsequent to the 1950s. These trends may show monthly or yearly fluctuations but if our hypothesis is correct, the mean level of activity around which the fluctuations occur should be higher than the mean level in the 1950s. In each case, in other words,

[100] In the case of these two newspapers, these data reflect only the mail received by those responsible for the letters-to-the-editor columns. Mail addressed to individual reporters and columnists or to other departments of the *Times* and the *Post* are not included in the figures. Likewise, the data for Senator Hart consist only of letters pertaining to public affairs and do not include those known as "case mail," which are estimated to constitute well over half of the letters received by members of Congress. (See Walter Gelhorn, *When Americans Complain: Governmental Grievance Procedures* [Cambridge: Harvard University Press, 1966], pp. 63–64.) Only the White House data are virtually all-inclusive. These are records of everything received in the White House except for three categories of mail: (1) telegrams (which were included in the tabulations only sporadically in less than half the years); (2) letters to Mrs. John F. Kennedy after the assassination of her husband (which totalled 757,231 between the weeks of December 5, 1963, and April 1, 1965); and (3) requests (or expressions of appreciation) for presidential memorial certificates honoring deceased veterans (which first became available as printed cards submittable to the White House in 1963 and which accounted for 674,724 pieces of mail between May 2nd of that year and November 10, 1965, when the submission of them waned and the category was dropped from the weekly reports). Otherwise the White House data include such regularly recurring categories of mail as messages to the President's family, requests for photographs, Christmas and birthday greetings, postcards from children and cranks, and letters to the Executive Office of the President as well as those dealing with public issues. The ensuing analysis separates issue mail (where identified) from the other categories by distinguishing between mail on local, national, and international questions on the one hand and "miscellaneous" mail on the other.

the terminal point of the trend line should be higher than its starting point. Likewise, if the presumption that Vietnam was not merely a momentary source of activity is valid, the terminal point in 1972 should not be lower than the level in, say, 1965. Presumably, too, the figures presented below should reveal a rate of increase in letter-writing activity which is greater than the rate of growth of the relevant population of potential letter-writers.

Table 2–1 presents a breakdown of the data in terms of the average weekly number of letters received per year.[101] Here it is clear that, for all four sources, the postwar years have been marked by substantial growth in the amount of mail received from the public. The upward trend is not continuous for any of the four sources, but the central tendency in each instance is one of growth. Using the average annual percentage of change in the letters received during the period for which records are available as a measure of central tendency, the data in Table 2–1 yield an average annual growth rate of 10.79 percent for *The New York Times*, 6.65 percent for the *New York Post*, 11.27 percent for Senator Hart, and 13.43 percent for the White House. In all four cases, moreover, the data for the 1960s and 1970s show an increase over those for the 1950s. Indeed, if for each source the most recent figures are compared with the figures for the first year of record, the data in Table 2–1 reveal that the weekly averages were more than doubled for the *Post, Senator Hart*, and the White House, and were almost four times as great in the case of the *Times*.

Perhaps the most conspicuous pattern depicted in Table 2–1 is the virtually continuous growth in the volume of mail received by the *Times*. With one exception, each annual weekly average exceeded the previous one, whereas the upward trends were not nearly as steady for the other three sources. The annual

---

[101] This unit of measurement has several advantages. It facilitates comparison among the four sources and at the same time permits handling of the fact that none of the sources supplied complete records. That is, the annual totals were divided by the number of weeks for which records were available. The number of weeks per year for which data were missing averaged less than one for the *Times*, twenty for the *Post*, two for Senator Hart, and three for the White House.

TABLE 2–1

AVERAGE WEEKLY NUMBER OF LETTERS RECEIVED
PER YEAR FROM THE PUBLIC BY FOUR SOURCES
(staggered by cycles of presidential terms)

	The Letters-to-the-Editor Department of The New York Times	The Letters-to-the-Editor Department of the New York Post	Senator Philip A. Hart of Michigan	The White House	
1949				16,688	1949
1950				17,672	1950
1951				15,671	1951
1952				9,018	1952
1953				20,155	1953
1954				12,767	1954
1955		110		14,117	1955
1956		150		15,233	1956
1957		136		12,606	1957
1958	233	119		10,041	1958
1959	244	134	456	10,760	1959
1960	340	170	436	12,579	1960
1961	330	144	559	28,652	1961
1962	343	136	689	29,921	1962
1963	367	147	506	28,052	1963
1964	388	158	624	35,438	1964
1965	458	153	748	35,000	1965
1966	541	172	678	26,653	1966
1967	596	193	615	24,597	1967
1968	704	234	1208	22,700	1968
1969	706	238	807	66,115	1969
1970	758		1185	52,030	1970
1971	885		1407	47,572	1971
1972	927		1022	43,706	1972

weekly average for the White House was less than the previous
year thirteen times and the equivalent figures for the *Post* and
Senator Hart were, respectively, five and six. These fluctuations
would appear to result partly from the cycle of presidential

terms[102] and partly from the ebb and flow of volatile issues, suggesting that those who write letters to public officials and to tabloids like the *Post* tend to be drawn more from the ranks of partisans and single-issue citizens whose participation in public

[102] As might be expected, this pattern is especially conspicuous in the White House data: the flow of mail tends to reach a peak either in the last or first year of a presidential term and to then decline in the middle years of a term. (A similar pattern, but less pronounced, is evident in the mail received by Senator Hart.) Even more apparent in the White House data is the enormous and seemingly permanent increase in the flow of mail that occurs, beginning in 1961, each time the party previously out of power gains the presidency. During all three of the Kennedy years (1961–1963) more than twice as much mail was received than in any of the four previous Eisenhower years, and the flow of mail during the first four years of Nixon's presidency was nearly twice as great as it was during the comparable years of the Johnson presidency. Why new plateaus of mail flow should be established with each new figure and party in the White House is not clear, but it is probably at least in part a function of the fact that each new individual evokes a response from whole new segments of the society, if only by virtue of being a change from the past. A new personality in the presidency with a different life style, as well as different policy commitments, probably attracts letters from like-minded or similarly styled persons who had not previously been moved to write. It is noteworthy, for example, that during the Eisenhower years letters classified as having been written by children averaged 262 per week, whereas the equivalent figure for the Kennedy years was 2,387 letters per week (a further comparison with the Nixon years is not presently possible, as the data supplied for 1969–1972 were not subcategorized at this level). Another explanation of the seemingly permanent increase in mail that accompanies the advent of a change of persons and parties in the White House is that they seek to enact new policies which, in turn, evoke reactions from proponents and opponents who have not previously had occasion to be aroused. Furthermore, the new policy orientations that new presidents and parties bring to the office necessitate continuous efforts to establish and sustain contacts with new groups and to mollify old ones, efforts that inevitably enlarge the daily conduct of public affairs and that are readily discernible in the fact that the average weekly number of letters received by the "White House Staff" (also categorized as "Secretariat and Executive Office Mail") rose from 3,298 in the Eisenhower years to 8,163 in the Kennedy years to 11,671 in the first Nixon Administration.

affairs between elections is momentary and sporadic. On the other hand, the pattern of the *Times* mail indicates that the slow expansion of the Attentive Public predicted by our growth hypothesis is confined mainly to the multi-issue citizens who enter and comprise the nationwide elite stratum of the society and who sustain their continuous involvement in public affairs through media such as the *Times*.

Nor are these isolated trends. Similar patterns can be seen in the data (Table 2–2) supplied by three other sources that had at least some record of the number of letters received or published

TABLE 2–2
LETTERS TO THE EDITOR RECEIVED OR PUBLISHED ANNUALLY BY THREE DAILY NEWSPAPERS

| | Number of letters received or published by | | |
Year	Ann Arbor News* (Michigan)	Democrat and Chronicle* (Rochester, N.Y.)	San Francisco Chronicle**
1954	105	—	—
1955	279	—	—
1956	407	—	—
1957	612	—	—
1958	594	1,783	7,577
1959	790	1,813	7,426
1960	823	2,199	10,936
1961	965	2,388	11,515
1962	1,114	2,279	11,720
1963	1,263	2,284	12,673
1964	1,415	2 575	15,743
1965	1,276	2,465	11,539
1966	1,316	2,421	11,790
1967	1,442	2,473	—
1968	1,683	2,316	—
1969	1,742	2,557	—
1970	2,093	2,220	14,140
1971	1,931	2,619	11,875
1972	1,950	2,545	11,437

— Data not available.
* The figures in this column are the number of letters published by the letters-to-the-editor department each year.
** The figures in this column are the number of letters addressed to the letters-to-the-editor department each year.

before and after the hypothesized turning point of the early 1960s.[103] These data are too crude to break down into weekly averages, but on an annual basis they all reflect a surge of letter-writing activity in the 1960s and 1970s. And again the figures for the last year of record are considerably greater than those for the first year, with the volume of mail received by the *Ann Arbor News* growing eighteenfold during the 1954–1972 period. In the case of the *Ann Arbor News*, moreover, the upward trend is relatively continuous, a pattern which again suggests, given the kind of town Ann Arbor is, that the validity of our growth hypothesis is due mainly to the expansion and politicization of elite groups in the society.

To attribute the stable growth patterns of *The New York Times* and the *Ann Arbor News* data to a growing and more active elite, however, risks obscuring the central finding that the overall trend is in the predicted direction for all seven recipients of mail from the public. Furthermore, since the seven recipients are located in different parts of the country, the data suggest that the upward trend is nationwide in scope.

Absolute figures could be misleading, of course. In themselves, they provide no indication as to whether there has also been an increase in the *relative* size of the Attentive Public. Our growth hypothesis predicted not only that the ranks of attentive citizens would show a continuous increase, but also that this growth would exceed that of the population as a whole. Conceivably the increases in the flow of mail could reflect merely increases in the circulations of the *Times* and the *Post*, in the population of Michigan, and in the overall population of the country. This

---

[103] As indicated in Table 2–2, two of the three sets of data consist of letters published rather than letters received. Although the number of published letters is not as reliable an indicator of citizenship activity as the number received, it does serve as at least a crude indicator. Except for papers like *The New York Times* that receive great quantities of letters every day, newspapers tend to publish all the serious letters they receive and leave out only crank and special interest mail. Hence the data in Table 2–2 serve as an indicator of citizenship activity, since papers are likely to expand the space allocated to their letters-to-the-editor columns if the flow of incoming mail warrants it.

TABLE 2–3
AVERAGE ANNUAL CHANGES IN THE WEEKLY
VOLUME OF MAIL RECEIVED BY *THE NEW YORK
TIMES*, THE *NEW YORK POST*, SENATOR PHILIP A.
HART, AND THE WHITE HOUSE COMPARED WITH
THE AVERAGE ANNUAL CHANGES IN THE
CIRCULATIONS OF *THE NEW YORK TIMES* AND
THE *NEW YORK POST* AND IN THE POPULATIONS
OF MICHIGAN AND THE UNITED STATES FOR
CORRESPONDING TIME PERIODS

	Average annual change in the weekly mail received by the source	Average annual change in the relevant population or circulation of the source
The New York Times (1958–1972)	+10.79	+2.39
The New York Post (1955–1969)	+6.65	+4.16
Senator Philip A. Hart (1959–1972)	+11.27	+1.23
The White House (1949–1972)	+13.43	+1.49

possibility is explored in Table 2–3, which compares the growth rates for the four main sources noted above with the corresponding changes in the different populations served by the recipients of the letters. Here it can be seen that this aspect of the growth hypothesis is fully affirmed. The growth rates for all four sources exceed—and, in three cases, are more than three times—the average annual increases in the corresponding populations for the same time periods.

Let us probe the data more deeply. In addition to predicting that attentiveness would be greater in absolute terms in the 1960s than in the 1950s, our growth hypothesis also forecast that the rate of growth in the Attentive Public would accelerate as a result of an increase in subjective political competence fostered by the success of the civil rights movement. If "the turning point of the early 1960s" is operationalized to mean 1963 (since that is the year when the President and the Congress first provided unmistakable evidence of a readiness to respond to citizenship activities on behalf of civil rights), the data in Table 2–1 are ambiguous with respect to this crucial element of our reasoning. Again using the annual average percentage of change as a measure of central tendency, the data for the *Post* clearly conformed to expectations, showing annual growth rates of 8.58 percent after 1963 and of 4.70 percent prior to 1963. On the other hand, the data for Senator Hart negated the hypothesis, with percentages of 9.94 after 1963 and 15.65 before 1963, while the data for the White House and the *Times* showed negligible differences, 13.55 and 13.28 percent for the White House and 11.23 and 10.47 for the *Times* for the pre- and post-1963 periods, respectively. It would seem, therefore, that the growing subjective political competence reflected in the overall growth rates depicted in Tables 2–1 and 2–2 cannot be clearly linked to the specific episodes through which the civil rights movement evoked responses from public officials. If these had an effect, they constituted only one of many factors that sustained the upward trend of attentiveness so readily apparent in the data.

In contrast, there is no ambiguity in the data with respect to our expectation that the growth of the Attentive Public would prove not to be a momentary consequence of the U.S.'s involvement in Vietnam. Despite the de-escalation of that involvement in 1971 and 1972, Tables 2–1 and 2–2 reveal that the amount of mail received in those two years by the *Times*, Senator Hart, the White House, the *Ann Arbor News*, and the *Rochester Democrat and Chronicle* exceeded by a large margin the comparable figures for 1963, the year before the Vietnam conflict began to escalate rapidly. Only in the case of the *San Francisco Chronicle* did the post-involvement figures for the 1970s show a return to pre-war levels, a finding which serves as a useful reminder that 1972 may not be an adequate measurement point and that data for a few more years must be examined before it can be concluded that the attenuation of the Vietnam issue did not lead to a corresponding decline in attentiveness. The need for such caution is further underlined by the fact that in three other cases—the White

House, Senator Hart, and the *Rochester Democrat and Chronicle* —the figures for 1972 were lower than those for 1971, possibly indicating the onset of a post-Vietnam decline. It bears repeating, however, that such a pattern is not evident for the *Times* or the *Ann Arbor News* and that, in any event, in all but one case the average weekly figures for 1972 are so much higher than the comparable figures for 1964 and 1965 that a society-wide return to pre-Vietnam levels of attentiveness seems unlikely.

In order to probe further whether the absolute and relative growth in the ranks of the Attentive Public was dominated by a single episode or arose out of greater competence and an inclination to range across a variety of issue-areas, the data were subcategorized in terms of the number of letters devoted to local, national, and international issues.[104] It will be recalled that our

---

[104] For the ensuing analysis, the categories used by the recipients to record the incoming letters were classified as local, national, international, or miscellaneous. A category was classified as local if in the judgment of the coder the letters it encompassed were "described as referring to events, persons, situations, etc., located exclusively" in New York, New Jersey, or Connecticut, in the case of *The New York Times* and the *New York Post*; in Michigan, in the case of Senator Hart's mail; or in a single community or state, in the case of the White House mail. A category was coded as national if it embraced letters "described as referring to events, persons, situations, etc., located in Washington, D.C., or elsewhere in the United States other than" the community treated as the local level. A category was classified as international if it included letters "described as referring to events, persons, situations, etc., external to the United States." Categories that spanned more than one of the three levels were coded in terms of the most remote level they spanned (i.e., the international level was treated as having precedence over the other two, and the national level as having precedence over the local level). All categories were "described in such a way that [if the coder was] unable (because of insufficient information, ambiguous description, etc.) to classify them as local, national, or international," they were coded as miscellaneous. Inter-coder agreement in the use of these four superimposed categories was 98.7 percent.

While our classification scheme can thus be regarded as reliable, it should be noted that high proportions of the letters received by the two newspapers and the White House were classified by the recipients as

growth hypothesis posits attentiveness as a generalized habit that leads citizens to move beyond the original issues that engaged their interest and to follow the course of events at all levels. If this is so, it follows that the trends for letters on local, national, and international issues received by each source all ought to rise at a greater rate than the growth trends of the relevant populations. Moreover, if the shrinkage factor is as crucial to the growth hypothesis as previously indicated, the rise ought to be especially pronounced for international issues, but not steep enough to account wholly for the growth reflected in the overall figures. Indeed, if our foregoing conclusion is correct that the Vietnam episode was not the only source of the recent intensification of citizenship between elections, the data on local and national issues should show increases during those periods when decreases at the international level might reasonably be attributed to the de-escalation of American involvement in Southeast Asia.

Figures 2–1 through 2–4 present graphically the data for each of the four sources at the three issue levels. Here it can be seen that our growth hypothesis is essentially upheld. Although the three trends for each of the sources fluctuate widely a number of times, in most of the twelve cases the fluctuations in more recent years occur at higher levels than those in the early years.

---

miscellaneous. Hence the miscellaneous category has a broad coverage that may include some letters addressed to public issues at the local, national, and international levels. Those who processed the letters at the time of their receipt appear to have used the miscellaneous category rather than a substantive one for single letters on isolated issues at any level. Whenever two or more letters were addressed to the same issue, the original recipients tended to create a new category and thereby give the letters a substantive classification. In addition, of course, presumably many of the letters originally classified as miscellaneous dealt with other than public issues, such as the weather, artistic performances, and similar matters of a nonpolitical nature. What proportion of letters classified as miscellaneous dealt with public issues and what proportion did not can thus not be determined, but the fact that unavoidably this category subsumes some of the others must be kept in mind when the data derived from our classification scheme are assessed.

Only the mail on local issues received by the White House and Senator Hart (Figures 2–1 and 2–2) remained largely constant throughout the years for which data are available, a finding which is consistent with the fact that these two sources serve national audiences far more extensively than do newspapers.[105] To be sure, Figure 2–1 reveals that letters on national and international issues came into the White House at the same rate in 1949 as they did in 1968, but this comparison is somewhat misleading, as the two trends are anything but constant during the intervening years and, as will be seen (Table 2–4), their intervening fluctuations generally reflect an increased flow of mail. In the cases of the two newspapers (Figures 2–3 and 2–4) and of letters on national and international issues to Senator Hart, moreover, the overall upward patterns are unmistakable, albeit occasional fluctuations render the trend lines ragged.

An even more clear-cut indication that the absolute and relative growth figures reflect the spread of attentiveness rather than a temporary upsurge linked to events of the 1960s is the frequency with which the three trends for each source move in contrary directions. This is particularly noticeable in Figure 2–3, where the line for mail on national issues received by the *Times* goes down (or up) almost every time the line for letters classified as international goes up (or down), with the result that the two lines cross each other seven times during the 15-year span. Similar patterns seem evident in the White House data (Figure 2–1), where the two lines cross eight times during a twenty-year period, and in the *Post* data (Figure 2–4), where the lines for local and national mail cross five times and move away from each other four other times. As for Senator Hart, although he receives more mail on national than international issues (due, no doubt, to the

---

[105] It must be noted in this connection that as a senior member of Congress, Senator Hart occupied several key committee posts during the period and thereby represented far more than simply his Michigan constituency. Furthermore, as indicated, "case" letters involving requests of particular constituents were not included among those from which his weekly summaries were compiled.

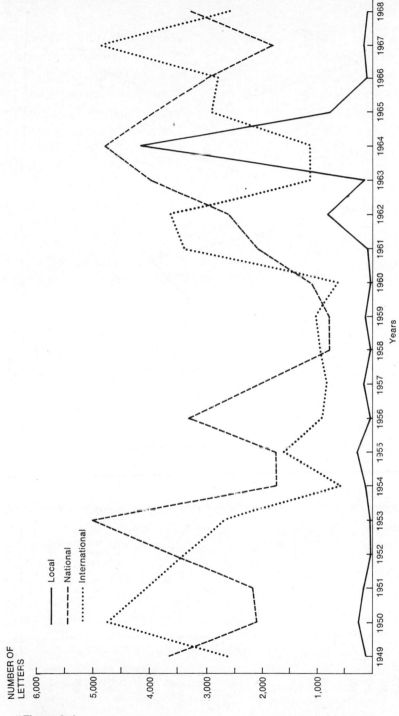

Figure 2–1
Comparison of the Average Weekly Number of Letters Received Per Year by the White House on Local, National, and International Issues, 1949–1968

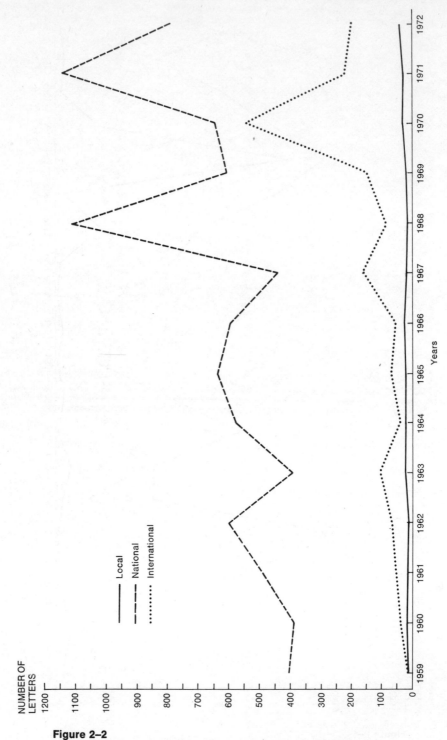

Figure 2–2

Comparison of the Average Weekly Number of Letters Received Per Year by Senator Philip A. Hart on Local, National, and International Issues, 1959–1972

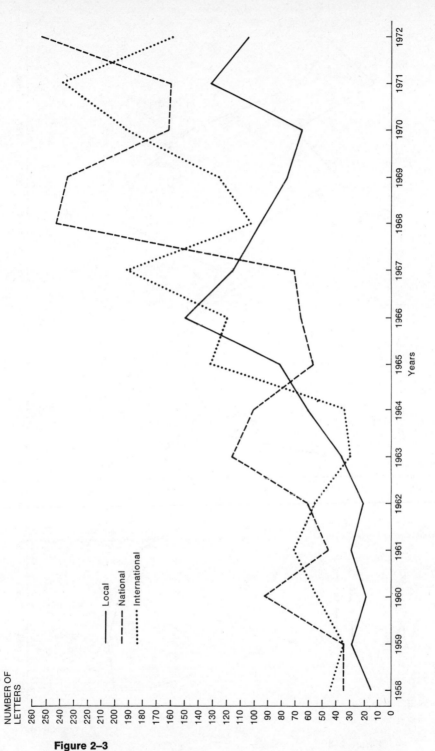

Figure 2–3

Comparison of the Average Weekly Number of Letters Received Per Year by the *New York Times* on Local, National, and International Issues, 1958–1972

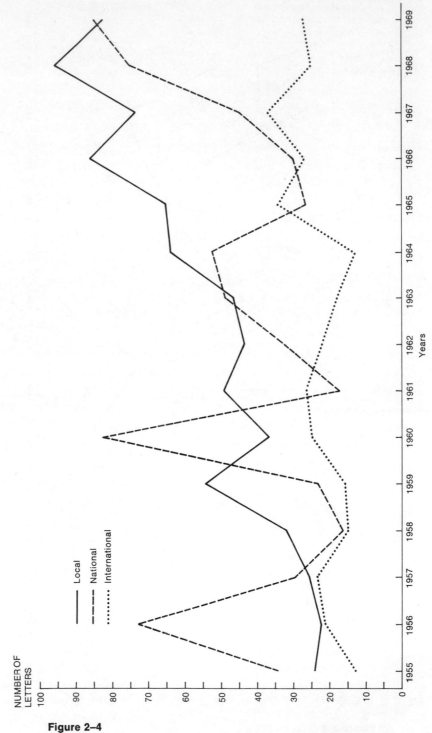

Figure 2–4
Comparison of the Average Weekly Number of Letters Received Per Year by the *New York Post* on Local, National, and International Issues, 1955–1969

fact that his work in Congress has been mainly on domestic problems) and more on international than local issues, a close inspection of Figure 2–2 reveals that the lines for mail on national and international issues diverged in as many years as they moved in the same direction. Furthermore, if the specific problem is whether these more detailed breakdowns of the data indicate that a society-wide return to pre-Vietnam levels of attentiveness lies ahead, there is at least one fluctuation that suggests otherwise. All four sets of comparisons reveal that the number of letters received on international issues tended to increase during the Vietnam conflict, but of the two for which the data extend through 1972, one (the *Times*) shows that mail on national issues rose to a new height at the same time that the pace of U.S. troop withdrawals from Vietnam quickened in 1972.

Taken together, in short, the fluctuations in the mail flows suggest that the overall increase in mail results from an expanding public involvement at all levels and not from a preoccupation with a single issue or type of situation, that attention turns to the national scene when international affairs are relatively quiescent and vice versa.[106]

Our expectations were not fully met, however, with respect to the question of whether the shrinkage factor fostered an especially pronounced growth in the flow of mail on international issues. As can be seen in Table 2–4, which compares the average annual rate of change in the mail received by the four sources on local, national, and international issues, the hypothesis was up-

---

[106] That the increase in letter-writing is due to a growing involvement in public issues, rather than to a sudden, erratic, and desperate spurt of activity generated by the hectic, crisis-ridden era of the 1960s, is further indicated by the stability of the flow of crank mail to the White House. Variously labelled "abusive and threatening" or "protective research" in the White House records, the number of letters classified in this category provide no signs whatever that a troubled era turned substantial numbers of people to hateful and extremist forms of expression: the average weekly number of crank letters received in the White House between 1951 through 1960 was 276, whereas the comparable figure for the 1961–1968 period was 261.

TABLE 2–4
AVERAGE ANNUAL RATE OF CHANGE IN THE
NUMBER OF LETTERS ON LOCAL, NATIONAL, AND
INTERNATIONAL ISSUES RECEIVED BY FOUR
SOURCES (in percentages)

| Source (years) | Rate for letters classified as | | | Rate for all letters received* |
	local	*national*	*international*	
The New York Times (1958–1972)	24.86	34.09	24.91	10.79
New York Post (1955–1969)	12.58	31.24	14.25	6.65
Senator Hart (1959–1972)	25.32	15.25	46.79	11.27
White House (1949–1972)	**	16.45***	34.82***	13.43

* The sum of the first three entries for each source does not correspond to the figure for all the mail received because the amount used to calculate the annual rates of change in the latter are much larger (and hence the percentage of change much smaller) than is the case for the local, national, and international categories.

** This figure (411.87) has not been included because it mainly reflects two enormous fluctuations in two different years (see Figure 2-1).

*** This percentage does not include changes for 1969–1972, as the data for this period could not be subcategorized.

held in the case of the two public recipients, but not in the case of the two newspapers. This partial disconfirmation of our hypothesis is reasonable if one assumes that expressions of concern over the ways in which the world's growing interdependence impinge on daily life are more likely to be addressed to officials of the federal government than to newspapers. Our hypothesis, however, posits the shrinkage factor as so potent that traces of its impact would be manifest in the flows of mail to all four sources, and for this the data do not provide full support.

SUMMARY

At the outset of this chapter four accounts of citizen behavior were presented and the question was posed of whether the two depicting citizen indifference to public affairs were descriptive of larger societal patterns. The data presented here indicate that they are not, that increasing numbers of people, and a growing proportion of the overall population, are attentive to public affairs in general and to local, national, and international affairs in particular. Indeed, the central tendencies of the data (summarized in Table 2–4) are in these respects so clear-cut and persistent that there is ample reason to conclude that our growth hypothesis has passed its initial test.[107] Based on an interpretation in which increasing degrees of objective political competence (derived from expanded educational opportunities) were expected to combine with mounting subjective political competence (fostered by the successes of the civil rights movement in the early 1960s) to generate slow and steady growth in the relative size of the Attentive Public, the hypothesis was upheld sufficiently to justify further exploration of it. Only the impact of the civil rights movement cannot be clearly discerned in the data, suggesting that our original reasoning exaggerated the degree to

[107] Several readers of an earlier version of this chapter questioned this conclusion on the grounds that possibly the data reflect more letter-writing on the part of the same citizens rather than increased activity among a widening number of people. Conceivably, it was argued, we have committed the same mistake that was made in the 1964 presidential election by Barry Goldwater, who apparently based part of his campaign strategy on the support evidenced in his mail, not realizing that many of the letters received were written by persons who had written earlier rather than by new adherents. (See Converse, Clausen, and Miller, "Electoral Myth and Reality," pp. 332–35.) In order to ascertain whether a similar pattern underlies the data presented here, a special analysis was made of the records of the one source, the *New York Post*, that included the names of the letter-writers in the weekly tabulations. The proportion of the number of persons who wrote only one letter during the years before and after the 1963 "turning point" was calculated, and this calculation clearly shows that our interpretation of the data is a reasonable one. In 1962, 1965, and 1966 the proportions of persons who wrote only one letter to the *Post* were, respectively, 87, 86, and 85 percent. Even if this slight decline pattern is interpreted as reflecting a trend toward more letter-writing on the part of the same people, it is hardly sufficient to account for the bulk of the increase in the *Post's* mail for those years (Table 2–1). The increase is such that it can only be viewed as also reflecting a trend toward more letter-writing on the part of more people.

which subjective political competence is susceptible to being profoundly altered by a single episode. On the contrary, the data gathered on the flow of letters to two newspapers, the President, and a U.S. Senator indicate that the increase in attentiveness stems from greater sensitivity to a wider range of issues. Even the Vietnam episode was found not to have been particularly dominant as a stimulus to greater attentiveness. A comparison of the mail flows to the four sources also led to the conclusion that the slow and permanent growth of the Attentive Public is probably due more to the politicization and expansion of elite groups than of segments of the mass public.

This is not to say, of course, that the dynamics of attentiveness and mobilizability have been adequately identified. Many of the key variables, especially those associated with the processes whereby experience in one issue-area is transferred to other areas, still need to be clarified, and their interaction with shifting degrees of objective and subjective competence still has to be probed. So do the processes through which greater attentiveness is translated into greater mobilizability. The analysis undertaken here, however, indicates that further investigation of the foundations and consequences of citizenship between elections is a worthwhile effort.

CHAPTER 3

FORMS OF CITIZENSHIP: SOME DISTINCTIONS AND DEFINITIONS

In order to gather and analyze empirical materials that will further our comprehension of how the Attentive Public performs its various roles and of when and why some of its members can be mobilized to provide support, we need to identify more precisely the similarities and the distinctions between attentive and mobilizable citizenship. The latter is a derivative of the former, and yet it also has special characteristics that must be delineated.

Unfortunately, the available literature offers little guidance along these lines. Not only has the concept of mobilizability been neglected, but contradictory and ambiguous formulations mark the many other concepts that are used to analyze the practices of citizenship. Neither a common terminology nor a shared conception of the phenomena involved can be found in the burgeoning research on the political orientations and activities that sustain citizenship between elections. Most notably, the concepts of involvement, activity, participation, and influence tend to be used in a variety of discrepant ways. For some researchers the involved citizen is one who is merely interested in public affairs; for others he need only be informed about them; for still others he must be both interested and informed;[1] and for a fourth group he is one whose interest and information also lead him to move physically about his community on behalf of some goal or organization.[2] In some studies political activity can take the form of reading a newspaper or talking about public issues with friends,[3] but in others such solitary behavior is not regarded as political action.[4] Frequent too are the inquiries that distinguish between apathetic and influential citizens, but that make no allowance for those who are neither apathetic nor influential.[5]

A measure of these varying usages and contradictory con-

---

[1] Indeed, the notion of high interest and high information served as the basis for the first definition of the Attentive Public to be introduced into the literature. Cf. Gabriel A. Almond, *The American People and Foreign Policy* (New York: Harcourt, Brace and Company, 1950), p. 138.

[2] Useful summaries of the various conceptual problems involved in delineating degrees and types of participation can be found in Lester W. Milbrath, *Political Participation: How and Why People Get Involved in Politics* (Chicago: Rand McNally, 1965); and Sidney Verba, "Democratic Participation," *The Annals*, Vol. 373 (1967), pp. 53–78.

[3] See, for example, James David Barber, *Citizen Politics: An Introduction to Political Behavior* (Chicago: Markham Publishing Company, 1969), p. 3; Donald J. Devine, *The Attentive Public: Polyarchical Democracy* (Chicago: Rand McNally, 1970), p. 120; and Fred E. Katz and Fern V. Piret, "Circuitous Participation in Politics," *American Journal of Sociology*, Vol. 69 (January 1964), pp. 367–73.

[4] Cf. Sidney Verba, Norman H. Nie, and Jae-on Kim, *The Modes of Democratic Participation: A Cross-National Comparison* (Beverly Hills: Sage Publications, 1971), pp. 9–11.

[5] For an incisive discussion of the nature and limits of the influence citizens can wield, see William A. Gamson, *Power and Discontent* (Homewood, Illinois: Dorsey Press, 1968), Chaps. 4 and 5. For an interesting

cerns is provided by the terminology that has evolved. The nomenclature of active citizenship is, to say the least, profuse: persons who extend their citizenship beyond voting on election day include, among others, the "visible" or "operative" public;[6] the "high participators";[7] the "active influentials";[8] "the spectators and the activists";[9] the "opinion leaders";[10] the "politists";[11] the "influentials" and the "interested";[12] the "leaders" and the "subleaders";[13] the "participating" or "active" citizens;[14] the "articulate public";[15] the "knowledgeables";[16] the "political class," the "political elite," the "political influentials," and the "political stratum";[17] the "hyperactives," the "power-seekers," the

---

empirical analysis from the perspective of the citizen, see Sidney Verba, "Political Participation and Strategies of Influence: A Comparative Study," *ACTA Sociologica,* Vol. 6 (1962), pp. 22–42.

[6] Philip E. Converse, "The Nature of Belief Systems in Mass Publics," p. 227.

[7] V. O. Key, Jr., *Politics, Parties, and Pressure Groups,* Chap. 21.

[8] Robert E. Agger, Daniel Goldrich, and Bert E. Swanson, *The Rulers and the Ruled: Political Power and Impotence in American Communities* (New York: John Wiley & Sons, 1964), Chap. 7.

[9] Robert E. Lane, *Political Life,* p. 94.

[10] Elihu Katz and Paul F. Lazarsfeld, *Personal Influence: The Part Played by People in the Flow of Mass Communications* (Glencoe, Illinois: The Free Press, 1955), *passim.*

[11] Alfred de Grazia, *Elements of Political Science* (New York: Alfred A. Knopf, 1952), Chap. 3.

[12] Kenneth P. Adler and Davis Bobrow, "Interest and Influence in Foreign Affairs," *Public Opinion Quarterly,* Vol. XX (Spring, 1956), pp. 89–101.

[13] Robert A. Dahl, *Who Governs,* pp. 90–96 and *passim.*

[14] Gabriel A. Almond and Sidney Verba, *The Civic Culture, passim.*

[15] Bernard C. Cohen, *The Political Process and Foreign Policy: The Making of the Japanese Peace Settlement* (Princeton: Princeton University Press, 1957), Chap. 3.

[16] Williams C. Rogers, Barbara Stuhler, and Donald Koenig, "A Comparison of Informed and General Public Opinion on U.S. Foreign Policy," *Public Opinion Quarterly,* Vol. 31 (Summer, 1967), p. 252.

[17] Herbert McClosky, "Consensus and Ideology in American Politics," *passim.*

"super-participants";[18] the "middlemen";[19] and the "attentive constituents."[20]

This chapter further contributes to the proliferation of concepts and terms, but the prevailing state of the literature leaves us no choice. We will not be able to make accurate assessments of current citizenship practices if we speak loosely of activity and fail to distinguish between involvement and leadership or participation and influence. To be sure, many of these concepts refer to overlapping phenomena and the lines between them are difficult to draw with great precision. Nevertheless, an effort must be made to specify concepts and operationalize definitions. Little would be accomplished by leaving the lines undrawn and using terms interchangeably. Our purposes are such that the overlap between the phenomena is not nearly as important as the distinctions between them, and it thus seems preferable to develop operational definitions that allow for exceptions than to ignore the distinctions in order to account for the exceptions. The latter procedure runs the risk of confounding the reader and misusing the data, whereas only some additional detail is the price of the former approach. The ensuing discussion may seem overly elaborate at times, but its utility should become apparent as soon as the analysis moves on to the tasks of deriving meaning from findings and ascribing causality to relationships.

The Concept of Participation

A good part of the confusion stems from different conceptions of the practices of citizenship, of what is encompassed when citizens participate in politics. Some analysts conceive participation broadly to include psychological as well as behavioral phenomena. A feeling of political efficacy and a sense of involvement

---

[18] James David Barber, *Citizen Politics*, p. 21.

[19] Dwaine Marvick, "The Middlemen of Politics," in William J. Crotty ed., *Approaches to the Study of Party Organization* (Boston: Allyn and Bacon, 1968), pp. 314–74.

[20] G. R. Boynton, Samuel C. Patterson, and Ronald D. Hedlund, "The Missing Links in Legislative Politics: Attentive Constituents," *Journal of Politics*, Vol. 31 (1969), pp. 700–21.

in how political issues turn out, for example, is regarded as a measure of participation.[21] Others conceive of it strictly in behavioral terms. Citizens must do things in order to be viewed as participants. Their feelings in the absence of action are regarded as having little relevance for the political process. The practices of citizenship are conceived to have psychological roots, but these are probed only in the context of behavior to be explained. As indicated above, however, even this narrow behavioral approach is differentially applied. Some analysts limit the behavior to be explained to that of communications which citizens transmit to governmental and nongovernmental leaders,[22] while others view the behavior through which information is acquired from the mass media and pondered through discussions with neighbors as a form of participation,[23] and still others conceive of discussions with family as participation but not the act of acquiring information through the mass media.[24] These five distinctions are bypassed by still others who define active citizens by asking public officials to specify those among their constituents whom they regard as knowledgeable and capable of giving good advice.[25]

Each of these diverse formulations is useful for certain purposes, but they differ in their relevance to our perspective, in which the practices of citizenship are seen as sustaining or hindering the generation, mobilization, and transference of support. The giving or withholding of support is primarily a behavioral

---

[21] For example, see Herbert McClosky, "Participation," in David Sills, ed., *International Encyclopedia of the Social Sciences* (New York: Macmillan, 1968), Vol. 12, pp. 252–64.

[22] "Political participation is the means by which the interests, desires, demands of the ordinary citizen are communicated. By political participation we refer to all those activities by private citizens that are more or less directly aimed at influencing the selection of governmental personnel and/or the decisions that they make" (Verba, Nie, and Kim, *The Modes of Democratic Participation*, p. 9).

[23] In addition to Barber and Devine (see footnote 3), see pp. 103–05.

[24] Donald R. Matthews and James W. Prothro, *Negroes and the New Southern Politics* (New York: Harcourt, Brace and World, 1966), pp. 37–38.

[25] G. R. Boynton, Ronald D. Hedlund, Samuel C. Patterson, "The Missing Links in Legislative Politics: Attentive Constituents," p. 702.

and not a mental or emotional phenomenon, so that here we shall eschew the broad conception of participation and only focus on psychological forms of involvement in politics as a means of probing the sources of observable behavior. On the other hand, since the separate acts whereby different citizens acquire and ponder information can be aggregated by the mobilizers of support (say, by investigating the ratings of television programs and the circulation figures of newspapers), we shall eschew the narrow behavioral formulation that limits participation to communicative acts that establish contact with officialdom. Instead, any action that directly or indirectly leads to contact with developments in the political arena is conceived to be a practice of citizenship and a form of participation. As elaborated below, we shall cope with the important differences between communicative and noncommunicative acts by distinguishing between first- and second-hand types of contacts.

The Distinction Between Personal and Public Affairs

Notwithstanding this broad behavioral approach to the concept of participation, however, not all contacts between citizens and government fall within its scope. Our concern is exclusively with participation in public affairs and any contacts which are established outside this realm are regarded not as a practice of citizenship, but as a business or personal practice. Citizenship is conceived to embrace the individual's roles in the larger society rather than his personal or occupational roles.[26] That is, one acts as a citizen of a polity when one relates oneself to matters that are of consequence for other than those in the immediate family or occupational group. Contacts with government that are unlikely to have effects beyond the personal world are seen not as an exercise of the rights of citizenship, but as a

---

[26] For a similar formulation in which this conception of citizenship is seen to be consistent with the requirements that modern polities, "democratic or dictatorial, multi- or single-party, guaranteeing private property or exercising state control of wealth," impose on their subjects, see Alex Inkeles, "Participant Citizenship in Six Developing Countries," *American Political Science Review,* Vol. 63 (December 1969), p. 1122.

carrying out of role requirements in systems other than the polity.[27] To be sure, the line between the world of personal and public affairs can sometimes be difficult to draw, but the distinction is nevertheless crucial from a perspective in which support building is a central process.

It should be stressed that some analysts explicitly reject this formulation, insisting instead that the practice of citizenship includes any activities through which individual citizens contact government officials, irrespective of whether the purpose and scope of the activity is highly personal or highly political.[28] A person who contacts his Congressman to ascertain why his social security check did not arrive or who applies to the city council for a zoning ordinance to allow him to enlarge his home is regarded as exercising his citizenship as much as is the person who marches in a protest rally or who presses the city council to pass an open housing ordinance. The reason for this conceptual merger of personal and public affairs is an obvious and legitimate one, namely, the experience of seeking to satisfy personal needs through recourse to government can contribute to a person's orientations and actions toward the larger, more remote world of public affairs. And, indeed, findings have been uncovered that suggest at least a slight relationship between the two forms of citizenship.[29]

The difficulty with this broad approach, however, is that it

[27] Walker implicitly develops this same conception by distinguishing between citizenship as a form of behavior and citizenship as a set of juridical rights: "A large commitment in time and energy must be made, even by a well-educated citizen, to keep informed of the issues and personalities in all levels of government. Most citizens are not able or willing to pay this kind of cost to gain the information necessary for effective political participation. . . . For most citizens the world of politics is remote, bewildering, and meaningless, having no direct relation to daily concerns about jobs or family life. . . . This group within our political system are citizens only from the legal point of view. . . ." Jack L. Walker, "A Critique of the Elitist Theory of Democracy," *American Political Science Review*, Vol. LX (June 1966), p. 291.

[28] The most elaborate formulation along this line is to be found in Verba, Nie, and Kim, *The Modes of Democratic Participation*, pp. 9–19.

[29] *Ibid.*, pp. 24–30.

allows for, even requires, a conception of citizenship in which self-initiated behavior occupies a central place.[30] It addresses itself to the situation in which the personal life of a citizen is marked by a grievance or need that can only be satisfied by a government action, so he initiates contacts with the appropriate officials. Such a sequence is a recurrent, even daily, aspect of the governmental process and it undoubtedly affects the skills and attitudes which underlie the responses of citizens to the more encompassing realm of public affairs. Yet, self-initiated behavior is probably more the exception than the rule with respect to the remote world of public affairs. In this world the citizen is endlessly bombarded with stimuli. The mail brings appeals for support; the newspaper contains calls for action on the part of public-spirited citizens; his friends claim that their political outlook is sound and urge him to write letters, attend rallies, or simply offer verbal concurrence; the television tube depicts speakers and situations that cry out for concern; organizations plead with their members to contribute time, money, or energy to help advance their causes. Most citizens, in other words, are not autonomous actors who calculate what ought to be done in public affairs, devise a strategy for achieving it, estimate their own resources, and then pursue the course of action most likely to achieve their goals. Their instrumental behavior is often suggested, if not solicited, by others, either directly in face-to-face interactions or indirectly through the mass media; either explicitly through calls for support by mobilizers or implicitly through the statements of leaders, journalists, and acquaintances that situations might be altered (or preserved) if support were available. Thus, to conceive of the practices of citizenship as being largely sustained by independent action toward the political arena initiated by individuals is to minimize the relational context in which citizens participate in public affairs.

This is not to imply that citizen participation in public affairs is uncalculated. On the contrary, most contacts with public affairs

---

[30] Cf. *ibid.,* Table 1 on p. 17.

are undoubtedly instrumental, and even when largely habitual, they are founded on some form of calculation as to how values can best be realized. Rather it is to suggest that ordinarily an individual's calculations are fostered by and focus on the stimuli that subsequently lead him to act. Unlike a decision to preserve or promote aspects of his personal world, in the world of public affairs the citizen concerns himself not with the question of whether or not to participate, but with whether or not to respond to a stimulus to participation.

To be sure, some citizens do get so moved by their consciences and by the course of events that they write unsolicited letters to officials or otherwise act autonomously toward issues outside their personal worlds. And surely it is also the case that such expressive, self-initiated acts may be tallied or otherwise aggregated by their recipients and offered as evidence of support. To the extent that the activities of citizens sustain public affairs between elections, however, they do so largely in a relational context, through the support-giving and support-building behaviors that initiate and give direction to the welter of instrumental acts in which citizens engage. Consequently, so as to avoid exaggerating the role of the autonomous citizen and to emphasize the process by which support is generated, mobilized, and transferred, we shall confine the concept of citizenship to those activities through which individuals become involved in public affairs.

Such a focus is important because the question of why citizens participate in public affairs is much more difficult to answer than that of why they establish contact with government in order to preserve or improve their personal affairs. Indeed, the latter is hardly a problem. Individuals turn to officials when they have needs and grievances that officials can handle. Why they become interested and involved in public affairs, however, is much less obvious. The world of public affairs is distant and complex, and impinges only indirectly on daily life at home and at work. Mobilizing people to act with respect to a remote and complicated issue must thus overcome extraordinary obstacles and precipitate intellectual, psychological, and political processes that are very different from those which underlie governmental contact stemming from narrow personal needs.

The Distinction Between Attentive and Mobilized Activity

It follows from the foregoing conception of participation that the distinction between attentiveness and mobilizability is not equated with the differences between passivity and activity. At no point in the ensuing analysis is the Attentive Public seen as consisting of passive observers. On the contrary, passivity and observation are viewed as mutually exclusive. Persons passive toward public affairs cannot observe them, since to observe is to engage in activity. To be sure, it is possible to "observe" public affairs inadvertently by, say, having the radio on during a newscast or being present when friends discuss political issues. In general, however, observation is a purposeful form of behavior and it will not be sustained for long by those whose orientation toward public affairs is one of passivity. Indeed, such an orientation is the defining characteristic of the Mass Public and thus can hardly be considered a trait of those in the Attentive Public.

In other words, being attentive to events through observing them is considered to be as much a form of activity as directly participating in them. To attend a lecture or listen to the news may not be as important as giving a lecture or making news by marching in a rally, but the former behaviors can be just as purposeful and consistent as the latter for those who undertake them. Thus, as used here, attentiveness is synonymous with participation. It consists of any form of intentional or habitual behavior through which a person relates himself to public affairs. It may take such solitary forms as the reading of newspapers or such social forms as the discussing of politics with friends. Attentiveness may even involve the writing of letters to officials or exchanging ideas with them in face-to-face situations.

Mobilizability also consists of activity through which people relate themselves to the course of events. As will be seen, many—though not all—of the activities of the Mobilizable Public take the same form as those undertaken by the Attentive Public. The main distinction between attentiveness and mobilizability lies in the relational nature of mobilized activity. For a member of the Attentive Public to be mobilized, there must be a second actor who provides a stimulus for him to act. This second actor, whom we shall call the "mobilizer," may be a friend, an organization, a political party, an official, or any other entity seeking the support of the "mobilizee." The mobilized act occurs only in response to a request for support, whereas an act of attentiveness can unfold in other than a relational context. The distinction between attentiveness and mobilizability, in short, is the difference between action and interaction. The attentive citizen may offer support as a part of his attentiveness, but he is stimulated to do so by the course of events and not by a specific request. Consequently, his offer is an isolated act and does not get interpreted as part of a support-building process. Often, in fact, the offer may not even be received, much less accepted, since the receiver is more interested in support that can be mobilized in visible and sizeable quantities. In the mobilized act, on the other hand, interaction occurs. A transfer of support takes place because the proffered support had been sought and is received and accepted by the mobilizer. The fact of the transfer, moreover, is usually widely recognized and is so interpreted by others as well as the parties to the relationship. Those who estimate the size of crowds at rallies or who report the success of fund-raising campaigns, for example, are tabulating, publicizing, and assessing the extent of support transference, either because they are actors with a stake in the amount transferred or because they are journalists or scholars with an interest in public affairs.

Mobilizability thus consists of attentiveness plus followership,[31] and is thus both similar to and different from attentiveness

---

[31] Although we shall assume throughout that attentiveness is a precondition of mobilizability, it must be acknowledged that it is possible to conceive of people who are mobilizable but inattentive and that such a conception points to a small minority of the Mobilizable Public who are not also members of the Attentive Public. Much depends on how atten-

in the forms it takes and the sources from which it derives. The differential sources are examined at great length in subsequent chapters, but it should be noted here that the foregoing is not to imply that the attentive act is somehow free of stimuli and that the mobilized act stems only from the stimulus of the mobilizer. As will be seen, attentiveness results from a multiplicity of sources, some of which may even involve interaction with other persons. Membership in a small group of friends who follow public affairs, for example, can easily generate pressure toward attentiveness on the part of one who might otherwise be inclined toward passivity. Such behavior, however, is generalized and does not pertain to identifiable acts of support-giving as does mobilizability. If the friendship group should become so agitated about

---

tiveness is defined. If it is conceived simply in terms of an interest in public affairs that is sufficient to result in sustained behavior toward them, then obviously the act of being mobilized is consistent with and derived from attentiveness. On the other hand, if clear-cut attitudes and a reasonable degree of information are posited as a necessary concomitant of attentiveness, then it is possible to imagine persons who are capable of being mobilized even though they do not comprehend the phenomena toward which their mobilized activity is directed. Persons whose loyalties to an organization are so deep and overriding that they will respond to its directions without considering or questioning them are examples of this phenomenon. Virtually every organization has some such persons on its rolls. They are the "loyal followers," the "hard workers," the "party faithful," or the "organizational technicians," and their mobilizability can be viewed as independent of their awareness of or concern about the course of events. However, since the first of these two conceptions is the one used here, conceptual room is not made for mobilizability that exists independent of attentiveness. From our perspective there is a limit to the loyalty of loyal followers. Their mobilizability is more certain, but it is not absolute and cannot be taken for granted under all circumstances. At the very least they see themselves as capable of withholding support and thus they have to maintain a modicum of awareness of public affairs in order to know when to provide or withhold it. Furthermore, support must be provided in some fashion and cannot be totally divorced from the situation in which it is to be applied. Hence the loyal follower must also be sufficiently acquainted with the course of events to know how to respond to demands on his loyalty.

an issue as to demand explicitly of its members that they write their Congressmen, then the initial source of attentiveness is transformed into a mobilizer and what would have been a simple act of attentiveness acquires the more complex characteristics of mobilization.

The mobilized act results not only from the efforts of a mobilizer. A host of other factors must be operative for the mobilizee if his support is to be successfully procured. His past experience, his attitudes toward policy questions, his conceptions of himself as a support-giver and of the political system's receptivity to support on particular issues—these are only a few of the variables that may determine whether he responds to the stimulus of those seeking his support. All the stimuli that foster attentiveness also undergird mobilizability and, in addition, the latter is generated by a number of variables inherent in the relationship between mobilizer and mobilizee.

To view mobilizability as relational is not to suggest that the relationship is a direct one between the parties involved. To refer to support being "requested," "given," "received," or "accepted" is to take some liberty with language in order to convey succinctly the essential meaning of an extraordinarily complex process. In fact, of course, members of the Mobilizable Public rarely meet those in the leadership structure who are seeking their support; or, if they do, it is usually across the great distances that separate those on the speaker's stand from those in the audience. Through his actions on the speaker's stand, the form letters he distributes, and the many other types of support-building behavior in which he engages, the mobilizer "requests" support for his policies. His requests may be directed to specific audiences, such as those on particular mailing lists, or they may be addressed to a general audience, such as those present for a speech or viewing it on television. Being moved by the speech or impressed by the letter, the mobilizee acts to "give" his support, either in a specific form that may have been requested, such as a financial donation, a letter to an official, or participation in a rally; or in a generalized form that may have been implicit in the stimulus, such as joining an organization, volunteering services, or arguing on behalf of the mobilizer's policies. Mobilizees may not be fully aware that the mobilizer's request served as the precipitating stimulus for their giving support; and the mobilizer is not likely to know exactly who the donors are of the support he "receives" and "accepts" when he annouces an increase in funds raised, cites a growth in organizational membership, or points to a rising wave of enthusiasm for his policies. But from the observer's point of view a relationship has been established and support has been transferred.

This relational conception gives rise to a number of methodological problems. Most notably, it requires us to come to terms with the question of empirically tracing the sequences of action and reaction whereby support is mobilized and transferred. How, for example, can one differentiate the voluntary contribution of support from the mobilized one? Would what appears to be a mobilized act have occurred in the absence of the mobilizer's stimulus? How direct must the appeal for support be for the researcher to treat it as a stimulus operating upon attentive citizens? How soon after the appeal has occurred must the response be forthcoming to be regarded as mobilization rather than attentiveness? Operational answers to such questions are extremely difficult to develop and they rarely satisfy all researchers.

Without minimizing the difficulties it presents, however, we have not abandoned the relational concept of mobilizability. Set forth below are operational definitions designed to embody it. They specify observable forms of juxtaposed behaviors and assume that juxtaposition reflects the process of mobilization. This solution seems preferable to abandonment of the concept because, as we have said, support is the currency of political systems and thus its generation, circulation, and transference must be analyzed. Although the measurement of influence is perhaps the most difficult methodological problem in all of social science, the exercise of influence—of which support mobilization is the political form—is also perhaps the most pervasive social phenomenon. It therefore cannot be ignored even if extraordinary methodological difficulties must be confronted. Subsequently we present data that we consider to reflect clear-cut evidence of support having been mobilized.[32] If the reader shares this interpretation, he should not find it too disconcerting to accept our assumption that by juxtaposing behaviors it is possible to cope with the main difficulties inherent in analyzing influence and to trace the response of mobilizable groups to the stimuli of their leaderships.[33]

The Identity of Attentive and Mobilizable Citizens

In order to develop a more precise conception of mobilizability, we must first specify our criteria for differentiating members of the Attentive Public from the mass and leadership segments of the society. While attentiveness to public affairs can take a variety of forms, it seems reasonable to presume that, whatever its form, it will ultimately be expressed through discussions with family and close friends. Except for the hermit, anyone who follows the course of events is bound eventually to communicate his concern, opinions, and ideas to those with whom he is most intimately acquainted.[34] Hence our overall definition of members of the Attentive Public is a simple one: such people are *those who communicate, with some regularity, ideas about public affairs to persons with whom they are closely associated (but not to persons whom they do not know).* Members of the mass public are excluded from this definition through the requirement that communication must occur with some regularity. Those who seldom engage in exchanging such ideas with family and friends are considered too passive toward public affairs to be ranked among the Attentive Public. Similarly, leaders are excluded from the definition by limiting the Attentive Public to

---

[32] See below, pp. 187–91.

[33] On the problems of measuring political influence, see especially James G. March, "An Introduction to the Theory and Measurement of Influence," *American Political Science Review*, Vol. XLIX (June 1955), pp. 431–51.

[34] For evidence supporting this presumption about the role of face-to-face communications, see Raymond A. Bauer, Ithiel de Sola Pool, and Lewis Anthony Dexter, *American Business and Public Policy: The Politics of Foreign Trade* (New York: Atherton Press, 1963), p. 187.

those who are unable to communicate their ideas to persons unknown to them. It will be recalled that the capacity to engage in this latter type of communication on a regular basis is the defining characteristic of a governmental or nongovernmental leader.[35]

Yet these exclusions do not fully demarcate the boundaries of membership in the Attentive Public. The question of what constitutes communication "with some regularity" also serves to exclude attentiveness that is confined to earth-shaking events. During a grave crisis, such as a presidential assassination or the outbreak of war, most citizens would probably discuss the crisis with their family and friends.[36] If extraordinary crises are the only times that public affairs are discussed, however, such behavior is obviously far removed from the phenomena in which we are interested. At the very least attentiveness involves exchanging ideas before and after crises reach a peak. Beyond saying this, however, little is gained by developing abstract specifications of how often the exchange of ideas must occur to constitute "regular" discussions. Such specifications are an operational problem that can be solved only in connection with a particular set of data. The operational meaning we have given to the word is presented below.[37] For the present, it is sufficient to note that communication which occurs "with some regularity" occurs more frequently than on a sporadic, crisis-generated basis.

To identify attentive citizens in this way, however, is not to limit attentiveness to the single act of discussing public affairs with family or friends. This is our operational measure of membership in the Attentive Public, not an exhaustive description of

---

[35] See above, p. 5.

[36] A measure of the extent to which information and ideas pulsate through the communications system at a time of grave crisis is provided by the astonishing finding that 92 percent of the American people were aware of John F. Kennedy's assassination within two hours after the event and that 99.8 percent knew about it within six hours. Cf. Paul B. Sheatsley and Jacob J. Feldman, "The Assassination of President Kennedy: A Preliminary Report on Public Reactions and Behavior," *Public Opinion Quarterly*, Vol. XXVIII (Summer, 1964), p. 192.

[37] Pp. 174–75.

the ways in which attentiveness is sustained by its members. Complex industrial societies offer citizens a wide variety of ways to relate themselves to public affairs. Some of these have already been mentioned and many others could be cited. Our definition asserts only that if any one of them is employed, discussion with family and friends is also likely to occur.

It should also be noted that our means of identifying attentive citizens involves observing a particular form of behavior and does not require the attribution of inferred characteristics. The definition purposely avoids treating attentiveness as based on a high level of information about public affairs, strong attitudes toward them, or extensive involvement in them. Such characteristics may accompany attentiveness, but it is the attentiveness and not the accompanying characteristics that has consequence for the political process. As previously indicated, to define attentiveness in terms of psychological characteristics such as information possessed and attitudinal strength is to run the risk of overlooking politically relevant behavior that may not be associated with these characteristics. The presence of associated characteristics is better determined by empirical inquiry than by definitional assertion.

Before turning to our overall definition of membership in the Mobilizable Public, it is necessary to introduce a distinction between two major ways in which people relate themselves to public affairs. While there is no need to develop an exhaustive catalogue of all the possible forms such behavior can take, the distinction between first- and second-hand contact with the course of events facilitates the task of identifying members of the Mobilizable Public. This distinction corresponds to the difference between participating in and observing public affairs. First-hand forms of attentive or mobilized activity involve relating oneself directly to one or more actors in the public arena. Writing newspapers, contacting officials, attending their speeches, joining picket lines, signing petitions, marching in protests, distributing pamphlets, and giving money are a few examples. Second-hand contact, on the other hand, is more indirect and distant. It does not involve being in touch with or in the presence of persons who are, at the time of the contact, acting in the public arena. Rather, second-hand contact is established through the media of communications, both mass and face-to-face, and is sustained by reading a newspaper, listening to a radio, discussing with a friend, and so on.

This distinction calls attention to a major difference between attentive and mobilized activity: the latter necessarily consists of first-hand contacts, while the former may not. One cannot respond to a mobilizer's appeal without contacting other actors. Attentive citizens can also relate themselves to the course of events on a first-hand basis, but this is not a necessary component of their attentiveness and they can rely exclusively on second-hand contacts and still be maximally attentive.

Our overall definition of mobilizability is derived from the foregoing considerations. In effect, the mobilized act is conceived to be attentiveness plus first-hand contact under a specific condition: members of the Mobilizable Public are *those who communicate, with some regularity, ideas about public affairs to persons with whom they are closely associated (but not to persons whom they do not know) and who, within a reasonable period after they have been urged to do so by actors seeking to mobilize their support, act in a manner that corresponds with the request to establish first-hand contacts with some aspect of public affairs.* It will be noted that this definition rests on the juxtaposition of two specific behaviors that must correspond, be "reasonably" close in time, and occur in sequential order. These three criteria of juxtaposition amount, in effect, to our solution of the problem of tracing influence. If the mobilizee engages in behavior that corresponds to that requested by the mobilizer, and if the former occurs soon after the latter, then influence is assumed to have occurred and the behavior to have been mobilized.[38]

---

[38] It must be added that this assumption refers to a preponderance, and not to all, of the juxtaposed behaviors. While it seems plausible to proceed as if most of the activity that occurs in the proper juxtaposition constitutes mobilization, conceivably some of it is the result of sheer coincidence rather than systematic causation. Quite possibly some of the behavior defined as mobilized in a situation was undertaken by people

The definitional requirement that the mobilizee's behavior must correspond to that requested by the mobilizer arises from the need to differentiate the mobilized actions from all the others he might stimulate. In calling for support, mobilizers frequently evoke opposition or other behaviors that are discrepant with their request. Yet, despite the political relevance of such inconsistent reactions, they must be kept separate from support mobilization if the latter is to be a meaningful concept. Exactly what constitutes correspondence is again an operational problem that can be solved only in connection with particular data. Suffice it to state here that the juxtaposed behaviors must manifestly corres-

---

who had no knowledge that previously a mobilizer had asked them to act exactly as they did. The definition makes no attempt to by-pass such coincidences for two reasons. One is that to attempt to eliminate them is to become hopelessly entangled in the influence problem and the dilemma of inferring intentions and cognitions. Secondly, it seems justifiable, in probability terms, to presume that coincidence will underlie only a small proportion of the juxtaposed behaviors in any situaion involving the Attentive Public. Given the large number of juxtaposed behaviors that can be discerned whenever a segment of the Attentive Public is mobilized, the likelihood of many of them occurring by chance is not very great. Accordingly, rather than take on the complexity of inferring intention and cognition in order to account for relatively few of all the observed activities, it seems preferable to accept the presence of coincidences in the context of the assumption that a preponderance of the juxtaposed behaviors represent causal sequences.

To be sure, while causal rather than chance factors are likely to account for a preponderance of the juxtaposed behaviors, it is also true that the juxtaposition can result from the systematic operation of processes other than the one in which mobilizers galvanize mobilizees into action. An obvious example is provided by the case of leaders who are slow to lead and whose sensitivity to issues thus often trails that of their followers. Once sensitive to an issue, such leaders may find themselves forced to satisfy the wishes of their followers by calling for support that is bound to occur anyway. No definition, however, could totally preclude the operation of systematic variables other than mobilization and one has to rely on the good judgment of the researcher to detect when they may be operative.

pond in some way. This means that considerable variation can mark operational definitions of correspondence. In one situation the definition might posit a simple correspondence in expressed or implied viewpoints, whereas in another the specific way in which the viewpoints are expressed or reflected may be relevant. If, for example, the mobilizer calls on mobilizees to convey a particular set of opinions to officials, then it probably would not matter whether they did so by mail, phone, or picket line as long as they conveyed opinions corresponding to the ones sought. If, on the other hand, the mobilizer called for a demonstration of support through attendance at a specific rally, then writing a letter in lieu of attending the rally would not be considered a corresponding behavior.

Much the same can be said about the requirement that the mobilizee's responses must occur within "a reasonable period" after the mobilizer's stimulus. Clearly, for example, corresponding activity undertaken several years after the stimulus cannot be viewed as a response to the stimulus. Members of the Attentive Public will have been exposed to too many other stimuli in the interim for the researcher to conclude with confidence that the activity was mobilized by the original stimulus. To be sure, the mobilization of support is a cumulative process. Each effort to generate support can contribute to the success of future efforts even if it is not in itself successful. The mobilized act, in other words, is not an isolated and impulsive behavior. It has a history and it derives from prior experience. One does not suddenly heed the bidding of a mobilizer and write one's Congressman without a host of other conditions being operative, including perhaps previous contacts with the mobilizer. The cumulative nature of support-building notwithstanding, empirical analysis of mobilizability must start with particular stimuli and with the particular responses they evoke. To do otherwise—to treat every mobilized act as merely a response to all previous experience—would make it impossible to trace the flow of influence and render the concept of mobilization unusable as an instrument of research. So as to insure that the mobilized act is linked to the specific stimulus of an identifiable mobilizer, therefore, the notion of a "reasonable" interval between the juxtaposed behaviors was introduced into the definition. How much time must elapse before the interval is considered unreasonably long is again a question that can be answered only with an operational definition constructed in the context of a particular set of data.

The Scope of Attentive and Mobilized Activity

It is not enough to differentiate personal affairs from public affairs and then define attentiveness and mobilizability as activity directed toward the latter. The world of public affairs is multidimensional. Unlike an election, it embraces phenomena that cannot be reduced to a single act of favoring or opposing a candidate. Yet, the tendency to treat all public affairs as similar to an election campaign marks many explanations of political behavior. Many investigators presume that the arena of public affairs encompasses the same phenomena at all times, whereas in fact its contents are constantly shifting as the concerns and problems of communities undergo continual change. Thus, in order to probe the dynamics of citizenship between elections, we need to break down the concept of public affairs into its components. These are issues which can then be clustered together in terms of the major types (what we shall refer to as "issue areas") that constitute the recurring concerns and problems of communities. Depending on the level of generality in which the investigator is interested, in other words, public affairs can usefully be conceived to be a complex of issues or issue areas.

By public issues we mean all those matters which, at any moment in time, have not been resolved to the satisfaction of all segments of the community and which are therefore the subject of dispute and the focus of support-mobilizing efforts. An issue becomes part of the complex of public affairs whenever a conflict arises in the community that cannot be resolved without the intervention of officialdom, that thus is being pressed upon or considered by government officials, and that has consequences for the entire community when it is resolved, whatever the solution may be and however it may be achieved.[39]

It is obvious that no individual can follow all the issues being pressed on or processed by government at any one time. Even if it were possible to do so in one's local community—which in large urban centers it probably is not—the fact that one is also a member of larger communities renders the task of attentiveness unmanageable. Local issues are not as numerous and technical as national and international ones, yet one is a member of communities at the local level as well and, as in a three-ring circus, the activity in all these arenas is simultaneous, continuous, and engrossing. The individual cannot watch it all at once.

Indeed, even the mass media have difficulty in this respect. Rare is the medium that can provide adequate coverage of all the conflicts spawned by the complexity of an industrial civilization. For all the electronic miracles in communications, most of the mass media are able to report only a few "big" issues in depth

[39] Following the earlier delineation of what actions derive from the role of citizen, the criteria of government intervention and community-wide consequence are included in this conception in order to distinguish public issues from private ones. Many of the conflicts that mark life *in* a community do not also become conflicts *of* the community because the disputants somehow manage to cope with them on their own, without disturbing the orderly course of events. When government intervention is required to facilitate conflict resolution, however, the dispute begins to lose its private character. At the very least the government intervenes in order to determine whether the public's interest is involved. Often the determination is a negative one and the intervention does not exceed adjudicative or administrative settlement of the dispute. Not every situation in which government intervenes, in other words, is considered a public issue. A conflict remains private if the governmental solution is not applicable to actors other than those who are parties to it. Most solutions achieved in domestic relations courts or through government arbitration of labor-management disputes, for example, have relevance only for those involved and thus never move beyond the status of private issues. Conflicts with consequences that exceed the welfare of the disputants, on the other hand, enter the arena of public issues as soon as the wider ramifications are recognized and arouse support-building behavior.

at any time and at best they can give only superficial and sporadic treatment to the remainder.[40] The problem is no simpler for top officials. The number of issues is so great and many of their dimensions so technical that the resources of government are hardly sufficient to keep top officials abreast of all the demands made upon them. It takes a vast bureaucracy to apprise them of all the attitudinal and behavioral trends that are unfolding in the public arena.

In short, public affairs are extremely complex and it is impossible for a citizen to relate himself to them in their entirety. He must carry, as it were, a "salience map" with which to pick his way across the political terrain.[41] Regardless of the strength of his motives and the extent of his capacities, he can be responsive only to some of the issues of the day and must be unresponsive to many, a circumstance that requires him to fall back on his salience map for guidance. There are, in short, limits to the scope of his attentive and mobilized activities.

What determines these limits and the selection of issues within them constitutes a primary concern of this book[42] and here we merely introduce the problem by identifying two basic dimensions of the scope of any citizen's attentiveness and mobilizability. One is the quantitative dimension of the number of issue areas toward which a citizen may be responsive. The second is the spatial dimension of the size and level of the community toward which attentiveness and mobilizability are likely to operate. To anticipate the ensuing discussion, it seems desirable to refine our definitions of the Attentive and Mobilizable Publics by making two distinctions. The first separates multi-issue citizens who communicate, with some regularity, at least two different kinds of ideas about local affairs to persons with whom they are closely

---

[40] For an incisive discussion of the factors that limit the range of issues covered by the mass media, see Bernard C. Cohen, *The Press and Foreign Policy* (Princeton: Princeton University Press, 1963), pp. 113–119.

[41] The concept of a salience map is developed in M. Kent Jennings and Harmon Zeigler, "The Salience of American State Politics," *American Political Science Review*, Vol. 64 (June 1970), pp. 523–25.

[42] See especially Chapter 12.

associated, from single-issue citizens whose regular communications to family and friends are confined to one local issue area. The second differentiates these two types from those who engage in single- or multi-issue activities with respect to national and international affairs.

Although empirical analysis must necessarily focus on particular issues and the conflicts they engender, the data and findings descriptive of issue behavior presented in the ensuing chapters are used as a basis for exploring similarities and differences at the more general level of issue areas. We are not so much interested in first- and second-hand contacts that are established with a particular conflict at a particular time as we are with patterns of attentiveness and mobilizability that can be discerned in a variety of situations. We want to know whether similar activities are precipitated by the same *type* of issue and, if so, what the differences are among various types of issues. Historically viewed, every issue is different from every other issue and our comprehension of the Attentive Public is not likely to be enriched unless we are prepared to move beyond this view and look for patterns of behavior in clusters of similar issues. It is this notion of types or clusters of issues that underlies the issue-area concept.[43]

The issue-area concept is not free of difficulties, however. Once the decision is made to cluster issues into areas the analyst immediately confronts the problem of how general each area should be and what issues should be classified in it. The problem is not easily solved and requires a delicate series of assumptions about the comparability of discreet patterns of action and interaction.[44] For example, does each foreign policy crisis lead to the same kind of behavior on the part of attentive and mobilizable citizens? Or is it erroneous to assume that the existence of conflict

---

[43] For a definition and formulation of this concept, see Rosenau, "Pre-Theories and Theories of Foreign Policy," in R. Barry Farrell, ed., *Approaches to Comparative and International Politics* (Evanston: Northwestern University Press, 1966), pp. 71–88.

[44] For an elaboration of the problem of classifying issues, see Rosenau, ed., *Domestic Sources of Foreign Policy* (New York: The Free Press, 1967), pp. 11–20.

abroad necessarily introduces a commonality into all external issues? Are there dimensions of attentiveness and mobilizability that make it reasonable to cluster rather than separate certain kinds of foreign and domestic policy issues? More specifically— and cast in terms of the empirical inquiry undertaken in subsequent chapters—is the behavior generated by a civil rights issue likely to resemble that associated with a treaty banning nuclear testing sufficiently to justify classifying the two issues in the same area?

The exact criteria used to distinguish issue areas and classify issues is again a matter of developing operational definitions that are appropriate to particular data. Whatever criteria are used, however, there would seem to be little reason to alter the assertion that the scope within which a citizen can follow the course of events is necessarily limited. A highly abstract scheme might be able to reduce public affairs to just a small number of issue areas;[45] but, short of that, the foregoing comments about the impossibility of keeping abreast of events is not changed by clustering together those similarly structured. Hence the question of what determines activity with respect to some issues and unresponsiveness with respect to others remains pertinent when cast in terms of issue areas. Accounting for the presence of some citizens in one area rather than another poses an important and intriguing challenge that has yet to be met in empirical research.

Multi-Area and Single-Area Activity

One limit to the scope of any citizen's attentiveness and mobilizability is, obviously, the number of issue areas to which he is ready to respond. Since he cannot respond to them all, the

---

[45] Two such schemes, both delineating four issue areas, can be found in Rosenau, "Pre-Theories and Theories of Foreign Policy," and Herbert J. Spiro, "Comparative Politics: A Comprehensive Approach," *American Political Science Review*, Vol. LVI (September 1962), pp. 577–95. For a formulation founded on three basic areas, see Theodore J. Lowi, "American Business, Public Policy, Case Studies and Political Theory," *World Politics*, Vol. XVI (July 1964), pp. 677–715.

scope of his activity is limited by the particular combination of factors that lead him to follow events in some areas and neglect them in others. Without exploring the dynamics of issue-area saliency at this point, a distinction can be usefully made between those citizens whose attentiveness is confined to only one area and those who are attentive to two or more areas. The former, whom we shall refer to as *single-area* members of the Attentive Public, may vary widely in terms of the area to which they are responsive, but they share the tendency to communicate ideas about issues in only one area to their family and friends. Likewise, the latter, whom we shall call *multi-area* persons, may differ considerably in the particular combination of areas that engage their attention, but they have in common a readiness to be active in at least two areas.[46]

Although there may be discernible differences among multi-area persons in terms of whether they are active in two, three, four, five, or more areas, the above distinction would seem to be especially important. Most notably, the distinction allows us to probe on the periphery of the Attentive Public where the line between it and the Mass Public becomes vague. That is, the concept of single-area behavior permits concentration on those members of the Attentive Public whose practice of citizenship between elections is founded on some special interest or preoccupation rather than on a more generalized concern about public affairs. Presum-

---

[46] It should be noted that this distinction refers to attentiveness over a span of time. A single-area person is not someone who is active with respect to only one area at a time. Rather such a person is attentive to only the same one area at *any* time. By "any" time, however, we do not mean a lifetime, but rather, say, several years. As noted in Chapter 2, there is always the possibility that habits learned in a single area will spill over into others and that with the passage of time some single-area citizens will thus become multi-area in their attentiveness. Likewise, a multi-area person is not conceived as active with respect to two or more areas at a time. Those who cannot handle issues in two or more areas simultaneously, but who move on to other areas as issues rise and fall, are considered multi-issue citizens because, to repeat, attentiveness is conceived in terms of behavior through time.

ably such persons become involved in the course of events sporadically and spasmodically, depending on the saliency of issues in the area of their interest or preoccupation, and in the intervals between bursts of activity they return to passivity and to the ranks of the Mass Public. The citizen of East European descent who becomes active only when issues encompassing the "homeland" arise, the zealot who becomes aroused by the course of events only when he perceives them menaced by the specter of communism, the worker who follows only issues pertaining to labor-management relations, the professor whose attentiveness to public affairs is confined to issues bearing on academic freedom, the mother whose apathy to the public arena temporarily gives way on the school-busing issue, the student who takes an interest only in foreign policy issues that may involve increased draft quotas for the armed forces—these are illustrative of single-area members of the Attentive Public. As their behavior suggests, single-area attentiveness is important because it introduces a measure of instability into the making of public policy. Unlike the more broad-gauged approach of multi-area citizens, the single-mindedness of single-area attentives can lead to an intensity of conviction and a lack of perspective that add impetuousness and unpredictability to the processes of support-building. Both as an unorganized audience and as organized groups, single-area persons often swell the ranks of the Attentive Public suddenly and, in so doing, contribute to the polarization of politics and the emergence of the "big" issues of the day. Indeed, there is much to be said for the hypothesis that the greater the proportion of single-area persons activated with respect to an issue, the longer that issue is likely to dominate the public affairs of a community.

It must be emphasized that thus far we have been referring primarily to *attentiveness* to a single area. Single-area *mobilizability* is a somewhat different matter. While those whose attentiveness is limited to a single area are presumably mobilizable only with respect to issues in that one area, it is easy to conceive of multi-area attentives who are only single-area mobilizables. Such persons are those who closely follow public affairs but who, perhaps for a variety of reasons, are so sensitive to the issues in a particular area that it is the only one in which their support is susceptible to mobilization. This phenomenon can be illustrated by revising and extending any of our earlier examples. Consider again persons of East European descent. Some of them may sustain continuous second-hand contact with public affairs and ordinarily refrain from engaging in first-hand activities. Yet, when an issue involving their ancestral lands arises, their involvement reaches the point where they will put all else aside when a mobilizer calls upon them to demonstrate support. Nor need this type of behavior stem from such direct and clear-cut sources. The factors that underlie mobilizability may, for complex and obscure reasons, be present in, say, the civil rights area for white, Protestant, upper-class citizens whose rights are not jeopardized, who are attentive to many issue areas, and who are responsive to the stimuli of leadership in only the one area.

One other aspect of single-area behavior needs to be mentioned. Discrepancies can arise between the boundaries of issue areas delineated by the observer and the boundaries that are meaningful for the actors who undertake attentive or mobilized behavior. While it is reasonable to expect a general coincidence between observers and actors in this respect, there is one kind of citizen whose activities are not easily categorized in an issue-area framework. We have in mind the individual who is so dominated by the issues of one area that he is unable to discern its boundaries and he treats it as encompassing a host of issues that both the observer and other actors regard as belonging to other areas. Some of our earlier examples hint at this discrepancy, the most obvious perhaps being the citizen for whom the specter of communism is so menacing that he perceives its evil influence at work in virtually every area that an observer might delineate. It seems erroneous, however, to classify his behavior with respect to the diverse issues as multi-area attentiveness or mobilizability. His presence in the several areas is real, but his activity is so undifferentiated among them that it cannot be viewed as consistent with our conception of multi-area activity. Although the terminology is somewhat awkward, our conceptual solution to this problem is to acknowledge the existence of such discrepant behavior by referring to it as *single-area dominant multi-area activity.*[47]

Local and National Activity

The scope of attentiveness and mobilizability is also limited spatially. That is, the geo-political boundaries of communities can also serve as demarcations of issue areas. Leaving aside for the moment the interplay among communities, one set of public affairs seems naturally to end and another to begin as one's observations move from community to community. For most Americans four communities are likely to be especially salient as foci of attentive and mobilized behavior: the home town, the state, the nation, and the world at large. For purposes of simplicity we shall cluster the first two of these together and treat them as the "local community," a combination which seems justifiable since both home town and state affairs have a proximity to the daily

[47] The identification of this form of behavior should not be interpreted as implying that other multi-area persons never permit their inclinations toward one area to prevail over their feelings toward another. The boundaries between areas are not conceived as impermeable and different areas are not regarded as equally salient for all persons. Hence the attentiveness and mobilizability of multi-area persons in one area may well be affected by events in another. Such cross-area effects, however, are not viewed as the consequence of single-area dominance if the pattern of dominance varies from time to time and area to area. Such variations are normal and expectable, and presumably they are randomly distributed throughout the Attentive Public, thus having no particular impact upon the policy-making process. Single-area dominant behavior, on the other hand, would seem to involve a concentrated set of processes that can have a systematic impact upon the role played by the Attentive Public. Therefore, just as single-area activity was distinguished from other types because it can introduce an unpredictableness into the policy-making process, so does single-area dominance appear to warrant identification as a special and extreme form of multi-area behavior.

life of a citizen that distinguishes them from national or international affairs.

It is the notion of proximity that makes analysis of the spatial scope of activity important. Different members of the Attentive and Mobilizable Publics are likely to ascribe different degrees of proximity to the various levels of public affairs. Some may be oriented only toward the local level and treat the national and international levels as too distant to warrant even attentiveness, much less mobilized actions. For others the national and international communities may be no more distant than local affairs and they will be active at all three levels. Still others may seem to reverse spatial perspective and find national and international issues more proximate and more worthy of attention than local issues.[48]

It follows that the policy-making roles of the Attentive and Mobilizable Publics are likely to be performed differently at each level as variations occur in the readiness of citizens to be active at each level. The public affairs of a local community, for example, are likely to be substantially altered if national or international events command the attention of its active citizens but they are not able to respond to issues in more than one community at a time. A common frustration of both local officials and those who oppose them in times of crisis is the inability to reach and mobilize the attentive citizen because he is preoccupied with the national scene.[49]

---

[48] For some empirical evidence that people are able to become involved in the world beyond the local community without maintaining an interest in local affairs, see Robert K. Merton, *Social Theory and Social Structure* (Glencoe, Ill.: The Free Press, 1957), Chap. X.

[49] A measure of this phenomenon is provided by situations in which national or international crises coincide with local elections. Under such circumstances the opposition candidates will often attempt to overcome them by associating their electoral campaign with the more salient larger issues and downplaying the less provocative local ones. In effect, they attempt to localize national and international issues. During the 1960's, for example, many candidates for local offices based their election campaigns largely on issues involving the war in Vietnam. Contrariwise, at

It seems desirable to combine the limitations on attentiveness and mobilizability and, doing so, eight kinds of members of the Attentive Public can be at least theoretically identified: (a) those who are single-area active at the local level and inattentive to national-international issues; (b) those who are multi-area active in local affairs and inattentive to national-international affairs; (c) those who are active in a single area at both the local and national-international levels; (d) those who engage in multi-area activities at all levels; (e) those who are multi-area active at the local level and only single-area active at the national-international level; (f) those who are active with respect to only a single local area but multi-area active at the national-international level; (g) those who are inattentive to local affairs and single-area active at the national-international level; and (h) those who are inattentive to local affairs and multi-area active at the national-international level. In all likelihood, of course, these eight types are not equally distributed throughout the population. Certain of them, such as type (f), may even prove hard to find in a community. Yet each type is theoretically possible and the relative predominance of the various types can have important consequences for the role of the Attentive Public and the course of public affairs.

In order to use these distinctions, criteria must be established for differentiating local issue areas from national-international ones and for classifying or otherwise dealing with those issues that bridge the two levels. We base our criteria on the identity of the officials involved in an issue who become foci of attentive and mobilized behavior on the part of the citizenry. If, in discussing an issue with family and friends, members of the Attentive Public mention only their home town or state officials, then we define it as being part of a local issue area. If reference is made only to federal officials, then an issue area at the national-

---

the national level candidates for office frequently seek to cope with a preoccupation with local issues by, in effect, nationalizing them. The use of the "crime-in-the-streets" issue in recent presidential campaigns provides an example of this process.

international level is seen as involved. Similarly, if both local and federal officials enter into the discussions, then the issue is viewed as involving a "mixed" area which spans the levels.[50]

Domestic and Foreign Policy Activity

In the two previous paragraphs we combined the national and international levels in order to stress the distinctive nature of local affairs. From another perspective, however, the distinction between national and international affairs is obviously important. Indeed, a central purpose of this book is to explore the question of whether conflicts over domestic policies arouse different forms of attentiveness and mobilizability on the part of different kinds of people than do foreign policy issues.[51]

Delineating the boundaries between foreign and domestic issues, however, is not as easy as it might seem at first glance. As technology shrinks the world and expands the interdependence of nations, both the foreign component of domestic affairs and the domestic component of foreign affairs grow apace. The "pure" foreign policy issue, in which the outcome is largely irrelevant to life within the national community, is becoming as obsolete as its domestic counterpart. Issues increasingly seem to be converging toward a mid-point between these two extremes, so that again reference can be made to a "mixed" issue-area that embraces

[50] These definitions might be challenged on the grounds that the perceptions of the Attentive Public are not always accurate, that occasionally the participation of one set of officials in the course of events may be quite informal and confidential, and thus beyond recognition. What, in other words, about issues in which the observer identifies communications and actions originating with officials of which the Attentive Public never becomes apprised? While such a circumstance is quite possible, it still would not undermine these definitions. Our concern is with public issues, not with private bargains or confidential deliberations. These may crucially affect the outcome of issues, but if the public never becomes aware of the participation of officials at another level, the latter are not relevant to support-building processes among the former and thus it does not seem inappropriate to exclude them from the definitions.

[51] See pp. 451–56.

conflicts in which the foreign and domestic components are thoroughly fused and indistinguishable from each other. In order to break away from the foreign-domestic dichotomy and give full recognition to the overlap between the two types, we shall employ a procedure similar to the one used to identify the mixed area between local and national issues. Again the identity of the officials who are perceived as active in an issue is the basis for operationalizing the boundaries between the foreign, mixed, and domestic areas. It is difficult to conceive of a controversy over international affairs that does not involve concern about the actions or reactions of officials of other governments. Hence, if no sustained mention is made of officials abroad and only national officials are perceived and discussed in connection with an issue, then that issue can be viewed as falling in the domestic area. Contrariwise, if the only officials consistently included in discussions of an issue are foreign ones and those national officials responsible for maintaining relations with the external world (i.e., the chief executive and officials of the foreign office), then the issue is considered to fall in the international or foreign policy area. Issues are classified in the mixed area whenever sustained reference is made to foreign officials and to national ones in addition to the chief executive and those in the foreign office.

Although further operationalization may be necessary in order to make empirical use of these distinctions, their general application can be readily illustrated. The Civil Rights Act of 1964, for example, would be classified as a domestic issue, since discussions of it referred only casually if at all to reactions abroad or to State Department officials, but focused intensely on the activities of the President, the Attorney General, members of Congress, and a variety of other officials. At the other extreme fall such issues as, say, the stability of the Congo, the situation in Berlin, and the unity of Western Europe. From the perspective of the United States, these are all foreign policy issues because in each instance the behavior of foreign officialdom, the President, and the top officers of the Department of State are central to any discussion of what policies are appropriate, while references to any others at the national level would be at most sporadic and infrequent. Mixed issues are exemplified by the 1963 nuclear test ban treaty and the foreign aid program. Senatorial approval was required for the treaty and each year's foreign aid funds must be authorized and appropriated by both houses of Congress. Hence legislators are bound to be as central to discussions of such issues as officials abroad and in the State Department.

This formulation also allows for major transformations in the nature of issues. Our conception of public issues is not a static one. Issues can change in significant ways and allowance must be made for those that do. The situation in Vietnam, for example, was radically altered as a public issue when bombings of North Vietnam were initiated in February, 1965. What had been a moderate debate became a heated one and the sphere of controversy was widened to include many new private and public actors. In effect, what was a foreign policy issue became a mixed one and our definitions permit reclassification accordingly. Domestic issues that become internationalized as an abrupt turn of events activates participation on the part of previously uninterested officials abroad and in the State Department are perhaps no less frequent. Conflicts that result in the outbreak of violence within a country are examples of mixed issues with such a history.[52]

SUMMARY

In this chapter we have posited the practices of citizenship as involving only public and not personal affairs. The attentiveness and mobilizability on which the practices are based have been defined in terms of specified forms of behavior. The characteristics usually associated with active citizenship, such as high levels of involvement, information, and strong attitudes, have been omitted from the definitions because it seems preferable to establish the association empirically rather than through conceptual formulation. Both attentiveness and mobilizability are conceived

---

[52] Cf. James N. Rosenau, ed., *International Aspects of Civil Strife* (Princeton: Princeton University Press, 1964), esp. Chap. 3.

to be activities through which people relate themselves to public affairs, either on the basis of first-hand contact with actors in the public arena or second-hand through the communications system. Of all the activities through which people can relate themselves to public affairs, the act of discussing such matters with family and friends has been singled out as the best measure of attentiveness. First-hand contact with public affairs preceded by a prior request for such action is the additional component that distinguishes a mobilized act from an attentive one.

The conceptualization of these forms of behavior has also allowed for the fact that one cannot be attentive to public affairs in their entirety. Distinctions have been drawn between persons who are active with respect to only a single area of public issues and those who are multi-area oriented, between those whose activities are confined to the local, national, or international levels and those whose scope cuts across two or more levels, and between those whose actions are directed primarily at issues in the domestic or mixed policy areas and those concerned about issues in the foreign policy area.

CHAPTER 4

MOBILIZING THE ATTENTIVE CITIZEN: AN INITIAL MODEL

Thus far our analysis has proceeded unrestrainedly at the level of interpretative speculation and moved cautiously at the level of detailed definition, but it has yet to be cast at the level of theory. We have suggested that the Attentive Public is growing in size and have identified the various forms its activities can take, but we have made no effort to assess the kinds of persons who are likely to be attentive or to uncover the sources from which their behavior springs. We have speculated that attentiveness is partly a matter of habit, but we have alluded only briefly to some of the dynamics of the habit. We have stressed that some attentive citizens are responsive to the appeal of mobilizers and some are not, but we have not attempted to explain the sources and dynamics of mobilizability.

Explanatory analysis of this kind is not easy. We cannot fall back on the literature for a general model of the dynamics of political action, since "no general theory of participation even approaches this ideal"; and yet we cannot proceed without such a model, since "participation appears to be a complex phenomenon that depends on a great many variables of different relative weights."[1] Thus we must construct our own elaborate model out of a set of integrated and testable hypotheses. To pave the way for systematic empirical inquiry such a model must be explicit, and it must also be elaborate, if we accept the premise that, like any behavior, the act of relating oneself to public affairs does not stem from a single source.

It seems clear that this premise is well founded. Neither the habit of attentiveness nor the inclination to respond to a mobilizer spring automatically from cumulative experience in high socio-economic statuses. Some persons who graduate from college never develop the habit, while others who do not finish high school acquire and maintain it for a lifetime. Nor do they stem simply from feeling strongly about an issue or being persuaded that one's self-interest is at stake in a situation. Attitudes do not always lead to action and not everyone with strong feelings toward an issue will undertake activities relevant to it. Self-interest may provoke attentiveness and heighten sensitivity to mobilizers, but people are also capable of involvement in remote situations that have little bearing on their personal lives or immediate concerns. In short, like all habits, attentiveness and mobilizability would seem to result from a complex of variables, each of which is necessary but none of which is sufficient to their establishment and maintenance.

Comprehension and comparison of the dynamics of attentiveness and mobilizability, therefore, require assessment of the contribution of a number of factors and it is to this task that we now turn. Our goal in this chapter is to outline a model that

[1] Herbert McClosky, "Political Participation," p. 256.

identifies the relevant variables and permits explanation of how, when, and why they combine to lead people to engage in the practices of citizenship between elections. In order to facilitate the analysis and enhance confidence in the empirical findings, we have identified and numbered those hypotheses derived from the initial version of the model that can be tested by the available data.[2] All the hypotheses have been cast in terms of the distinctions drawn in the previous chapter and the variables embraced by the research instrument.[3] Chapters 6 through 12 test these hypotheses against our data, while Chapter 13 refines the model in the light of these tests.

SOME UNDERLYING PREMISES

The essential components of our model of citizenship between elections are presented in Figure 4–1. Here it can be seen that the citizen's posture toward his environment is conceived to result from the way in which his current behavior, as conditioned by his past experiences and channeled by his present responsibilities, interacts with his attitudes and perceptions to produce orientations toward personal affairs exclusively or also, either because of the efforts of mobilizers or for other reasons, toward one or more issues of public affairs.

Also discernible in the diagrammatic presentation of the model are several of its main premises. One is that apathy, attentiveness, and mobilizability are all products of the same variables. Depending on their relative intensities and the particular con-

---

[2] It must be emphasized that these hypotheses were derived from propositions built into the model and developed prior to inspection of the data. Such a procedure facilitates analysis by indicating which of the many data should be examined and it enhances confidence in the generalizability of the findings by allowing for confirmation of prior reasoning.

[3] Since the instrument does not encompass all the variables contained in the model (personality variables are the most conspicuous omission in this regard), formal hypotheses have not been derived for those which cannot be explored in our data. However, their place in the model and our expectations as to their operation are noted in the ensuing presentation.

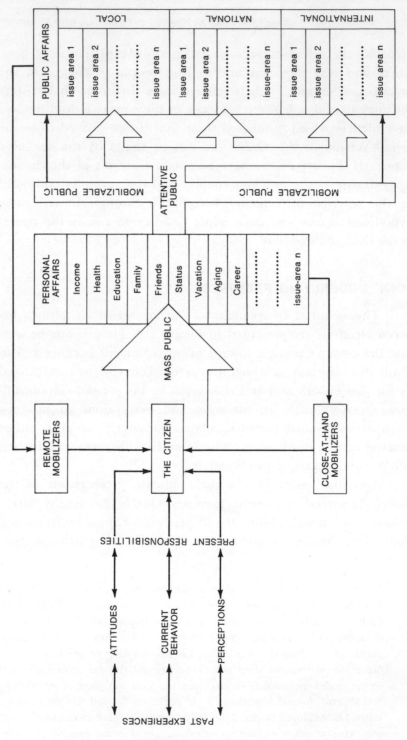

Figure 4–1

The Attentiveness Model

figuration they form as they interact, these same variables can produce attentiveness, inattentiveness, or mobilizability. All citizens are concerned about personal affairs and whether they become members of the Attentive, Mobilizable, or Mass Publics, and how they behave once there, is conditioned by their previous experience, shaped by their attitudes and perceptions, restricted by their present responsibilities, and affected by feedback from their current behavior. Moreover, they are all subjected to the appeals of mobilizers. What distinguishes the three publics is the form taken by each of the variables and the interaction among them.

A second main premise—suggested by the two-way arrows in Figure 4–1—is that the variables comprising the model are interdependent. The model presumes that for attentiveness to come into being, none of the main variables can be operating so as to be contrary to it. If even one of them operates in the direction of apathy, attentiveness cannot persist. New circumstances can alter such a discrepant variable and render it conducive to active citizenship, in which case attentiveness is likely to develop. More specifically, for the habit of attentiveness to be established and maintained, a citizen's social background must allow him to hold certain attitudes and undertake certain activities, but his attitudes must not be inconsistent with his activities and the latter must not negate the former; and, in turn, both the attitudes and activities must shape and be shaped by his perceptions and his present responsibilities, thus producing orientations that are further channeled by the nature of events in the arena of public affairs. Stated differently, "We may note that when a number of the more effective determinants of active citizenship combine their influence, the result is a very sharp increase in the proportion who manifest that characteristic [to a large] degree. That is to say, the impact of the determinants is apparently cumulative." [4]

It is important to stress, however, that the interdependence posited by the model does not require that all the main variables

---

[4] Alex Inkeles, "Participant Citizenship in Six Developing Countries," p. 1140.

contribute to attentiveness, but only that they all operate so as not to detract from it. This dimension is important because it allows for the possibility that the various sources of attentiveness will combine in different ways for different citizens. Other researchers have analyzed samples of citizens in five countries, including the United States, and found that high degrees of political participation result from both extensive involvement in voluntary organizations and occupancy of certain social statuses, but that the social status route to participation is associated with attitudinal variables which reinforce the propensity to participate while the organizational activity route does not depend on such concomitant attitudes.[5] Such a finding does not undermine the basic premise of our model, however, since there is no evidence that the direct link between organizational activity and political participation is sustained by cynicism, a low sense of efficacy, or any of the other attitudes that foster apathy and alienation.

Some extreme examples will perhaps help to clarify the interdependency of the variables that underlie attentiveness. Consider, for instance, a woman whose background, attitudes, perceptions, and statuses are conducive to public affairs, but who is nevertheless apathetic toward them because none of her present activities produce the kind of feedback necessary to maintain attentiveness. If such a person should marry a government official, her daily experiences would probably bring her into much closer contact with public affairs and alter the only condition opposing her entry into the Attentive Public. On the other hand, if she is a highly religious person who believes that the course of events is determined only by God, such a marriage might not pull her out of the Mass Public. A less hypothetical illustration of the circumstances under which attentiveness may be established is provided by the conclusion reached in Chapter 2 that the ranks of the Attentive Public were permanently enlarged when previously apathetic citizens became engaged in civil rights activities. In this instance the discrepant variable was the state of public

[5] Norman H. Nie, G. Bingham Powell, Jr., Kenneth Prewitt, "Social Structure and Political Participation: Developmental Relationship, II," *American Political Science Review,* Vol. 63 (1969), pp. 812–13.

affairs. Those who entered the Attentive Public via the civil rights issue must have had all the other prerequisites to attentiveness or the emergence of the issue would not have aroused them. It took such a situation to engage their concern about the course of public affairs but, once engaged, they were also responsive to events in Vietnam and elsewhere.

A new job, which is so time-consuming that its occupant no longer has time to read the daily newspaper, illustrates how a variable that was previously consistent with the other variables in the interdependent set becomes discrepant and leads to a diminution or extinction of attentiveness. Failing health is a similar example. Still another is the obverse of the civil rights sequence noted above. If a person is repeatedly thwarted in his efforts to contact officials and influence policy, his attitudes toward his own political competence might be altered sufficiently to alienate him from public affairs and direct his interests into other areas.

Attentiveness is thus conceived as a dynamic process. It grows and declines in response to changes in any of its components. Even the "past experience" variable is dynamic: if one's background is not so constricting as to allow for its reinterpretation in the light of current activities and new attitudes, perceptions, or responsibilities, then it can be said to be susceptible to interaction with the other variables.

This is not to imply, however, that attentiveness is unstable or constantly changing. As previously indicated, it is partly a habit—a characteristic way of responding to particular stimuli— as well as a calculated assessment of how each stimulus should be handled, and habits tend to be enduring. Indeed, one analyst provides cogent evidence that for some citizens the habit of attentiveness is acquired in childhood:

> Our findings suggest that much political behavior is to be explained as habitual. It is not directly derived from the intellectual, economic, social, or characterological features of actors. It is an aspect of life style that has been accepted uncritically since childhood by a relatively small number of people in the society. They may come from diverse ethnic, religious, occupational, or social backgrounds. They may exhibit the gamut of personality types.

They are distinguished only by their political involvement, an interest they acquired when other children built model airplanes or engaged in nonpolitical "street corner" pastimes. Such people, though a very small part of the total population, make up a large portion of the political participants.[6]

Whatever the time span over which the attentiveness habit is nourished, our model presumes that it is as difficult to establish and hard to break as any other habit. If one is used to skipping the first section of a newspaper and turning to the sports or entertainment pages, it will take unusual circumstances to alter this pattern and incorporate the front page into one's reading habits. Similarly, much would have to happen for a regular viewer of the evening news to abandon that practice.

On the other hand, as indicated by the evidence cited in Chapter 2 that the Attentive Public is growing, change does occur and the strength of habits does fluctuate, even if only gradually. Given circumstances that intensify the saliency of certain issues, the front page can catch the individual's eye and eventually become the focus of recurring interest. In short, the model is flexible. It presumes that attentiveness and mobilizability are to some extent habitual, but it consists of variables which, if they vary sufficiently, can alter prevailing habits and foster new ones. By building in issues as a major variable, it also allows for the possibility that some citizens are—or become—selective in their behavior and do not respond unthinkingly to all stimuli.

As will be seen in the hypotheses derived from the model, the interdependence of its variables is no less for the propensity to respond to mobilizers than for the habit of attentiveness. In-

[6] Robert H. Salisbury, "The Urban Party Organization Member," *Public Opinion Quarterly*, Vol. XXIX (Winter, 1965–66), p. 564. For other analysts who conceive of the practices of citizenship to be sustained by habitual modes of behavior, see Barber, *Citizen Politics*, p. 18; Angus Campbell, "The Passive Citizen," *ACTA Sociologica*, Vol. 6 (1962), p. 16; and Matthews and Prothro, *Negroes and the New Southern Politics*, p. 70.

deed, mobilizability requires all the variables to be conducive to responsiveness simultaneously—at precisely the time when the mobilizer appeals for support—and thus its maintenance involves an especially delicate balance among them. The delicacy of this balance is accentuated further by the fact that mobilizability necessitates a readiness to commit substantial—and normally scarce—time, energy, and resources. Through reliance on second-hand contacts, attentive persons can be spectators at the arena of public affairs, but those who are mobilizable must enter it and be active in it—and they must do so at a time and in a manner decided by someone else. In addition, because mobilized behavior consists of first-hand contacts with the course of events, it cannot be undertaken in private. For all kinds of reasons, ranging from shyness to fear of retaliation, such open behavior is repugnant to many people, thus rendering even more delicate the balance underlying mobilizability. The woman whose marriage to a government official precipitated her attentiveness may not become mobilizable if her friends deride such overt activity. The man for whom the civil rights situation served as the final stimulus to attentiveness may not be mobilizable, even with respect to civil rights, because his perceptions of the policy-making process do not accord much consequence to action by the citizenry.

Still another reason for the delicacy of the balance on which the propensity toward mobilizability rests is the mobilizer himself. His identity and style can be a crucial variable in the process whereby citizens respond to appeals for support. For reasons that we shall explore at length in Chapter 11, people are more responsive to some mobilizers than to others *even* when they all make the same appeal on the same issue. One person may heed a friend's urgings but resist those of the President of the United States, whereas another's sensitivities may be exactly the opposite. Some persons may be responsive to bombastic appeals over television and others may be moved by closely reasoned requests for support sent through the mails.

The delicate balance that fosters and sustains mobilizability between elections is further indicated by the absence of nationwide norms supporting such a propensity. Mobilizers usually have little difficulty generating support during election campaigns because the norm that one should accord support through one's vote is pervasive and intense. Similarly, attentiveness between elections is reinforced by the widely shared and articulated American value that one should follow closely the course of events. Neither precedents nor their consciences, however, remind Americans of a responsibility to respond to a mobilizer who seeks support that cannot be given in a voting booth. The propensity to respond to a request for support between elections thus has no societal foundation on which to rest.[7] It must therefore be self-generating and its strength depends on the way in which the other variables are patterned.

It is little wonder, then, that the proportions of mobilizable persons cited in Chapter 2 are so small. All the factors that inhibit attentiveness to public affairs also impede mobilizability, and the latter must overcome a number of additional obstacles in order to persist. Stated somewhat differently, it is hardly surprising that political change is normally slow and incremental. If the mobilization of support on behalf of remote issues is the essence of politics,[8] then an especially complex and subtle task confronts those who wish to bring pressure to bear on the course of events between elections.

Responsiveness to a mobilizer is delicate and dynamic, but it is far from being impetuous or random. We have not meant to suggest that instability is a central characteristic of the phenomena in which we are interested. Mobilizability involves not an impulse, but a propensity; not a tendency toward capriciousness, but a stable disposition to be responsive to certain kinds of stimuli.

---

[7] It should be noted that this is not necessarily characteristic of mobilizability. There are societies where norms encouraging the propensity are strong and widespread, where people lead their lives expecting to turn out for meetings and rallies when the appropriate mobilizer requests it. Communist countries are examples in this regard.

[8] For elaborations of this conception, see Neil A. McDonald, *Politics: A Study of Control Behavior* (New Brunswick, N.J.: Rutgers University Press, 1965), and also Rosenau, *The Scientific Study of Foreign Policy* (New York: The Free Press, 1971), Chap. 7.

Like the habits of the attentive person, the propensies of the mobilizable one are rooted deep in his experience, his value system, and his attitude structure. Momentary circumstances may prevent a response to a mobilizer's appeal in a specific situation, but the propensity is not so fragile that such an effect will carry over to subsequent situations. It is precisely because of this stability, in fact, that most mobilizers can always count on a few loyal followers even when they are unable to bring all the variables into the delicate balance that would evoke support-giving action from many potential followers in the Attentive Public.

One other premise underlying our model needs to be made explicit. It is that neither the habit of attentiveness nor the propensity toward mobilizability are conceived to be established or sustained by an invariant causal sequence. The ensuing analysis necessarily focuses on one set of variables of the model at a time, but the order in which they are considered is not meant to outline a causal priority or suggest that some of the variables are more crucial to the maintenance of attentiveness or mobilizability than others. What is cause for one person may be effect for another and both the cause and effect may be the consequence of other variables for a third person. In a fourth case the variables may interact in a mutually reinforcing fashion. Some people, for example, are led to participate in the work of public affairs organizations by their attitudes toward specific issues, while others are led to the same behavior by the requirements and responsibilities of their occupational roles and these, in turn, foster similar attitudes.

In view of the many ways in which the relevant variables are hypothesized to combine to foster and preserve attentive and mobilized behavior and given the limitations of the data developed here, there would seem to be little advantage in constructing a causal model at this time. Such a model would have to be so complex that it might actually confound rather than clarify analysis. Hence our model makes no claims along these lines. For our purposes it is sufficient to presume that the main variables are interdependent, each shaping and being shaped by the others in such a way as to perpetuate, diminish, or intensify the habit of attentiveness and the propensity toward mobilizability. In order to justify this presumption and provide an overview of the model before each of its parts is subjected to intensive examination, the nature of the main variables must be outlined.

THE MAJOR VARIABLES

Current Behavior

Let us emphasize the interdependence of the model by outlining first those variables that are at the same time products and sources of attentiveness and mobilizability. These comprise all the activities through which citizens establish contact with public affairs. While such current behavior is obviously an expression of the habit of attentiveness or the propensity to respond to mobilizers, it is also posited as having a feedback effect on these orientations. That is, the citizen has reactions to his own behavior, and each of his activities stimulates, reinforces, or curbs his readiness to undertake further activity. If, for example, he neither discussed public affairs with family and friends nor exposed himself to the mass media, he could not acquire the minimum amount of information necessary to sustain interest in the course of events. The discussions and the mass media accounts may not change his attitudes or perceptions, but without such experiences he might well become inattentive. Similarly, the letters members of the Attentive Public write to officials ordinarily are answered, encouraging the continuance of this form of activity or, at least, not allowing it to decline through frustration and disillusionment. The psychological dynamics whereby the current behavior of citizens feeds back to become a source of subsequent predispositions have been succinctly described by Himmelstrand:

> Basic to our approach ... is the assumption that the political involvement of the ordinary citizen depends to a large extent on the goodness-of-fit or affinity between the politically relevant predispositions and political aspects of his environment. If there is such a fit, an exchange is likely to

occur between the individual and his environment, the individual being emotionally gratified in the process. Next time he encounters this particular aspect of his environment he will anticipate emotional gratification; he will feel involved. According to these assumptions the amount of exchange taking place is as important as the goodness-of-fit between environment and individual predispositions.[9]

In order to develop hypotheses about how the activities of Attentive and Mobilizable citizens can be expected to differ, the current behavior variable can be subcategorized in terms of the distinction between first- and second-hand contacts with public affairs. Since our data are especially rich with respect to letter-writing and organizational activities, we shall treat these as illustrative of first-hand contacts and, for the same reason, our analysis of the second-hand forms of contact will focus on face-to-face discussions and mass media consumption.

In general, the model posits members of the Attentive Public ("the Attentives"), compared to those in the Mobilizable Public ("the Mobilizables"), as less likely to undertake first-hand activities and equally likely to establish second-hand contacts. The first part of this prediction derives from the conception that the Mobilizables must necessarily engage in first-hand activities when responding to requests for their support, whereas the Attentives can, by definition, remain in the spectator role and relate themselves to public affairs through second-hand routes. Hence it was reasoned that the Mobilizables, being more disposed to direct action and being reinforced by the experience of responding to appeals for support, would be likely to maintain a wide variety of first-hand contacts in addition to those resulting from their acquiescence to the appeals of mobilizers. The Attentives, not being so inclined, would probably sustain such activity on a less extensive scale. More specifically, the following relationships were posited:

[9] Ulf Himmelstrand, "A Theoretical and Empirical Approach to Depoliticization and Political Involvement," *ACTA Sociologica*, Vol. 6 (1962), p. 97.

Hypothesis I: *Independent of mobilizing attempts by an outside source, the letter-writing behavior of Mobilizables as compared to Attentives will be (a) characterized by a greater number of letters (b) addressed to a greater variety of public officials (c) about a greater number of public issues. Similarly, the organizational activities of Mobilizables as compared to Attentives will show (d) membership in a greater number of organizations, (e) more frequent participation in the decision-making processes of organizations that take stands on public issues, and (f) more frequent attendance at meetings at which these issues are discussed.*[10]

On the other hand, since second-hand contacts are equally necessary to membership in both groups, there would seem to be no reason to expect differences in this regard:

Hypothesis II: *There will be no difference between Mobilizables and Attentives in (a) the number of public issues they discuss on a face-to-face basis, (b) the frequency with which they engage in such discussions, or (c) the extent to which they rely on the mass media of communications for information about public issues.*[11]

At first glance Hypotheses Ic and IIa might seem contradictory. If the Mobilizables can be expected to write letters on a greater number of issues than the Attentives, the stronger attitudes that presumably contribute to this tendency (Hypotheses X and XI) might also be expected to lead them to discuss more issues with family and friends than do the Attentives. Until data confirm such reasoning, however, it has been rejected on the grounds that second-hand contacts, requiring less time and energy than first-hand contacts, do not require greater attitudinal strength and thus the Attentives can be expected to discuss as many issues on a face-to-face basis as the Mobilizables. More succinctly,

---

[10] The test of this hypothesis is presented in pp. 209–11, 217–18, 221–23.
[11] The test of this hypothesis is presented in pp. 226–29, 234–37.

Hypothesis III: *There will be no difference between the proportions of Mobilizables and Attentives who show single-area and multi-area attentiveness.*[12]

Past Experience

Included here are all those aspects of an individual's social background and personal history that may bear upon his present citizenship activities and orientations. The skills and perceptions through which a citizen relates himself to public affairs are likely to be conditioned by what he has previously experienced. Present-day responsibilities and situational circumstances can reduce or translate the relevance of social background, but they are unlikely to erase it. There are numerous findings indicating that the roots of attentiveness and mobilizability are sown, to a greater or lesser degree, in childhood and family experience, in exposure, or the lack of it, to religious values and training, in varied contacts with the culture of a particular region, in formal education, in the opportunities or deprivations associated with socio-economic status, in political affiliations and attachments, and in all the other events and conditions at each stage of life that foster orientations operative in succeeding stages.

The dynamics of attentiveness and mobilizability attributable to personal history, in other words, are conceived to rest on either "background" or "personality" variables. The distinction between these two major subcategories involves the difference between psychological variables that are uniform among many people and those that tend to be of idiosyncratic kind. To assess the impact of being, say, white or Negro, young or old, Catholic or Protestant, college or high school educated, is to estimate the psychological consequences of widely shared experiences, whereas to probe the impact of, say, parental authority, sibling rivalry, or marital problems is to investigate the psychological results of experiences that are not systematically distributed among large

---

[12] The test of this hypothesis is presented in pp. 235, 238.

numbers of individuals. Certain kinds of personality traits—such as self-esteem, a tendency to dominate or be dominated, the ability to feel comfortable in interaction situations—may systematically flourish in certain occupational roles, including political roles.[13] Most personality variables, however, seem likely to operate idiosyncratically, and since the available data do not allow for more than a brief exploration of those that may be linked to occupational roles,[14] only the background variables have been built into the model and systematically investigated in subsequent chapters. But this is not to deny the possible relevance of personality variables. At many points in the ensuing chapters, we shall have occasion to speculate about whether they may underlie findings that cannot otherwise be explained.[15]

While not all of them are hypothesized to be equally relevant to the dynamics of attentive or mobilizable behavior, eleven background variables are subjected to empirical examination in later chapters. These are sex, race, age, region, marital status, party, religion, occupation, education, income, and foreign travel. It will be noted that the impact of some of these variables stems from present responsibilities as well as past experiences. Many years in one occupation, for example, can contribute to a person's posture toward public affairs, but so can the present statuses and roles he occupies in that field. His citizenship activities can thus reflect both the outlook of, say, the business community and the specific responsibilities of his role as a corporation executive.

---

[13] Cf. Lester W. Milbrath and Walter W. Klein, "Personality Correlates of Political Participation," *ACTA Sociologica*, Vol. 6 (1962), pp. 53–66.

[14] See below, pp. 433–34.

[15] Even if our data permitted a more thorough assessment of the relevance of personality variables, however, the resulting interpretations would hardly be more than speculative. For, as one observer notes, "The fact is that we do not know a great deal about the significance the basic personality needs have in the political life of the electorate" [Angus Campbell, "The Passive Citizen," *ACTA Sociologica*, Vol. 6 (1962), p. 12]. For a review of what is known about the relationship between political behavior and personality, see Fred I. Greenstein, *Personality and Politics: Problems of Evidence, Inference and Conceptualization* (Chicago: Markham, 1969).

Similarly, a woman's activities may be shaped by attitudes acquired through the accumulation of many experiences as a female and by the opportunities to devote time and energy to public affairs that result from her present role of housewife. Although we shall not attempt to examine the past and present consequences of the background variables separately, the model does contain several "present responsibilities" variables (see below) that bring together and treat as a unit all those aspects of the background variables that, at a given time, operate to provide or block access to public affairs.

Two contradictory considerations had to be resolved to formulate hypotheses about the background variables. On the one hand, there is substantial evidence that socio-economic status affects the practice of citizenship. Whether measured by education, income, race, occupation, or some combination of these and other background variables, the finding consistently emerges that citizens are more politically active the higher their status.[16] On the other hand, we view mobilizability as a specialized form of active citizenship but not as an indicator of especially intense activity. Viewed in this way, there is no reason to expect that the association between the socio-economic variables and political activity will distinguish attentive and mobilizable citizens in the same way it does passive and attentive citizens. Consider, for example, the education variable. Many studies have shown that the more formal education a person has, the more likely he is to be politically involved. Once a person becomes attentive to public affairs, however, how might his educational experiences be relevant to the degree to which he is mobilizable? He may never have finished high school, but if he is attentive might he not be just as sensitive to the appeals of mobilizers as someone with similar affiliations, attitudes, and perceptions who possesses a

---

[16] One analyst, writing in 1964, reports finding eighteen systematic empirical studies that affirm this association between the background variables and political activity. See William Erbe, "Social Involvement and Political Activity: A Replication and Elaboration," *American Sociological Review*, Vol. 29 (1964), pp. 198–215.

Ph.D.? Is it not likely that the behavior of highly educated mobilizables will be more like that of poorly educated mobilizables than like that of highly educated attentives?

Resolution of these considerations was achieved in the following manner. Each background variable was considered to consist of resources and predispositions, either of which can facilitate or interfere with a person's readiness to establish contacts with public affairs.[17] About each variable it was then asked, first, whether the resources or predispositions it embraced were likely to differentiate the composition of the Attentives from that of the Mobilizables and, second, whether they were also likely to underlie behavioral differences within and between each group. For a variety of reasons elaborated in connection with the analysis of each variable in Chapter 7, the first step in this procedure led to the general conclusion that, with three exceptions (sex, religion, and occupation) the two groups would not be significantly differentiated along socio-economic dimensions. The composition of the Attentives and Mobilizables was expected to differ in terms of sex, religion, and occupation for a variety of reasons. In the case of the sex variable, both interfering resources and predispositions were judged to be sufficient (for women) to make for differentiation, whereas, in the case of religion, facilitating predispositions (for Jews) were expected to produce differences. A variety of interfering and facilitating resources and predispositions were considered to produce differences among occupations. Time, for example, tends to be more available to students and lawyers than to engineers or blue-collar workers. Citizens whose work involves concern about the welfare of communities (such as social workers and clergymen), on the other hand, are more likely to be predisposed toward mobilizability than are those for whom such a concern is less central. In short, two basic propositions were derived with respect to the socio-economic composition of the Attentives and Mobilizables:

Hypothesis IV: *The composition of the Attentives and Mobilizables is not likely to differ in terms of their (a) age, (b)*

[17] This conception is elaborated below, pp. 246–49.

race, (c) region, (d) marital status, (e) party affiliations, (f) education, (g) income, and (h) foreign travel experience.[18]

Hypothesis V: *The composition of the Attentives and Mobilizables is likely to differ in terms of their (a) sex, (b) religious affiliations, and (c) occupation.*[19]

This is not to say, however, that the interdependence of the model is limited to sex, religion, and occupation insofar as the background variables are concerned. The role of some of the other variables was expected to become more evident when the prediction (in Hypothesis I) that the Mobilizables would establish more first-hand contacts than the Attentives was tested within and between socio-economic subgroups. Most of the background variables were not expected to introduce different patterns of letter-writing or organizational activity among either the Attentives or the Mobilizables or to offset the differences between them predicted in Hypothesis I. We expected, however, that the resources that facilitate specific kinds of mobilizability would be differentially distributed among specific subgroups of the variables. It seemed likely, for example, that it would be easier for the aged to write letters than to be active in organizations. Hence the predicted gap between the Mobilizables and Attentives in letter-writing was expected to persist at all age levels, but to disappear or be significantly narrowed among the elderly in the case of organizational activity. Similarly, the capacity of the less educated Mobilizables to attend organizational meetings is probably greater than their ability to write letters, so that the differences between them and their counterparts among the Attentives predicted in Hypothesis I are likely to mark their organizational activities but to be narrowed or eliminated in the case of their letter-writing activities. Following this line of reasoning, two general propositions were derived:

---

[18] The test of this hypothesis is presented in Chapter 7 (*passim*).

[19] The tests of Hypotheses Vb and Vc are presented in pp. 275–76 and 308–310. Hypothesis Va could not be tested because of an effort to achieve the same proportions of men and women in the Attentives and Mobilizables (see pp. 171 and 185).

Hypothesis VI: *The differences predicted in Hypothesis I between the letter-writing and organizational activities of Attentives and Mobilizables will not be eliminated except for segments of these groups which share certain social background variables that reduce the individual's resources below the level necessary for the performance of first-hand contacts.*[20]

Hypothesis VII: *Except for sex, religion, occupation, and those variables embracing subgroups in which the resources available are not sufficient for the performance of first-hand contacts, among neither the Attentives nor the Mobilizables will letter-writing and organizational activity be affected by any of the background variables.*[21]

Attitudes

This component of the model provides the evaluative dimension of attentiveness and mobilizability. The norms of American culture make it extremely difficult to be both interested in public issues and neutral about their outcomes,[22] with the result that involvement in an issue is normally accompanied by judgments about how it should be resolved. Such judgments in turn require a person to have beliefs about the importance of the issue, and it is these two types of beliefs that are conceived here to comprise the attitude variables. The first of these will be referred to as the "importance" variable, with the scale from low to high importance corresponding to the increase in the extent to which the solution of an issue is regarded as central to the conduct of public affairs. The second will be called the "extremity" variable, with the range from low to high extremity in the increasing scope of

---

[20] The test of this hypothesis is presented in Chapter 7 (*passim*).

[21] The test of this hypothesis is presented in Chapter 7 (*passim*).

[22] For evidence that other cultures may allow for a harmonious linkage between neutrality and interest, see Elliott McGinnies, "Some Reactions of Japanese University Students to Persuasive Communications," *Journal of Conflict Resolution*, Vol. IX (December 1965), p. 488.

the governmental action deemed necessary to resolve an issue.

Although attitudes do not necessarily lead to behavior, activity with respect to an issue is more likely if it is both considered important and extreme measures are deemed necessary to resolve it. If the value of either variable is low, the probability of action is reduced, and it drops further if both variables are weak. Furthermore, it seems reasonable to presume that this relationship exists for all kinds of citizenship activity, that the degree of both first- and second-hand contacts with a public issue will reflect the importance attached to it and the extremity of beliefs about its resolution. A number of propositions relevant to the Attentive and Mobilizable Publics follow from these considerations:

Hypothesis VIII: *Attentives and Mobilizables are likely to attach high importance to and evidence extreme beliefs about at least one of the issues comprising public affairs at any moment in time.*[23]

Hypothesis IX: *The more importance Attentives and Mobilizables attach to an issue, the more extreme will be their beliefs about it.*[24]

Hypothesis X: *The more importance Attentives and Mobilizables attach to an issue, the more likely will they be to establish (a) first-hand and (b) second-hand contacts with it.*[25]

Hypothesis XI: *The more extreme the beliefs of Attentives and Mobilizables about an issue, the more likely will they be to establish (a) first-hand and (b) second-hand contacts with it.*[26]

[23] The test of this hypothesis is presented in pp. 325–30.
[24] The test of this hypothesis is presented in pp. 330–32.
[25] The test of this hypothesis is presented in pp. 333–34.
[26] The test of this hypothesis is presented in pp. 333 and 335.

Hypothesis XII: *Mobilizables will tend to (a) attach more importance to and (b) evidence more extreme beliefs about an issue than will Attentives.*[27]

Perceptions

This component of the model provides the cognitive dimension of attentiveness and mobilizability. It encompasses the processes by which citizens structure and organize public affairs. In order to judge issues and act with respect to them, an individual must have some views about what values are at stake, what actors are contesting them, and how they might be resolved. These notions may be quite simple and even inaccurate, but attentiveness and mobilizability will be more likely if they have sufficient detail and coherence for importance and meaning to be ascribed to events and action toward them initiated.

Among the many possible perceptions of public affairs, two clusters of them are selected for close empirical exploration in subsequent chapters. One cluster, which we call the "information" variables, involves the extent of information about public issues that a citizen perceives himself and the general public to possess. It seems reasonable to presume that in order to support their involvement in the political process, members of the Attentive and Mobilizable Publics will be inclined to see themselves as well informed about issues. At the very least, they are likely to justify their public activities by seeing themselves as more informed about an issue than the citizenry in general. The relationships between the information-possessed variable and the other components of the model follow rather simply. An active citizen is likely not only to develop perceptions that reinforce each other, but also to make his perceptions consistent with his attitudes and behavior. He will thus tend to see himself as more informed about those issues about which he feels strongly and with respect to which he is active. It also follows that since mobilizables engage in a more direct form of political activity than attentives, they

---

[27] The test of this hypothesis is presented in pp. 336–38.

are likely to perceive themselves as better informed than do the attentives. Stated more formally, our model yields five propositions about this cognitive dimension of attentiveness and mobilizability:

> Hypothesis XIII: *Attentives and Mobilizables are likely to perceive themselves as well informed about at least one current issue of public affairs.*[28]

> Hypothesis XIV: *Attentives and Mobilizables are likely to perceive themselves as more informed about current issues than the general public.*[29]

> Hypothesis XV: *The more informed about a public issue Attentives and Mobilizables perceive themselves to be, the more importance they are likely to attach to it and the more extreme is their attitude toward it likely to be.*[30]

> Hypothesis XVI: *The more informed about public affairs Attentives and Mobilizables perceive themselves to be, the more likely will they be to establish first- and second-hand contacts with current issues.*[31]

> Hypothesis XVII: *Mobilizables are likely to perceive themselves as more informed about public affairs than are Attentives.*[32]

The other cluster of perceptions included in the model are called the "competence" variables. These involve the extent to which citizens perceive individuals, groups, and the general public as capable of influencing officials and, through them, public affairs. Such variables are considered central to the model because there is mounting evidence that "if an individual believes he has

[28] The test of this hypothesis is presented in pp. 346–48.
[29] The test of this hypothesis is presented in pp. 349–51.
[30] The test of this hypothesis is presented in pp. 351–52.
[31] The test of this hypothesis is presented in pp. 353–54.
[32] The test of this hypothesis is presented in pp. 355–56.

influence, he is more likely to attempt to influence the government. A subjectively competent citizen, therefore, is more likely to be an active citizen." [33] Similarly, it would seem that for a person to be responsive to the appeals of a mobilizer, he must perceive officials as receptive to public opinion and believe that coordinated individual actions can exert at least some influence on the outcome of issues. Indeed, it seems reasonable to expect that his first-hand activities will vary in direct relation to his feelings of political competence. Much the same can be anticipated with respect to the relationship between subjective competence and the strength of a mobilizable individual's attitudes. In addition, he is likely to develop perceptions that support his subjective competence and to see interest groups as playing a role in the resolution of issues, the groups with which he is affiliated or sympathetic being perceived as having the greatest influence. Attentiveness, on the other hand, would seem to be much less dependent on a sense of civic competence. One can be a spectator at the arena of public affairs even if one perceives that only officials can enter it. Attentives are also likely to seek a balance between their attitudes and activities on the one hand and their perceptions of citizen competence on the other; but since their activities are minimal, compared to the Mobilizables, this balance seems unlikely to require as high a degree of perceived competence. In short, five more propositions can be derived:

> Hypothesis XVIII: *Attentives and Mobilizables are likely to perceive (a) the individual citizen, (b) the interest group, and (c) the general public as possessing high competence to influence public affairs.*[34]

> Hypothesis XIX: *The more Attentives and Mobilizables perceive the individual, the group, and/or the general public as possessing the competence to influence public affairs,*

---

[33] Sidney Verba, "Political Participation and Strategies of Influence: A Comparative Study," *ACTA Sociologica*, Vol. 6 (1962), p. 23.

[34] The test of this hypothesis is presented in pp. 358–65.

the better informed about current issues are they likely to perceive themselves.[35]

Hypothesis XX: *The more Attentives and Mobilizables perceive the individual, the group, and/or the general public as possessing the competence to influence public affairs, the more importance are they likely to attach to current issues and the more extreme are their beliefs toward the issues likely to be.*[36]

Hypothesis XXI: *The more Attentives and Mobilizables perceive the individual, the group, and/or the general public as possessing the competence to influence public affairs, the more likely will they be to establish first- and second-hand contacts with current issues.*[37]

Hypothesis XXII: *The Mobilizables are likely to perceive the individual citizen, the interest group, and the general public as possessing more competence to influence public affairs than are the Attentives.*[38]

Present Responsibilities

Whatever the extent of his subjective competence, the statuses and roles a person occupies can enhance or limit his ability to relate himself to public affairs. Some statuses and roles afford more opportunities for citizenship than others, either because the performance of the roles requires involvement in public affairs or because the responsibilities attached to the statuses encourage a felt obligation to be involved in such matters. It seems reasonable to expect that the greater a citizen's responsibilities, the more inclined he will be to perceive himself and others as capable of influencing officials. Compare, for example, a businessman who heads a large firm engaged in international

[35] The test of this hypothesis is presented in pp. 365–67.
[36] The test of this hypothesis is presented in pp. 367–72.
[37] The test of this hypothesis is presented in pp. 373–80.
[38] The test of this hypothesis is presented in pp. 380–82.

trade with the chief executive of a small advertising company. The former will doubtless be obliged to travel more widely and follow world politics more closely than the latter. Having greater access to public affairs, the trader is thus likely to be more capable of undertaking activities with respect to them than the advertiser and this greater capacity is in turn likely to foster greater confidence in his ability to affect the course of events. Responsibility, in other words, breeds responsibility, and, in a society that values responsible citizenship, this relationship would seem bound to result in greater attentiveness on the part of those whose statuses and roles require the exercise of responsibility in personal or professional affairs. For the same reason it seems likely that mobilizable citizens will have greater responsibilities than their attentive counterparts.

Rather than re-examining all the social background variables to determine how they might subsume current responsibilities that foster or limit the practice of citizenship, our data permit us to include in the model three other variables that bring together and synthesize the requirements and responsibilities of all the statuses and roles a person occupies. One of these we shall call the "objective proximity" variable. It refers to the degree to which a citizen's occupational roles, apart from his personal inclinations, place him in touch with public affairs. Viewed in the context of the foregoing paragraph, this yields:

> Hypothesis XXIII: *The more objectively proximate Attentives and Mobilizables are to public affairs, the more likely will they be (a) to write officials about issues, (b) to be active in organizations, (c) to discuss public affairs on a face-to-face basis, (d) to hold strong attitudes toward issues, (e) to perceive themselves as informed about issues, and (f) to perceive individuals and groups as competent to influence officials.*[39]

> Hypothesis XXIV: *The objective proximity of Mobilizables to public affairs is likely to be greater than that of Attentives.*[40]

---

[39] The test of this hypothesis is presented in pp. 395–401.
[40] The test of this hypothesis is presented in pp. 391 and 402.

The second synthesizing variable is that of "domestic travel," by which is meant nonvacation travel. If we assume that the more widely a person moves around the country, the more he will be brought into contact with public affairs, predictions similar to the two previous ones follow:

> Hypothesis XXV: *The wider the domestic travel of Attentives and Mobilizables, the more likely will they be (a) to write officials about issues, (b) to be active in organizations, (c) to discuss public affairs on a face-to-face-basis, (d) to hold strong attitudes toward issues, (e) to perceive themselves as informed about issues, and (f) to perceive individuals and groups as competent to influence officials.*[41]

> Hypothesis XXVI: *The domestic travel of Mobilizables is likely to be greater than that of Attentives.*[42]

The third synthesizing variable is comprised of all those aspects of a person's present statuses and roles that accord him public recognition and thus reflect his leadership responsibilities. We shall refer to it as the "opinion-making potential" variable,[43] but this designation should not be allowed to obscure the fact that it encompasses responsibilities relevant to the course of public affairs. Again the context of the previous analysis points to clear-cut expectations:

[41] The test of this hypothesis is presented in pp. 395–401.

[42] The test of this hypothesis is presented in pp. 393 and 402.

[43] The variable has been given this label because of its prior use as a means of assessing a person's access to the communications system. It will be recalled that the degree of access determines whether or not a person is a member of the leadership public. While those who receive a high score on the scale of opinion-making potential would not be regarded as members of the Attentive or Mobilizable Publics, those whose scores fall below the cut-off point for leadership do vary in the degree to which their responsibilities provide them access to the communications system and it is these variations that are being measured in the present context. See below, pp. 177 and 179, for a discussion of where this cut-off point is most appropriately drawn.

Hypothesis XXVII: *The higher the opinion-making potential of Attentives and Mobilizables, the more likely will they be (a) to write officials about issues, (b) to attend organizational meetings, (c) to discuss public affairs on a face-to-face basis, (d) to hold strong attitudes toward issues, (e) to perceive themselves as informed about issues, and (f) to perceive individuals and groups as competent to influence officials.*[44]

Hypothesis XXVIII: *The opinion-making potential of Mobilizables is likely to be greater than that of Attentives.*[45]

The Appeal of the Mobilizer

The derivation of hypotheses with respect to this component is an especially precarious enterprise and, since there are no relevant data, it amounts to little more than guesswork. We have already stressed that mobilizability is a relational phenomenon, that it can occur only in the context of interaction between the seeker and the giver of support. Thus, virtually by definition, the identity and performance of the mobilizer must be variables in the model. Exactly how these variables may operate to produce mobilizability, however, is far from clear and there are few either theoretical or empirical insights into how the process unfolds in a political context.[46] It is not enough to assert that the mobilizer

---

[44] The test of this hypothesis is presented in pp. 395–401.

[45] The test of this hypothesis is presented in pp. 394 and 402.

[46] At a more general level, of course, there are some experimental investigations of the process by social psychologists as well as by those interested in the effects of advertising on the behavior of consumers. See, for example, Herbert I. Abelson, *Persuasion: How Opinions and Attitudes Are Changed* (New York: Springer, 1959); Carl I. Hovland, Irving L. Janis, Harold H. Kelley, *Communication and Persuasion: Psychological Studies of Opinion Change* (New Haven: Yale University Press, 1953); C. I. Hovland and W. Weiss, "The Influence of Source Credibility on Communication Effectiveness," *Public Opinion Quarterly,* Vol. 15 (1951), pp. 635–50; and Elihu Katz and Paul F. Lazarsfeld, *Personal Influence: The Part Played by People in the Flow of Mass Communications* (Glencoe, Ill.: The Free Press, 1955).

must be charismatic, as to use the charisma label is not to elucidate the processes that lead mobilizees to respond. Nor does it
help very much to know from electoral research that voters are
more sensitive to pressures from family and friends than from
politicians trying to win their support. It is not the voter who
concerns us but the attentive citizen between elections, and it is
possible that he could differ from the voter and be more sensitive
to the appeals of organizations and officials in the remote world
of public affairs than to the urgings of intimates and associates in
the close-at-hand personal world.

Because there are not clear guidelines, we return to the
assumption that it is precisely the remoteness of public affairs
that renders politics so complex and support-building so delicate.
If it is the case that the complexity and delicacy of political
mobilization stems from the fact that mobilizees know distant
mobilizers less well and interact with them less often on a narrower range of matters than close-at-hand ones, then it seems
logical to presume that even members of the Attentive Public will
be less likely to respond to the appeals of mobilizers the greater
the spatial, temporal, and functional distance that separates them.
The relationship of Attentives and Mobilizables to organizations
and officials is of course less remote than is the case with the Mass
Public. Attentives and Mobilizables, being in the habit of relating
to public affairs, tend to be familiar with the policy goals and
operating modes of the main actors in the issue areas that interest
them. Nevertheless, it seems unwarranted to conclude that this
familiarity resembles a close personal friendship. Close-at-hand
relationships include sharing much more than a concern about
public affairs, and thus an appeal from a friend to write a letter
on an issue would seem to tap a much more extensive reservoir of
support than would the same appeal from an organization or an
official. Similarly, an organization appealing to its members would
seem able to draw on a wider base of support than would the
official making a comparable appeal to them, since a citizen can
work in an organization and know its goals and activities first-
hand, whereas he can generally observe officials only at large
meetings or through the mass media.

From the foregoing considerations these overall propositions were framed:

Hypothesis XXIX: *Attentives and Mobilizables will perceive themselves[47] as more responsive to the appeals of a close friend than to those of organizations to which they belong on a given issue.[48]*

Hypothesis XXX: *Attentives and Mobilizables will perceive themselves as more responsive to the appeals of an organization to which they belong than to those of politicians and public officials on a given issue.[49]*

Some qualifications of these propositions, however, are necessary. Since the model attributes stronger attitudes and more extensive first-hand activities to the Mobilizables than to the Attentives, it seems reasonable to expect differences in the degree of their responsiveness to different mobilizers. Virtually by definition the Mobilizables are likely to be more responsive than the Attentives irrespective of the identity of the mobilizers, but this difference is likely to be greater the more distant the mobilizer, given the stronger attitudes, greater subjective competence, and more extensive first-hand contacts attributed to the former. Hence these somewhat more specific propositions were derived:

Hypothesis XXXI: *Mobilizables will perceive themselves as more responsive to the appeals of any mobilizer on a given issue than will Attentives.[50]*

Hypothesis XXXII: *The differences in the self-perceived responsiveness between the Mobilizables and Attentives will*

---

[47] The data used to test all the hypotheses pertaining to the identity of the mobilizer consist more of self-perceptions than actual behavior and thus it seems desirable to frame the hypotheses in terms of this limitation.

[48] The test of this hypothesis is presented in pp. 409–10, 422–28.

[49] The test of this hypothesis is presented in pp. 422–28.

[50] The test of this hypothesis is presented in pp. 410–17.

be greater on a given issue if the mobilizer is an organiza-
tion or public official than if he is a close friend.[51]

Although Mobilizables can be expected to be more responsive to any mobilizer than Attentives, there is no reason to anticipate that the two will also differ in how their mobilizability
interacts with the other factors that underlie their predispositions
to be involved in public affairs. Consistent with our assumption
that the major variables of the model are interdependent, both
groups can be expected to reveal a balance between their receptivity to the appeals of mobilizers and their attitudes, perceptions,
and behavior. Furthermore, it seems plausible to anticipate that
this receptivity will be linked to the degree to which submissiveness is inherent in a status or role, since to respond to a mobilizer
is, in one sense, to submit to his authority. The expectation of
interdependence thus yields two additional propositions:

Hypothesis XXXIII: *Mobilizables and Attentives will be
likely to perceive themselves as more responsive on a given
issue to the appeals of any mobilizer, (a) the stronger their
attitudes, (b) the more information they perceive themselves
to possess, (c) the greater their perceived competence, (d) the
greater their present responsibilities, and (e) the more extensive their first- and second-hand contacts.*[52]

Hypothesis XXXIV: *Greater self-perceived responsiveness
to the appeals of mobilizers on a given issue is likely to be
exhibited by (a) women as compared to men, (b) young persons as compared to old persons, (c) white collar workers
as compared to corporation executives, (d) blue collar
workers as compared to artists, (e) pre-college educators as
compared to college educators, and (f) engineers as compared to students.*[53]

[51] The test of this hypothesis is presented in pp. 410, 412–18.
[52] The test of this hypothesis is presented in pp. 428–32.
[53] The test of this hypothesis is presented in pp. 432–34.

The Appeal of Issues

The foregoing hypotheses contain the qualification "on a given issue" because it seems obvious that the appeal of mobilizers will not be equal across all the issues to which citizens might respond. As stressed in Chapter 3, members of the Attentive Public cannot be concerned about every aspect of public affairs. Some matters will be more stimulating than others and the role of the mobilizer can be expected to fluctuate accordingly. It seems clear that if both the issue and the mobilizer are highly salient, the likelihood that a member of either the Attentive or Mobilizable Publics will respond will also be high and it will decline substantially if both are of low salience. It is harder to predict what the likelihood of response will be when the salience of the issue and the mobilizer are discrepant or when the salience of both is moderate rather than either high or low. Posing the problem in these terms highlights how little is known about the dynamics of issue-areas.

Lacking research findings relevant to this problem, our intuitive approach is to anticipate that the appeal of issues will ordinarily be more powerful than the appeal of mobilizers. What is involved, in effect, is a conflict between two sets of attitudes, one toward the actors who call for action in the public arena and the other toward the action itself. Unlike voters, attentive and mobilizable citizens do not act with respect to the merits of actors. Their attitudes, perceptions, information, and activities are all focused on unfolding events, in which the interaction among actors is the means through which values are pursued and resources allocated. Some citizens probably reverse this priority and attach greater importance to the appeal of mobilizers than to the appeal of issues, differentiating their responses to issues according to the source that appealed for support. But given the nature of citizenship between elections, it seems reasonable to expect that such persons, whom we shall refer to as "source oriented," would be far less numerous than those at the other extreme for whom only the issue matters. If the issue is viewed as unimportant, then the "issue oriented" person will not respond to any mobilizer, whereas he will be responsive to appeals from any and every source if the issue is important. Stated more formally:

> Hypothesis XXXV: *Issue-oriented Attentives and Mobilizables are more likely than their source-oriented counterparts (a) to attach importance to an issue, (b) to hold extreme attitudes toward the issue, and (c) to feel they possess information about the issue.*[54]

> Hypothesis XXXVI: *Mobilizables, being more responsive to appeals for support than Attentives, (a) are likely to perceive their mobilizability as less issue oriented and more source oriented than are the latter, but (b) both groups are likely to be more issue than source oriented.*[55]

On the question of what makes an issue salient, however, the initial version of the model takes no position. It distinguishes among local, national, and international issues, and among domestic, foreign, and mixed issues, but no effort is made to hypothesize about how each of these areas is affected by the other variables of the model. The dynamics of issue-area behavior has not been sufficiently explored to warrant meaningful predictions about the relative salience of issues in each area. Hence it seems wiser to assume at this stage merely that some issues have wide appeal and others do not, and that such differences have consequences for the attitudes and behavior of citizens. Subsequently, after the behavior associated with issues of high and low salience have been contrasted, an effort to refine and extend our conception of issue-area phenomena will be undertaken.

It should be noted that in eschewing initial hypotheses about issues, we have rejected an alternative procedure. We could have developed hypotheses based on the notion that political behavior is motivated by self-interest, differentiating issue areas in terms of the kinds of values that appeal to the immediate needs and wants

---

[54] The test of this hypothesis is presented in pp. 464–65.
[55] The test of this hypothesis is presented in pp. 461–63.

of various groups of citizens. We used this notion to explain many forms of single-area behavior and thus it might seem logical to extend the same reasoning to those who engage in multi-area activities. To make such an extension, however, would be to ignore the limits of the self-interest conception, particularly the abundant evidence that citizens are capable of engaging in attentive and mobilized activity with respect to values that are only remotely related to their self-interests.[56] The voluntary associations that espouse general interests may not be as numerous as those that champion special interests, but many of them do nonetheless, and their contribution to citizenship between elections cannot be discounted. People who are active in such organizations—say, whites who work for civil rights for blacks, conservationists who can be mobilized on behalf of unborn generations, rich persons who are concerned about the plight of the poor, childless couples who can be aroused by the need for better schools, Americans attentive to the standard of living of undernourished Asians—simply do not fit into the self-interest mold. It is probably true that such behavior on behalf of goals remote from one's immediate needs and wants soothes one's conscience and enhances one's self-image, but to view this as merely a form of self-interest is to extend the concept so widely that it is bereft of meaning and utility.[57]

These qualifications of the self-interest conception seem so pertinent to the behavior of the multi-area citizens who comprise the stable and permanent core of the Attentive and Mobilizable Publics that it seemed preferable to leave our initial model incomplete rather than bias it with hypotheses founded exclusively on that conception of behavior. Such hypotheses are necessary to

---

[56] For a systematic inquiry into the role of remote values in political behavior, see James Q. Wilson and Edward C. Banfield, "Public-Regardingness as a Value Premise in Voting Behavior," *American Political Science Review*, Vol. LVIII (December 1964), pp. 876–87.

[57] For a persuasive plea on behalf of extending political research beyond the self-interest conception, see Christian Bay, "Politics and Pseudo-Politics: A Critical Evaluation of Some Behavioral Literature," *American Political Science Review*, Vol. LIX (March 1965), pp. 39–51.

the model, but they are best framed after we have examined the behavior of multi-area citizens who can be mobilized by a general interest organization on behalf of humane and remote values.

SUMMARY

In order to probe the dynamics of attentive and mobilized behavior, an initial model has been constructed that identifies seven main sets of variables as underlying forms of citizenship and that posits a delicate interdependence among them. For a person to be attentive or mobilizable, his (1) current behavior, (2) past experience, (3) attitudes, (4) perceptions, and (5) present responsibilities must all operate together to bring it about and so must the appeal of (6) the mobilizers seeking support and of (7) the issues being contested in the arena of public affairs. The operation and interaction of the variables are summarized in thirty-six formal hypotheses that, in effect, posit attentive citizens as quite different from those who are also mobilizable.

In general, the hypotheses predict that, in comparison to Attentives, Mobilizables are likely to have more first-hand contacts with public affairs, to have stronger attitudes toward issues, to perceive themselves as more informed and more competent to influence the outcome of issues, to have present responsibilities that accord them greater proximity to and responsibility for public affairs, to see themselves as more responsive to the appeals of friends, organizations, and officials for support, and to be more oriented toward the Mobilizers seeking their support than toward the issue involved. The model also anticipates occupational, sex, and religious differences in the backgrounds of Attentives and Mobilizables, but otherwise there appears to be no reason to expect the two types to differ in their past experiences. Most notably, while education has been found to distinguish apathetic citizens from active ones, the model does not posit this variable as central to the differences between those who engage in attentive and mobilized forms of activity. In addition, the two groups are not expected to differ in the extent to which they establish second-hand contacts with public affairs. The model offers no hypotheses as to the kinds of issues that are salient for Attentives and Mobilizables, there being reasons to postpone consideration of this point until after empirical data have been examined.

Several characteristics of the model must be stressed. First, while it is a psychological model in the sense that assumptions about intra-individual processes explicitly underlie the hypotheses, our main concern is with the impact of external stimuli upon behavior and in this sense it is a socio-political model. Our research focus is cast at the micro level, but only in order to probe the larger question of whether micro phenomena, taken together, add up to potential consequences for political processes at the macro level. We are interested in processes that are systematically related to the responses of broad groups of people and not in idiosyncratic forces that originate in the individual's psychological makeup. Political activity can serve personality factors and it can be an irrational substitute for unfulfilled needs, but although the model does not preclude the possibility that personality variables may operate as important sources of active citizenship, they are not central to it. What concerns us is not whether the dynamics of attentiveness and mobilizability are conscious or subconscious, rational or irrational—probably they are all of these—but whether they integrate social and political experience in such a way as to become the basis for citizenship between elections.

Secondly, and relatedly, the model places great emphasis on the delicate interdependence of its main variables because of the implications that follow for the macro political process. If the empirical analysis upholds the assumption of interdependence and does not reveal a predominant single source of mobilizability, it will be possible to extrapolate from this to the macro level and conclude that the polity is essentially stable and not vulnerable to gross distortion by a charismatic demagogue. In and of themselves, many of the thirty-six hypotheses are not particularly important. Taken alone, for example, it matters little whether or not a citizen's perception of his amount of information is closely related to his first- or second-hand activities. Nor is there anything earthshaking about such questions as whether responsibility breeds responsibility, whether mobilizable citizens perceive themselves as more competent than do their attentive counterparts, or whether women are more mobilizable than men. To confirm such hypotheses is to add to the storehouse of knowledge, but the value of such knowledge lies in whether the cumulative pattern of the data depicts interdependence. If it does, if enough hypotheses are affirmed to warrant the conclusion that the initial assumption of interdependence was justified, then the implications for the direction and adaptability of the political system are far different than if most of the hypotheses are negated and only a few factors emerge as central to the dynamics of mobilizability. It is for this reason that the model has been elaborated in such detail and that the ensuing empirical analysis digs so deeply into the data.

Thirdly, it must be emphasized that in its present form the model is hardly more than an outline. The hypotheses are internally consistent, but the concepts and findings of social science relevant to them have not been indicated. Nor has the reasoning underlying each hypothesis been fully developed. Only the barest minimum necessary to guide the sifting of social science materials and the analysis of empirical data has been provided, a procedure that has also enabled us to depict the model in its entirety before intensively examining each of its parts.

Finally, even in outline form the model is cast in highly tentative terms. The hypotheses pave the way for the analysis of empirical data, but they were developed prior to the analysis and thus must be viewed as rudimentary and provisional until they have been put to empirical test. As will be seen, the empirical data make expansion and refinement of the model possible.

Before the data can be analyzed, however, they must be introduced and both the opportunities they afford and the limits they impose must be clearly specified. It is to this task that we now turn.

CHAPTER 5

OPPORTUNITIES FOR CITIZENSHIP: SOME EMPIRICAL MATERIALS

I saw the ladies myself [through the window]. I recognized why they were here. There were a great number of them. It was in the rain. I understood what they were trying to say and, therefore, I considered that their message was received.

John F. Kennedy[1]

As previously indicated—and as suggested by these press conference remarks that an American President made in response to a question about the utility of a "Women Strike for Peace" demonstration in front of the White House—there were ample opportunities for citizenship between the elections of the early 1960's. In the foreign policy area, the period was marked by crises

---

[1] Quoted in *The New York Times,* January 16, 1962, p. 18.

in *the Congo* and *Berlin*, by strains and stresses in *Western unity* following France's veto of British entry into the Common Market, and by the persistence of *balance of payments* problems. The domestic area was dominated by the issue of *civil rights*, but the question of *federal tax reduction* and the perennial problem of *agricultural surpluses* were also matters of concern. In the mixed area, too, there was much for attentive and mobilizable citizens to respond to during this period: they could hardly be unaware, for example, of the controversy over *tariff reduction* proposals in 1962, the debate over *nuclear testing* in 1963, the agitation over the war in *Vietnam* in 1964, and the recurring dilemma of *foreign aid*.[2]

In addition to having been outlets for activity on the part of interested citizens, several of these situations also provide unique opportunities for the researcher interested in analyzing the behavior of the Attentive and Mobilizable Publics in different issue-areas. Two situations in particular, the ratification of the nuclear test ban treaty of 1963 and the civil rights legislation of 1964, were especially conducive to both citizenship and scholarship. Not only did they both involve matters close to the personal lives and values of many people, but, unlike Vietnam and the other foreign policy issues, governmental deliberations about them were conducted publicly and the key officials were therefore open to relevant communications from the citizenry. More importantly, in both situations there was uncertainty throughout the deliberations about the outcome of crucial votes in Congress.

In the case of the civil rights bill, the sources of the uncertainty were obvious. The bill contained provisions so much

---

[2] The eleven italicized issues do not, of course, exhaust the list of matters that occupied the attention of citizens and officials alike during the period. All three areas were marked by episodes just as important as— and, in the case of two situations involving Cuba, perhaps more important than—those cited. These eleven issues have been mentioned, however, because exactly as italicized, they were built into the research instruments used to generate data. The reasons for selecting these particular eleven are elaborated below, as is the reasoning underlying their distribution among the three areas (pp. 441–46).

stronger than any ever approved by Congress in the past that emasculating amendments were sure to be introduced. Even if these could be overcome, Southern Senators were likely to resort to the filibuster, a tactic that had never failed them as a means of preventing the enactment of thoroughgoing civil rights legislation. Notwithstanding the vigor of the civil rights movement, whether the bill's central features would survive and a filibuster be overcome was never clear until the votes were tallied in both the House and Senate.

Similar uncertainty prevailed in the case of the test ban treaty. Legally a two-thirds majority in the Senate was required, but even wider approval was desirable politically in order to demonstrate, as President Kennedy put it in a press conference, "that we are as determined to achieve . . . a just peace as we are to defend freedom." [3] Six weeks prior to the signing of the treaty on July 25, 1963, the President had enunciated this new emphasis upon peaceful accommodation with the Communist world in a speech at American University and the treaty was designed as the first step in this direction. However, many Senators were uncommitted, others were skeptical, and some had publicly announced their conclusion that above ground tests were vital to national security and that their vote would thus be against ratification. Furthermore, the civil rights bill, which at the time was just beginning its passage through the legislative mill, posed a danger that one biographer called "the President's chief concern . . . [namely,] that enough Southern Democrats might combine with Republicans to prevent the two-thirds vote [required for ratification of the treaty]. Angered by his civil rights bill, they would be hoping to use the treaty as a bargaining counter and follow the lead of Armed Services Committee Chairman Russell, who was opposed." [4] Additional uncertainty about the outcome was fos-

---

[3] September 12, 1963, quoted in Harold W. Chase and Allen H. Lerman, eds., *Kennedy and the Press: The News Conference* (New York: Thomas Y. Crowell, 1965), p. 491.

[4] Theodore C. Sorensen, *Kennedy* (New York: Harper & Row, 1965), p. 737.

tered by a nationwide poll taken early in the summer that "found general public approval [of the treaty], but fewer than 50 percent giving 'unqualified approval.' " [5] Whether greater public enthusiasm could be generated also seemed problematic. The President "felt sure the great majority of the people were for it," but "he was not sure they could make themselves heard in time," citing as evidence the fact that in the week after his American University speech only 896 letters on the subject were received by the White House, whereas during the same period "28,232 people had sent letters about a freight rate bill." [6]

For the citizen inclined to be concerned about nuclear testing and civil rights, in short, all the incentives to action were present at that time. The issues were important. The procedure for their resolution was clear and it allowed for participation by any citizen. The balance of forces in both situations was so delicate that any support a citizen gave or that a leader mobilized seemed consequential and capable of affecting the course of events.

In view of these circumstances, it is hardly surprising that efforts to mobilize support for and against the treaty and the civil rights bill were particularly intense. Many officials, organizations, and individuals extended themselves in ways that went well beyond ordinary support-building procedures. A measure of the extraordinary efforts that pervaded the test ban controversy is provided by the President himself:

> ... to reduce the large number of uncommitted Senators, he worked through unofficial as well as official channels. A series of telephone calls and off-the-record meetings encouraged the creation of a private "Citizens' Committee for a

---

[5] *Ibid.*

[6] Arthur M. Schlesinger, Jr., *A Thousand Days: John F. Kennedy in the White House* (Boston: Houghton Mifflin Company, 1964), p. 910. The author quotes Kennedy as dismissing these figures with "disgust," saying, "That is why I tell people in Congress that they're crazy if they take their mail seriously." As noted below, however, shortly thereafter the President was clearly eager to generate mail from the grass roots in support of the treaty.

Nuclear Test Ban," a bipartisan group of prominent leaders organized to mobilize support. The President, beginning with an off-the-record meeting in the Cabinet Room, advised them which Senators should hear from their constituents, approved their newspaper and TV advertisements, counseled them on their approach to the unconvinced, and suggested particular business and other leaders for them to contact.[7]

Whether all the activity by Kennedy and the individuals and organizations he mobilized was the decisive factor in the outcome of the Senate's deliberations is hard to estimate. Senators were undoubtedly persuaded by a variety of considerations, not the least of these being the reasoning and assurances given them by Administration witnesses in committee hearings. But it was also the case that "public opinion polls indicated a marked swing in favor of the treaty—80 percent by September" [8]—and on the 24th of that month the Senate consented to ratification by a vote of 80 to 19, or fourteen more than the necessary two-thirds. It seems reasonable to presume that the widespread activity that had been generated and the extensive support that had been mobilized were not irrelevant to this outcome.

Much the same can be said about the disposition of the civil rights bill in 1964. While it would be erroneous to see members of Congress as acting only in response to the pressures of public opinion, the correlation between the direction and extent of the pressure on the one hand and the tallies recorded in roll call votes on the other is unmistakable. President Johnson extended himself on behalf of the civil rights bill as much as his predecessor had on the test ban treaty and, as previously noted, the activity of the Attentive and Mobilizable Publics was particularly vigorous. This activity reached a peak as the vote to close off the Southern filibuster in the Senate neared and, as in the test ban situation, it was especially intense in states where Senators were uncommitted. These were mainly Senators from nonurban states who had no rea-

---

[7] Sorensen, *Kennedy*, p. 739.
[8] Schlesinger, *A Thousand Days*, p. 913.

son to be overly concerned about civil rights and who had traditionally been resistant to the idea of voting for closure. Church groups and an association of seventy-nine organizations interested in civil rights, known as the "Leadership Conference on Civil Rights," were particularly active in these rural states and are credited with having been "instrumental in stirring up interest in the civil rights issue." [9] The relevance of such activities to the outcome of the situation seems evident in the following facts: the provisions of the bill were not materially altered; the House of Representatives passed the bill on February 10 by a 290 to 130 vote, the Senate filibuster was broken on June 10 by a 71 to 29 vote (or four more than required), and on June 19 the Senate approved the measure by a vote of 73 to 27.

The actual role of the mobilized support in the two situations, however, is less important for our purposes than the fact that it occurred. Except for elections, there are not many opportunities to observe nationwide mobilization efforts in which highly specific stimuli are employed on behalf of broad civic concerns rather than narrow special interests. Yet this was the kind of behavior that the test ban treaty and the civil rights bill evoked from leadership groups and their organizations, thus providing an unusual natural laboratory in which the student of politics could gather and analyze data relevant to citizenship between elections.

PROFILE OF AN INQUIRY

Among the many organizations that were moved to undertake extraordinary support-building measures in the test ban and civil rights situations was the Americans for Democratic Action (ADA), a nationwide, loosely structured, and politically liberal organization that was founded after World War II and that describes itself as composed of "progressives dedicated to the achievement of freedom and economic security for all people

---

[9] Symposium, *Congress and the Nation, 1945–1964: A Review of Government and Politics in the Postwar Years* (Washington, D.C.: Congressional Quarterly Service, 1965), p. 1936.

everywhere, through education and democratic political action." [10]
On September 4, 1963, one week after the Senate Foreign Relations Committee concluded its hearings on the test ban treaty and five days before the Senate began to debate it, the Washington headquarters of ADA made a first-class mailing to some 31,000 persons on its rolls, urging them to establish immediate first-hand contacts with members of Congress and the President on behalf of the treaty. YOU MUST ACT NOW the message proclaimed in bold headlines and red ink. In finer print it emphasized that the Senate had rejected the League of Nations, that opponents to the treaty were "doing battle with their pens," so much so that "their letters have tilted the mail 9 to 1 *against* the treaty in some states." Accordingly, the message argued, "Only a deluge of letters supporting the treaty and urging a 'yea' vote can win the overwhelming approval needed for this crucial forward step." The recipients were then given the appropriate addresses and instructed to write four letters, one each to their Senators their Representative, and the President: "Tell them you and your neighbors want this treaty," the appeal concluded. "Raise your voice as if the treaty depends on you alone. Tomorrow will be too late to wish you had."

The message was sent out in the form of a large card, attached to which was a smaller card that could be easily torn off along a perforated line. On one side of the smaller card was the ADA's Washington address and place for a 4-cent stamp. The other side consisted of a CONFIRMATION OF ACTION ON THE TEST BAN TREATY, which the recipient was asked to sign and return after indicating the officials to whom he had written. The purpose of this additional step was to give recipients "a sense of closure," the theory being that they would be more likely to write officials if they could tell someone that they had done so.[11] Since the ADA's appeal constituted the specific stimulus for much of the mobilized behavior analyzed in subsequent chapters,

---

[10] Quoted in Clifton Brock, *Americans for Democratic Action* (Washington, D.C.: Public Affairs Press, 1962), p. 17.

[11] Interview with Mr. Richard Lambert, ADA Director of Organization.

both the message and "closure" cards are reproduced in black and white as Appendix C on pages 512 and 513 exactly as they came through the mails to the recipients.

The 31,000 persons to whom the appeal was sent did not constitute the entire ADA mailing list.[12] The number on the list is close to 39,000, but cards were sent only to those who resided in states where one or more Senators' position on the treaty was in doubt. About 1,800 of these did not reach the addressees for various reasons and were returned by the post office. All told, then, 29,200 persons, or approximately three-fourths of ADA, were the targets of the mobilization effort. Of these, 1,380, or 4.7 percent, completed and returned the card. From the view of the researcher, these are 1,380 Americans known to have engaged, at a moment in political history, in two mobilized acts, one of writing to officials and the other of informing the mobilizer that they had done so.[13]

On January 16, 1964, some four months after the original mobilization effort, a ten-page questionnaire was sent to the 1,380 persons who had been mobilized and to 1,580 additional names

---

[12] The organizational structure of ADA is such that it is more accurate to refer to its "mailing list" than to its "membership." The roll of members consists of all those who pay dues in an ADA chapter, whereas the mailing list also includes those who have at some time or another participated in some way in an ADA activity. A succinct summary of the structure of this mailing list is provided by Brock (*Americans for Democratic Action*, p. 33), who notes that after an initial surge of membership, "by the end of 1959 ADA's organization had contracted to 43 chapters in 14 states, and it could count only 18,000 paid-up members in these chapters. However, by including at-large members unaffiliated with any chapter, inactives who have paid no dues but consider themselves ADAers, and a large number of people who contribute money and work but do not bother to take out membership cards, it might be possible to swell ADA's total to something approaching 40,000."

[13] As stressed below, our knowledge of these two acts is not exactly identical. We can be less confident that the first occurred than the second, since the former requires the presumption that the respondents actually wrote the letters they reported when they returned the card.

drawn from the ADA mailing list who had not been mobilized.[14] The questionnaire did not require the respondent to identify himself because it was believed that anonymity would maximize both the rate of the return and the integrity of the response. It was sent under the letterhead of the Center of International Studies of Princeton University, along with a covering letter that stressed the anonymity of the survey and that it was being conducted as part of a larger inquiry into the policy-making process. "Please understand," the letter read, "that we are not trying to make a case for or against any particular policy or program. Our concern is solely that of gaining insight into the processes of foreign policy formation." The letter made no mention whatsoever of the test ban treaty or of ADA, noting merely that "the enclosed questionnaire . . . comes to you . . . as a result of our sampling procedures." The questionnaires sent to the two groups were identical except for a fictitious "project number" on the first page that differentiated them and indicated whether or not the respondent had been mobilized by the ADA appeal. They consisted of fifty-eight items designed to explore the hypotheses in our model.[15]

Later in 1964, both the ADA and this researcher went through the entire procedure again in connection with the civil rights bill. On March 19 of that year, ten days after the Senate

---

[14] These additional names were drawn at random after insuring that their distribution matched the two dimensions of the mobilized group, sex and region, that could be ascertained from the returned cards. The proportion of men and women from each region was fixed to correspond to the equivalent figures for the mobilized group. More questionnaires were sent to the unmobilized group because it was deemed desirable, both for statistical and substantive reasons, to achieve roughly the same absolute number of returns from both groups and because earlier experience had confirmed the hypothesis that questionnaires are more likely to be returned by those who complete organizational forms than by those who do not. Cf. James N. Rosenau, "Meticulousness as a Factor in the Response to Mail Questionnaires," *Public Opinion Quarterly*, Vol. 28 (Summer, 1964), pp. 312–14.

[15] A copy of the questionnaire is reproduced in Appendix A.

began debate on a motion to take up the House-passed bill and one week before the vote to take it up precipitated the Southern filibuster, the Washington headquarters of ADA made another first-class mailing. This time the ink was blue and the message concerned civil rights, but the card was identical in size and format to its predecessor. Again it proclaimed YOU MUST ACT NOW and gave reasons why letters were necessary to overcome the filibuster. And again a CONFIRMATION OF ACTION ON CIVIL RIGHTS was attached in order to provide a sense of closure. The civil rights "confirmation" also provided space to request additional information on the subject from the ADA, but, as can be seen in Appendix C, mobilization stimuli in the test ban and civil rights areas were for all practical purposes identical.

The entire mailing list was subjected to the civil rights stimulus, but fewer were mobilized than in the test ban case. Allowing for cards returned by the post office, approximately 37,000 persons received the civil rights appeal and, of these, 1,004, or 2.7 percent returned the card to ADA. Of the 1004, 267 had also responded to the nuclear test appeal, so that a total of 737 new names of mobilizable citizens were derived from the ADA mailing list.

About five months subsequent to the ADA's second mobilization effort, on September 10, 1964, a second research procedure was undertaken with respect to the 737 persons who had returned the civil rights, but not the test ban, card and an additional 939 addresses drawn from the ADA rolls of individuals who had neither responded to either appeal nor been among the non-respondents surveyed in the test ban mailing.[16] On that date essentially the same questionnaire was mailed under the same auspices and in the same format. The covering letter was identical, as was the size, type, sequence, and pagination of the questionnaire. And again two fictitious "project numbers" were used to distinguish the mobilized from the unmobilized respondents. The

---

[16] Unfortunately circumstances prevented matching the two groups in terms of sex and region. On the other hand, it was again possible to try to match the two groups in terms of absolute size by surveying a larger number of persons in the unmobilized sample.

only differences between the two questionnaires were some minor changes to account for events that had occurred in the interval between the two mailings. One change involved the replacement of an an entire question [#57] [17] with one [#59] that could not be asked until after passage of the civil rights bill.[18] The only other changes were slight alterations in the stems of four questions [#20, 43, 44, and 52] to allow for intervening events with respect to civil rights, the Congo, federal tax reduction, and foreign aid. Each alteration was made with a view to not disturbing the essential meaning of the question and no alterations were made in the wording of the choices that followed the stems.[19] Indeed, the effort to insure that the test ban and civil rights samples were exposed to the same conditions even went to the extreme of not amending the second questionnaire to include an item that had been inadvertently omitted from the first.[20]

It is not unreasonable, in short, to claim that both the action and the research stimuli were, for all practical purposes, identical in the two situations. The circumstances under which the respondents acted in the two situations were not the same because of what transpired in public affairs during the eight months that separated the action stimuli and during the nine that elapsed

[17] Bracketed numbers refer to the number of the question as it appears in the questionnaire reproduced in Appendix A. Questions were not given numbers in the questionnaires actually mailed so as to avoid calling attention to its length and discouraging its completion.

[18] This replacement, however, came at the end of the questionnaire and did not affect the order of the questions. In addition, the replacement occupied an identical amount of space on the last page as its predecessor and thus did not affect the general format of the questionnaire.

[19] An example of the minor nature of the changes in the stems is the alteration made in the question on attitudes toward federal tax reduction [#44] that was necessitated by the fact that the tax bill had been enacted in the interval between the two mailings. The first version of the stem read, "The President has asked Congress for $10 billion tax reduction, how much of a reduction do you think Congress should have approved?"

[20] An undetected typing error resulted in the omission of the President from the list of officials in Question #3 to whom the respondents wrote letters. Fortunately this was not the case in Question #10, which probed the same behavior and thus compensated for the omission.

between the two mailings of the questionnaire, but at least it can be said that neither the ADA's appeals nor the researcher's instruments contributed to these differences.

A SAMPLE OF 3,362 ATTENTIVE CITIZENS

The combined total of the two sets of questionnaires was 4,636. Of these, 3,362 were completed and returned in an envelope provided for the purpose. This amounts to an overall response rate of 72.5 percent, a surprising figure given the size, complexity, and focus of the questionnaire. It exceeds by a considerable margin the 60.6 percent rate recorded in 1958 by a sample of 1,067 national leaders who received a similarly long questionnaire under the same auspices and with a covering letter that also promised anonymity and denied ulterior purpose.[21] Perhaps this difference between the two rates of response is a quantitative measure indicator of the probable fact that attentive citizens have more time available than leaders for coping with the inquiries of the social scientist. Whatever the explanation,[22] the figure of 72.5 percent is clear testimony that success was achieved in surveying a segment of the Attentive Public rather than a conglomeration of attentive and apathetic citizens.

The extent to which the respondents reported themselves as active in public affairs provides further evidence that the 3,362 questionnaires offer an opportunity to probe and compare the dynamics of attentiveness and mobilizability. Eighty-seven percent of the entire sample reported that they discussed public affairs with family [#41a] or close friends [#41b] "invariably" or "often." [23] This figure is four times greater than the equivalent

---

[21] See James N. Rosenau, *National Leadership and Foreign Policy*, Appendix A.

[22] For additional thoughts on why questionnaires of this sort evoke remarkable responses, see Rosenau, *National Leadership and Foreign Policy*, pp. 373–74.

[23] If neither the two frequencies nor the two types of intimates are clustered together, the overall data reveal that discussions with friends are

one previously cited for a sample of the general public and three times greater than the aforementioned proportion of those in another cross-sectional sample who reported following public affairs "regularly." [24]

This disparity widens even further if our operational definition of what distinguishes members of the Attentive and Mass Publics[25] is relaxed to include those in the ADA sample who engage in such activity "sometimes": under these circumstances another 8 percent would be classified as attentive, leaving only one-half of one percent who said they "hardly ever" held such discussions with family or friends, a similar proportion who reported that they "never" did, and a final 4 percent who did not provide a codable answer to either part of the question.

Further indication that attentive citizens were surveyed can be obtained by considering membership in "organizations which publicly express their viewpoints on national or international problems" [#1] as a measure of attentiveness. In one national sample, 24 percent cited such an affiliation;[26] and in another, 31 percent said they belonged to one or more such organizations and 7 percent specified two or more.[27] In contrast to such findings, 85 percent of the ADA sample cited at least one organizational membership, 70 percent listed at least two, 49 percent at least three, 29 percent at least four, 18 percent at least five, and 10 percent said they belonged to no less than six organizations of this type.[28] Similarly, where one survey of four communities found

---

slightly more widespread, but do not occur quite so frequently as do discussions with family: while 30 percent said they "invariably" entered into discussions with family and 46 percent reported doing so "often," the comparable figures for such behavior with close friends were 25 and 56 percent.

[24] See above, pp. 27–28, for these comparable data.

[25] See above, pp. 103–09, for a discussion of the operational basis for distinguishing between these two segments of the public.

[26] Almond and Verba, *The Civic Culture*, p. 306.

[27] Woodward and Roper, "Political Activity of American Citizens," p. 874.

[28] However, these figures are not nearly as impressive as comparable ones for Dahl's sample of 281 "subleaders" in New Haven (*Who Governs,*

no more than 15 percent in any of them who "attended meetings at which policy matters were major subjects of consideration," [29] the equivalent figure for the ADA [#2] sample was 77 percent. Indeed, 6 percent reported that "on the average" they attended "organizational meetings where national or international problems are discussed" every week, 20 percent specified once a month, 15 percent six times a year, 19 percent three times a year, and 17 percent once a year.[30]

Much the same can be said about letter-writing practices. Where only 13 percent of one sample of the general public was found to have talked or written to Congressmen or other public officials "in the past year" [31] and where the equivalent figures for a sample of "influentials" and one of "interesteds" were, respectively, 38 and 35 percent,[32] 78 percent of the ADA respondents said they wrote at least one to three letters a year to members of Congress alone [#10b] and this figure swells to 81 percent if other federal officials are included [#10c, d]. The letter-writing activities of the ADA group even exceeded those of a sample of local party officials, 69 percent of whom reported writing "their congressman or senator." [33]

By any reasonable standard of activity, in short, persons entered on the rolls of the ADA are not likely to be apathetic members of the Mass Public. This, of course, does not mean that

---

p. 173.) Forty-seven percent of the subleaders, for example, specified membership in five or more organizations. This figure is considerably larger than the equivalent one for the ADA, providing the first clue in response to the question, examined on pp. 177–81, of whether the ADA sample was drawn from the ranks of the leadership stratum, rather than the Attentive Public.

29 Agger, Goldrich, Swanson, *The Rulers and the Ruled*, p. 268.

30 Of the remainder, 20 percent responded "never" and 3 percent did not provide a codable answer.

31 Woodward and Roper, "Political Activity of American Citizens," p. 874.

32 Kenneth P. Adler and Davis Bobrow, "Interest and Influence in Foreign Affairs," *Public Opinion Quarterly*, Vol. XX (Spring, 1956), p. 96.

33 Lewis Bowman and G. R. Boynton, "Activities and Role Definitions of Grassroots Party Officials," *Journal of Politics*, Vol. 28 (February 1966), p. 140.

they will necessarily be found among the Attentive Public. It is conceivable that, instead of reaching attentive citizens, the questionnaire went to leaders—to those who hold positions that provide them with the capacity to regularly circulate their opinions to unknown persons as well as to their family and close friends. It will be recalled that, in our operational definition, those with this capacity were also excluded from membership in the Attentive Public in order to differentiate it from the leadership as well as the mass stratum of the society.[34]

The questionnaire contained ten items [#6, 7, 8, 9, 12, 13, 18, 24, 25, 26] intended to ascertain whether the survey reached leadership ranks. These items were identical to those which, in an earlier inquiry, comprised an index of "opinion-making potential" that was used to assess the leadership capacities of 647 national leaders. The responses of the ADA and leadership samples to each item can be compared in Table 5–1 and the distribution of the index scores recorded by the two samples are presented in Figure 5–1.[35]

Comparisons of both the raw and processed data reveal that we did survey members of the Attentive Public rather than those in leadership ranks. The mean index scores compiled by each group demonstrate this even more succinctly: while the national leaders recorded a mean score of 49.0, the equivalent for the ADA respondents was 18.0.[36]

Exactly where the line should be drawn dividing leaders from followers is essentially an arbitrary matter. If it is drawn between the lowest and the four other ranges on the scale,[37] then two-thirds of the ADA sample would be classified in the Attentive

---

[34] See above, pp. 103–04.

[35] For the procedures and weights used to derive the score for each individual, see Rosenau, *National Leadership and Foreign Policy*, pp. 144–45 and 392–95.

[36] Three percent of the leaders and 2 percent of the ADA group did not provide sufficient responses to permit derivation of index scores.

[37] For an elaboration of the kinds of leadership capacities associated with the lower, lower middle, middle, upper middle, and upper ranges on the scale of opinion-making potential, see Rosenau, *National Leadership and Foreign Policy*, pp. 146–47.

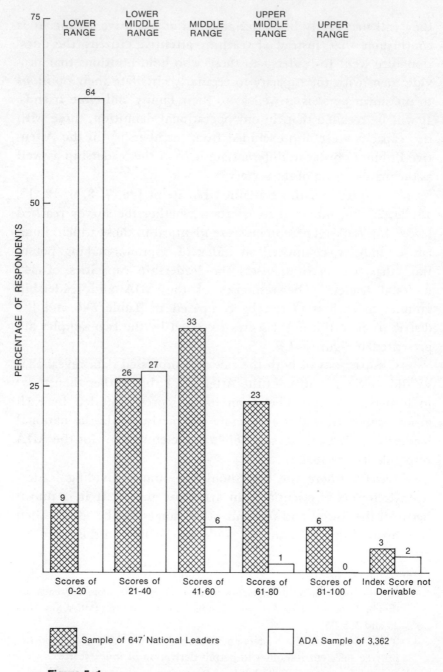

Figure 5–1

Distribution of the Attentive and Leadership Samples in Five Ranges of the Opinion-Making Potential Index

Public. If it is operationalized between the two lower ranges on the one hand and the middle and upper two on the other—a not unreasonable distinction—then 91 percent of the sample can be considered attentive citizens. However, instead of eliminating the remaining 7 percent who would thus be classified as leaders from further consideration, it seems preferable simply to presume that the sample is composed predominantly of attentive citizens and to use the scale of opinion-making potential as an instrument for examining whether distinctive attitudinal and behavioral patterns are associated with the minority who circulate opinions to unknown others as well as to family and friends.[38]

To conclude that an overwhelming proportion of the respondents are members of the Attentive Public, however, is not to demonstrate that they had political orientations similar to those of the mobilizer and that they were thus susceptible to being mobilized on the issues for which the ADA sought support. While it seems reasonable to presume that those on the ADA's mailing list shared its liberal political outlook, it is useful to note several data that indicate the extent of this homogeneity. The most general of these concerns the party affiliations of the respondents [#33], and it clearly suggests that their distribution on the conventional political spectrum which places Democrats to the left of Republicans was far from what would be normal for any randomly selected group of 3,362 Americans. Only 42 respondents —or 1 percent of the total—considered themselves a Republican, and another 9 responded in such a way as to be classified as a "qualified Republican." On the other hand, 2,201 said they were Democrats and another 145 were classified as "qualified Democrats," a total of 70 percent of the sample. Nor does it seem unlikely that the remainder were also to the left of center: 25 percent regarded themselves as Independents and 2 percent speci-

---

[38] Similar reasoning underlies a decision not to eliminate from the sample the even smaller minority (3 percent) who do not regularly discuss public affairs with either family or friends and who can thus be viewed as members of the Mass Public.

TABLE 5–1
RESPONSES TO TEN ITEMS COMPRISING THE
INDEX OF OPINION-MAKING POTENTIAL BY THE
ATTENTIVE AND LEADERSHIP SAMPLES (in
percentages)

Bracketed question numbers refer to the present survey	ADA Sample (n = 3362)	National Leadership Sample* (n = 647)
[#6] Are you in any way responsible for the writing of press releases?		
Yes	14	50
No	84	45
Codable answer not given	2	5
[#7] Do you have some voice in determining the contents of any publication?		
Yes	16	59
No	81	36
Codable answer not given	3	5
[#8] Have you ever written a book?		
Yes	12	25
No	87	72
Codable answer not given	1	3
[#9] Have you ever written an article published in a magazine circulated nationally and sold at newsstands?		
Yes	9	39
No	90	58
Codable answer not given	1	3
[#12] Do items appear in the newspaper in which quotations are attributed to you?		
Quote often	1	9
Occasionally	9	38
Very rarely	59	39
†Never	20	7
Codable answer not given	11	7

[#13] Do the requests you receive to give lectures or talks on any subject average about

Twenty or more a month	0	5
Ten a month	0	9
Five a month	3	21
†Two to four a month	1	3
One a month	9	26
†Less than one a month or four to eleven a year	34	20
†One to three a year	13	3
†None	31	6
Codable answer not given	9	7

[#18] About how many times a *YEAR* do you appear on a television or radio program?

†52 or more	0	2
†20 to 51	0	5
†10 to 19	1	9
†7 to 9	0	1
†4 to 6	2	15
†1 to 3	14	26
†Less than one a year	17	7
†None	61	26
Codable answer not given	5	9

[#24] Do you participate in the deliberations of any organizations which take stands on public issues?

Yes	51	70
No	44	25
Codable answer not given	5	5

[#25] If you wanted to disseminate a new idea, about how many people could you reach with it?

A million or more	2	18
†Between 100,001 and 999,999	0	4
One hundred thousand	3	12
Fifty thousand	3	10
Ten thousand	9	20
One thousand or less	73	20
†Qualitative comment indicating inability to calculate size	2	4
†Qualitative comment indicating that size varies	1	2
Codable answer not given	7	10

TABLE 5–1 (continued)

Bracketed question numbers refer to the present survey	ADA Sample (n = 3362)	National Leadership Sample* (n = 647)
[#26] Are you ever asked to lend your name to advance worthy causes?		
Quite often	15	48
Occasionally	35	39
Very rarely	47	11
Codable answer not given	3	2

* These data taken from James N. Rosenau, *National Leadership and Foreign Policy*, Ch. V.

† Category developed out of written responses.

fied the Socialist Party or other parties to the left of the Democrats.[39]

Although there is no reason to expect that the attitudinal homogeneity of the sample extends across all eleven of the issues included in the questionnaire, it tends to hold up with respect to the two specific situations that led ADA officials to undertake their mobilization efforts.[40] Uniformity of outlook is especially conspicuous in the case of the test ban treaty. In response to a five-point scale on which to locate their opinions of the treaty [#45], 84 percent selected one of the extreme alternatives and described their attitude as "very favorable," while another 8 percent selected the next point and said they were "somewhat favorable." [41] There was less unanimity in the case of the civil rights bill, but again virtually the entire sample was clustered around the two positive points on the scale. Asked "How much of an extension of civil

[39] Another 2 percent did not provide a codable answer.

[40] For the degree to which heterogeneity prevailed on the other issues, see Tables 8–1 and 8–2 below.

[41] Of the remainder, 1 percent reported themselves as "neutral," 1 percent as "somewhat unfavorable," 4 percent as "very unfavorable," and 2 percent did not provide a codable answer.

rights should Congress approve?" [#20], 50 percent selected "an unlimited extension," 41 percent "a great extension," 5 percent "somewhat of an extention," 1 percent "a very small extension," and 1 percent "no extension." [42]

In sum, since the respondents were predominantly members of the Attentive Public, since they were distinguished by their shared attitudes toward the test ban treaty and civil rights, and since these were also shared with the mobilizer who appealed for their support, it seems plain that both the ADA officials and the researcher managed to contact persons whose outlooks and behavior conformed to the respective requirements of political action and systematic analysis.

A SAMPLE OF 1,704 MOBILIZABLE CITIZENS

Of the 4,636 questionnaires, 2,117 went to persons who had been mobilized by the ADA stimulus and 2,519 to those who had not. Four-fifths of the former group and two-thirds of the latter returned the questionnaire, confirming our expectation that the mobilizable individuals would have a higher response rate. We thus succeeded in achieving a rough balance between the absolute size of the two groups: of the 3,362 returned questionnaires, 50.7 percent were completed by the mobilized group ("the Mobilizables"), and 49.3 percent by the unmobilized sample ("the Attentives").

The question immediately arises as to whether in fact the 1,704 Mobilizables and 1,658 Attentives differ along the dimension which is defined as differentiating them. That is, did significantly more of the Mobilizables than the Attentives write letters as requested by the ADA stimulus? While both the question and the data relevant to it are more appropriately analyzed below, when the responses to the test ban and civil rights mailings are compared, an affirmative answer can usefully be noted here.

[42] The final 2 percent did not select an alternative or otherwise supply a codable answer.

Two questionnaire items [#4c and 4h] were specifically designed to test the validity of assuming that the two groups differed in terms of the behavior reported in the "confirmation" cards returned to the ADA, and in both instances it seems clear that the Mobilizables were vastly more susceptible to the stimulus than were the Attentives (see Table 5–3).

Representativeness was also achieved with respect to the other two dimensions of the surveyed population that were known in advance. Neither group differed significantly from the two larger populations out of which they emerged as self-selected samples in the relative proportions of men and women from each of four regions[43] who comprised the Mobilizables and Attentives.[44]

---

[43] Except for Hawaii and Alaska, which have been assigned to the Far West category, the states comprising the four regions are the same as in the earlier study (see Rosenau, *National Leadership and Foreign Policy*, p. 60).

[44] In this instance, a *chi square* (χ^2) test was used to contrast the difference between the samples and the populations. The differences did not prove to be significant at the .001 level, the level of significance used throughout the analysis. That is, irrespective of the particular statistical test used, the ensuing chapters are organized mainly around quantitative differences or correlations whose probability of occurring by chance is less than one in a thousand (P < .001). Cogent arguments have been made against the use of tests of significance in research such as is reported here. While there is much to be said for these arguments, we concluded we would feel more secure with the guidelines offered by such tests than without them. So many differences and relationships are examined in the next seven chapters that it seemed necessary to establish, before the data were processed, a criterion that would determine independently of the observer's judgment whether he should attempt to interpret an observed relationship in the data. At no point, on the other hand, is the .001 cut-off used as an absolute basis for attributing meaning to findings. In some cases speculation is offered about the meaning of differences which fall short of the cut-off and in other instances differences exceeding the cut-off are not seen as particularly meaningful. Nevertheless, the use of the tests and the .001 level were deemed an essential point of departure for the investigation of such a great quantity of data. The choice of such a rigorous cut-off point was considered necessary on the grounds that the large number of respondents rendered the con-

The data serving as the basis for these comparisons are presented in Table 5–2.

The effort to render the Mobilizable and Attentive groups similar to each other in terms of sex and region was less successful. As noted below, it proved impossible to control for these variables in the civil rights mailing without sacrificing similarity in the total size of the two groups.[45] Thus, as can be seen by contrasting

---

TABLE 5–2

SEX AND REGION DISTRIBUTION OF QUESTION-NAIRES MAILED TO AND RETURNED BY THE MOBILIZABLES AND THE ATTENTIVES (in percentages)

	THE MOBILIZABLES				THE ATTENTIVES			
	Men		Women		Men		Women	
	Questionnaires		Questionnaires		Questionnaires		Questionnaires	
Region (n =)*	mailed (1251)	returned (986)	mailed (866)	returned (690)	mailed (1599)	returned (1087)	mailed (920)	returned (535)
Northeast	38	38	46	45	32	35	35	37
Midwest	32	34	25	24	27	25	21	23
South	8	7	6	7	16	15	19	16
Far West	21	20	22	22	25	25	25	23
Other (foreign, District of Columbia) and Unknown	1	1	1	2	0	0	0	1
Total	100	100	100	100	100	100	100	100

* An additional 64 of those who returned the questionnaire (28 of the Mobilizables and 36 of the Attentives) did not indicate their sex.

---

ventional cut-off points of .05 and .01 less reliable as a basis for distinguishing between chance and substantive distributions. Actually, many of the findings presented in the ensuing chapters were significant at the .00000001 level. However, we have not indicated the degree of significance beyond $P < .001$, since to do so would be to convey a misleading sense of precision.

45 See footnote on p. 52.

the second with the sixth and the fourth with the eighth columns of Table 5–2, there are significantly greater proportions of Southern men and women among the Attentives and, correspondingly, significantly more Northeastern women and Midwestern men among the Mobilizables.[46]

A SAMPLE OF 1,104 TEST BAN MOBILIZABLES AND 600 CIVIL RIGHTS MOBILIZABLES

Like the ADA stimulus, the questionnaire evoked a larger response in the test ban situation than in the civil rights situation: 76 percent of the 2,960 questionnaires sent in the first mailing were returned, but only 70 percent of the 1,676 in the second mailing came back. Of the 2,186 questionnaires returned in the test ban situation, 1,104 were completed by persons who had also returned the "confirmation" card to the ADA, while the other 1,082 were filled out by those who had not sent back the card. Henceforth we shall refer to the former as "Test Ban Mobilizables" and to the latter as "Test Ban Attentives." Similarly, in the case of the 1,176 questionnaires returned in the civil rights situation, the 600 respondents who had also answered the ADA's appeal will be called the "Civil Rights Mobilizables" and the 576 who completed the questionnaire but not the "confirmation" card will be designated the "Civil Rights Attentives."

Since the ensuing analysis rests on the assumption that the four groups actually differed in the ways our nomenclature for them indicates, the relevant data must be presented and analyzed with care. All that can be asserted with complete certainty is that the Test Ban and Civil Rights Mobilizables returned the card to the ADA and that their unmobilized counterparts did not. The step from this knowledge to the conclusion that only the former two groups engaged in letter-writing activity in response to the ADA appeal is a large one and cannot be made by fiat. It could

---

[46] In the case of the regional comparison, $\chi^2 = 75.53$ with three degrees of freedom (df), and $P < .001$; for sex, $\chi^2 = 23.66$, df $= 1$, $P < .001$.

well be that the distinction between those who did and did not return the "confirmation" cards is merely one of mail-answering habits rather than of mobilizability. It is conceivable that a large proportion of the respondents were mobilized but only half of them were led by their letter-writing habits to inform the ADA. Or possibly none were mobilized but half of them intended to do as the ADA requested and thus returned the "confirmation" card. In order to assess these possibilities, the questionnaire contained items that asked whether, "in the last three years," the respondent had written a letter to an official on "nuclear testing" [#4c] and/ or "civil rights" [#4h]. Such questions, however, raise two obvious additional problems. One is that some respondents may have written letters on these issues before receiving the ADA's appeal, in which case their affirmative answers do not necessarily reflect mobilizability. The other is that several months elapsed between the ADA's stimulus and our questionnaire, and some respondents who had been moved to act by the former might have forgotten about this action by the time they received and completed the latter.

The evidence from these items must therefore be overwhelming in order to clear away doubts about the meaning of the "confirmation" card and validate the assumption that the groups differed in the degree of their mobilizability. If the difference between the Test Ban Mobilizables and Attentives who reported writing a letter on nuclear testing is not substantial, and if the difference between the two civil rights groups with respect to a letter on that subject is not equally substantial, then we would not be justified in going beyond the certain but trivial knowledge that half the sample returned a card to the ADA and half did not.

Happily, however, the findings are unambiguous. Few differences in the entire study are as sizable as those between the Test Ban Mobilizables and the Test Ban Attentives on the question of writing a letter on nuclear testing and between the Civil Rights Mobilizables and the Civil Rights Attentives on writing a letter about civil rights. As can be seen in Table 5–3, both mobilizable groups contained at least double the proportion of letter-writers on their respective issues than did their unmobilized counterparts.[47]

To be sure, 13 percent of the Test Ban Mobilizables and

TABLE 5–3
RESPONSES TO ITEMS #4c AND 4h BY THE TWO MOBILIZABLE AND TWO ATTENTIVE GROUPS (in percentages)

(n =)	Test Ban Mobiliz- ables (1104)	Test Ban Attentives (1082)	Civil Rights Mobiliz- ables (600)	Civil Rights Attentives (576)
#4c				
Reported having written a letter to an official on nuclear testing in last 3 years	87	39	57	34
Did not report having written such a letter in last three years	13	59	43	65
Did not provide a codable answer to Item #4c	0	2	0	1
Total	100	100	100	100
#4h				
Reported having written a letter to an official on civil rights in last 3 years	73	46	94	47
Did not report having written such a letter in last 3 years	27	52	6	51
Did not provide a codable answer to Item #4h	0	2	0	2
Total	100	100	100	100

[47] Statistically, too, the mobilizability assumption is fully upheld; for the comparison between the two test ban groups on Item #4c, $\chi^2 = 515.28$, df $= 1$, P $<.001$; for the difference between the two civil rights groups on Item #4h, $\chi^2 = 297.92$, df $= 1$, P $<.001$.

6 percent of the Civil Rights Mobilizables did not report behavior consistent with the meaning attributed to the act of having returned the "confirmation" card to the ADA. However, these proportions do not seem sufficient to jeopardize the mobilizability assumption. On the contrary, the magnitude of the proportions who reported the appropriate behavior (87 percent of one group and 94 percent of the other) warrants added confidence that we did survey samples of persons who are responsive to leadership in public affairs.

Nor is this conclusion offset by the findings (Table 5–3) that nearly two-fifths of the Test Ban Attentives reported writing a letter on the treaty and that nearly half of the Civil Rights Attentives wrote on civil rights. We are not comparing activity and passivity, but attentiveness and mobilizability. Hence it is to be expected that many of these ADA Attentives engaged in letter-writing activity. The 39 percent of the Test Ban Attentives and 47 percent of the Civil Rights Attentives who reported such activity on these issues may be viewed as an indication of the degree to which attentive but not mobilizable citizens are ready to initiate first-hand contacts with the course of events. However, the mobilizability assumption is not undermined by this readiness, given the large differences between these figures and those for the two mobilizable groups. In this context, these large differences may be said to reflect the degree to which attentiveness can be translated into political action by leaders who seek to mobilize support.

Similar considerations apply to the finding that more than half of the Civil Rights Mobilizables reported having written a letter on nuclear testing and that more than two-thirds of the Test Ban Mobilizables cited similar behavior with respect to the civil rights bill. Such behavior indicates that both mobilizable groups were readier than their unmobilized counterparts to engage in first-hand forms of activity, an indication that is supported by other data[48] and is a predictable difference between the

---

[48] See pp. 219 and 225 below.

two types of citizens. Furthermore this behavior can be viewed as upholding rather than negating the mobilizability assumption because the two mobilizable groups recorded different degrees of activity with respect to each issue. If this had not been the case, if both groups had been equally active with respect to both issues, then it would have to be conceded that a greater propensity to first-hand forms of contact had been surveyed rather than responses to a mobilizer's efforts. Yet, over and above the 57 percent of the Civil Rights Mobilizables who wrote letters on nuclear testing were the 87 percent of the Test Ban Mobilizables who undertook such behavior, and over and above the 73 percent of the latter who wrote about the civil rights bill were the 94 per cent of the former who did so. Statistically both these differences proved to be significant[49] and substantively they might be said to represent the degree to which attempts to mobilize support can produce behavior on the part of activists that would not otherwise occur.

The data in Table 5–3 provide one other reason for confidence in the assumption that we surveyed groups that were mobilized on specific issues. It might be argued that only 73 percent of the Test Ban Mobilizables had written a letter on civil rights because that issue had not yet fully developed at the time they were surveyed. This line of reasoning would predict that they would have matched the 94 percent figure of the Civil Rights Mobilizables if they had received the questionnaire nine months later. At least a partial answer to this argument is provided by a comparison of the two unmobilized groups. If the circumstances of public affairs at the time of the second mailing were so different from those of the first as to raise the general level of activity and mobilizability, the behavior of the unmobilized group surveyed in the second mailing should reflect this at least to some extent. Yet such was not the case. Thirty-nine percent of the Test Ban Attentives and 34 percent of the Civil Rights Attentives

---

[49] For the comparison of their behavior with respect to nuclear testing, $\chi^2 = 219.03$, df $= 1$, P$<.001$; in the case of the difference in their letters on civil rights, $\chi^2 = 151.14$, df $= 1$, P$<.001$.

wrote letters on nuclear testing and 46 and 47 percent of these groups wrote, respectively, on civil rights. Neither of the differences were significant. In other words, the behavior of the two unmobilized groups was comparable in the two situations, whereas the behavior of those who were mobilized was not. Although it does not offer conclusive proof, this finding seems to indicate that the susceptibility of the two mobilized groups to mobilization was issue-specific.

While there is thus ample reason to conclude that the two groups surveyed in the test ban and civil rights situations were sufficiently similar in size and sufficiently different in composition to permit exploration of the dynamics of mobilizability and issue sensitivity, it must be remembered that the effort to achieve similarity in terms of sex and region was only partially successful. Table 5–4 presents the relevant data and here it can be seen that the circumstances of the civil rights mailing gave rise to the problem. Neither the sex nor region differences between the two test ban groups proved to be significant, whereas those between the civil rights groups were.[50] These differences stemmed from the failure to achieve, for both men and women, a higher proportion of Easterners and Midwesterners among the Civil Rights Attentives and a correspondingly lower representation of Southerners and Far Westerners. As noted earlier, however, this failure is not as serious as the data in Table 5–4 might seem to indicate. It merely means that these differences are among the many dimensions of the data that need to be taken into account as the analysis proceeds.

METHODOLOGICAL LIMITATIONS

Historical situations offer opportunities for research, but they also impose limitations. The materials we have gathered with regard to a large sample of attentive and mobilizable citizens that

---

[50] For the sex differences between the Civil Rights Mobilizables and the Civil Rights Attentives, $\chi^2 = 30.08$, df $= 1$, P$<$.001; for the region differences, $\chi^2 = 182.11$, df $= 3$, P$<$.001.

TABLE 5-4
SEX AND REGION DISTRIBUTION OF QUESTION-
NAIRES RETURNED BY THE MOBILIZABLES (M)
AND ATTENTIVES (A) IN THE NUCLEAR TEST BAN
AND CIVIL RIGHTS SITUATIONS (in percentages)

	TEST BAN SITUATION				CIVIL RIGHTS SITUATION			
	Men		Women		Men		Women	
Region	M	A	M	A	M	A	M	A
(n =)*	(632)	(665)	(452)	(394)	(354)	(422)	(238)	(141)
Northeast	39	42	41	44	36	23	50	17
Midwest	31	28	23	26	39	21	27	13
South	7	6	7	7	7	28	5	41
Far West	22	24	26	21	17	27	16	28
Other (foreign, District of Columbia) and Unknown	1	0	3	2	1	1	2	1
Total	100	100	100	100	100	100	100	100

* An additional 64 (20 of the Test Ban Mobilizables, 23 of the Test Ban Attentives, 8 of the Civil Rights Mobilizables, and 13 of the Civil Rights Attentives) did not indicate their sex.

engaged in the behavior attributed to them at two significant moments of modern political history are unique, but they are not without imperfections. The limits of their use must thus be at least briefly noted.

The Problem of Representativeness

The most troublesome methodological questions concern the meaning of the empirical materials. Were the persons who returned the questionnaire representative of those who received it? Were those who received it representative of those on the ADA mailing list? Is the ADA mailing list representative of the active stratum of the citizenry? In short, do the questionnaire findings provide insights about the Attentive and Mobilizable Publics in general or only about a single group that is not organized around a special interest and that is distinguished by its liberal approach to politics? Would the data have yielded the same patterns if the questionnaire had also been completed by an equal number of persons who possessed "conservative" political orientations? How different would the results have been if a special rather than a civic interest group had been surveyed? [51]

The first two of these questions can perhaps be easily answered. With a response rate of nearly 75 percent, it seems reasonable to presume that those who returned the questionnaire were representative of those who received it. Likewise, half of those who received the questionnaire were representative of the 37,000 persons on the ADA mailing list and half were not. The Mobilizables were unrepresentative precisely because the survey was designed to assess the unique behavior of those who were responsive to appeals for support. As previously noted, on the other hand, the other half of the questionnaires went to a group that was randomly selected after an effort to control for sex and region had been made.[52] For all practical purposes, in short, the Attentives can be viewed as a representative sample of the ADA

---

[51] For a discussion of the differences between these two major types of interest groups, see James N. Rosenau, *Public Opinion and Foreign Policy, An Operational Formulation* (New York: Random House, 1961), pp. 62–64.

[52] More precisely, since the ADA mailing list is organized alphabetically by persons within cities, the randomizing procedure was carried out in two stages in the test ban situation. First, cities within the four states of each region with the most persons on the mailing list were selected at random and then a table of random numbers was used to choose the men and women in the selected cities to whom the questionnaire would be sent. In the case of the civil rights mailing, the desirability of sending out the questionnaire before the 1964 presidential campaign got into full swing seemed so great that the procedure could not be fully repeated. Due to the lack of time, the ADA could not be asked to provide another list of names and thus those not sifted out by the table of random numbers in the first mailing had to be used. In effect, the first stage of the procedure was repeated, but not the second (which is why the sex and regional distributions of the Civil Rights Attentives depicted in Table 5–4 are so discrepant).

list, but the problem of representativeness does not arise in the case of the Mobilizables.

The question of the extent to which generalizations about the Attentive and Mobilizables Publics can be based on data supplied by citizens on the ADA mailing list is much more difficult to answer. A lot depends on the analytic approach preferred by the observer. If he is inclined to emphasize the unique, never-to-be repeated dimensions of political actors and events, then he is likely to see the ADA as having a specific history and a particular point of view that distinguish it from any other organization and that differentiate its adherents from any other identifiable segments of the Attentive and Mobilizable Publics. Strictly speaking, in other words, the ensuing analysis can be viewed only as a case study and its findings as relevant only to the small group of 37,000 persons on the ADA's rolls. On the other hand, if the observer believes in stressing the similarities of actors and the recurring nature of events, then he will not be content with an idiographic approach to the data and will probe them for wider relevance. From such a nomothetic perspective, the ADA appears as one of many general interest organizations that take stands on public issues and that thereby enable their adherents to sustain membership in the Attentive and Mobilizable Publics. Viewed in this way, it is appropriate to treat the findings as indicative of the nature of active citizenship and to generalize from the ADA sample to a larger population.

Our own inclination is to achieve a compromise between these two analytic approaches by treating the data as findings about the ADA on the one hand and as bases for revising our hypotheses about the Attentive and Mobilizable Publics on the other. Such a procedure should inhibit unwarranted claims about the meaning of the data even as it also enables us to take advantage of the insights they provide into the dynamics of citizenship between elections. This perspective toward the data should allow us to add to comprehension about the behavior and attitudes of one group of active citizens and at the same time point the way to further analysis of the many other groups that comprise the Attentive Public.

There still remains the problem of the nature of the larger

population about which it is appropriate to hypothesize. Most importantly, there is the question of whether persons on the ADA's mailing list should be treated as representative of any attentive or mobilizable citizens or only of those who are politically liberal. Again our response is in the nature of a compromise. We shall proceed with special care in the case of findings that appear to be closely associated with attitudinal direction, but we shall not avoid generalizing simply because liberal-mindedness may underlie particular forms of attentiveness and mobilizability. Attitudinal direction is not the only determinant of the nature and content of citizenship behavior. As our initial model indicates, other variables can contribute to making people responsive to public affairs and in these cases the liberal-mindedness of those comprising the sample is not an obstacle to generalization.

Furthermore, in some respects the liberals in the Attentive Public can be treated as quite similar to their conservative counterparts. The two types may have sharply different views about a wide range of political questions, but they would seem to share an inclination to be concerned about a variety of remote issues. Unlike the millions who form the Mass Public, they are not neutral or apathetic, and they share a commitment to the idea that what happens in the distant world of public affairs is important. Stated differently, they hold attitudes toward the same or similar objects even though these are different or even opposite in direction. Accordingly, it is quite conceivable that those at the two ends of the attitude direction scale have more in common with each other in style, intensity, and form of citizenship than they do with the behavior of persons located toward the center.[53] However, since we did not gather comparable materials for persons

---

[53] It has been found, for example, that the more extreme a person's attitude, the greater will be its intensity. Translating this finding into the present context, it suggests that there will be greater similarity between the attitudinal intensities of extreme liberals and conservatives than between the attitudinal intensities of either group and those who are more neutral politically. For an elaborate presentation of the finding and a discussion of its implications, see Samuel A. Stouffer, *et al.*, *Measurement and Prediction* (Princeton: Princeton University Press, 1950), Chap. 7.

on the rolls of, say, the American Legion or the John Birch Society, such relationships between attitudes and action cannot be probed.[54] We are only saying that while there are respects in which it is appropriate to interpret the behavior of those on the ADA rolls as characteristic of any member of the Mobilizable Public, generalizations about findings in which attitudinal variables are considered to be operative must be regarded as especially tentative insofar as they are applicable to the conservative stratum of the Attentive Public.

Of course, the distinction between liberals and conservatives is not the only problem of generalization we shall face. The ADA is also distinguished by the wide range of its concerns, raising the question of the extent to which findings depicting the behavior of its adherents can be said to apply to persons who are mobilized by a special interest organization with a very narrow range of concerns. Throughout the ensuing chapters our general posture toward problems of this sort will be along the lines already indicated; namely, to recognize their existence and to point out how they may limit the relevance and scope of our interpretations.

The Problem of Intervening Time (1)

One other question about the representativeness of the ADA sample requires comment. In the years since the survey was conducted, seemingly substantial shifts have occurred in the modes and norms of participation. Today's first-hand forms of contact

[54] For some evidence supporting our speculation that, discrepant attitudes notwithstanding, members of such groups engage in citizenship practices similar to those of persons on the ADA mailing list, see Fred W. Grupp, "Political Activists: The John Birch Society and the ADA" (New York: Paper presented to the Annual Meeting of the American Political Science Association, mimeo., 1966); and Hannah Wartenberg and Wagner Thielens, Jr., *Against the United Nations: A Letter-Writing Campaign by the Birch Movement* (New York: Bureau of Applied Social Research, 1964).

are even more public than they were in the 1963–1964 period. An active citizen at that time was likely to communicate his attitudes mainly through letters to officials, while now he might be also likely to join in a demonstration. As indicated in Chapter 2, the intensification of the Vietnam conflict after February 1965, fostered widespread use of a variety of new techniques for expressing opinions and mobilizing support that seem to require a greater commitment to public affairs than those prevalent in earlier periods. Unfortunately the questionnaire developed to generate the data analyzed here did not anticipate the teach-in, the march, or any of the other forms of nonviolent (and violent) protest that have marked citizenship between elections in the post-1965 period and thus it asked no questions about such activities. Only letter-writing and organizational activities were probed, and while the latter may measure a variety of forms of protest indirectly, it would be misleading to assume that current citizenship practices were adequately explored by the questionnaire. Thus we must ask whether the new forms of first-hand contact are not so different as to have altered the habit of attentiveness and the propensity to be mobilized to a degree that renders the ensuing data obsolete. Would the socio-economic background of a mobilized group, either liberal or conservative, surveyed today be similar to the one analyzed here? Does attentiveness today require greater or lesser attitudinal strength than was the case prior to 1965? Does the currently active citizen need a greater or lesser sense of civic competence to sustain his involvement than did his pre-1965 counterpart?

The importance of such questions about the behavioral representativeness of the ADA sample cannot be minimized, but we believe it would not be fruitful to avoid generalizing simply because our data were generated in a particular context. We are interested in the interaction of variables and it seems reasonable to presume that the ways in which this occurs have not changed greatly even though new citizenship practices have developed. Furthermore, letter-writing and organizational activities are still very much in vogue among active citizens and there is evidence that they are practiced more widely than the newer forms of first-hand contact.[55] In the absence of comparable data about the new citizenship practices we can only speculate about the relevance of our findings to those who employ them, but our guess is that at least the nonviolent forms of protest that emerged after 1965 have not greatly altered the dynamics of citizenship between elections. We must nonetheless proceed with caution in generalizing beyond the letter-writing and organizational means of establishing contact with public affairs, and wherever possible we shall seek to minimize this limitation of our data by taking note of inquiries into the new, post-1965 citizenship practices and comparing their findings with our own, attempting to identify the continuities as well as the disjunctions that have marked attentive and mobilizable citizens in recent years.

The Problem of Intervening Time (2)

Another perhaps less troublesome problem of time is that nine months elapsed between the mailings of the questionnaire to the test ban and civil rights samples. While both the ADA stimulus and the questionnaire were virtually identical for both groups, each responded at a unique moment in history. It is true that no major political event intervened between the two mailings. Both occurred after the assassination of President Kennedy and before the 1964 presidential campaign reached its peak. Yet the assassination was undoubtedly more salient for those who responded to the first than for those who responded to the second mailing, whereas the campaign was probably more keenly anticipated by those who were exposed to the second mailing than by those reached in the first. In addition, the war in Vietnam had become an increasingly central focus of public affairs during the nine-month period, even though it had not yet become an extensive American commitment. Contrariwise, Congress adopted the

---

[55] Cf. Sidney Verba and Richard A. Brody, "Participation, Policy Preferences, and the War in Vietnam," *Public Opinion Quarterly*, Vol. XXXIV (Fall, 1970), p. 326.

bill to reduce taxes during this period and the issue subsequently declined. In short, the world changed in a variety of ways between January and September of 1964. No two moments of history are ever the same and differences between them may underlie different predispositions toward the researcher's queries on the part of the individuals surveyed.

This problem does not arise in our comparative analysis of the Mobilizables and the Attentives, since both groups consisted of roughly the same proportion of respondents from the two mailings. When we attempt to identify issue-area differences by comparing the Test Ban and Civil Rights Mobilizables, however, the problem of intervening time must be confronted. Whenever a comparison yields a difference between the two groups, we must face the question of whether the finding stems from issue-area differences or from the different circumstances of public affairs that prevailed when the questionnaires were completed. The solution to this problem lies in the availability of comparisons between the Test Ban and Civil Rights Attentives, to which we resorted earlier when assessing the validity of our assumption that we had in fact surveyed the groups that had been mobilized specifically on two separate issues. Since the two Attentive groups were randomly selected and are not differentiated in terms of their behavior in two issue-areas, they can be viewed as control groups for the purpose of assessing the effects of intervening time. Any attitudinal or behavioral differences between them that are uncovered (and that persist after controlling for social background distinctions between them) can be interpreted as stemming from intervening changes in the circumstances of public affairs. When the responses of the two unmobilized groups are similar, then it seems warranted to conclude that the changing course of events was not the determinant of the differences between the responses recorded by the Test Ban and Civil Rights Mobilizables. Thus, in order to attribute a difference between responses to an item in the two mailings of the questionnaire to issue-area sources, the responses of the two Mobilizable groups must be significantly different from each other, while the responses of the two Attentive groups must not differ significantly. Under these circumstances historical factors cannot be said to account for the difference between the Test Ban and the Civil Rights Mobilizables, since the same factors did not produce corresponding differences between their unmobilized counterparts.

The Problem of Self-Reported Data

Throughout the chapters that follow we have used, for obvious stylistic reasons, short-hand descriptions that may make it seem as if we are mistaking reported behavior for actual behavior. The reader's patience would surely give out if every reference to an activity was prefixed by an adjectival reminder that the occurrence of the activity was reported by those described as having undertaken it. Yet such is the case with all but one of the data derived from the questionnaire survey. The only act that can be said to have actually occurred is the one of returning or not returning the "confirmation" card to the ADA. For everything else we must rely on the estimates, recollections, and predictions of their own behavior made by the respondents in response to the questionnaire items. This reliance poses a number of problems that cannot be ignored even if the imperatives of style prevent their constant reiteration.

A variety of factors can distort what a person recalls or predicts about his behavior. He may unknowingly exaggerate the extent of his activity in order to maintain a sense of importance. Or distortion may result from the "social desirability" phenomenon, the tendency to respond to the researcher's inquiry in terms of what is conceived to be socially valued or accepted.[56] Communicating one's opinions to officials, for example, is considered to be an integral part of responsible citizenship, so that members of the Attentive Public, who are presumably committed to the value of shouldering such responsibilities, may find it difficult to

---

[56] For a full discussion of this phenomenon, see Allen L. Edwards, *The Social Desirability Variable in Personality Assessment and Research* (New York: Dryden Press, 1957).

give a response that falls toward the low end of the scale when asked to estimate the number of letters they write annually to members of Congress [#10b]. Those who never write such letters might not give a distorted response, but those who write only one or two might be inclined to report a higher estimate.[57] To the extent that the social desirability variable is operative, the pattern of responses will tend to measure political norms rather than political behavior.

Undoubtedly there are also factors that lead some people to minimize their information, accomplishments, and activities, but most of those that operate systematically would seem to foster exaggeration. As several experienced researchers have observed, "A person sensitive to the importance of appearing well informed may collect opinions as avidly as small boys collect butterflies." [58]

The self-reporting problem is thus the bane of survey research and can never be completely solved. The best that can be done is to recognize its existence and allow for its operation in the

[57] A concrete illustration of the operation of the social desirability variable can be discerned in the discrepancy between the overall responses to two items. In response to Item #41, 87 percent of the 3,362 respondents reported that they discussed "public affairs" with family and friends "invariably" or "often." Yet when requested in Item #49 to cite issues around which such discussions "invariably" or "usually" focused, only 76 per cent of the sample cited such a frequency for any of the eleven issues listed. Part of this discrepancy can be attributed to the fact that the listing of issues was not exhaustive and contained no local issues, so that some of those who comprised the 11 percent difference might have cited a higher frequency if the item had been open-ended. On the other hand, discrepancies between the responses to a general question and specific questions derived from it are a common phenomenon in survey research. It seems probable that some among the 11 percent conformed to socially desirable norms by asserting that they discussed public affairs frequently even as they more accurately reported engaging in a lesser extent of activity in the context of particular issues.

[58] Angus Campbell, Philip E. Converse, Warren E. Miller, and Donald E. Stokes, *The American Voter*, p. 173. See also their discussion on pp. 93–96.

interpretation of findings. In some instances the probability of exaggeration would seem to be low and the responses can be taken more or less at face value. Certain forms of behavior, such as whether or not one has appeared on television or written a book, are easy to assess and difficult to distort. In other cases, especially those involving the prediction of future behavior, the likelihood of distortion seems high enough to put aside the requirements of style and stress repeatedly that self-reported rather than actual behavior is being analyzed. As will be seen, for example, the items that asked the respondents to assess their mobilizability under three different conditions [#14, 42, 53] may have yielded data pertaining as much to their norms about mobilizability as to their actual mobilizability, compelling us to use some ungainly language in order to avoid losing sight of the distinction between norms about behavior and behavior itself.

The problem can thus be kept under control through explicit and careful interpretation, although it is not solvable.[59] In the case of this survey, moreover, such control is facilitated by the availability of an independent measure of response accuracy. The difference between those who did and did not return the "confirmation" card not only serves a basic substantive purpose but also provides a methodological check on the reliability of the data. In these terms, the aforementioned 13 percent of the Test Ban Mobilizables and 6 percent of the Civil Rights Mobilizables who did not report writing a letter on their respective issues demonstrate that allowance must be made for the potential discrepancy between actual and reported behavior.

Miscellaneous Problems

Besides the limitations imposed by the representativeness of the sample, the time interval between mailings, and the nature of self-reported data, the questionnaire itself poses a host of method-

---

[59] For a further discussion of the self-reporting problem, see Carl I. Hovland and Irving L. Janis, *Personality and Persuasibility* (New Haven: Yale University Press, 1959), pp. 249–250.

ological problems that can affect the meaning and significance of the findings. The order of the items, the meaning of the alternatives within items, the coding of written responses substituted for the provided alternatives, the disposition of unanswered items —these are only some of the more obvious problems that must be faced if the findings are to reflect substantive phenomena rather than the structure and content of the questionnaire itself. We shall identify and try to deal with these problems as they arise with respect to particular questions, but it is useful to note several relevant points here. The order of the eleven parts of the eight issue questions was randomized to prevent the respondents from developing routinized responses. Wherever possible the items were constructed with five alternatives in order to maximize the variability of the responses, but sometimes the highest alternative of the scaled items was located to the left and sometimes to the right of the page so as to prevent another form of routinization. Both the written and the checked responses were coded in terms of an explicit set of coding rules; daily spot checks by the coders clearly established that no systematic errors entered into the coding process; and a punch verification system was used when the coded data were transferred to cards for machine processing in order to insure accuracy at this stage.

On the other hand, there are also some methodological limitations to record. The time requirements of the situation prevented systematic pre-testing of the questionnaire and its items and, regrettably, the orders of the questions on each page and of the pages in each questionnaire were the same for all the respondents. In addition, an exact measure of inter-coder reliability was not made.[60]

The problem posed by uncodable responses and unanswered questions requires more extended comment. Unlike interviews, mailed questionnaires inevitably result in items that are not answered adequately by all the respondents. If the pattern of un-

---

[60] Roughly every thirtieth questionnaire was coded twice and a single coding error was uncovered in fewer than one-tenth of these. As indicated, the errors were not patterned in any way.

codable responses is extensive, or if particular items are skipped over frequently, then interpretation of the results becomes extremely difficult. The analyst cannot be sure of what the omissions mean or of how his interpretations would be altered if the respondents had answered more diligently. Happily this problem is not particularly relevant in this instance. As might be expected of attentive citizens, the 3,362 ADA respondents appear to have completed the questionnaire with discrimination and thoroughness. Two-fifths of them answered every one of the fifty-eight questions and more than 90 percent did not omit more than five questions. All told, thirty-seven questions were skipped over by fewer than 3 percent of the respondents and forty-four by less than 5 percent. Only one question was omitted by as much as one-tenth of the sample.

Although there was a tendency on the part of some respondents not to answer every part of the large, multi-part questions, in general the omissions were not extensive enough to cast doubt upon the legitimacy of interpreting those answers that were supplied. Nor were they enough to justify dropping the worst offenders from the sample (in this case, say, 253 respondents who skipped over six or more questions). To drop them is not to eliminate the problem, and it would give up the data that they did supply. Hence it was decided not to alter the sample and to cope with the problem through explicitness—by including the "uncodable" and "no answer" proportions at every stage of the presentation and by calling attention to those that are sufficient to raise the possibility of alternative interpretations of the data.

SUMMARY

Survey research must ordinarily focus on past situations or hypothetical ones. Not being able to structure the course of events to meet his analytic purposes, the survey researcher must perforce ask his respondents, "What did you do when such and such happened?" or "What would you do if such and such should occur?" In neither case can the researcher be sure that the respondents did in fact do what they reported or that they would in fact do what they predicted.

The present inquiry avoids much of this uncertainty. Data pertaining to citizenship between elections were gathered from 3,362 members of the Attentive Public, 1,704 of whom, at either of two moments of recent political history, are known to have responded to efforts to mobilize their support ("the Mobilizables") and 1,658 who are known not to have responded to the same efforts ("the Attentives"). The efforts were undertaken by the Americans for Democratic Action, a liberally oriented organization concerned with major political issues, and directed at persons on its mailing list. The latter were asked to write members of Congress on behalf of the 1963 test ban treaty and the 1964 civil rights act and to confirm having done so to the ADA. A ten-page questionnaire, sent in two waves, was returned by 1,704 of the Mobilizables who confirmed one of the two actions and by 1,658 of the randomly selected Attentives who did not. The former consisted of 1,104 Test Ban Mobilizables and 600 Civil Rights Mobilizables, while the latter included 1,082 Test Ban Attentives and 576 Civil Rights Attentives.

The responses to a number of the items in the questionnaire clearly indicate that virtually all of the 3,362 respondents were members of the Attentive Public. Unlike the results of inquiries into other segments of the citizenry, the members of the ADA sample proved to be almost uniform in their high concern for public affairs and their strong inclination to engage in citizenship between elections. Other data also demonstrate that most of the respondents did not possess sufficient opinion-making capacities to be classified as leaders rather than as members of the Attentive Public.

The questionnaires also yielded unambiguous evidence that the Test Ban and Civil Rights Mobilizables wrote many more letters on their respective issues than their unmobilized counterparts. This finding reinforces the presumption that the Mobilizable and the Attentive groups are in fact differentiated by the extent of their mobilizability and that any differences uncovered between them are, after allowance has been made for the operation of other variables, a reflection of the process whereby some citizens can and others cannot be moved to action.

Several methodological problems that limit interpretation of the data have been noted. None of these is considered unmanageable and none of them offsets the advantages of knowing that the persons surveyed engaged in the behavior which the inquiry is attempting to probe.

CHAPTER 6

THE DYNAMICS OF CURRENT BEHAVIOR

The ensuing presentation has two purposes. One is simply to depict the first- and second-hand activities of the Attentives and Mobilizables which, as such, reflect the differences between them. To identify and comprehend the sources of behavior, it is useful to start with a clear conception of the nature and frequency of that behavior. No less important than the description of these activities, however, is the analysis of them as major explanatory variables of our model. It will be recalled that the model treats current behavior as an independent as well as a dependent variable. For both Attentives and Mobilizables, their own activities are conceived as serving to either reinforce or inhibit further activity, thus adding to the reasons for expecting the two groups to differ in their first-hand contacts and to be undifferentiated in their second-hand forms of behavior. Such a feedback process occurs because while active citizens often respond to others' stimuli, their first-hand contacts with public affairs themselves usually evoke a response of some kind. Letters to officials generally produce replies.[1] Organizational activity provides the rewards of interaction with similarly oriented people.[2] Involvement in protest rallies yields verbal and nonverbal approval from other participants.

As we present the behavioral data, therefore, we shall also assess whether they conform to the predictions made in the first three hypotheses of the model. Let us begin this twofold task by looking at the first-hand contacts with public affairs made by members of the Attentive and Mobilizable Publics.

LETTER-WRITING ACTIVITIES

When the ADA asked those on its mailing list to write their Senators, it was carrying forward a time-honored American tradi-

---

[1] For lengthy accounts of the extent to which officials have institutionalized the process of replying to all the mail they receive, see David J. Olson, "Citizen Grievance Letters as a Gubernatorial Control Device in Wisconsin," *Journal of Politics,* Vol. 31 (1969), pp. 741–55; John D. C. Little, Chandler H. Stevens, and Peter Tropp, "Citizen Feedback System: The Puerto Rico Model," *National Civic Review,* Vol. 60 (April 1971), pp. 191–98; and "New System Speeds Replies to Foreign Affairs Mail," *Department of State Newsletter,* March 1967, pp. 30–31.

[2] There are considerable data indicating that because of these rewards organizational participation is cumulative, that people get more involved in more organizations the more active they become. Cf. William Erbe, "Social Involvement and Political Activity: A Replication and Elaboration," *American Sociological Review,* Vol. 29 (1964), pp. 198–215. See also David Horton Smith and Richard D. Reddy, "The Impact of Voluntary Action Upon the Volunteer/Participant," in David Horton Smith, ed., *Voluntary Action Research: 1973* (Lexington, Mass.: Lexington Books), pp. 169–237.

tion. For generations the idea of expressing one's concern about public affairs to one's representatives in government has been a popular norm in this country. Although not so deeply engrained as the dictate to enter the voting booth on election day, it is nonetheless a tradition that extends well back into the 19th century.[3]

As in other matters, however, the gap between letter-writing norms and behavior is substantial. Despite the aforementioned signs of a slow but continual growth in the ranks of the Attentive Public, all the available data reveal that far more people believe in this form of citizenship than actually practice it.[4] As previously noted, the practice is confined to roughly 15 percent of the adult population and is a regular practice for only about 3 percent.[5] Yet, as we have seen, persons on the ADA mailing list are among this small minority, since it will be recalled that four-fifths of our respondents reported letter-writing activities. When this overall figure is broken down in terms of the number of letters written by the Attentives and Mobilizables, however, it becomes clear that the practice of letter-writing is neither evenly distributed throughout the Attentive Public nor amounts to an uncontrolled or indiscriminate airing of views. Further breakdowns of the responses in terms of the addressees of the letters and the issues mentioned in them indicate that the first-hand contacts with public affairs that active citizens establish between elections are purposeful and selective.

Table 6–1 presents the breakdown of the frequency of letters to various addresses. Here can be found clear-cut support for our expectation (Hypothesis Ia, b) that the Mobilizables, being more predisposed to direct action, would engage in more letter-writing than the Attentives. With respect to local, state, national, and

---

[3] For a history of political letter-writing practices in the United States, see Leila A. Sussmann, *Dear FDR: A Study of Political Letter-Writing* (Totowa, N.J.: The Bedminster Press, 1963), Chap. 1.

[4] Cf. V. O. Key, Jr., *Public Opinion and American Democracy* (New York: Alfred A. Knopf, Inc., 1961), pp. 418–419.

[5] See above, p. 27.

TABLE 6-1

PERCENTAGE DISTRIBUTION AND STATISTICAL COMPARISON OF THE RESPONSES OF THE 1,704 MOBILIZABLES (Ms) AND 1,658 ATTENTIVES (As) TO ITEM #10

[#10] All told, about how many letters a year do you write to the types of persons listed at the left? (in percentages)

		None	1–3	4–6	7–9	10 or more	Codable answer not given	Total	Mean number of letters	χ²	df	P
a.	United Nations officials or delegates											
	Ms	79	19	1	0	0	1	100	.49	45.93	2	<.001
	As	85	12	0	0	0	3	100	.27			
b.	Members of Congress											
	Ms	5	58	23	6	7	1	100	3.52	564.72	4	<.001
	As	35	48	10	2	2	3	100	1.91			
c.	The President											
	Ms	28	64	5	1	1	1	100	1.70	512.60	2	<.001
	As	66	29	2	0	0	3	100	.73			
d.	Other Federal executive officials											
	Ms	71	23	4	1	0	1	100	.74	40.44	3	<.001
	As	78	16	2	0	1	3	100	.53			
e.	State officials (executive or legislative)											
	Ms	41	45	10	2	1	1	100	1.69	156.59	4	<.001
	As	61	31	4	1	0	3	100	.98			
f.	Local officials											
	Ms	65	29	4	1	0	1	100	.93	65.08	3	<.001
	As	76	18	3	0	0	3	100	.60			
g.	Newspaper editors											
	Ms	49	36	9	2	3	1	100	1.58	73.48	4	<.001
	As	61	29	4	1	2	3	100	1.07			
h.	Others											
	Ms	92	4	1	1	1	1	100	.30	10.36	3	ns*
	As	92	3	1	0	1	3	100	.18			

* ns = not significant.

international officials, both executive and legislative, and also in the case of newspaper editors [#10a, b, c, d, e, f, g], the Mobilizables reported writing significantly more letters annually than did the Attentives.[6] The substantial extent of these differences is summarized in the fact that the mean number of letters to all seven types of addressees reported by the Mobilizables was 1.52, whereas the equivalent figure for the Attentives was 0.87.

Besides affirming the general expectation of greater first-hand contacts on the part of the Mobilizables, there are other noteworthy findings in Table 6–1. One of these is the large degree to which letter-writing is a correlate of mobilizability. Not only did the Mobilizables exceed the Attentives in this respect, but in absolute terms there were hardly any in the group who did not report writing at least one letter to at least one kind of official. Only 5 percent of the Mobilizables who provided a codable response did not cite letters to members of Congress, and one-fourth of these mentioned letters to other types of officials, leaving less than 4 percent who apparently never resorted to letter-writing at all.

This finding is not particularly surprising, given that their claim to have written a letter to officials was the initial basis for identifying the Mobilizables. What is startling, however, is the place of the President in their letter-writing practices. The ADA appealed to them to communicate with Capitol Hill, not the White House, and while Table 6–1 reveals that more of their letters were directed toward the former than the latter, nearly three-fourths of the Mobilizables reported writing the President. More importantly, the Mobilizables differed sharply from the Attentives in their orientations toward the President.[7] Few items,

---

[6] Only with respect to "others" [#10h] was the difference between the two groups not significant. A wide variety of addressees were written in by those few (122 Mobilizables and 74 Attentives) who indicated one or more letters in response to this residual question. These included "friends," "magazines," "radio commentators," "television stations," "industrial concerns with a political image," "national church officials," "labor unions," "foreign embassies," "people in the news," "people who write newspapers themselves," etc.

[7] For additional indications of this difference, see Chapter 11.

in fact, turned up a difference between them as wide as the 38 percentage points that separated the proportions who responded that they did not write letters to the President.[8] Stated more substantively, while the Attentives reported writing fewer letters to the President than to state officials and newspaper editors, the exact opposite was the case for the Mobilizables, who wrote to the President more often than to any other leaders save members of Congress.

It might be argued that the special salience of the White House for the Mobilizables merely reflects an orientation toward national affairs that is also evident in the difference between the number of their letters to members of Congress on the one hand and to state and local officials on the other. Table 6–1 does depict their greater concern with actors on Capitol Hill than with those in City Hall or the Statehouse, but this is hardly a sufficient explanation since it also reveals the same pattern for the Attentives.[9] Furthermore, if the Mobilizables' pronounced predisposition to write the President reflects only an intense orientation to issues at the national level, then the Mobilizables would have also written other federal executive officials to a noticeable extent. Yet this was not the case. The Mobilizables reported writing more letters to state and local officials than to officers of the executive branch

[8] Indeed, this difference is so large and was so unexpected that a special check was made to determine whether it reflected a coding or programming error.

[9] That the distinction between national and local orientations is also as readily discernible at the receiving end of the mail as at the sending end requires only a comparison between the flow of letters to the President outlined in Chapter 2 and the finding that the governors of "North Carolina, Georgia, Michigan, California, Texas, and New York all average well over 100 letters a day" (Coleman B. Ransome, Jr., *The Office of Governor in the United States* [University, Ala.: University of Alabama Press, 1956], p. 128). For additional data on the relative degree to which local, state, national, and international affairs are of concern to attentive citizens, see M. Kent Jennings and Harmon Zeigler, "The Salience of American State Politics," *American Political Science Review*, Vol. 64 (1970), pp. 523–35.

other than the President. Thus there seems to be more to their orientations toward the White House than merely concern about national affairs.

Two other lines of explanation are possible. One employs the same reasoning that previously led us to hypothesize (XXXI) that Mobilizables are likely to be more responsive to the appeals of officials than are Attentives and interprets the finding as a reflection of rational calculation. Being readier to express their concerns through first-hand contacts, and presumably possessing stronger attitudes and greater subjective competence,[10] Mobilizables are more inclined to go directly to the heart of political authority. Hence 71 percent of those in our sample were not content just to carry forward the "write your Congressman" tradition and wrote their representative in the White House as well, whereas the equivalent figure for the Attentives, who are more inclined to observe than participate in public affairs, was 31 percent.[11]

---

[10] The hypotheses attributing these characteristics to the Mobilizables were at least partly confirmed (see below, Chaps. 8 and 9).

[11] Further evidence that first-hand contacts are partly guided by rational calculations of the locus of authority is discernible in the finding (Table 6–1) that both the Attentives and the Mobilizables sent fewer letters to U.N. officials than to any of the other leaders listed. Or at least such an interpretation is plausible if it is assumed, as seems reasonable, that the former have yet to acquire as much authority relative to the domain of public affairs that falls within their purview as is possessed by local, state, and national officials with respect to issues encompassed by their responsibilities. Still another indication along these lines is provided by the responses to an item [#3b,c] that distinguished between letters written to Senators and Representatives. Assuming that the former, being fewer and having wider constitutional responsibilities, possess greater political authority than the latter, it would follow that if active citizens do engage in such calculations, their communications with Senators would be more extensive than with Representatives. Such proved to be the case. For both the Attentives and the Mobilizables, the proportion who reported writing "a letter in the last three years to a member of the U.S. Senate" was seven percentage points higher than those who said they wrote members of the House. On the other hand, for evidence that rational calculation alone does not explain the behavior of persons who

The second line of reasoning is more speculative and focuses on nonrational, perhaps even subconscious, processes that might account for the salience of the President for the Mobilizables. Besides being attracted by his constitutional and political authority, many people are inclined to treat the President as a symbol of values that extend beyond current issues. A number of studies have revealed that the White House and its occupant are seen as standing above the din of current politics, as carrying forward all the historic forces that have made for progress and unity, and as thus embodying all that is good and wise. The President is the first political object of whom Americans become aware as children and from childhood on he assumes, irrespective of his identity, heroic stature for most citizens.[12] One observer notes that he may even perform a function similar to that of religion, that

> ... the absence of ritual in American politics, the absence of an aristocratic or monarchic tradition, and the self-conscious secularization of political life may obscure the extent to which political commitment in the United States contains a prime component of primordial religious commitment. ... And the President is the appropriate focus of this commitment, for ... he is the concrete human individual whom one can see, on whom one can focus attention, and with whom one can share common human emotions, and yet he

---

write letters to officials, see the "surprisingly high proportion" of letter-writers who did know how the Congressmen they wrote on foreign trade policy voted on the issue (Bauer, Pool, and Dexter, *American Business and Public Policy*, p. 216).

[12] Fred I. Greenstein, *Children and Politics* (New Haven: Yale University Press, 1965), Chap. 3; Robert D. Hess and David Easton, "The Child's Image of the President," *Public Opinion Quarterly*, Vol. XXIV (Winter, 1960), pp. 632–44. Hess and Easton conclude that there is not a very great danger that in adulthood criticism of an occupant of the role will spill over to the role itself, that their data "suggest that one of the factors that prevents this from occurring is a strong parental-like tie with respect to the President's role itself, developed before the child can become familiar with the contention surrounding the incumbent of the office" (p. 644).

is something transcending his concrete human aspects, for he is also the symbol of the nation.[13]

Given this many-faceted symbolic role, it follows that,

> Writing to the President, as compared to both the administrative agencies and departments under him and Congress, may fulfill needs rather different from those satisfied in other cases. The President is a father figure in a way legislators seldom are, and letter writers may turn to him for vague, undefined help, or in order to complain of some general situation, or merely as a means of assuaging a general anxiety.[14]

Granting that the President serves such symbolic functions, why should he be any more of a symbol for the Mobilizables than for the Attentives? Our answer to this question can be only speculative, but it may be that, feeling stronger about, and being more ready to act on behalf of, remote values, Mobilizables develop a greater need than Attentives to personify the complex social collectivities that they care so much about, and they thus attach greater significance to the occupant of the White House. Perhaps, too, their greater readiness to respond to appeals for support reflects a more general sensitivity to and submissiveness toward authority, which would further reinforce their inclination to correspond with the President.[15]

---

[13] Sidney Verba, "The Kennedy Assassination and the Nature of Political Commitment," in Bradley S. Greenberg and Edwin B. Parker, eds., *The Kennedy Assassination and the American Public* (Stanford: Stanford University Press, 1965), p. 354.

[14] Robert E. Lane, *Political Life: Why People Get Involved in Politics* (Glencoe, Ill.: The Free Press, 1959), p. 72. This special character of writing to the President is also noted by V. O. Key, Jr., *Public Opinion and American Democracy*, p. 418.

[15] To the extent that greater submissiveness to authority is a distinctive feature of the Mobilizables' behavior, it is confined to the President and does not particularly mark their behavior toward other political exec-

Whatever the proper explanation of the White House's greater salience for the Mobilizables, it would seem to be one of their central characteristics. As will be seen in Chapter 11, this characteristic even dominates the respondent's perceptions of their own mobilizability. Indeed, it is such a pervasive phenomenon that we shall have occasion to recur to its implications for the processes of support-building that ensue between elections.

The data in Table 6–1 also provide empirical support for the observation in Chapter 1 that the activities of the Attentive Public can be highly misleading as clues to the trends of mass opinion. It can be seen that a large number of the respondents wrote to more than one public official and also to newspaper editors. This is especially true of the Mobilizables, more than half of whom wrote at least one letter to members of Congress, the President, state officials, and newspaper editors, but it is also discernible in the responses of the Attentives. Summarizing the pattern in terms of the overlap between private and public leaders, 99 percent of the Mobilizables who wrote letters to editors also wrote to officials in Washington and 67 percent said they wrote to state or local officials. The equivalent figures for the Attentives were 81 and 53 percent. This tendency of the same

utives. The difference between them and the Attentives is not nearly so pronounced in the case of State Governors. The executive-legislative distinction at the state level was included in another letter-writing item [#3e, f] and again both Mobilizables and Attentives reported more communications with legislators than with chief executives: 51 percent of the former reported having written "a letter in the last three years to a member of your State Legislature" and 39 percent said they wrote "the Governor of your State," and the equivalent figures for the latter were 31 and 22 percent. However, the forty percentage points that separated the Mobilizables and Attentives in their letters to the President is substantially greater than the seventeen points that differentiated them in regard to Governors. That feelings about political authority should be more extensive toward the chief executive of the federal government than toward those in state governments is hardly surprising, however. It is a difference that has also been found to have roots in childhood experience. Cf., Greenstein, *Children and Politics*, p. 37.

people to write repetitively has been uncovered by other researchers, who note that "as these few people write more and more letters over time, they are counted again and again," and since members of the Attentive and Mobilizable Publics tend to have stronger attitudes than those who comprise the Mass Public, the "letter opinion" that circulates through government offices and media columns and the "public opinion" that is recorded in polls can be highly discrepant.[16]

The repetitiveness of letter-writing does not necessarily stem from a preoccupation with a single issue. Of the eleven issues listed as choices in Item #4, 71 percent of the Mobilizables reported mentioning at least two of them in their letters to officials, 17 percent cited four, and 3 percent mentioned six or more. Since the listing did not include state or local issues, these percentages are probably an underrepresentation of the issues covered in their letters.[17] Even among the Attentives, those who did write letters often wrote about more than one issue: 41 percent wrote about at least two, 8 percent about four, and 2 percent about six or more.

Table 6–2 presents an additional breakdown of the issue coverage of the letters written by both groups and it provides further support for the expectation (Hypothesis Ic) that the Mobilizables would write letters on a wider assortment of issues than would the Attentives. The table lists the proportion of each group who reported mentioning each issue in their letters. It can be seen that the Mobilizables were more active on six of the issues, while the two groups did not differ significantly on the other five. In these data we also come upon the first indication that the

[16] Philip E. Converse, Aage R. Clausen and Warren E. Miller, "Electoral Myth and Reality: The 1964 Election," *American Political Science Review*, Vol. LIX (June 1965), p. 333.

[17] In fact, 6 percent of the Mobilizables and 7 percent of the Attentives appended other issues to their responses to Item #4. These consisted of a miscellany ranging from "Indian affairs" to "medicare," from "narcotics problem" to "civil defense," from "school aid" to "birth control aid for foreign countries," etc.

TABLE 6–2
DISTRIBUTION OF THE RESPONSES OF THE 1,704
MOBILIZABLES AND 1,658 ATTENTIVES TO ITEM #4

[#4] If you [wrote to at least one official in the last three years], which of the following problems were mentioned in your letter (or letters)?

Issues*	Percentage of the Mobilizables Attentives who responded affirmatively		Statistical comparison of the responses of the two groups to each issue		
			$\chi^2 =$	$df =$	P
Agricultural surpluses	6	4	1.89	1	ns**
Balance of payments	2	1	.66	1	ns
Berlin	7	5	6.15	1	ns
Civil rights	81	47	390.30	1	.001
The Congo	4	2	5.36	1	ns
Federal tax reduction	13	7	26.93	1	.001
Foreign aid	31	19	59.38	1	.001
Nuclear testing	76	37	501.05	1	.001
Tariff reduction	5	3	3.70	1	ns
Vietnam	11	6	18.51	1	.001
Western unity	5	2	14.25	1	.001

* In all the tabular listing of issues, the latter have been rearranged into alphabetical order so as to facilitate comparison. See Appendix A for the order in which the issues were listed in the questionnaire itself.

** ns = not significant.

Mobilizables and Attentives differed most extensively with respect to the issues that both regard as important.[18] All five of the issues about which both groups wrote the most letters were among the six in which they reported different degrees of letter-writing. In contrast, not more than 7 percent of either group wrote letters on the five issues where the differences between them were not significant.

In order to facilitate the analysis of letter-writing practices in subsequent chapters, an index was constructed out of responses to the two relevant items [#3 and 10].[19] Scores in the first decile

[18] For other indications of this pattern and a discussion of its possible meaning, see pp. 337–38, 418–19, 45.

[19] For the weights and rules used to construct the index, see Appendix B.

of "the index of letter-writing activity" reflect virtually no activity of this sort and those in the top four deciles represent a great amount of activity. Nineteen percent of the respondents fell in the lowest category and were designated the "nonwriters," while 5 percent tallied scores in the highest category and are clustered together as the "steady" writers. The 19, 36, and 20 percent whose scores fell in three intervals (11 to 20, 21 to 41, and 41 to 60) between these extremes shall be called, respectively, the "sporadic," "occasional," and "frequent" writers.[20] As can be seen in Table 6–3, the Occasional, Frequent, and Steady writers were mostly Mobilizables, while the Sporadic and Nonwriters were mostly Attentives. More specifically, the Mobilizables recorded a mean index score of 35 and the Attentives one of 22, a difference that proved to be significant.[21]

TABLE 6–3
DISTRIBUTION OF THE SCORES RECORDED BY THE 1,704 MOBILIZABLES AND THE 1,658 ATTENTIVES ON THE INDEX OF LETTER-WRITING ACTIVITY (in percentages)

	Mobilizables	Attentives
Nonwriters	5	32
Sporadic Writers	17	21
Occasional Writers	43	29
Frequent Writers	27	13
Steady Writers	7	2
Score unknown	1	3
	100	100

ORGANIZATIONAL AFFILIATIONS AND ACTIVITIES

Since the achievement of the goals of many voluntary associations requires that they keep abreast of the course of events, take stands on relevant issues, and otherwise participate in the political

[20] The remaining 1 percent did not provide sufficient responses to justify the derivation of an index score.

[21] $\chi^2 = 528.20$, df = 5, P<.001.

process, involvement in the activities of such organizations and exposure to their communications constitutes a form of first-hand contact with public affairs. The officers and staff of an association are, as they move to advance its interests, actors in the arena of public affairs and their efforts to inform and mobilize the membership are part of the larger political process. The newsletters, bulletins, and other messages that link the association's members, being designed to maintain loyalties and orient attitudes, are in the nature of political documents and serve as central channels of communication in the political system.[22] Mere affiliation with—must less active participation in—an association that concerns itself with public affairs thus provides contacts that are more direct than, say, reading a newspaper or engaging in discussions with friends. As Almond and Verba put it, "Voluntary associations are the prime means by which the function of mediating between the individual and the state is performed. Through them the individual is able to relate himself effectively and meaningfully to the political system." [23]

It is hardly surprising, then, that one of the least ambiguous and most persistent findings of inquiries into political behavior is the close relationship between membership in voluntary associations and involvement in public affairs. Irrespective of whether they are active or passive members, those affiliated with associations have consistently been shown to be more politically involved than nonmembers and the data also show that the more associations a person belongs to and the more he participates in their affairs, the more active he is likely to be politically.[24] Organizational

---

[22] For an elaboration of the nature and role of these "organizational media," see Rosenau, *Public Opinion and Foreign Policy: An Operational Formulation* (New York: Random House, 1961), pp. 83–96.

[23] *The Civic Culture*, p. 300.

[24] See, for instance, the data in Howard E. Freeman and Morris Showel, "The Political Influence of Voluntary Association," in William N. McPhee and William A. Glasser, eds., *Public Opinion and Congressional Elections* (New York: The Free Press, 1962), Chap. 8; Almond and Verba, *The Civic Culture*, Chap. 11; Key, *Public Opinion and American Democracy*, pp. 504–05; Robert R. Alford and Harry M. Scoble, "Sources of Local Political Involvement," *American Political Science*

activities seem to be so central to the practices of citizenship that one analyst reports finding that more individuals "would attempt to work through other formal organized groups than would attempt to work through political parties," [25] while another offers persuasive evidence that "political participation is at least as highly associated, if not more so, with organizational involvement as with socio-economic status." [26] These organizational affiliations need not be primarily political in character. The data indicate that affiliations with any type of organization are likely to promote citizenship activity. According to one student of voting behavior, "We find in our own research . . . that in urban populations the degree of political involvement is highly related to the actual number of group memberships which a person reports. Those individuals who belong to none of the social organizations which characterize American urban life are likely to care little about political matters and to participate little in on-going events." [27]

The earlier finding that persons on the ADA mailing list reported more extensive organizational affiliations and activities than have samples of the general population[28] is thus consistent with the results of prior research, as is the confirmation of our expectation (Hypotheses Id, e, f) that the Mobilizables and Attentives would also be differentiated along these lines. As can be seen in Table 6–4, the Mobilizables reported belonging to [#1] and participating in the deliberations of [#24] more public-issue oriented associations more frequently [#2] than did the Attentives,[29] albeit the latter can hardly be said to have avoided these kinds of first-hand contacts. All in all, the Mobilizables averaged

Review, Vol. 62 (1968), p. 1197; and Verba and Nie, *Participation in America,* pp. 186–200.

[25] Sidney Verba, "Political Participation and Strategies of Influence: A Comparative Study," *ACTA Sociologica,* Vol. 6 (1962), p. 30.

[26] William Erbe, "Social Involvement and Political Activity," p. 213.

[27] Angus Campbell, "The Passive Citizen," *ACTA Sociologica,* Vol. 6 (1962), p. 13.

[28] See pp. 175 and 76.

[29] For the difference in their responses to Item #1, $\chi^2 = 97.25$, df = 7, P<.001; for Item #2, $\chi^2 = 70.36$, df = 5, P<.001; and for Item #24, $\chi^2 = 48.91$, df = 6, P<.001.

TABLE 6-4

DISTRIBUTION OF THE RESPONSES OF THE 1,704
MOBILIZABLES AND 1,658 ATTENTIVES TO ITEMS
#1, 2 AND 24 (in percentages)

[#1] Do you belong to any organizations which publicly express their viewpoints on national or international problems?

	Mobilizables	Attentives
*Yes	90	81
*No	6	14
Question not answered	4	5
	100	100

If yes, to about how many organizations?

	Mobilizables	Attentives
**One	10	14
**Two	22	21
**Three	21	18
**Four	12	10
**Five	8	7
**Six to ten	12	6
**Eleven or more	1	1
Answered yes, but did not specify number	4	4
	90	81

[#2] On the average, how often do you attend organizational meetings where national or international problems are discussed?

	Mobilizables	Attentives
*Every week	7	5
*Once a month	23	17
*Six times a year	16	14
*Three times a year	19	18
*Once a year	16	18
*Never	16	25
Codable answer not given	3	3
	100	100

[#24] Do you participate in the deliberations of any organizations which take stands on public issues?

	Mobilizables	Attentives
*Yes	58	47
*No	39	50
Question not answered	3	3
	100	100

If yes, about how many organizations?

	Mobilizables	Attentives
**One	19	17
**Two	19	15
**Three	10	8
**Four	4	3
**Five	2	1
**Six or more	2	1
Answered yes, but did not specify number	2	2
	58	47

* Provided alternative.
** Category developed out of written responses.

membership in 3.4 organizations, participation in 1.4, and attendance at 8.6 meetings per year, whereas the equivalent mean figures for the Attentives were 2.7, 1.0, and 6.3. These data seem to indicate that the more contacts a person has with the affairs of voluntary associations, the more likely he is to be responsive to appeals for support. It would, of course, be unwarranted to conclude that organizational activity causes mobilizability, since still another characteristic of mobilizable citizens may account for the relationship; or, more likely, several factors may contribute to it. Yet a causal explanation of how organizational activity and mobilizability may interact independently of other variables is suggested by the data. To be mobilizable is, in part, to appreciate the virtues of cooperative endeavor and cumulated support, and it seems reasonable to speculate that participation in organizational activities contributes to positive dispositions toward cooperating with mobilizers as a means of realizing shared aspirations.

The fact that the vast majority of both the Mobilizables and Attentives belonged to more than one organization is consistent with a recurrent finding that, in the United States, membership in voluntary associations tends to be multiple in nature. Indeed, the tendency toward multiple memberships is far more pronounced for these two groups than for the samples of other studies. For example, Almond and Verba found that 55 percent of the organization members in their American sample belonged to more than one organization,[30] and Scott's survey yielded a multiple membership figure of 40 percent,[31] but in our sample as many as 63 percent of the Attentives and 81 percent of the Mobilizables who reported belonging to one organization also cited other memberships. Some analysts interpret such data as a sign of political viability in the United States. Multiple membership is seen as exposing the organizationally active individual to dissimilar political stimuli that produce cross-pressures and serve to reduce his intolerance of political opposition. In subjecting this reasoning

[30] *The Civic Culture*, p. 320.
[31] John C. Scott, Jr., "Membership and Participation in Voluntary Associations," *American Sociological Review*, Vol. 22 (June 1957), p. 318.

to empirical verification, however, one observer failed to find support for it and suggested the possibility that multiple membership exposes active citizens to homogeneous rather than hetereogeneous experiences.[32] Our inquiry did not yield any systematic findings on this aspect of multiple membership, but a few isolated data were inadvertently uncovered that lend greater weight to the homogeneous point of view. Two percent of both the Attentives and the Mobilizables wrote in the names of the organizations to which they belonged and, of the entries that included two or more associations, none suggest that persons on the ADA list are exposed to cross-pressures through their varied organizational affiliations. If those who identified their memberships are typical of the entire sample, these respondents belong exclusively to organizations that are essentially similar to the ADA in their postures toward public affairs. A typical entry, for example, was made by a person who cited affiliations with the "League of Women Voters, Consumers League, Democratic Party, NAACP, ADA, ACLU."

In order to facilitate subsequent analysis, equal weight was given to the membership and participation dimensions of associational affiliations and these were combined to create an "index of organizational activity." [33] The index consists of six intervals, with the scores in the lowest (0 to 9) being recorded by respondents who neither belonged to any organizations nor attended any meetings and the scores in the highest (81 to 100) by those who reported membership in at least six organizations and weekly attendance at their meetings. The former designated the "Inactive" cluster,

---

[32] Sidney Verba, "Organizational Membership and Democratic Consensus," *Journal of Politics*, Vol. 27 (August 1965), pp. 467–97.

[33] For the weights and rules used to construct the index, see Appendix B. Here it will also be found that the index scores were compiled out of the responses to Items #1 and #2 and that Item #24 was not included. This exclusion was necessitated by the presence of the same item in the index of opinion-making potential (see Table 5–1). Since this overlap would render spurious any results stemming from a cross-tabulation of the two indices, it seemed necessary to omit Item #24 from the organizational activity index.

accounted for 7 percent of the respondents. The latter, the "Extremely Active" category, also encompassed 7 percent. The 15, 24, 27, and 19 percent whose scores fell in the intervals (9 to 20, 21 to 40, 41 to 60, 61 to 80) between these extremes are labeled, respectively, "Slightly," "Occasionally," "Moderately," and "Highly" active.[34] The distribution of the scores among the Mobilizables and Attentives is presented in Table 6–5, which reveals in summary form the extent to which the organizational activities of the former exceeded those of the latter.[35] The mean index score registered by the Mobilizables was 50.2, while that of the Attentives was 41.3.

Before concluding the analysis of the first-hand forms of contact with public affairs, it is useful to note the relationship between them, since other researchers have found that these forms of activity tend to be positively correlated.[36] Do high scores on the

TABLE 6–5
DISTRIBUTION OF THE SCORES RECORDED BY THE 1,704 MOBILIZABLES AND 1,658 ATTENTIVES ON THE INDEX OF ORGANIZATIONAL ACTIVITY
(in percentages)

	Mobilizables	Attentives
Inactive	4	10
Slightly Active	12	18
Occasionally Active	23	26
Moderatively Active	28	25
Highly Active	23	15
Extremely Active	9	5
Score not determined	1	1
	100	100

[34] One percent did not answer either item of the index and were not given a score.
[35] For the differences between the two groups, $\chi^2 = 111.06$, df $= 5$, P$<.001$.
[36] Cf. Lane, *Political Life*, pp. 93–94; Sussmann, *Dear FDR*, p. 138.

index of organizational activity imply comparable scores for letter-writing, or are active citizens more selective in their modes of behavior? A few respondents demonstrated that such selectivity is possible,[37] but overall the data show a positive correlation between the two sets of index scores for both the Mobilizables and the Attentives.[38] Exactly three-fifths of the Steady Writers in both groups, for example, were classified among the Extremely or Highly Active on the organizational scale and, at the low end, nearly half of the Nonwriters in both groups were among the Inactives or Slightly Actives with regards to organizational work.

CONTACT THROUGH THE MASS MEDIA

Let us turn now to those aspects of current behavior considered to be second-hand forms of contact with public affairs. We have argued that such behavior is equally necessary to membership in the Attentive and Mobilizable Publics and that therefore the two groups would not be differentiated in this regard. This expectation proved to be largely accurate with respect to contacts established through the mass media (Hypothesis IIc), but not nearly as valid in the case of face-to-face communications (Hypotheses IIa, b). Let us look first at the findings about contacts through the mass media.

The questionnaire contained three items designed to probe such contacts. One called for an indication of the types of media on which the respondents relied for information about foreign affairs [#15], while the other two asked about specific magazine [#16] and newspaper [#17] media. The responses to these items are presented in Tables 6–6 and 6–7. In both it can be plainly seen that the Attentives and Mobilizables do not differ very greatly either generally or specifically in their exposure to the mass media.

---

[37] To cite the most extreme cases of selectivity, one of the 155 Steady Writers in the overall sample was classified as inactive in organizations and six of the 624 Nonwriters were among the Extremely Active on the organizational scale.

[38] For the Mobilizables, $r = .40$, df $= 1,678$, P$<.001$; for the Attentives, $r = .45$, df $= 1,601$, P$<.001$.

TABLE 6-6
DISTRIBUTION OF THE RESPONSES OF THE 1,704
MOBILIZABLES AND 1,658 ATTENTIVES TO ITEMS
#15 AND #16

[#15] On what sources do you rely for information about foreign affairs?***

Source	Percentage of the Mobilizables Attentives who indicated reliance		Statistical comparison of the responses of the two groups to each source		
			$\chi^2 =$	$df =$	P
a. Word of mouth*	26	25	1.05	1	ns*****
b. Newspapers*	90	88	3.90	1	ns
c. Magazines*	95	95	.00	1	ns
d. Radio or television*	70	73	2.74	1	ns
e. Columnists or commentators*	82	82	.24	1	ns
f. Organizational media**	12	6	37.51	1	.001
g. Books**	9	9	.49	1	ns
h. Governmental documents**	1	1	1.07	1	ns
i. Travel**	1	1	.00	1	ns
j. Other**	6	8	2.42	1	ns

[#16] More specifically, on which of these sources do you rely for information about foreign affairs?****

a. *Life**	15	19	8.31	1	ns
b. *Harper's**	27	28	.03	1	ns
c. *Foreign Affairs**	12	12	.57	1	ns
d. *New Republic**	47	40	17.19	1	.001
e. *US News & World Report**	10	14	15.09	1	.001
f. *Saturday Evening Post**	9	10	.44	1	ns
g. *Newsweek**	24	24	.01	1	ns
h. *The Reporter**	41	40	1.17	1	ns
i. *Time**	24	26	.57	1	ns
j. *London Economist**	3	4	.13	1	ns
k. *Atlantic**	18	18	.34	1	ns
l. *Reader's Digest**	8	13	24.15	1	.001
m. *Progressive***	6	6	.18	1	ns
n. Other**	11	7	18.18	1	.001

   * Provided alternative.
  ** Category developed out of written responses.
 *** One percent of both the Mobilizables and Attentives did not provide a codable answer to Item #15.
**** Nine percent of the Mobilizables and seven percent of the Attentives, presumably consisting mainly of nonmagazine readers, did not provide a codable answer to Item #16.
***** ns = not significant.

TABLE 6–7

DISTRIBUTION OF THE RESPONSES OF THE 1,704 MOBILIZABLES AND 1,658 ATTENTIVES TO ITEM #17 (in percentages)

[#17] How often do you read *The New York Times*?

	Every day	Sundays only	Once in a great while	Never	Uncodable and no answer	Statistical comparison of the responses of the two groups
Mobilizables	26	20	40	13	1	$\chi^2 = 4.29,$
Attentives	24	20	42	12	2	df $= 3$, ns*

* ns = not significant.

In twenty of the twenty-five media listed in Table 6–6, the differences between the extent of their contacts were not significant.[39]

Further analysis of three of the five exceptions to this finding suggests that only a slight modification of the original hypothesis that the Mobilizables and Attentives would not be differentiated in their contacts with the mass media is necessary to account for them.[40] In one of the three exceptions (the *New Republic*) the Mobilizables reported greater reliance than did the Attentives, and the opposite was true in the other two cases (the *Reader's*

[39] Both groups, however, differ considerably in their reading habits from members of the Attentive Public with conservative political attitudes. See Fred W. Grupp, Jr., "The Magazine Reading Habits of Political Activitists," *Public Opinion Quarterly*, Vol. 33 (1969), pp. 103–06.

[40] Two of the five do not negate the hypothesis because one is a residual category of "other" magazines and another amounts, in effect, to a first- rather than a second-hand form of contact (that is, it is entirely consistent that the Mobilizables should append comments indicating significantly greater reliance on "organizational" media than the Attentives, since the phenomena encompassed by this derived category consist of first-hand contacts virtually by definition).

Digest and *U.S. News & World Report*). The first of these exceptions involves the most outspoken and action-oriented of the
magazines listed, while the last two are much less explicitly
oriented toward solving problems. It could thus be argued that
magazines with signed, solution-oriented articles have greater
appeal for a mobilizable person than for his unmobilizable counterpart, and that the latter exceeds the former in preferring
unsigned synopses in magazines that aim to summarize rather than
recommend. In order to pursue this possibility, the respondents
who reported reliance on any of three of the more descriptive,
less explicitly policy-oriented "news" magazines (*Newsweek,
Time,* and *U.S. News & World Report*), but not on any of three
of the more analytic and openly judgmental "opinion" magazines
(*Atlantic, Harper's* and the *New Republic*), were clustered together for comparison with those who cited at least one of the
"opinion" and none of the "news" magazines. Thirty-four percent
of the Mobilizables and 30 percent of the Attentives were classified
in the opinion magazine category; the equivalent figures for the
news magazines were 15 and 21 percent.[41] Although the direction
of both of these differences is consistent with the argument derived
above, only the second of them proved to be significant.[42] This
outcome affirms the validity of the original hypothesis and at the
same time suggests a possible reformulation of it: Attentive and
Mobilizable citizens will not differ from each other with respect
to the types of mass media through which they establish second-
hand contact; but they are likely to differ in their use of particular
media within each type, with the Mobilizables preferring the more
provocative and less descriptive media.

Table 6–6 indicates that, whatever their differences, both
the Mobilizables and the Attentives prefer the printed media
(newspaper or magazines) to the electronic media (radio or tele-

---

[41] In addition, 23 percent of the Mobilizables and 22 percent of the
Attentives did not report reliance on either type of medium and 28 percent of the former and 27 percent of the latter reported both types.

[42] $\chi^2 = 16.32$, df $= 1$, P$<.001$.

vision). Such a preference is also shared by leadership groups,[43] but the reverse has been found to characterize the mass public.[44] Active citizens diverge from leadership groups in the extent of their reliance on the electronic media and in their lesser reliance on word-of-mouth. Attentives and Mobilizables may prefer reading to listening or viewing, but more than two-thirds of both groups did indicate reliance on the electronic media and this proportion is considerably greater than has been found in leadership samples.[45] Presumably this difference stems partly from the fact that leaders are not at home as much as members of the Attentive Public and thus have less time for and access to the television screen. Partly for the same reason, but perhaps also because a leader tends to be in direct contact with others leaders, two-fifths of the national leadership sample said that they relied on word-of-mouth for information about foreign affairs,[46] whereas only one-quarter of the Mobilizables and Attentives indicated such reliance. This is not to say, of course, that attentive citizens shy away from face-to-face communication. On the contrary, we have already indicated that discussing public affairs with family and friends is a defining characteristic of the Attentive Public. But, obviously, to discuss such matters with others is not to rely on them for information, and it is with respect to this aspect of face-to-face communication that the Mobilizables and Attentives differ from those in leadership positions.[47]

One other aspect of the data on the mass media is worthy of

[43] Cf. Rosenau, *National Leadership and Foreign Policy*, p. 190, and Kenneth P. Adler and Davis Bobrow, "Interest and Influence in Foreign Affairs," *Public Opinion Quarterly*, Vol. XX (Spring, 1956), pp. 93–95.

[44] For example, see Almond and Verba, *The Civic Culture*, Table 9, p. 94; Alfred O. Hero, *Mass Media and World Affairs* (Boston: World Peace Foundation, 1959), pp. 112–13; and Robert W. Hattery, *"Great Decisions –1962"—A Survey of Kit Buyers in Two Wisconsin Communities* (Milwaukee: University Extension Division, The University of Wisconsin-Milwaukee, n.d.), pp. 32–34.

[45] Less than one-fifth of both the samples listed in footnote 43 indicated reliance on electronic media.

[46] Rosenau, *National Leadership and Foreign Policy*, p. 190.

[47] Indeed, since virtually the entire sample reported frequent conversations

note. Unlike certain leadership groups, majorities of whom have been found to rely on the same medium, members of the Attentive and Mobilizable Publics apparently derive information from a variety of sources. The three magazines most frequently cited by both the Mobilizables and the Attentives were all distinguished by a "liberal" approach to public affairs,[48] but none of them was cited by a majority of the respondents or even by many more than those who indicated reliance on the more conservatively oriented news magazines. Even those that are like-minded in their general posture toward public issues—such as persons on the ADA mailing list—do not turn to a single source to the same extent that the responsibilities of leadership appear to make national leaders turn to *The New York Times*[49] or business leaders to *The Wall Street Journal.*[50] It seems that all a highly attentive or mobilizable person needs to sustain his orientations is a vast array of second-hand contacts with public affairs.

FACE-TO-FACE COMMUNICATION

Perhaps no form of contact with public affairs requires less effort than talking about them. No special equipment is needed, no money must be invested, and it is not necessary to plan ahead and set time aside. Talking about public affairs requires even

---

about public affairs with family and friends, the sizable discrepancy depicted in Table 6-6 between their reliance on word-of-mouth and on the mass media implies that the two forms of second-hand contact serve quite different purposes. In the ensuing analysis of the data on face-to-face communication, this implication becomes even more clear-cut.

[48] *The Reporter* is now defunct.

[49] *National Leadership and Foreign Policy*, p. 193. Nor can it be said that the proportion of the ADA sample who reported reading the *Times* (Table 6–7) would have been higher if more respondents had come from New York and its environs, as geographic remoteness did not prevent national leaders from developing access to the *Times*. Among the Far Westerners, Southerners, and Midwesterners, in the leadership sample, 46, 55, and 60 percent cited, respectively, this paper, whereas the equivalent regional figures for the entire ADA sample who said that they read it either daily or only on Sunday were 28, 29, and 25 percent.

[50] Bauer, Pool, and Dexter, *American Business and Public Policy*, p. 162.

less forethought than watching a television program or reading a newspaper.[51] All that is needed is another person who at least partially shares one's interest.

The ease with which second-hand contact can be established through face-to-face communication led to the prediction (Hypotheses IIa, IIb, and III) that the Mobilizables and Attentives would not differ in this regard. It was reasoned that the Attentives, being concerned about public affairs, would be as ready to discuss them with the persons who are part of their daily routines as would the Mobilizables. Yet face-to-face communication is a dynamic process and we experienced some hesitation in deriving this expectation. It is possible that the factors that propel Mobilizables into the arena of public affairs are strong enough to heighten the political content of their daily conversations. It may even be that talking about public affairs is a primary precipitant of, if not a prerequisite to, participating in them. Students of electoral behavior have found that a high frequency of political conversations often distinguishes the voter from the non-voter and those with firm convictions from those with neutral attitudes.[52] Similarly, studies of businessmen, farmers, housewives, physicians,[53] and participants in the "Great Decisions" programs of the Foreign Policy Associa-

---

[51] It should be noted, however, that there is considerable evidence indicating that the two forms of second-hand contact are not independent of each other. Indeed, one researcher has found that "Both the number of newspapers read and the time spent with newspapers have a stronger relationship with discussion frequency than traditional demographic predictors such as education, income, occupation level, age, or sex." See Charles K. Atkin, "Anticipated Communication and Mass Media Information-Seeking," *Public Opinion Quarterly*, Vol. XXXVI (1972), p. 191. For another analysis of the interaction between the face-to-face and mass media forms of communication, see Jerome Becker and Ivan Preston, "Media Usage and Political Activity," *Journalism Quarterly*, Vol. 46 (1969), pp. 129–34.

[52] Bernard R. Berelson, Paul F. Lazarsfeld, and William N. McPhee, *Voting: A Study of Opinion Formation in a Presidential Campaign* (Chicago: University of Chicago Press, 1954), p. 120.

[53] Bauer, Pool, and Dexter, *American Business and Public Policy*, Chap. 11.

tion[54] have found that personal contact is an immediate determinant of action. Another study found that face-to-face communication serves as a crucial step in the circulation of information and opinions contained in the mass media.[55] All of these findings, however, pertain mainly to contrasts between interested and uninterested persons, whereas we are concerned about the differences betwen two interested groups, one of which expresses itself through responsiveness to appeals for support. The personal and political worlds may overlap and interact in a much different way once a person enters the Attentive Public and develops a readiness to be mobilized.[56] In constructing the model, therefore, the findings of other inquiries were not considered as necessarily relevant and the initial expectation of no differences between the face-to-face communication of the Attentives and Mobilizables was allowed to stand.[57]

Two main items of the questionnaire were used to test this reasoning. One of these inquired into the frequency with which

[54] Alfred O. Hero, *Voluntary Associations in World Affairs Communication* (Boston: World Peace Foundation, 1960), p. 21.

[55] Elihu Katz and Paul F. Lazarsfeld, *Personal Influence: The Part Played by People in the Flow of Mass Communications* (Glencoe, Ill.: The Free Press, 1955), Chap. XII. See also Bradley Greenberg, "Person-to-Person Communication of News Events," *Journalism Quarterly*, Vol. 41 (1964), pp. 336–42.

[56] For example, as will be seen, we have uncovered some evidence that for neither the Mobilizables nor the Attentives are conversations with friends perceived to be a prime stimulus to the establishment of first-hand contacts with public affairs (see Table 11–1).

[57] This conclusion was reinforced by the one study which did compare two groups of active citizens, one comprised of 41 "Givers" of opinions on public affairs on a face-to-face basis and the other of 34 "Askers" of opinions. The study found that while the Givers and Askers both deviated along a number of dimensions from 127 "Inactives" who neither gave nor asked for opinions about public affairs through word of mouth, they were similar to each other in almost every respect, including the extent of their second-hand contacts. Cf. Verling C. Troldahl and Robert Van Dam, "Face-to-Face Communication about Major Topics in the News," *Public Opinion Quarterly*, Vol. XXIX (Winter, 1965–), pp. 626–34.

different issues entered into discussions with "friends and acquaintances" [#49] and the other into the frequency with which public affairs were discussed with various types of persons who are part of daily routine [#41].

Let us look first at the responses to the former. These are presented in Table 6–8. Here it is evident that the data bearing on the original hypothesis are somewhat inconclusive. On the one hand, the initial reasoning was upheld for most of the eleven issues. The Mobilizables engaged in significantly greater face-to-face communication than the Attentives only with respect to two issues, whereas on the other nine the responses of the two groups were not significantly differentiated. The two exceptions to the pattern are important, however. The Mobilizables reported greater face-to-face communication on the two issues, civil rights and nuclear testing, that had been the focus of their mobilized activity. This finding suggests that our initial model underestimated the feedback of current behavior. The finding cannot be attributed simply to the more extreme attitudes toward civil rights and nuclear testing held by the Mobilizables. They did attach more importance to these issues and felt more extremely about them than the Attentives, but this was also the case for several of the other issues.[58] If attitudinal strength were the only determinant of face-to-face communication, then the two groups would have also differed significantly on these other issues. The fact that civil rights and nuclear testing were the only two issues which the Mobilizables talked about more frequently would thus seem to indicate that being mobilized to establish first-hand contact with an issue heightens a person's involvement in it and this in turn increases his second-hand contacts with it. Having responded to the mobilizer's appeal, perhaps at least partly due to strong attitudes, the mobilizable person must then justify to himself the effort he has expended. He must, in the language of cognitive theory, bring his attitudes and behavior into balance. One way to do this is to develop even stronger attitudes. Another is to talk with friends and acquaintances about the issue and about his

[58] See Chapter 8.

activities with respect to it, thus enhancing the importance of the latter.

If this interpretation of the data is correct, face-to-face communication is not only an immediate determinant but also an immediate consequence of action and thus might even be said to serve as its reinforcement.[59] This conclusion is hardly startling, but it indicates an important underlying dynamic of mobilizability that we shall have occasion to note again.

That feedback from current behavior plays such a role is pinpointed even more sharply when we observe, in Table 6–8, that the two issues on which the two groups differed from each other were also the two issues on which they were seemingly most involved. More than a quarter of both groups reported talking about civil rights with a frequency at the highest point on the scale and nearly one-sixth recorded such a response for the nuclear testing issue. In contrast, no more than 3 percent of either group registered a response at the high point of the frequency scale for the other nine issues. Thus, the feedback from the Mobilizables' activity differentiates their behavior from that of the Attentives even with respect to issues that have intense appeal for both groups.

It must be stressed that the Mobilizables and Attentives did not differ in their face-to-face communication about the nine issues that had not been the focus of mobilized activity, suggesting that the feedback effect is not powerful enough to spill over into other issue-areas. Further support for our initial expectation (Hypothesis III) of no differences between the groups in this regard is provided by the finding that they did not differ in the proportion of each group that evidenced multi- and single-area attentiveness. For the Mobilizables these proportions were 56 and 44 respectively, while the comparable figures for the Attentives

---

[59] It will be recognized that this reinforcement concept underlay the reasoning that led the ADA to include a "confirmation card" in its mobilization effort. The card was included on the grounds that people are more likely to act if they can tell others they have done so, and this wisdom of the practitioner is brilliantly affirmed in Table 6–8.

TABLE 6–8
PERCENTAGE DISTRIBUTION AND STATISTICAL COMPARISON OF THE RESPONSES OF THE 1,704 MOBILIZABLES (Ms) AND 1,658 ATTENTIVES (As) TO ITEM #49

[#49] How often do your conversations with friends and acquaintances turn to each of the problems listed at the left? (in percentages)

		Never	Hardly ever	Some-times	Usually	Invariably	Codable answer not given	Total	χ^2	df	P
Agricultural surpluses	Ms	17	38	34	5	1	5	100	5.61	4	ns*
	As	15	37	37	5	1	5	100			
Balance of payments	Ms	30	42	20	2	0	6	100	14.19	4	ns
	As	25	44	22	3	1	5	100			
Berlin	Ms	4	20	59	11	1	5	100	3.64	4	ns
	As	4	22	58	10	2	4	100			
Civil rights	Ms	1	1	19	43	33	3	100	24.69	4	.001
	As	2	2	23	42	28	3	100			

Statistical comparison of the responses of the two groups on each issue

									χ^2	df	
The Congo	Ms	10	35	43	6	1	5	100	8.51	4	ns
	As	10	39	40	5	1	5	100			
Federal tax reduction	Ms	7	22	51	13	2	5	100	3.58	4	ns
	As	6	22	52	12	3	5	100			
Foreign aid	Ms	3	16	63	13	2	3	100	3.01	4	ns
	As	4	18	61	12	2	3	100			
Nuclear testing	Ms	1	6	40	33	16	4	100	43.09	4	.001
	As	2	12	41	27	14	4	100			
Tariff reduction	Ms	19	44	29	3	0	5	100	8.14	4	ns
	As	15	44	31	3	1	5	100			
Vietnam	Ms	4	25	53	13	2	3	100	9.09	4	ns
	As	6	24	52	11	3	4	100			
Western unity	Ms	12	32	41	9	1	5	100	1.12	4	ns
	As	11	34	40	9	1	5	100			

*ns = not significant.

were 51 and 49,[60] a difference which approached but did not exceed the significance level.[61]

The responses to Item #41, presented in Table 6–9, provide further insight into the dynamics of face-to-face communication. Once again, our initial reasoning is both supported and negated. Support is provided by the finding that the Mobilizables and Attentives did not differ in the extent to which they discussed public affairs with "professional associates," one main group of persons who are part of daily routine. Our expectations are countered by the finding that the Mobilizables reported more frequent discussions with "family" and "close friends" than did the Attentives. Moving beyond persons in the immediate daily environment, the evidence is also inconsistent: Table 6–9 reveals that the Mobilizables reported more discussions with "clergymen," "politicians," and "journalists" than did the Attentives, but the two groups did not differ with respect to "educators," "merchants," and "business executives."

An interpretation of these findings must at best be speculative, but the outlines of a meaningful pattern can be discerned in spite of the inconsistencies. If it is true, as students of voting behavior have found, that "people mostly discuss politics with other people like themselves," [62] then it is interesting to examine the character of the groups with whom the Mobilizables reported more frequent face-to-face communications. Besides family and friends, these groups—clergymen, politicians, and journalists—all consist of persons who deal with undifferentiated audiences and who are necessarily concerned about a broad range of issues. Unlike educators, businessmen, or professional associates, who maintain highly specific relationships with the students, customers, clients, and others in their daily environment, clergymen, poli-

---

[60] The distinction between multi- and single-area attentiveness was operationalized in terms of whether the respondents reported having conversations with friends and acquaintances "invariably" or "usually" on more or less than two of the eleven issues.

[61] $\chi^2 = 9.75$, df $= 1$, $.002 > P < .001$.

[62] Berelson, Lazarsfeld, and McPhee, *Voting*, p. 102.

ticians, and journalists share a responsibility for informing, uplifting, encouraging, and otherwise serving heterogeneous clients. Their relationships to their clients range across a variety of matters, many of them having to do with public affairs. They often espouse causes and champion interests, and they can thus be said to be among the main mobilizers of the society. Indeed, even when clergymen, politicians, and journalists are not directly issuing appeals for support of their own goals, their access to large heterogeneous audiences attracts other mobilizers to turn to them for assistance in launching or sustaining support-building efforts. In short, they are precisely the persons with whom citizens are likely to come into contact when they are mobilized into activity outside the home and friendship group.

Viewed in this way, perhaps the most noteworthy aspect of the data in Table 6–9 is the large degree to which the respondents, and especially the Mobilizables, reported face-to-face communication with politicians. Well over half of the Mobilizables and more than two-fifths of the Attentives said that they engaged in such communication at least "sometimes." These proportions are more than twice as large as the comparable figures for random samples of citizens in a variety of communities,[63] indicating the large extent to which the current behavior of active citizens is self-sustaining. The more they join organizations, attend meetings, write officials, and discuss public affairs, the more they establish contacts with political leaders, contacts which in turn reinforce the very practices that led to them in the first place. Citizenship between elections appears to be a seamless web of interdependent activities.

SUMMARY

Comparison of the Attentives and Mobilizables in terms of the extent and nature of their contacts with public affairs generally confirmed the expectation that the Mobilizables would estab-

---

[63] See Agger, Goldrich, Swanson, *The Rulers and the Ruled*, p. 268; and Matthews and Prothro, *Negroes and the New Southern Politics*, p. 40.

TABLE 6–9

PERCENTAGE DISTRIBUTION AND STATISTICAL COMPARISON OF THE RESPONSES OF THE 1,704 MOBILIZABLES (Ms) AND 1,658 ATTENTIVES (As) TO ITEM #41

[#41] How frequently do you discuss (in person, by phone, or by mail) public affairs with members of the groups listed at the left? (in percentages)

		Never	Hardly ever	Some-times	Often	Invariably	Codable answer not given	Total	Statistical comparison of the two groups on each type χ^2	df	P
Family	Ms	1	3	14	45	33	4	100	23.25	4	.001
	As	2	3	18	46	27	4	100			
Close friends	Ms	0	1	13	57	27	2	100	18.70	3	.001
	As	0	1	18	55	23	3	100			
Professional associates	Ms	7	8	26	36	12	11	100	5.03	4	ns*
	As	7	8	27	38	10	10	100			

								Total		df	p
Clergymen	Ms	32	20	21	13	5	9	100	27.48	4	.001
	As	39	20	20	10	3	8	100			
Educators	Ms	12	13	35	25	7	8	100	13.11	4	ns
	As	15	16	53	24	5	7	100			
Politicians	Ms	16	21	34	16	6	7	100	77.16	4	.001
	As	25	25	27	12	3	8	100			
Journalists	Ms	34	26	21	6	3	10	100	29.10	4	.001
	As	40	28	14	5	2	9	100			
Merchants	Ms	29	33	25	5	0	8	100	6.18	3	ns
	As	28	31	25	7	1	8	100			
Business executives	Ms	29	28	26	8	1	8	100	10.03	4	ns
	As	27	26	28	10	1	8	100			

*ns = not significant.

lish more first-hand contacts than the Attentives, but that the two groups would not differ in their second-hand contacts. Two forms of first-hand contact, the writing of letters to officials and activity in voluntary organizations, were examined, and in both cases the Mobilizables were found to be considerably more active than the Attentives. In the case of letter-writing, they reported a significantly greater volume of mail than the Attentives to seven different types of officials at all levels of government. Both groups wrote members of Congress more often than any other officials, but the Mobilizables also evidenced a noteworthy inclination to write the President. Indeed, the salience of the White House for the Mobilizables was so striking that it was interpreted as a major finding reflecting more than a concern with politics at the national level. The more frequent letter-writing of the Mobilizables was not confined to a single issue, as they reported writing more letters than the Attentives on six of eleven different issues.

The findings pertaining to organizational activities were equally clear. Although multiple membership characterized both groups, the Mobilizables were found to belong to significantly more organizations, to attend organizational meetings more frequently, and to participate in the deliberations of more organizations than the Attentives. Not surprisingly, letter-writing and organizational activity were positively correlated in both groups.

The two forms of second-hand contact that were examined were mass media consumption and face-to-face communication. In the case of contacts with the mass media, the expectation of no difference between the Mobilizables and Attentives was unmistakably affirmed. Comparisons of their contacts with ten general types of mass media and fifteen specific media yielded significant differences in only one of the former and four of the latter. Two of these differences, moreover, can be explained on methodological grounds, while the remainder were interpreted as suggesting the possibility that the Attentives prefer less provocative and more descriptive media than the Mobilizables. Both groups were found to be similar to leadership groups in their preference for printed media over the electronic forms of communication.

The data on face-to-face communication were not so clearly

arrayed. Although the Mobilizables and Attentives did not differ in the extent to which they reported discussing nine of eleven issues with friends and acquaintances, the Mobilizables exceeded the Attentives in their discussions of civil rights and nuclear testing. This finding was interpreted as reflecting feedback from current behavior, since these were the two issues on which they were known to have been mobilized. Contrary to expectations, the Mobilizables reported discussing public affairs in general with family, close friends, clergymen, politicians, and journalists more frequently than did the Attentives. The anticipated absence of differences between them in this respect held only for discussions with professional associates, educators, merchants, and business executives. The more extensive conversations with family and friends were judged to be further reflections of feedback, while the other differences were explained in terms of the identity of these groups. They were seen as mobilizers with whom citizens are likely to come into contact when they are mobilized into activity outside the home and friendship group.

CHAPTER 7

THE IMPACT OF PAST EXPERIENCE

Although the seeds of attentiveness and mobilizability may be sown in prior experiences in various social statuses, many of these background factors seem unlikely to give rise to one rather than the other form of citizenship. The initial version of our model thus did not anticipate that the backgrounds of the Attentives and Mobilizables would differ as much from each other as from the more apathetic Mass Public. Differences were expected only with respect to sex, religious affiliations, and certain occupational statuses, which were viewed as providing predispositions and resources that are more necessary to the maintenance of mobilizability than to the sustenance of attentiveness.[1] In addition, it

[1] In some respects the impact of occupation can be viewed as the result of present responsibility rather than as the product of past experience.

was reasoned that, except in a few extreme cases, the differences between the Mobilizables and Attentives in their readiness to establish first-hand contact with public affairs would persist even when the effects of the eleven background variables were taken into account. These expectations were embodied in four main hypotheses (IV–VII), and the ensuing analysis aims to put them to empirical test. An additional purpose is to identify, as we proceed through an examination of each background variable, the points at which the Attentives and Mobilizables, whatever the differences between them, deviate from the general population.

For the purposes of assessing how the background variables may underlie citizenship between elections, each one is conceived to consist of resources and predispositions that facilitate and interfere with a person's readiness to respond to mobilizers or otherwise establish first- or second-hand contact with public affairs. At any moment in time both the facilitating and interfering resources and predispositions are operative. The extent to which people relate themselves to public affairs is determined by whichever type of resources and predispositions operates most strongly.

Consider, for example, the resources and predispositions inherent in the role of woman. Its facilitating resources include the time many women have available for political activity and its facilitating predispositions include the recent stress on greater equality with men. On the other hand, the energy required for home-keeping and child-rearing and the traditional societal norm that a woman's place is in the home are among its interfering resources and predispositions. Which set of resources and predispositions will prevail depends on which aspects of the role are most salient and on what other roles the person occupies. The background of a highly educated woman who earns a large income as a lawyer, or who favors the values of the women's liberation movement, may contain experiences and talents that enable her to surmount the obstacles interposed by her sex role.

However, the interaction between the latter and the practices of citizenship is separately analyzed in Chapter 10.

In short, the extent to which an individual becomes involved in citizenship activities at any point in time will be partly the result of the combined potencies of the variables comprising his or her social background. As previously noted, all the available evidence indicates that the likelihood of such involvement is maximized when considerable education combines with a substantial income and with the other dimensions of high socio-economic status. It remains to be seen, however, whether this or any other combination of variables differentiates Mobilizables from Attentives. We have hypothesized that for the most part they do not, but the facilitating and interfering resources and predispositions encompassed by the background variables may be so numerous that our original estimates may require revision.[2]

By the resources inherent in a variable is meant the capacities which it does or does not provide for greater or lesser citizenship activity. Young people have more physical energy with which to be politically active than old people; educated citizens have more intellectual resources upon which to draw for effective political action than their uneducated counterparts; wealthy persons have more time available for participation in public affairs than those who are poor. In general, in other words, youth, education, and wealth are facilitating resources, while old age, illiteracy, and poverty are interfering resources. The resources supplied by a variable depend, of course, on the kind of first- or second-hand contacts involved. The young have more stamina than the old with which to participate in organizational activities, but this difference is much less relevant to letter-writing activities. The educated are more able to write letters than the uneducated, but the two are not likely to differ in their capacities to attend a rally or march in a picket line.

Beyond the objective capacities they provide, however, whether or not an individual utilizes the resources at his disposal

---

[2] The idea of assessing the resource and predispositional dimensions in terms of facilitating and interfering factors parallels the treatment of similar phenomena in Carl I. Hovland and Irving Janis, eds., *Personality and Persuasibility* (New Haven: Yale University Press, 1959), Chap. 12.

depends on the subjective inclinations they foster. It is at the point where resources are translated into action that predispositions become relevant. Young people have more physical energy than old people, but the latter are likely to have a stronger sense of the responsibilities of citizenship. The educated are more articulate than the uneducated and they are thus also more likely to feel competent to undertake political action. The wealthy have more time than the poor and have a greater stake in the political system; they are thus more likely to be active with respect to it. As in the case of resources, the predispositions encompassed by a variable can vary from one form of activity to another. Trade union members, for example, are probably more inclined to engage in organizational activity than artists, but the latter may be more disposed to write letters to officials than the former.

The background variables differ considerably in the resources and predispositions they contribute to a person's behavior. Some of them are predominantly predispositional, while others are a mix of resource and predispositional elements. Examples of the former type are race, region, religion, and party affiliations. Each of these can contribute to a person's orientation toward public affairs, but they are not particularly relevant to the resources at his disposal. The resources—physical capability, intellectual skill, time, money, and/or influence—derive mainly from variables such as age, sex, marital status, occupation, income, and/or education, which can also contribute importantly to a citizen's predispositions toward public affairs.

The balance between the resources and predispositions contributed by a variable needs to be stressed because it is central to our estimate of whether the variable would differentiate the Attentives and Mobilizables. We reasoned that the interfering resources and predispositions which accompany the female sex role, the facilitating predispositions associated with certain religious groups, and the differential resources and predispositions inherent in certain occupations were sufficient to render the composition of the two groups different on these dimensions (Hypothesis V). With respect to the other eight background variables, however, there seemed to be no reason why the resources and predispositions of active citizens should be systematically related to whether they became members of the Mobilizable Public (Hypothesis IV). To be sure, a minimum set of facilitating resouces and predispositions are necessary to start a person on the road to active citizenship and, as previously indicated, all the available research indicates that those with high socio-economic statuses are more likely than those with low status to possess this minimum. Yet, all that follows from this conclusion is that the social profiles of the Mobilizables and Attentives should deviate in a similar way from the general population. It does not warrant the expectation that high status will underlie mobilizability. Indeed, it does not even support the expectation that high status will be associated with the extent to which attentive or mobilizable citizens write letters to officials or are active in organizations. Given appropriate circumstances, attentive and mobilizable women will put aside their housework, those who are uneducated will manage a letter, those who are poor will find a dollar to contribute, and those who are elderly will ignore their aches and pains.

Our estimates of the balance between resources and predispositions also served as the basis for predicting the outcomes of comparisons of the first-hand contacts established by the various subgroups of Mobilizables and Attentives within each background category. While the composition of the two groups was not expected to differ for eight of the eleven background variables, it did seem possible that many of these variables might underlie behavioral differences between them. That is, we anticipated (Hypotheses VI and VII) that certain mobilizable subgroups would lack the wherewithal to establish more of certain types of first-hand contacts than their counterparts among the Attentives. The very old among the Mobilizables, for example, seemed less likely to respond to an appeal to be organizationally active than to appeals to write letters.

In sum, the ensuing analysis is carried out in three steps. First, the existing literature on each variable is summarized by way of ascertaining how both the Attentives and Mobilizables may be expected to differ from the rest of the citizenry. Second, the two groups are compared to determine whether the variable introduces differentiation into their ranks. Third, the letter-writing and organizational activities of the two groups are analyzed in order to see whether the variable introduces differentiation within and between their subgroups.

AGE

"Born in this century." Thus did John F. Kennedy, in describing the new generation to whom leadership passed with his inauguration, give vigorous expression to the widely shared idea that age matters in politics. Conceptions of the consequences of age, however, are not entirely consistent. The young are said to be more idealistic and forward-looking, the old more skeptical and conservative. On the other hand, the former are alleged to be too busy pursuing the fruits of life to implement their idealism, while the latter are viewed as possessing more skills and time with which to relate themselves to public affairs and express their skepticism. There are thus two contradictory images in continuous competition: the image of the youthful protester who can, but rarely does, vigorously carry his message to anyone who will listen; pitted against the image held by many Congressmen of little, grey-haired widows who, having nothing better to do, write a never-ending stream of letters to officials.[3]

These conflicting popular images can be seen as confirming our conception of the age variable as a mix of resource and predispositional factors. Social science findings also reveal that where one is in the life cycle tends to influence both the quality and quantity of one's citizenship activity. Consistent with the inconsistency of the popular images, younger persons have been found to be both more forward-looking in their outlooks[4] and less con-

---

[3] Cf. Daniel M. Berman, *In Congress Assembled: The Legislative Process in the National Government* (New York: The Macmillan Company, 1964), p. 56.

[4] See, for example, Kenneth J. Gergen and Kurt W. Back, "Aging, Time Perspective, and Preferred Solutions to International Conflicts," *Journal of Conflict Resolution*, Vol. IX (June 1965), pp. 177–86.

sistent in their level of political activity[5] than older persons. The latter finding is especially clear-cut in the case of electoral behavior, where "there is a steady and at times spectacular increase of vote participation as a function of age," [6] but it is also discernible in the data on citizenship activities between elections. Contacts with public affairs tend to peak among the middle-aged and then to decline somewhat among the elderly; but both groups have been found to exceed young adults in the extent of their second-hand contacts, and even the decreased first-hand contacts of the elderly rarely dip below those of the younger group.[7] Consumption of news in the mass media, for example, "reaches a peak somewhere between the ages of thirty and fifty, and thereafter drops off slightly," [8] whereas membership and participation in organizations occur at roughly the same rate for the younger and the older groups and at a higher rate for those in their middle years.[9]

There is a simple explanation for the variations in degree of activity among different age groups if we hypothesize that facilitating predispositions increase with age. As people grow older, they acquire a greater sense of involvement and responsibility for community affairs and they become increasingly disposed to

[5] Cf. Julian L. Woodward and Elmo Roper, "Political Activity of American Citizens," p. 877; and John Crittenden, "Aging and Political Participation," *Western Political Quarterly*, Vol. 16 (June 1963), pp. 323–31.

[6] Campbell, et al., *The American Voter*, p. 494.

[7] One exception here is that of contacts established through peace groups, where one study found that "the older the individual, the less likely [he is] to be in the peace organization." See William Erbe, "Interest in a Peace Organization," *Journal of Conflict Resolution*, Vol. X (March 1966), p. 78.

[8] Wilbur Schramm and David M. White, "Age, Education, and Economic Status as Factors in Newspaper Reading: Conclusions," in Wilbur Schramm (ed.), *The Process and Effects of Mass Communication* (Urbana: University of Illinois Press, 1954), p. 71.

[9] Cf. Lane, *Political Life*, p. 78; John C. Scott, Jr., "Membership and Participation in Voluntary Associations," p. 324; and James Curtis, "Voluntary Association Joining: A Cross-National Comparative Note," *American Sociological Review*, Vol. 36 (October 1971), p. 876.

establish contact with public affairs.[10] However, at a certain point —perhaps as retirement approaches—age introduces interfering resources that offset some of the facilitating predispositions. The "sense of citizen duty" has been found to remain high among the elderly,[11] but their "sense of political efficacy" declines,[12] presumably due to an increase in interfering resources, and as a result the tendency to establish contact with public affairs is "highest in the prime of life, and generally declines among the aged." [13] This decline is less discernible in the statistics on electoral behavior because the biennial or quadriennial act of entering a voting booth is a simple one and, except for the infirm, is more dependent on a person's sense of civic duty than on the resources he can command.[14] Continuous or regular contact, however, requires not only a sense of responsibility but considerable energy, and this resource tends to become increasingly scarce with advancing years, making the aforementioned patterns for citizenship between elections more pronounced.

Although the data on the ADA sample are largely consistent with the foregoing, they contain a few surprises. Since the Mobilizables and Attentives are all active citizens, it follows from the preceding analysis that both groups should prove to be considerably older than the Mass Public. In this respect the responses to the age item [#29] conform to expectations. As can be seen in Table 7–1, which compares the age structure of the Mobilizables and Attentives with that of two samples of the general population, both of the former consisted of fewer people under forty-five years

---

10 Cf. Lane, *Political Life*, p. 219.

11 Angus Campbell, Gerald Gurin, and Warren Miller, *The Voter Decides* (Evanston: Row, Peterson and Company, 1954), p. 197.

12 *Ibid.*, p. 191. See also Thomas J. Agnello, Jr., "Aging and the Sense of Political Powerlessness," *Public Opinion Quarterly*, Vol. XXXVII (Summer 1973), pp. 251–59.

13 Dahl, *Who Governs*, p. 273.

14 But some evidence of such a decline has been discerned in the behavior of voters. See Ben Arneson and William Eells, "Voting Behavior in 1948 as Compared with 1924 in a Typical Ohio Community," *American Political Science Review*, Vol. 44 (June 1959), pp. 432—34.

of age and more over fifty-five than either of the latter. What is surprising about the distribution of their ages, however, is the large proportion found in the oldest bracket. There are no precedents in previous research for nearly two-fifths of the respondents being past middle age or—breaking down the data in the fourth row of Table 7–1—for more than one-fifth of both the Mobilizables and Attentives reporting themselves as having passed the retirement age of sixty-five. All in all, including 3 percent of both groups who reported themselves as over eighty, the Mobilizables averaged fifty years of age and the Attentives forty-nine years.[15]

Is this finding indicative of the age structure of most segments

---

TABLE 7–1

AGE DISTRIBUTION OF THE MOBILIZABLES, THE ATTENTIVES, AND TWO RANDOM SAMPLES OF THE GENERAL POPULATION (in percentages)

Age Groups*	The Mobilizables	The Attentives	Michigan SRC Sample of the 1956 Presidential Election**	McClosky's National General Population Sample (January, 1958)***
Under 35	17	17	30	28
35–44	20	21	26	24
45–54	19	18	19	20
55 +	39	38	25	28
Age unknown	5	0	—	—
Total	100	100	100	100
(n =)	(1,704)	(1,658)	(1,762)	(1,484)

* For the Mobilizables and Attentives, add one year to the listed age brackets (i.e., under 36, 36–45, 46–55, 56 +).

** As reproduced in Herbert McClosky, "Consensus and Ideology in American Politics," *American Political Science Review*, Vol. LVIII (June, 1964), p. 381.

*** *Ibid.*

---

[15] Furthermore, these means portray the respondents as younger than they actually were. Those who described themselves as occupationally retired, but who did not answer the item on age, were coded as sixty-six years old and no doubt the age of most of the respondents so classified exceeded this figure.

of the Attentive Public or is it unique to the ADA? In the absence of comparable data for other groups, such a question is not easily answered. It is true that the biggest influx into ADA occurred when it was established after World War II and that it was an influx sustained by adults who matured in the 1930's and who wished to perpetuate the values associated with Roosevelt's New Deal. These values were less appealing to those who matured in the 1950s, and therefore the disproportionately large number of older ADA members in the 1960's may reflect an imbalance between the organization's appeal to pre- and post-war generations.[16] It is equally plausible, however, to argue that the data merely add support for, or at least illustrate, the earlier findings that depict political activity as generally increasing with age. Previous studies have all involved samples of the general population, but the ADA respondents are a sample of the Attentive Public and thus what emerges is an age structure that has been, so to speak, purified of the passive and inactive elements present in the other samples. If this is the case, the ADA is perhaps typical rather than unrepresentative of other groups of attentive citizens. Some groups, of course, such as those composed of students, are linked to a particular stage of the life cycle and would not be composed disproportionately of those at the older end of the age scale, but other groups for which age is not a structural characteristic may well resemble the ADA in this respect. There would seem to be some validity to the impression of Congressmen that an inordinate amount of their mail comes from older persons who have time to devote to such pursuits.

Notwithstanding the disproportionate number of older people, the data indicate that citizenship activities tend to peak in the middle years. Figure 7–1 depicts the mean scores on the

[16] For an incisive analysis indicating that the age variable can reflect generational differences as well as stages in the life cycle, see Neal E. Cutler, "Generational Succession as a Source of Foreign Policy Attitudes: A Cohort Analysis of American Opinion, 1946–1966," *Journal of Peace Research*, 1 (1970), pp. 33–48; and Eugene S. Vyeki and Richard W. Dodge, "Generational Relations in Political Attitudes and Involvement," *Sociology and Social Research*, Vol. 28 (January 1964), pp. 155–65.

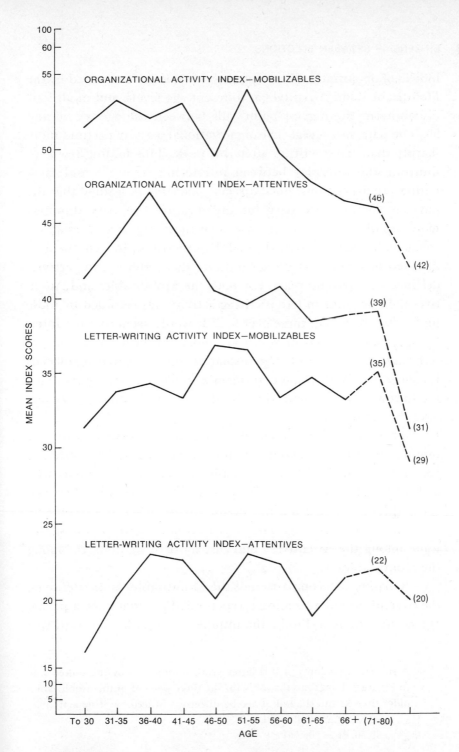

Figure 7–1

Distribution by Age Groupings of the Mean Scores Recorded by the Mobilizables and Attentives on the Indices of Organizational and Letter-Writing Activity

indices of organizational and letter-writing activity recorded by the Mobilizables and Attentives at different age levels, and in all four distributions the highest point falls between the ages of 36 and 55. The data also reveal that organizational activity declines more sharply than letter-writing after this peak. This finding seems to illustrate the interplay between interfering resources and facilitating predispositions, since it seems plausible to assume that the physical energies necessary for organizational activity diminish more rapidly with advancing age than those required to establish contact with public affairs through letter-writing. Indeed, the data depicted in Figure 7–1 do not indicate that letter-writing activity declines with passing years. For both the Mobilizables and Attentives the low point in letter-writing activity was recorded by those under 30 rather than those over 65.[17] It would seem that the interfering predispositions of youth are more inhibiting than the interfering resources of old age insofar as the act of writing officials is concerned. With respect to organizational activity, in contrast, the lowest point for both the Mobilizables and Attentives occurs after the age of sixty.

These inferences from the data are consistent with our original expectations about the differential impact of interfering resources on different forms of first-hand contact (Hypothesis VII) and they are also borne out statistically. The relationship between age and letter-writing was not significant in either group, but the relationship between age and organizational activity was significant among the Attentives[18] and just short of significance among the Mobilizables.[19]

Turning to a comparison of the Mobilizables and Attentives, the data affirm our reasoning (Hypothesis IVa) that once a person enters the Attentive Public the number of years he has lived will

---

[17] A special breakdown of this latter group—indicated by the dotted line in Figure 7–1—reveals that only for the three percent of the Mobilizables older than 81 can the toll of age be discerned in letter-writing activity.

[18] $\chi^2 = 62.85$, df $= 20$, P$<.001$.

[19] $\chi^2 = 39.36$, df $= 20$, $.001 < P<.01$.

be irrelevant to whether or not he is responsive to the appeals of a mobilizer. As can be seen in Table 7–1, the Mobilizables and Attentives did not differ significantly in their distribution along the age scale. Likewise, the data uphold our expectation (Hypothesis VI) that the stronger tendency of the Mobilizables as compared to the Attentives to establish first-hand contacts would not be affected by age. We had wondered whether the resources available to the elderly for organizational activity might make the elderly among the Attentives and Mobilizables more nearly alike insofar as their organizational activities were concerned, but even this attribution of limited strength to the age variable proved unwarranted. Figure 7–1 reveals that on both the letter-writing and organizational activity indices the scores recorded by the Mobilizables in every age group, including the elderly, proved to be significantly higher than those registered by their counterparts among the Attentives.[20] Not even the interfering resources associated with advancing age, in short, offset the characteristics that distinguish Mobilizables from Attentives.

SEX

Few findings of social science are as consistent and pervasive as those pertaining to sex differences. The attitudes and behavior of men and women have been found to differ in a wide variety of ways and in all kinds of circumstances. Traceable largely to expectations that are built into the culturally defined male and female roles, starting early in childhood and continuing through

[20] For the comparison of the organizational activities of the Mobilizables and Attentives under 35, $\chi^2 = 25.14$, df $= 5$, P$<.001$; for those between 36 and 50, $\chi^2 = 29.32$, df $= 5$, P$<.001$; for those between 51 and 65, $\chi^2 = 47.56$, df $= 5$, P$<.001$; and for those over 65, $\chi^2 = 20.39$, df $= 5$, P$<.001$. For the comparison of the letter-writing activities of those in the two groups under 35, $\chi^2 = 112.44$, df $= 4$, P$<.001$; for those between 36 and 50, $\chi^2 = 155.58$, df $= 4$, P$<.001$; for those between 51 and 65, $\chi^2 = 149.67$, df $= 4$, P$<.001$; for those over 65, $\chi^2 = 99.41$, df $= 4$, P$<.001$.

all stages of the life cycle, differences between men and women are found in their interests, talents, pleasures, aspirations, and self-concepts.[21] Thus how a person assesses and relates to social situations depends in large part on his or her particular adaptation to the sex-role standards defined by society.

Political situations are no exception in this regard and there is ample evidence showing that there are substantial differences in the political activities and attitudes of men and women. In the United States, as in most societies, the male role provides facilitating predispositions toward politics, while the female role tends to be comprised of interfering predispositions.[22] Notwithstanding some evidence of change (noted below) which may be hastened if the values of the women's liberation movement become increasingly pervasive, public affairs are still widely regarded as the bailiwick of men. They are expected, both by themselves and by women, to be interested in and knowledgeable about such matters.[23] Conversely, women are generally expected to be submissive and to leave public affairs to men.[24] Indeed, the interfering predispositions of their roles are such that many still view politically active women as unfeminine. Sex typing of this sort is even evident in the writings of such an astute political analyst as V. O. Key, who, noting

[21] For analyses of these differences, their origins, and their consequences, see Eleanor E. Maccoby, ed., *The Development of Sex Differences* (Stanford: Stanford University Press, 1966); and Jerome Kagan, "Acquisition and Significance of Sex Typing and Sex Role Identity," in Martin L. Hoffman and Lois Wladis Hoffman, eds., *Review of Child Development Research* (New York: Russell Sage Foundation, 1964, Vol. 1), pp. 137–67.

[22] One exception here is the finding that "women are as likely to be active in organizations as men" (Verba and Nye, *Participation in America*, p. 181), which suggests that not all the predispositions inherent in the female role are of an interfering kind.

[23] See, for example, Myron Brenton, *The American Male: A Penetrating Look at the Masculinity Crisis* (New York: Coward-McCann, 1966), and Charles W. Ferguson, *The Male Attitude: What Makes American Men Think and Act as They Do?* (Boston: Little, Brown & Co., 1966).

[24] Cf. Martin Gruberg, *Women in American Politics: An Assessment and Sourcebook* (Oshkosh, Wis.: Academia Press, 1968), pp. 26–38.

that men are more active than women, added that nevertheless "there can be no denying that a junior-league type with the political fever is a truly awesome spectacle." [25] In addition to interfering predispositions, the female role also seems to contribute interfering resources, at least for married women with young children, who often find it hard to give much time to political activities away from home.[26]

That sex-role expectations and requirements exert a powerful influence on behavior seems clearly evident in the available data. Boys have been found to be more politically oriented and knowledgeable than girls;[27] and among adults it has been found that men are more likely to vote,[28] to avoid the "no opinion" category in surveys,[29] to join voluntary associations,[30] to discuss politics,[31] to watch news and public affairs programs on television,[32] to be informed about world affairs,[33] to write letters to officials,[34] and to report engaging in more political activity than women.[35] The differences are just as impressive at the attitude level: women

[25] *Public Opinion and American Democracy*, p. 331.

[26] In a recent survey involving about 2,000 questionnaires returned by women, for example, "more than half said that they should like to be involved in politics, but cited lack of time, family obligations, and a general suspicion of politics as their stumbling block" (*Ladies Home Journal*, August 1972, p. 6).

[27] Greenstein, *Children and Politics*, Chap. 6.

[28] Campbell, et al., *The American Voter*, p. 484.

[29] Greenstein, *Children and Politics*, p. 109.

[30] Scott, "Membership and Participation in Voluntary Associations," p. 324; Lane, *Political Life*, p. 78; and Almond and Verba, *The Civic Culture*, p. 393.

[31] Almond and Verba, *The Civic Culture*, p. 390.

[32] Steiner, *The People Look at Television*, p. 173.

[33] See, for example, Don D. Smith, " 'Dark Areas of Ignorance' Revisited: Current Knowledge About Asian Affairs," *Social Science Quarterly*, Vol. 51 (December 1970), pp. 671–72; and Stanley J. Morse and Stanton Peele, "A Study of Participants in an Anti-Vietnam War Demonstration," *Journal of Social Issues*, Vol. 27 (1971), p. 130.

[34] Sussmann, *Dear FDR—A Study of Political Letter-Writing*, p. 144.

[35] Woodward and Roper, "Political Activity of American Citizens," p. 877.

have generally been found to feel less involved in public affairs,[36] to have a lower level of political concept formation[37] and to express less subjective political competence[38] than men. In addition, differences in male and female attitudes toward the substantive issues of public affairs have been consistently uncovered.[39]

There are some contradictions among these general findings, however. Even before the advent of the women's liberation movement, some of the differences between men and women began to narrow in the United States. Most notably, differences in voting turnout have disappeared among the college-educated[40] and those pertaining to a sense of involvement in public affairs were also found to be "fairly well obliterated or even reversed among college-educated men and women." [41] Similarly, although men write more political letters and belong to more organizations than women, the differences in letter-writing are steadily diminishing[42] and women have been found to be more active than men once they join an organization.[43] There is even some evidence that the two sexes join voluntary associations in equal numbers[44] and that, with the exception of students, women are more likely than men to join in demonstrations (a finding that can "perhaps be accounted for by female nonstudents having more free time than

[36] Campbell, et al., *The American Voter*, pp. 489–90.

[37] *Ibid.*, pp. 491–2.

[38] *Ibid.*, 490–1; Almond and Verba, *The Civic Culture,* p. 212.

[39] For example, see Sidney Verba and Richard A. Brody, "Participation, Policy Preferences, and the War in Vietnam," *Public Opinion Quarterly*, Vol. XXXIV (1970), p. 329.

[40] Campbell, et al., *The American Voter*, pp. 486–7; and V. O. Key, *Public Opinion and American Democracy,* p. 331.

[41] Campbell, et al., *The American Voter*, p. 489.

[42] Sussmann, *Dear FDR—A Study of Political Letter-Writing,* p. 144.

[43] Almond and Verba, *The Civic Culture*, pp. 315–16; and Scott, "Membership and Participation in Voluntary Associations," p. 320. The former suggest that this discrepancy between membership and activity may be due to "the smaller size of the organizations to which women belong."

[44] Cf. Murray Hausknecht, *The Joiners: A Sociological Description of Voluntary Association Membership in the United States* (New York: The Bedminster Press, 1962), pp. 31, 37, 72, and 84.

males in this category").[45] It would seem, in other words, that at least some of the interfering predispositions built into the female sex role are breaking down as women acquire more education and equality in an increasingly industrialized society.[46]

Both the general pattern of sex differences in political activity and the trend toward the narrowing of these differences are discernible in a comparison of the Attentives and Mobilizables (Table 7–2). Men predominated in both groups and the disproportion is particularly striking if the groups are compared to samples of the electorate and the population as a whole.[47] Although there is some reason to question the validity of the proportions of men and women in both groups,[48] it seems warranted to attribute at least some of the differences displayed in Table 7–2 to the operation of societal values with respect to sex-role standards. When the focus shifts to the first-hand contacts established by the men and women in each group, however, the differences between them are erased and, in one case, even reversed. Contrary to expectations (Hypothesis VII), the data clearly reveal that, once women enter the Attentive Public, the interfering predispositions of their female role tend to lose their relevance. The letter-writing scores of the two sexes did not differ significantly among either the

---

[45] Morse and Peele, "A Study of Participants in an Anti-Vietnam War Demonstration," p. 119.

[46] Such a conclusion seems particularly valid when the political behavior of American women is compared with that of women in somewhat less industrialized societies. Cf. Almond and Verba, *The Civic Culture*, p. 390ff.

[47] The differences between the Attentives and Mobilizables in Tables 7–2, however, cannot be interpreted as a negation of our expectation (Hypothesis Va) that men would also be more predominant among the Mobilizables than the Attentives. Because of the aforementioned (pp. 184–86) effort to achieve comparable proportions of men and women in both groups, Hypothesis Va could not be tested.

[48] It seems conceivable, if not probable, that sex role typing is such that when a married couple joins an organization like the ADA, it is the husband who is formally listed as the member. Consequently, an exaggerated number of men may have received the original ADA mailings and the subsequent questionnaires.

TABLE 7–2

SEX DISTRIBUTION OF THE MOBILIZABLES, THE ATTENTIVES, THE ELECTORATE, AND THE GENERAL POPULATION (in percentages)

	The Mobilizables	The Attentives	Michigan SRC Sample of the 1956 Presidential Election*	1960 Census*
Men	58	66	45	48
Women	40	32	55	52
Sex unknown	2	2	—	—
Total	100	100	100	100
(n =)	(1,704)	(1,658)	(1,762)	

* As reproduced in Herbert McClosky, "Consensus and Ideology in American Politics," *American Political Science Review,* Vol. LVIII (June, 1964), p. 381.

Attentives or the Mobilizables. Mobilizable men and women did not differ in their scores on the index of organizational activity, but among the Attentives, women registered significantly higher scores on this index than men.[49] Fifty-four percent of the Attentive women and 41 percent of the Attentive men compiled scores that fell in the highest three intervals of the organizational activity scale.

Two explanations of this unanticipated finding seem plausible. One attributes it to a facilitating predisposition of the female role; namely, that women tend to see themselves as more socially responsive than men. This would also explain the finding of other studies that women are more active than men once they join an organization.[50] The second explanation attributes the lesser organ-

[49] $\chi^2 = 33.84$; df $= 5$, P$<$.001.

[50] Further support for the social responsiveness argument is provided by Hausknecht (*The Joiners,* p. 73), who found that women outnumber men in religious, civic, and service organizations. The author interprets this finding in terms of sex role identity on the ground that "most of the organizations comprising [these categories] have functions which might be termed as 'succorance,' 'supportive,' or, more invidiously, 'do-goodism'—all implying behavior more congruent with the orientations traditionally associated with the roles of wife and mother."

izational activity of the Attentive men to an interfering resource in the male role; namely, that occupational requirements leave men less time than women to engage in this form of attentiveness. These explanations are neither mutually exclusive nor inconsistent with the absence of differences among the Mobilizables. Mobilizable men are virtually by definition as socially responsive as women, and they thus write as many letters to officials and they overcome occupational hurdles to engage in as much organizational activity. What is inconsistent with this interpretation is that Attentive women did not report writing more letters than Attentive men, suggesting the need for further specification of how sex roles are related to different types of political activity.

Within each sex, the sizeable differences in the extent to which Attentives and Mobilizables engage in first-hand forms of contact remain. The Mobilizable women reported significantly more letter-writing and organizational activities than did the Attentive women,[51] and the same was true for the comparison of the two groups of men.[52] Contrary to expectations (Hypothesis VI), apparently neither the resources nor predispositions associated with either sex role make a difference once a person acquires the propensity to be responsive to the appeals of a mobilizer.

An analysis of the proportion of men and women in the Attentive and Mobilizable Publics at various ages provides additional insights into the ways in which sex-role factors foster and hinder citizenship between elections. The data depict sharply different age patterns for the two sexes. As can be seen in Table 7–3, men tend to leave the Attentive and Mobilizable Publics as they age, while women tend to enter them.[53] In both groups there were fewer men in each of the two older age groups than in any

[51] For the difference in their scores on the letter-writing index, $\chi^2 = 216.65$, df $= 5$, P<.001; for the difference in organizational activity, $\chi^2 = 28.96$, df $= 5$, P<.001.

[52] For the letter-writing differences between Mobilizable and Attentive men, $\chi^2 = 292.38$, df $= 5$, P<.001; for the difference in their scores on the organizational activity index, $\chi^2 = 74.64$, df $= 5$, P<.001.

[53] For the difference in the age distributions of the Mobilizable men and women, $\chi^2 = 95.29$, df $= 4$, P<.001; for the same comparison among the Attentives, $\chi^2 = 29.03$, df $= 4$, P<.001.

TABLE 7–3
AGE AND SEX DISTRIBUTION OF THE
MOBILIZABLES AND ATTENTIVES (in percentages)

Age Groups	Mobilizables		Attentives	
	Men	Women	Men	Women
To 35	23	8	18	15
36–45	23	17	23	19
46–55	18	21	21	15
56–65	15	19	16	21
Over 65	17	31	17	26
Age unknown	4	4	5	4
Total	100	100	100	100
(n =)	(986)	(690)	(1,087)	(535)

of the three younger age groups, whereas almost the opposite pattern prevailed for the women.[54]

These findings again suggest that occupational factors in the male role and predispositional and resource aspects of the female role lead to differences in behavior. In the case of the men, the thinning of their ranks occurs at those points in the life cycle when presumably their occupational responsibilities are greatest. The relevance of these responsibilities is further demonstrated by the fact that once men pass the retirement age of 65, their numbers in the Attentive and Mobilizable Publics show a slight upturn even though their life expectancy at this point declines markedly. As for the women, their numbers increase at those ages where the responsibilities of keeping a home and raising children taper off.[55] The data for the women in Table 7–3 can be interpreted in terms of the diminution of an interfering predisposition as well as of an

[54] Age distributions virtually identical to these for organizational activity on the part of men and women in two nationwide samples of the general population can be found in Hausknecht, *The Joiners*, pp. 41–42.

[55] For findings indicating that child-rearing responsibilities even interfere with casting a ballot on election day, see Campbell, et al., *The American Voter*, pp. 486–88.

interfering resource. That is, the distribution of the data can also be viewed as indicating that women fulfill the expectations of being a woman in their earlier years and are thus less subject to such constraints in their later years. For a variety of reasons, in short, it seems clear that as women move through the life cycle, their lives become increasingly compatible with political activity.

Another indication that women tend to be freed of certain sex-role constraints when they become attentive to public affairs is to be found in the data on face-to-face communication. Although our initial model did not require analysis of these data, the foregoing interpretation led us to hypothesize that, while occupational factors might limit the kinds of persons with whom women come into contact, those in the Attentive and Mobilizable Publics would be free of the feminine sex-role inhibition against discussing public affairs outside the circle of close friends and family. More precisely, we anticipated that while men would report more frequent discussions than women with professional associates and others in the world of business, the two sexes would not differ in the frequency of their face-to-face communication with actors in the arena of public affairs. These expectations were essentially upheld by a sex breakdown of the previously presented (Table 6–8) responses to Item #41: while both the Mobilizable and Attentive men reported significantly more face-to-face communication than did their female counterparts with professional associates, merchants, and business executives,[56] the two sexes did not differ in either group in their conversations with politicians. On the other hand, the standard sex-role differences are more manifest with respect to clergymen and journalists, whom we have identified as also likely to be among those with whom active citizens come into contact. Attentive men and women did not differ in

---

[56] For the difference between Mobilizable men and women with respect to professional associates, $\chi^2 = 46.45$, df $= 4$, P$<.001$; for merchants, $\chi^2 = 24.16$, df $= 3$, P$<.001$; for business executives, $\chi^2 = 37.19$, df $= 4$, P$<.001$. For the difference between Attentive men and women with respect to professional associates, $\chi^2 = 33.07$, df $= 4$, P$<.001$; for merchants, $\chi^2 = 26.22$, df $= 3$, P$<.001$; for business executives, $\chi^2 = 44.41$, df $= 4$, P$<.001$.

their communication with clergymen, but Mobilizable men reported significantly greater discussions with them than did Mobilizable women, and in the case of journalists, the men in both groups reported more discussions than did the women.[57]

MARITAL AND FAMILY STATUS

Notwithstanding some impressionistic evidence that young single women have turned to politics in order to find a husband,[58] the available findings of social science indicate that married people are more likely than either those who never marry or those who are widowed or divorced to undertake citizenship activity. Married persons not only turn out in greater numbers than unmarried persons at election time,[59] but they also participate more actively in voluntary associations[60] and are more likely to make financial contributions to peace research.[61] This difference has been uncovered in other countries as well as in the United States and it has led to the widely shared interpretation that a number of important facilitating predispositions are associated with marriage: "The almost universal difference between single and married people . . . may, like the age differences to which it is linked, reflect lesser cross-pressures among the married, who have a more stable existence, more homogeneous ties in the community, and, especially among the workers, less geographic and social mobility." [62]

----

[57] For the difference between the Mobilizable men and women with respect to clergymen, $\chi^2 = 24.35$, df $= 4$, P$<$.001; for journalists, $\chi^2 = 29.99$, df $= 4$, P$<$.001. For the difference between Attentive men and women with respect to journalists, $\chi^2 = 20.40$, df $= 4$, P$<$.001.

[58] See Harry F. Waters, "The Disenchanted: Girls in the City," *The New York Times Magazine*, February 6, 1966, p. 28.

[59] Cf. Lane, *Political Life*, p. 218.

[60] Cf. Scott, "Membership and Participation in Voluntary Associations," p. 325; and Hausknecht, *The Joiners*, p. 35.

[61] Jerome Laulicht and Norman Z. Alcock, "The Support of Peace Research," *Journal of Conflict Resolution*, Vol. X (June 1966), p. 201.

[62] Seymour Martin Lipset, *Political Man: The Social Bases of Politics* (Garden City: Doubleday & Co., 1960), p. 212.

Although traces of this pattern can be discerned in the ADA data, our central finding is one of no differences between single and married persons. As can be seen in Table 7–4, the composition of the Mobilizables and Attentives did not differ significantly in this respect. In addition, there were no significant differences between either the letter-writing or the organizational activity scores of the married and single men among the Mobilizables, the married and single women among the Mobilizables, the married and single men among the Attentives, or the married or single women among the Attentives.[63] The irrelevance of the marital status variable is further indicated by the finding that Mobilizable mar-

---

TABLE 7–4
MARITAL STATUS OF THE MOBILIZABLES, THE
ATTENTIVES, AND THE GENERAL POPULATION
(in percentages)

	Single	Married	Divorced-Widowed	Un-known	Total	(n)
Nationwide Sample*	21	69	10	—	100	(119,333)
Men	25	70	5	—	100	(57,470)
Women	19	68	13	—	100	(61,863)
The Mobilizables	19	66	13	2	100	(1,704)
Men	15	81	3	1	100	(986)
Women	25	48	26	1	100	(690)
The Attentives	16	71	11	2	100	(1,658)
Men	12	81	6	1	100	(1,087)
Women	24	54	21	1	100	(535)

* "Current Population Survey," Bureau of the Census of the U.S. Department of Commerce, as reproduced in *The Statistical History of the United States from Colonial Times to the Present* (Stamford, Conn.: Fairfield Publishers, Inc., 1965), p. 15. The sample includes persons "14 years old and over" and the percentages are "standardized for age." The sample was surveyed in March, 1957.

---

63 Although included in Table 7–4, the divorced-widowed category was omitted from the statistical comparisons because in important respects it encompasses the characteristics of both the married and single statuses, thus tending to confound the differences between them.

ried men and women registered significantly higher letter-writing and organizational activity scores than did their Attentive counterparts,[64] and the same differences prevailed among single men and for letter-writing activity among single women.[65]

While these findings had all been anticipated (Hypotheses IVc, VI, and VII), some evidence that marriage provides facilitating predispositions can be seen in the eight comparisons between the married and single respondents. In all eight, the mean scores recorded by the married respondents exceeded those of their unmarried counterparts, although the differences were not significant; and the same pattern held for both sexes, in both groups, for both forms of first-hand contact. The consistency of these differences suggests that the diminution of cross-pressures with marriage is not totally irrelevant to membership in the Attentive Public.

A comparison of the marital status of the Mobilizables and Attentives on the one hand and the general population on the other reveals that it is true only for men. As can be seen in Table 7-4, there are proportionately more married Mobilizable and Attentive men than there are in the population as a whole, while the reverse is true for women. Thus, for women, marriage seems to be an interfering resource as much as it is a facilitating one.

One other aspect of family status needs to be noted. The number of children or other dependents for whom adults are responsible might be expected to affect political attitudes and activities. Young children can serve as an interfering resource because considerable time must be allocated to their care, but they might also foster facilitating predispositions if a person feels a greater

---

[64] For the difference in letter-writing activity between Mobilizable and Attentive married men, $\chi^2 = 219.30$, df $= 4$, P$<.001$; for the difference in organizational activity, $\chi^2 = 61.51$, df $=5$, P$<.001$. The comparable figures for the married women were $\chi^2 = 110.20$, df $= 4$, P$<.001$, in the case of letter-writing activity, and $\chi^2 = 23.62$, df $= 5$, P$<.001$, in the case of organizational activity.

[65] For the difference in letter-writing activity between Mobilizable and Attentive single men, $\chi^2 = 64.44$, df $= 3$, P$<.001$; for the difference in organizational activity, $\chi^2 = 31.92$, df $= 5$, P$<.001$. The figures for the letter-writing activities of single women were $\chi^2 = 74.55$, df $= 3$, P$<.001$.

stake in the affairs of the community as the size of his or her family grows. This aspect of family status has not been the subject of extensive inquiry. There is some evidence that married persons with one child are less active in public affairs than those who are childless or have two or more children,[66] but on the whole there are no social science findings on the extent to which children and other dependents affect political behavior.

While the absence of relevant data made it seem unwise to include formal hypotheses about parenthood in our original model, the questionnaire included an item [#32] along these lines. The data from this item, presented in Table 7–5, show that having children is hardly a bar to attentiveness and mobilizability. Even allowing for the single persons (who accounted for a preponderance of those who provided no answers as well as of those who said they were childless), more than three-fifths of both the Attentives and Mobilizables reported themselves to be parents and roughly half of both groups reported having at least two children. Equally

---

TABLE 7–5
PARENTHOOD AND POLITICAL ACTIVITY AMONG
THE MOBILIZABLES AND ATTENTIVES

	The Mobilizables			The Attentives		
	Mean scores on index of			Mean scores on index of		
Number of		letter-writing	organizational		letter-writing	organizational
Children	Percent		activity	Percent		activity
None	19	32	49	18	19	40
One	14	35	50	14	21	40
Two	25	35	51	27	20	40
Three	16	36	54	17	22	45
Four or more	8	37	54	9	25	46
Unknown	18			15		
Total	100			100		
(n =)	(1,704)			(1,658)		

---

[66] Cf. Scott, "Membership and Participation in Voluntary Associations," p. 325; and Milbrath, *Political Participation*, p. 135.

striking is the fact that letter-writing and organizational activity do not diminish in either group as the family size increases.[67] On the contrary, the data in Table 7–5 tend to indicate that both kinds of activity increase, although not significantly, along with family size. Or, more cautiously, it can at least be said that once a person becomes attentive or mobilizable, even four or more children do not hinder his or her citizenship activities.

The Attentives and Mobilizables did not differ significantly in the size of their families.[68] As was the case for marital status, however, it is again evident that the tendency of the Mobilizables toward first-hand contacts operates independently of social background. They reported more letter-writing and organizational activity than did Attentives regardless of the number of children.[69]

RACE

The data comparing the political activities of blacks and whites are scarce and difficult to interpret. In most surveys, except for those dealing with voting and campaign activities, the races are usually so unevenly represented that comparison of their behavior

[67] For a similar finding in which married women with children reported more organizational activity than those who were childless or single, see Eli Ginzberg and Associates, *Life Styles of Educated Women* (New York: Columbia University Press, 1966), p. 67.

[68] Nor did they differ in the number of others dependent upon them: 33 percent of the Mobilizables said they had no such dependents, 12 percent cited one, 4 percent cited two or more, and 51 percent did not provide a codable answer to the query. The equivalent figures for the Attentives were 31, 15, 5 and 49 percent.

[69] For the letter-writing differences between those in the two groups with no children, $\chi^2 = 106.15$, df $= 4$, P$<.001$; with one child, $\chi^2 = 70.37$, df $= 4$, P$<.001$; with two children, $\chi^2 = 169.60$, df $= 4$; P$<.001$; with three children, $\chi^2 = 71.73$, df $= 4$, P$<.001$; with four or more children, $\chi^2 = 30.20$, df $= 4$, P$<.001$. For the differences in organizational activity between those in the two groups with no children, $\chi^2 = 22.91$, df $= 5$, P$<.001$; with one child, $\chi^2 = 25.18$, df $= 5$, P$<.001$; with two children, $\chi^2 = 44.82$, df $= 5$, P.<001; with three children, $\chi^2 = 24.80$, df $= 5$, P$<.001$; with four or more children, $\chi^2 = 12.35$, df $= 5$, $.001> $ P $<.05$.

in response to common stimuli is at best superficial.[70] Such is the case here. Although it ·champions civil rights, the ADA has apparently not attracted many blacks to its ranks. As can be seen in Table 7–6, the proportion of blacks among both the Attentives and Mobilizables was only 2 percent.[71]

Table 7–6 also reveals what obviously follows from this, that

TABLE 7–6
RACE DISTRIBUTION OF THE MOBILIZABLES, THE ATTENTIVES, AND THE GENERAL POPULATION
(in percentages)

Race	The Mobilizables	The Attentives	McClosky's National General Population Sample (January, 1958)*
White	92	89	93
Black	2	2	7
Race unknown	6	9	—
Total	100	100	100
(n =)	(1,704)	(1,658)	(1,484)

* As reproduced in Herbert McClosky, "Consensus and Ideology in American Politics," *American Political Science Review,* Vol. LVIII (June, 1964), p. 381.

[70] Indeed, even students of voting behavior have been prevented from pursuing all the implications of their data in this regard by "the limited number of cases available to us" (Campbell, et al., *The American Voter,* pp. 282–83). For an exception in which the number of cases is sufficient to allow for systematic comparisons across racial lines, see Donald R. Matthews and James W. Prothro, *Negroes and the New Southern Politics* (New York: Harcourt, Brace & World, 1966).

[71] Although an inordinately high proportion of both groups did not answer the race item [#28], apparently feeling that such a query constituted a violation of civil rights, it seems doubtful whether the two percent figure would have been much larger if all the respondents had answered. The comments appended to the question indicate annoyance that rights were being violated by its inclusion; but, of these commentators, those who identified their race were primarily white.

the proportion of blacks on the mailing list of the ADA is less than the equivalent figure for a nationwide sample. Due to their lesser education, income, and occupational opportunities, blacks have generally been found to be less politically active than whites.[72] Moreover, with the growth of the civil rights movement and of a sense of racial identity, the number and size of black political action organizations has also grown in recent years, probably reducing further the number of blacks in organizations like the ADA.

There are a number of exceptions to the finding that blacks participate less than whites in the political process. Under circumstances when the interfering resources inherent in their minority status are at a minimum, blacks have been found to be as active as whites. Indeed, often the status of a deprived minority seems to foster facilitating predispositions that can offset the interfering resources and lead blacks to participate at higher rates than whites.[73] Once blacks enter the Attentive and Mobilizable Publics, in other words, their minority status becomes irrelevant to their citizenship between elections. Hypotheses IVb, VI, and VII thus anticipated that the Attentives and Mobilizables would not differ in their racial composition, that the differences in their letter-writing and organizational activities would not be affected by race, and that the whites and blacks in both groups would report similar degrees of first-hand contact with public affairs. These predictions could not be subjected to tests for statistical significance because of the small number of blacks in the sample, but inspection of the data in Tables 7–6 and 7–7 suggests that the hypotheses would have been confirmed.

RELIGION

The political activities of adherents of various religions have been found to differ, but few analysts trace these variations to

---

[72] Cf. Woodward and Roper, "Political Activity of American Citizens," p. 877; and Milbrath, *Political Participation*, p. 138.

[73] See, for example, Dahl, *Who Governs*, pp. 294–96; and Agger, Goldrich, and Swanson, *The Rulers and the Ruled*, p. 269.

TABLE 7-7
MEAN SCORES RECORDED ON THE INDICES OF
LETTER-WRITING AND ORGANIZATIONAL ACTIVITY
BY BLACKS AND WHITES AMONG THE
MOBILIZABLES AND ATTENTIVES

Race (n =)	Mean scores on index of letter-writing activity		Mean scores on index of organizational activity	
	Mobilizables	Attentives	Mobilizables	Attentives
Whites	34 (1,549)	21 (1,443)	50 (1,550)	42 (1,473)
Blacks	37 (34)	22 (38)	58 (34)	39 (37)

theological precepts. While different citizenship practices can readily be inferred from the ideological structure of all the religions claiming followers in the United States,[74] it seems doubtful whether this structure actually organizes and channels behavioral predispositions. Rather, as one analyst puts it, "The relationship between politics and religion is based on organizational pressure, group interaction and identity, and group interest, not theology.[75]

These group pressures, interactions, identities, and interests are, however, not to be minimized. Some religions seem to foster facilitating predispositions and others interfering predispositions, with the result that persons with different religious affiliations have been found to differ in the nature and scope of their contacts with public affairs. Some of these variations are closely related to other background variables, but the predispositions derived from religious factors are not erased when the other variables are taken into account.[76] For example, due apparently to aspects of their

[74] For a coherent set of inferences along these lines, see René de Visme Williamson, *Independence and Involvement: A Christian Reorientation in Political Science* (Baton Rouge: Louisiana State University Press, 1964), Chap. VI.

[75] Lane, *Political Life*, p. 247.

[76] Cf. James C. Davies, *Human Nature in Politics: The Dynamics of Political Behavior* (New York: John Wiley and Sons, 1963), p. 228.

culture and their status as a minority group, Jews have been found to establish much closer ties to public affairs than those of other faiths.[77] Indeed, except in comparison to professional intellectual groups ("where Jews are heavily represented"), they prove to be "more internationalist and liberal than . . . any other segment of American society," even when education, income, and occupational factors are held constant.[78] Similarly, the higher rate of organizational activity among Protestants than Catholics has been attributed to differences in the authority structure of their respective churches.[79] In turn, and excepting those in the upper socio-economic class, Catholics have been found to establish more extensive contacts with public affairs than those who profess no religious affiliation,[80] a difference that might be due, at least in part, to the latter's lack of affiliative experience. In contrast, those without church affiliations have been found to be more responsive to appeals for financial support than those with such affiliations.[81]

To a considerable extent, the responses of the ADA sample

[77] Cf. Lawrence H. Fuchs, *The Political Behavior of American Jews* (Glencoe, Ill.: The Free Press, 1956), Chap. XI; Alfred O. Hero, Jr., *Americans in World Affairs* (Boston: World Peace Foundation, 1959), pp. 72–75; Lane, *Political Life*, pp. 68, 75; and Stanley J. Morse and Stanton Peele, "A Study of Participants in an Anti-Vietnam War Demonstration," *Journal of Social Issues*, Vol. 27 (1971), p. 119.

[78] Hero, *Americans in World Affairs*, p. 73. In this connection it is noteworthy that a comparison of public attitudes toward the Korean and Vietnam conflicts yielded the finding that "Jews seem to be about the only subgroup of all those sorted by demographic questions in surveys whose position on the two wars differs." John E. Mueller, "Trends in Popular Support for the Wars in Korea and Vietnam," p. 372.

[79] Hausknecht, *The Joiners*, pp. 54–55. For other findings that indicate distinctive political behavior on the part of Catholics, see Gerhard Lenski, *The Religious Factor* (Garden City, N.Y.: Doubleday & Co., 1961), Chaps. 4 and 8; and Robert R. Alford, *Party and Society: The Anglo-American Democracies* (Chicago: Rand McNally & Co., 1963), p. 245.

[80] Cf. Scott, "Membership and Participation in Voluntary Associations," p. 322; Milbrath, *Political Participation*, p. 137; and Erbe, "Interest in a Peace Organization," p. 79.

[81] Laulicht and Alcock, "The Support of Peace Research," p. 201.

proved to be consistent with these findings. The number of Jews among the Attentives and Mobilizables suggests that facilitating predispositions lead this group to establish especially close ties to public affairs. As can be seen in Table 7–8, the proportion of Jews on the ADA mailing list and responsive to its support-building efforts was considerably greater than that found in a random sample of Americans. It can also be seen that this overrepresentation of Jews was accompanied by an underrepresentation of Catholics, a finding that is also consistent with other findings showing that Catholics engage in organizational activity less than do Protestants.

The expectation that the effect of religion would persist among members of the Attentive Public (Hypothesis Vb) was also upheld in that the composition of the Mobilizables and Attentives differed significantly along religious lines.[82] Inspection of

---

TABLE 7–8
RELIGIOUS DISTRIBUTION OF THE MOBILIZABLES,
THE ATTENTIVES, AND THE GENERAL POPULATION
(in percentages)

Religion	McClosky's National General Population Sample (January, 1958)*	The Mobilizables	The Attentives
Catholic	22	4	3
Jew	2	25	31
Protestant, other, and no answer	76	71	66
Protestant		48	44
Other		1	1
No religion		19	18
Codable answer not given		3	3
Total	100	100	100
(n =)	(1,484)	(1,704)	(1,658)

* As reproduced in Herbert McClosky, "Consensus and Ideology in American Politics," *American Political Science Review*, Vol. LVIII (June, 1964), p. 382.

---

[82] $\chi^2 = 16.67$, df $= 3$, P$<.001$.

Table 7–8, however, reveals that the sources of this difference were not those we had anticipated. There were not more Jews among the Mobilizables than among the Attentives nor more individuals without religious affiliations among the Attentives than among the Mobilizables. Both groups contained roughly the same proportion of persons who reported no religious affiliations and the different composition of the two groups was due largely to the lower mobilizability of the Jews and the higher mobilizability of the Protestants.

The data on letter-writing and organizational activities reveal the limits of the relevance of religious affiliations and experiences for citizenship between elections. Contrary to expectations (Hypothesis VII), the Catholics, Jews, Protestants, and non-religious respondents among the Mobilizables did not record significantly different degrees of both forms of first-hand contact. On the other hand, while the predispositions derived from past experiences in religious roles thus seem to be reduced to the point of not being operative when attentiveness takes the form of mobilizability, such a reduction does not necessarily occur after an individual enters the Attentive Public. As anticipated, the four religious groups among the Attentives did differ significantly in their letter-writing and organizational activities.[83]

A comparison of the mean scores recorded by each religious group among the Mobilizables and Attentives on the two activity indices provides some indications of the nature of past experience in religious roles that is relevant to membership in the Attentive Public. As can be seen in Table 7–9, one is the behavior of Protestants, whose facilitating predispositions apparently persisted sufficiently to lead them to record the highest mean scores in all four of the sets listed. Even more striking is the distinctive behavior of the Attentive Catholics. Plainly they made the major contributions to the differences reported in the previous paragraph by engaging in much less letter-writing and organizational activity than any of the other religious groups. This disparity is partic-

---

[83] For the distribution of their letter-writing activity scores, $\chi^2 = 37.07$, df = 9, P < .001; for their organizational activity scores, $\chi^2 = 48.50$, df = 12, P < .001.

TABLE 7–9

MEAN SCORES RECORDED ON THE INDICES OF
LETTER-WRITING AND ORGANIZATIONAL ACTIVITY
BY RELIGIOUS GROUPINGS AMONG THE
MOBILIZABLES AND ATTENTIVES

Religious Affiliation (n =)	Mean scores on index of letter-writing activity		Mean scores on index of organizational activity	
	Mobilizables	Attentives	Mobilizables	Attentives
Catholics	34	15	41	27
	(68)	(47)	(68)	(51)
Jews	33	18	49	41
	(430)	(505)	(429)	(517)
Protestants	35	23	52	44
	(816)	(709)	(818)	(719)
None	34	20	50	40
	(314)	(287)	(311)	(290)

ularly evident in the case of organizational activity, which it will be recalled is consistent with findings relevant to the political behavior of Catholics among the general population. The effect of Catholic predispositions on organizational activity is also revealed by the fact that Mobilizable and Attentive Catholics did not differ significantly in their scores on this index. This is the only comparison for either kind of activity within the four religious groups that did not conform to our expectation (Hypothesis VI) that the Mobilizables would be more active than the Attentives.[84]

In sum, the effect of religion on citizenship between elections is selective. It seems to facilitate attentiveness for Jews and mobilizability for Protestants, and it appears to interfere with the

[84] For the differences in the letter-writing scores of the Catholics in each group, $\chi^2 = 27.79$, df $= 3$, P$<$.001; for the Jews, $\chi^2 = 180.21$, df $= 4$, P$<$.001; for the Protestants, $\chi^2 = 195.06$, df $= 4$, P$<$.001; for those with no religious affiliations, $\chi^2 = 111.05$, df $= 4$, P$<$.001. For the differences in the organizational activity scores of the Jews in each group, $\chi^2 = 32.62$, df $= 5$, P$<$.001; for the Protestants, $\chi^2 = 44.88$, df $= 5$, P$<$.001; for those with no religious affiliations, $\chi^2 = 28.19$, df $= 5$, P$<$.001.

organizational activities of Attentive Catholics. Otherwise it is not potent enough to erase the greater readiness of Mobilizables than Attentives to establish first-hand contacts.

REGION

Although the mounting pace of industrialization has weakened the effect of regional subcultures on norms and attitudes, social science findings still reveal regional differences in political behavior. At the very least, most surveys show the behavior of Southerners to be distinctive. Cross-sections of Northeasterners, Midwesterners, and Far Westerners tend to be more similar than they are different in opinion and activity, but comparable cross-sections of Southerners are usually discrepant enough to suggest that the South persists "as a region with a special subculture." [85] Indeed, the growing uniformity of the other regions is such that researchers have tended to limit regional analysis to two regions, the South and the Non-South.[86] World War II, it is noted, brought Midwestern isolationism to an end and thus erased regional differences on foreign policy questions,[87] and industrialization has

---

[85] Lane, *Political Life*, p. 308. See also Robert R. Alford, *Party and Society: The Anglo-American Democracies* (Chicago: Rand McNally & Co.), and V. O. Key, Jr., *Public Opinion and American Democracy*, p. 107.

[86] For example, see Campbell, et al., *The Voter Decides*, p. 166; and Campbell, et al., *The American Voter*, pp. 477–80. For a challenging exception in which the systematic analysis of poll data yield the conclusion that industrialization has not lessened regional differences and that "the strongest evidence for a divergence is between the Northeast and each of the other regions," see Norval D. Glenn and J. L. Simmons, "Are Regional Cultural Differences Diminishing?" *Public Opinion Quarterly*, Vol. 31 (Summer, 1967), pp. 176–93.

[87] Cf. Key, *Public Opinion and American Democracy*, p. 106. It should be noted, however, that some observers have impressionistically perceived residents of large port cities to be much more concerned about foreign policy questions than those of inland communities. Apparently, for example, the outlooks of persons in San Francisco, Boston, and New Orleans have more in common with each other than with those of other cities in their regions. See *The New York Times*, October 12, 1964, p. 19.

had a similar effect with respect to most domestic policy questions. The most notable exception is the issue of race. Due to this complex problem, as well as a slower rate of industrialization and a unique set of historical circumstances, Southern political culture still remains distinct from the rest of the nation. Southerners have been found not only to vary considerably in their attitude toward racial issues, but also to join fewer organizations than those from other regions,[88] to have a lesser sense of civic duty,[89] and in general to "have far lower levels of political participation than do other Americans." [90] There is some evidence that Far Westerners also differ from Northeasterners and Midwesterners, in their attitudes and level of participation,[91] but these differences are not nearly as marked as those that distinguish Southerners.[92]

Both the growing regional uniformity and the persistent deviance of the South can be discerned in the ADA data. The interfering predispositions fostered by Southern ties are evident in a comparison of the regional distribution of the ADA sample and the population as a whole. As can be seen in Table 7–10, Southerners do not enter the Attentive Public in numbers proportionate to their place in the Mass Public. Whether the same is true for

[88] Lane, *Political Life*, p. 78.

[89] Campbell, et al., *The American Voter*, p. 480.

[90] Key, *Public Opinion and American Democracy*, p. 104.

[91] For example, Key notes in *Public Opinion and American Democracy*, p. 108, that "the odds are that the Far West has an attitudinal differentiation on foreign policy that turns attention westward rather than toward Europe" and that "a more marked concern for civil liberties also seems to characterize the West." The somewhat lesser degree of political activity on the part of Far Westerners is evident in the data presented by Lane in *Political Life*, p. 78. In addition, see Alfred de Grazia, *The Western Public* (Stanford: Stanford University Press, 1954), and Don D. Smith, " 'Dark Areas of Ignorance' Revisited," p. 672.

[92] For extensive inquiries into the political subculture of the South, see Alfred O. Hero, Jr., *The Southerner and World Affairs* (Baton Rouge: Louisiana State University Press, 1965); Charles O. Lerche, Jr., *The Uncertain South: Its Changing Patterns of Politics in Foreign Policy* (Chicago: Quadrangle Books, 1964); and V. O. Key, Jr., *Southern Politics in State and Nation* (New York: Alfred A. Knopf, 1949).

TABLE 7–10
REGIONAL DISTRIBUTION OF THE MOBILIZABLES,
THE ATTENTIVES, AND THE GENERAL POPULATION
(in percentages)

Region	McClosky's National General Population Sample (January, 1958)*	The Mobilizables	The Attentives
Northeast	28	40	35
Midwest	36	30	24
South	20	7	15
Far West	17	21	25
Other and unknown	—	2	1
Total	101	100	100
(n =)	(1,484)	(1,704)	(1,658)

* As reproduced in Herbert McClosky, "Consensus and Ideology in American Politics," *American Political Science Review*, Vol. LVIII (June, 1964), p. 382. In this sample persons from West Virginia were classified as Northeasterners, whereas in the ADA they were classified as Midwesterners. However, since only five West Virginians were among the 4,636 persons who were sent the questionnaire, this discrepancy does not distort the patterns depicted.

their membership in the Mobilizable Public cannot be directly inferred from the data,[93] but later we will present some indirect evidence that it is.

The data in Table 7–10 also show that the Midwest was underrepresented, and the Northeast and Far West overrepresented, in the ADA sample as compared to the population as a whole. The overrepresentation of the Northeast is due in part to the tendency of Jews, who are concentrated in New York, to join liberal organizations like the ADA,[94] but the disproportionate

[93] In view of the aforementioned effort (p. 171) to control the region variable in compiling the sample of Attentives, the distributions of the Mobilizables and Attentives in Table 7-10 cannot be directly compared. Consequently Hypothesis IVc cannot be subjected to a direct test.

[94] In contrast to the 35 percent of the Mobilizable Northeasterners who were Jewish, 19, 12, and 21 percent of those from, respectively, the Midwest, South, and Far West were Jews. The comparable figures for the Attentives were 41, 31, 26, and 22 percent.

numbers of Far Westerners stems partly from the tendency of many older persons, with the facilitating predispositions of age, to spend their retirement years in California.[95] The distributions in Table 7–10 probably also reflect urban-rural differences among the regions, with urban individuals engaging in more political activity than those in rural communities.[96] Unfortunately our questionnaire did not identify urban-rural differences.

A comparison of the first-hand contacts established by the respondents from the four regions confirms our expectation (Hypothesis VII), that a growing uniformity has diminished the impact of the regional variable for those citizens who become actively involved in public affairs. Neither among the Mobilizables nor the Attentives did the four regions differ significantly from each other in either their letter-writing or organizational activities. The mean letter-writing scores of the Attentive Northeasterners, Midwesterners, Southerners, and Far Westerners were respectively, 20, 20, 20, and 22, and the equivalent figures for the regional groupings among the Mobilizables were 34, 33, 36, and 35. Similarly, the Attentives from the Northeast, Midwest, South, and Far West recorded mean organizational activity scores, respectively, of 40, 41, 42, and 44, and the comparable scores for the Mobilizables were 49, 51, 51, and 51.

Both the general lack of impact of the regional variable and the residue of its strength for Southerners are evident in comparisons of the first-hand contacts reported by the Mobilizables and Attentives in each region. As had been predicted (Hypothesis VII), the former reported greater letter-writing activity than the latter in all four regions.[97] With respect to organizational activities, Mobilizable Northeasterners and Midwesterners recorded significantly greater scores than their counterparts among the

[95] Three-tenths of the Mobilizables and one-quarter of the Attentives from the Far West were over the age of 65. None of the other regions had such large proportions of older persons.

[96] Cf. Milbrath, *Political Participation*, pp. 128–29; and Campbell, et al., *The American Voter*, pp. 410–16.

[97] For the Northeast, $\chi^2 = 219.66$, df = 4, <.001; for the Midwest, $\chi^2 = 150.38$, df= 4, P<.001; for the South, $\chi^2 = 55.81$, df = 3, P<.001; and for the Far West, $\chi^2 = 109.81$, df = 4, P<.001.

Attentives,[98] but although in the same direction, the differences between the Mobilizables and Attentives were not significant among Southerners and Far Westerners. The absence of difference among the Southerners in this regard may reflect the interfering predispositions that citizens from this region must overcome to enter the Attentive Public in the first place, while the lack of difference among the Far Westerners is perhaps attributable to the aforementioned finding that a substantially greater number of persons over 65 resided in that region.

PARTY IDENTIFICATION

Inquiries into the contribution of party identification to citizenship activity are marked by inconsistency. On the one hand, several voting studies have found it to be the most potent background variable. In the words of one team of researchers, "Evidently no single datum can tell us more about the attitude and behavior of the individual as presidential elector than his location on a dimension of psychological identification extending between the two great parties." [99] Another investigator conceded that some people shift their vote in a particular election, but stressed that "over the long run party identification has more influence over a person's vote decision than any other single factor." [100] On the other hand, quite the opposite has also been found with equal clarity: "We must conclude that, for many people, calling oneself a Democrat or a Republican does not imply a serious obligation to exert oneself on behalf of that party, even to the extent of voting for it." [101]

Nor is the available evidence on the extent of activity during elections any more consistent than that pertaining to the voting

---

[98] For the Northwesterners, $\chi^2 = 55.52$, df= 5, P<.001; for the Midwesterners, $\chi^2 = 41.13$, df = 5, P<.001.

[99] Campbell, et al., *The American Voter*, pp. 142–43.

[100] Lane, *Political Life*, p. 300.

[101] Campbell, Gurin, Miller, *The Voter Decides*, p. 108.

decision itself. One inquiry, for example, found that "the less an individual is committed to one of the two major parties and the more his political predisposition is uncrystallized, the less likelihood there is of his voting." [102] Another came to the even more general conclusion that "the stronger the individual's sense of attachment to one of the parties, the greater his psychological involvement in political affairs." [103] Still another investigation, however, presented data indicating that "there are insignificant differences among independents and party identifiers on every activity that would seem to constitute areas of expected differences." [104]

Underlying these seeming inconsistencies are different conceptions of what it means to be an "independent" citizen. Researchers who consider party identification to be a potent variable view Independents as those persons who are not committed to a political party because they are essentially uninterested in politics, but who see it as more socially desirable to attribute their irregular voting pattern to independence than to disinterest. On the other hand, in studies that ascribe a minimal role to party identification the Independent is seen as a person who is neither partisan nor apathetic but whose irregular voting behavior stems from other structured criteria. This type of Independent is involved in public affairs even though his posture toward them is not associated with a political party. He has been found to resemble the party identifiers in his propensities to vote, discuss politics, and follow public affairs in the mass media, but to resemble the apathetic citizen in his lack of partisan conviction.[105]

---

[102] Samuel J. Eldersveld, "The Independent Vote: Measurement, Characteristics, and Implications for Party Strategy," *American Political Science Review*, Vol. XLVI (September 1952), p. 747.

[103] Campbell, et al., *The American Voter*, p. 143.

[104] Robert E. Agger, "Independents and Party Identifiers: Characteristics and Behavior in 1952," in Eugene Burdick and Arthur J. Brodbeck, eds., *American Voting Behavior* (Glencoe, Ill.: The Free Press, 1959), p. 320.

[105] Cf. Alan S. Meyer, "The Independent Vote," in William N. McPhee and William A. Glaser, eds., *Public Opinion and Congressional Elections* (Glencoe, Ill.: The Free Press, 1962), pp. 72–73.

These findings about the operation of party identification during elections suggest the utility of exploring how the distinction between party identifiers and Independents may be relevant to the behavior of active citizens, although the small number of Republicans in the ADA sample (see Table 7–11) prevents a full investigation of the role of the party variable. In the first place, the finding that "the individual who has a strong and continuing involvement in politics is more likely to develop a commitment to one or the other of the major parties" [106] led us to expect that the ADA sample would be composed largely of party identifiers. Secondly, since members of the Attentive Public who designate themselves as Independents are similar to the involved rather than the apathetic type of independent voter, we predicted (Hypothesis VII) that neither among the Mobilizables nor the Attentives would the Democrats and Independents differ in their first-hand contacts with public affairs. Given this lack of strength of the party identification variable, it was also anticipated (Hypothesis VI) that among both Democrats and Independents the Mobilizables would report greater letter-writing and organizational activity than the Attentives.

With regard to party composition, both the Mobilizables and Attentives were expected to be composed mainly of Democrats, but the voting studies do not provide a basis for predicting whether similar or different proportions of each group would consider themselves to be Independents. Nor is a logical solution to the problem easily developed. On the one hand, it seems conceivable that the readiness to respond to the appeals of a mobilizer requires a belief in the virtues of organized effort that is less likely to be held by a person who sees himself as independent in politics than by one who identifies with a political party. In other words, party commitment may also facilitate mobilizability. On the other hand, few party identifiers are also active in party affairs, thus suggesting that the commitment to party may be more symbolic than behavioral. As one study concludes, "It may be that for many people party identification does not have the capacity to stimulate overt activity, but does have the power to command

[106] Campbell, et al., *The American Voter*, p. 144.

support on the psychological level of preferences and attitudes." [107]
In the absence of any substantive basis for choosing between these
conflicting rationales, it seemed wiser to make the conservative
prediction that the Mobilizables and Attentives would not be
differentiated in their party affiliations (Hypothesis IVe).

The responses to Item #33 negated our conservative approach. The two groups differed significantly in their party
affiliations[108] and, as can be seen in Table 7–11, this difference was
due to the greater inclination of the Mobilizables to consider
themselves Democrats and the greater tendency of the Attentives
to see themselves as Independents. This finding suggests that
mobilizability and party loyalty are underlain and supported by
similar psychological processes. Identifying oneself with a party
organization may not create the readiness to respond to appeals
for support, but the two variables apparently reinforce each other.

The data in Table 7–11 also reveal that, despite the greater

TABLE 7–11
PARTY IDENTIFICATION OF THE MOBILIZABLES,
THE ATTENTIVES, AND THE GENERAL POPULATION
(in percentages)

Party	The Mobilizables	The Attentives	Michigan Survey Research Center Sample of Sept. 1953*	Oct. 1956*	Oct. 1958*
Identifiers	76	70	75	73	76
Republicans	1	1	30	29	29
Democrats	73	67	45	44	47
Other parties	2	2	—	—	—
Independents	22	29	18	24	19
Identity unspecified or unknown	2	1	7	3	5
Total	100	100	100	100	100
(n =)	(1,704)	(1,658)	(1,023)	(1,772)	(1,269)

* As adapted from Angus Campbell, *et al., The American Voter,* p. 124.

[107] Campbell, Gurin, and Miller, *The Voter Decides,* p. 108.
[108] $\chi^2 = 18.05$, df = 2, P<.001.

number of Independents in their ranks, the Attentives consisted predominantly of party identifiers. Thus, the initiative and interest which lead to membership in the Attentive Public apparently do not produce such independence of mind as to lead citizens to think of themselves as above or apart from partisanship and the party battle. On the contrary, the main finding of the voting studies, that strong involvement in politics and commitment to party are directly linked, is corroborated by the fact that seven out of every ten Attentives associated themselves with a party. Table 7–11 also shows that the proportions of Independents in the Attentive and Mobilizable Publics are roughly the same as that in the electorate as a whole.

The data also upheld our reasoning that the kind of Independents to be found in the Attentive Public do not differ from the party identifiers in their first-hand contacts. The letter-writing and organizational activity scores registered by the Democrats and Independents did not differ either among the Mobilizables or the Attentives. The Mobilizable Democrats recorded significantly higher scores on both indices than the Attentive Democrats,[109] and the same difference held between the two groups of Independents.[110]

There is one respect, however, in which independent voters and attentive citizens do diverge sharply. Voting studies reveal that the former, whether apathetic or interested, tend to be young and that a "steady increase in strong party attachments" becomes manifest as voters age.[111] Indeed, insofar as the voter is concerned, "it is a matter of particular interest that party identification does not decline in significance in the later years of life; on the contrary, strong party attachment is more common among people of retire-

---

[109] For the difference in letter-writing, $\chi^2 = 378.21$, df $= 4$, P $<.001$; for the difference in organizational activity, $\chi^2 = 67.13$, df $= 5$, P $<.001$.

[110] For the difference in letter-writing, $\chi^2 = 124.52$, df $= 4$, P $<.001$; for the difference in organizational activity, $\chi^2 = 44.48$, df $= 5$, P $<.001$.

[111] Campbell, et al., *The American Voter*, p. 161. For similar findings, see Eldersveld, "The Independent Vote," p. 751, Lane, *Political Life*, p. 300; and Crittenden, "Aging and Political Participation," pp. 327–30.

ment age than it is at any other period." [112] For reasons that are not entirely clear, this relationship between age and party identification was almost exactly reversed among both the Mobilizables and Attentives. As can be seen in Table 7–12, the proportion of Democrats in both groups declines steadily with age while the proportion of Independents rises.[113] Moreover, this is not a spurious relationship, as it was not entirely erased by the two other background variables, region and religion, that were significantly related to party identification among either the Mobilizables or the Attentives.[114] Table 7–12 reveals considerable regional variation in party identification,[115] but the age pattern nevertheless persisted in two of the regions and was manifest more weakly in a third.[116] Much the same was true for two of the four religious groups.[117]

The discrepancy between the interaction of age and party among voters on the one hand and attentive citizens on the other

[112] Campbell, et al., *The American Voter*, p. 165.

[113] These divergent patterns fell short of statistical significance in the case of the Mobilizables, but were enough to be significant among the Attentives ($\chi^2 = 34.61$, df $= 4$, P$<.001$).

[114] The region-party relationship was significant among both groups (for the Mobilizables, $\chi_m^2 = 28.60$, df $= 3$, P$<.001$; for the Attentives, $\chi^2 = 67.13$, df $= 3$, P$<.001$), but only among the Mobilizables was the religion-party relationship significant ($\chi^2 = 33.10$, df $= 3$, P$<.001$).

[115] It is interesting to note that regional variation in party identification is much greater for the Mobilizables and Attentives than for the population as a whole. In the electorate only the Southerners deviated in the degree of their party loyalty, but in the ADA sample both the Southerners and the Far Westerners varied substantially from the Northeasterners and Midwesterners in this respect. Indeed, the party identifiers were even more numerous among the Mobilizable and Attentive Far Westerners than among their Southern counterparts.

[116] With the Mobilizables and Attentives clustered together to facilitate statistical analysis, the age-party relationship proved to be significant among Northeasterners ($\chi^2 = 29.09$, df $= 4$, P$<.001$) and Southerners ($\chi^2 = 19.23$, df $= 4$, P$<.001$). It was almost significant among Far Westerners ($\chi^2 = 14.50$, df $= 4$, $.006>$P$<.005$).

[117] Namely, the Protestants ($\chi^2 = 20.63$, df $= 4$, P$<.001$) and the Jews ($\chi^2 = 14.39$, df $= 4$, $.007>$P$<.006$).

TABLE 7-12

RELATION OF PARTY IDENTIFICATION TO AGE, REGION, AND RELIGION AMONG THE MOBILIZABLES, THE ATTENTIVES, AND THE GENERAL POPULATION (in percentages)

| | The Mobilizables | | | | The Attentives | | | | General Population* | | |
	Democrats	Independents	Republicans, other, no answer	Total (n =)	Democrats	Independents	Republicans, other, no answer	Total (n =)	Party identifiers	Independents	Total (n =)
Age**											
To 35	75	18	7	100 (282)	77	19	4	100 (278)	75	25	100 (2,791)
36 to 45	78	20	2	100 (346)	74	24	2	100 (348)	77	23	100 (2,302)
46 to 55	74	23	3	100 (328)	67	30	3	100 (310)	79	21	100 (1,892)
56 to 65	72	25	3	100 (286)	60	37	3	100 (285)	80	20	100 (1,418)
Over 65	69	26	5	100 (383)	60	34	6	100 (342)	85	15	100 (1,124)

*Region****

Northeast	71	25	4	100 (690)	56	40	4	100 (579)	72	28	100 (809)
Midwest	68	26	6	100 (505)	65	30	5	100 (395)	74	26	100 (1,084)
South	77	17	6	100 (118)	77	21	2	100 (254)	84	16	100 (842)
Far West	83	13	4	100 (359)	78	17	5	100 (409)	74	26	100 (410)
Religion											
Catholic	85	10	5	100 (68)	84	13	2	100 (51)			
Jewish	74	25	1	100 (431)	69	30	1	100 (518)			
Protestant	77	18	5	100 (824)	68	28	4	100 (726)			
No religion	63	33	5	100 (315)	64	31	5	100 (292)			

* As adapted from Angus Campbell, et al., *The American Voter*, pp. 158, 162.

** For the general population, subtract one year from the listed age brackets (i.e., to 34, 35–44, 45–54, 55–64, over 64).

*** In the ADA sample persons from Maryland and West Virginia were classified, respectively, as Northeasterners and Midwesterners, whereas in the sample of the general population they were classified as Southerners. The former sample also includes Hawaiians and Alaskans (as Far Westerners), but the latter was surveyed before statehood was granted and thus presumably includes no such persons.

is somewhat puzzling. The increase in partisanship observed in voters as they age is generally attributed to the development of greater political awareness as people mature and acquire both a growing stake and a wider acquaintanceship in the community.[118] But presumably the same could be said about the Attentive Public and we did so earlier when we noted that its ranks include a disproportionate number of older people and that its youngest members tend to establish fewer first-hand contacts than their elders. In the case of the Attentives and Mobilizables, however, this increased politicization with maturity seems to be associated with a decrease rather than an increase in party loyalty.

One possible explanation of this unexpected relationship between age and party is that, as they age, citizens become increasingly sensitive to the differences among issues and increasingly aware of the broad areas of gray that lie between black or white solutions. Since their concern with public affairs persists between elections, when the party battle tends to be quiescent, they develop a growing recognition of the limits beyond which party loyalties are useful as a source of thoughts and values about the course of events. It is possible, in other words, that their strong attachment to a party is slowly eroded by the very factors that sustain their attentiveness.

This interpretation might seem to run counter to another finding of the voting studies. It has been found that, the longer a voter has identified himself with a party, the stronger is his attachment to it, so that "as time passes, stress of increasing severity must be required to induce him to shift his allegiance to the opposing party, or even to cast a vote 'away' from his party." [119] Upon closer examination, however, this finding tends to support our interpretation that attentiveness undermines party loyalty. Or at least it seems reasonable to presume that attachment to the idea

---

[118] For a full exposition of this explanation of the relationship between age and partisanship uncovered by the voting studies, see Campbell, et al., *The American Voter, pp.* 161–65.

[119] Campbell, et al., *The American Voter*, p. 163.

of being an Independent also gathers strength as people age, in which case the data in Table 7–12 can be viewed as reflecting a growing resistance to the appeals and candidates of a particular party that some attentive citizens acquire as they get older.

In short, further investigations of how the age-party relationship operates between elections is clearly needed. Until comparable data are gathered from other segments of the Attentive Public, the generalizability of the relationship uncovered here remains speculative. However, our finding makes it clear that there are limits to the extent to which the conclusions of the voting studies can be projected into other areas of citizenship behavior.

EDUCATION

Social science has yet to uncover many laws of political behavior, but the close correlation between education and political activity is so pervasive in the findings of systematic research that it might well qualify for such status. As one analyst puts it, "Perhaps the surest single predictor of political involvement is number of years of formal education." [120] Whatever the lawful properties of educational experience may be, it is clear that it contributes facilitating resources and predispositions. The data show unambiguously that the more formal education a person acquires, the more likely he or she is to participate in the political process. Educated persons are more likely to vote,[121] to write letters to officials,[122] to join organizations,[123] to discuss politics,[124] to feel politically competent,[125] and to follow the publics affairs content

[120] Angus Campbell, "The Passive Citizen," *Acta Sociologia,* Vol. 6 (1962), p. 20.

[121] Cf. Campbell, et al., *The American Voter,* pp. 477–78.

[122] Cf. Sussmann, *Dear FDR,* p. 136; Hadley Cantril, ed., *Public Opinion, 1935–1946* (Princeton: Princeton University Press, 1951), p. 703; Bauer, Pool, and Dexter, *American Business and Public Policy,* p. 214.

[123] Hausknecht, *The Joiners,* pp. 17, 24; Scott, "Membership and Participation in Voluntary Associations," pp. 320–21.

[124] Almond and Verba, *The Civic Culture,* p. 121.

[125] *Ibid.,* p. 204.

of the mass media[126] than are those without an education.[127] In addition, the more formal education a person has the less is he likely to be interested in local politics, a finding that "echoes the well-known propensity of the better off and better educated to be more concerned than lower status people with broader environments." [128]

The impact of formal schooling even tends to be manifest at adjacent educational levels: the person with an advanced degree is more active than the college graduate, who is more active than the high school graduate, who in turn is more active than the person whose education ended with grade school. Moreover, the relationship has been found to prevail across cultural and class lines.[129] It is also as evident in developing societies as in developed ones. A study of six developing societies concluded that education "emerges as one of the most important factors in stimulating active citizenship in competition with any other source of influence." [130] Although education is closely associated with socio-economic status and occupation, its effects have nonetheless been found within all statuses and occupations.[131] There is no study that has shown its impact to disappear when other social background variables are controlled. On the contrary, education tends to erase many of the effects of other variables. It even "erases the contrasts between men and women in the gross types of political participation" [132] and thus is generally regarded "as the best predictor of these forms of participation." [133]

[126] Steiner, *The People Look at Television*, p. 177; Lane, *Political Life*, p. 82; and Hattery, *"Great Decisions—1962": A Survey of Kit Buyers in Two Wisconsin Communities*, p. 33.

[127] For more general data along these lines, see Woodward and Roper, "Political Activity of American Citizens," p. 877.

[128] Kent Jennings and Harmon Zeigler, "The Salience of American State Politics," *American Political Science Review*, Vol. 64 (1970), p. 531.

[129] Almond and Verba, *The Civic Culture*, pp. 94, 121–22, 304–05.

[130] Alex Inkeles, "Participant Citizenship in Six Developing Countries," *American Political Science Review*, Vol. 63 (1969), p. 1139.

[131] Cf. Key, *Public Opinion and American Democracy*, p. 330.

[132] *Ibid.*, p. 331.

[133] Campbell, et al., *The American Voter*, pp. 476–77.

Some of the reasons for the lawful effects of education are not difficult to discern. A number of analysts have noted that formal education provides skills that make the establishment of contact with public affairs easier and more likely.[134] Many ideas, as well as the techniques for acquiring, analyzing, and assessing ideas on one's own are learned in school.[135] In addition to such facilitating resources, moreover, education appears to foster facilitating predispositions. People like to use their skills. Thus the more educated, being better able to form and express opinions, are more inclined than the less educated to seek out and discuss information pertaining to public affairs and, in so doing, to enjoy the sense of responsibility that accompanies the use of their intellectual resources.[136] These facilitating predispositions are given added momentum by the fact that a person's education places him "in social situations where he meets others of like educational attainment, and this tends to reinforce the effect of his own education." [137]

The data from the ADA sample corroborate both the potency of the education variable and our expectation that it was not powerful enough to erase the distinction between Attentives and Mobilizables. Its effects are most evident in a comparison of the educational backgrounds of the two groups with that of the population as a whole. Consistent with the findings of other studies, our sample of active citizens reported considerably more years of formal education than has been found among inactive individuals. As can be seen in Table 7–13, the proportion of college graduates in the ADA sample was as much as four times greater than the equivalent figures for samples of the general public. Equally striking are the responses to Item #38, which show that more than

---

[134] For a wide-ranging analysis of the relationship between education and politics, see James S. Coleman, ed., *Education and Political Development* (Princeton: Princeton University Press, 1965).

[135] For impressive data showing an unmistakable relationship between education and the holding of ideas about political issues, see Key, *Public Opinion and American Democracy*, pp. 332–36.

[136] For data depicting the close correlation between education and a sense of responsibility, see *ibid.*, pp. 325–26.

[137] Almond and Verba, *The Civic Culture*, p. 379.

TABLE 7–13

EDUCATIONAL DISTRIBUTION OF THE MOBILIZABLES, THE ATTENTIVES, NATIONAL LEADERS, AND THE GENERAL POPULATION (in percentages)

Level of Educational Attainment	The Mobilizables	The Attentives	National Leaders*	American Institute of Public Opinion Sample (January, 1958)**	Michigan Survey Research Center Sample of 1956 Electorate**	McClosky National General Population Sample (January, 1958)**
Item #37						
Did not attend college	13	15	9	84	81	73
Attended college for less than four years	13	14	24	—	—	—
Graduated from college	72	70	65	16	19	27
Codable answer not given	2	1	2			
Total	100	100	100	100	100	100
(n =)	(1,704)	(1,658)	(647)	(3,024)	(1,762)	(1,482)

Item #38

Did not attend graduate or professional school	30	36	31
Attended graduate or professional school	19	16	20
Obtained a postgraduate or professional degree	46	45	43
Codable answer not given	5	3	6
Total	100	100	100
(n =)	(1,704)	(1,658)	(647)

* As reproduced in James N. Rosenau, *National Leadership and Foreign Policy: A Case Study in the Mobilization of Public Support* (Princeton: Princeton University Press, 1963), pp. 107–108.

** As reproduced in Herbert McClosky, "Consensus and Ideology in American Politics," *American Political Science Review*, Vol. LVIII (June 1964), p. 382.

three-fifths of both ADA groups had some graduate or professional experience and that more than two-fifths obtained an advanced degree. We do not have comparable data for samples of the general public, but the extent of their college attendance makes it highly unlikely that the amount of advanced training they would report would be anything like that of the ADA sample. This difference would seem to be a clear indication of the magnitude of the facilitating resources and predispositions provided by education. As can be seen in Table 7–13, the data on advanced training for our sample also compare favorably with those reported for a sample of national leaders.[138] Leaders in public affairs may have greater access to the communications system than do members of the Attentive Public (see Table 5–1 and Figure 5–1), but the two groups do not differ in the amount of formal training they bring with them when they are moved to participate in the political process.

It is also important to note the limits of education. An examination of the first two columns of Table 7–13 reveals that the Mobilizables and Attentives did not differ in terms of education. Neither the item that dealt with the college level [#37] nor the one concerned with postgraduate education [#38] yielded a significant difference between the two groups. This finding had been expected (Hypothesis IVf) on the grounds that, once a person enters the Attentive Public, the predispositions and skills acquired through years of formal education have little bearing on whether or not he is responsive to appeals for support. Education may, as indicated below, affect the extent to which mobilizable citizens establish some forms of first-hand contact, but it does not seem to

---

[138] The data in Table 7–13 are not the only findings that support such a comparison. Item #38 also asked for a specification of the advanced degrees obtained, and here again the attainments of both the Mobilizables and Attentives compare favorably with those of national leaders. For example, 9 percent of the national leaders reported having a Ph.D. and 12 percent said that they had a terminal master's degree in arts, science, and business or public administration (Rosenau, *National Leadership and Foreign Policy*, p. 108), and these two types of degrees were reported, respectively by 10 and 19 percent of the Mobilizables and 11 and 17 percent of the Attentives.

be among the complex of factors that lead them to be mobilizable in the first place.

While the data affirm that the impact of the resources acquired through educational experience would be discernible in certain first-hand contact established by the Mobilizables and Attentives and not in others, they did so quite differently than had been anticipated. It had been expected (Hypothesis VI and VII) that the impact of education would affect the extent of letter-writing rather than the degree of organizational activity. We reasoned that the less educated Mobilizables would not have the facilitating resources necessary to sustain the practice of letter-writing, whereas this lack would not be likely to affect their inclination to be active in voluntary associations. Quite the opposite proved to be the case. The letter-writing scores of the Mobilizables and Attentives did not reflect any influence of the education variable. Thus, at each educational level, the Mobilizables registered significantly high letter-writing scores than their counterparts among the Attentives,[139] but within neither group were the differences in the letter-writing practices of those at the various levels significant. These patterns were substantially reversed with respect to organizational activity. Here education seems to matter. As can be seen in Table 7–14, the more years of formal education undergone by the Mobilizables and Attentives, the more organizational activity they undertake. The scores on this index differed significantly across educational levels among both the Mobilizables and the Attentives.[140] These effects of ed-

---

[139] For the difference between the Mobilizables and Attentives who never attended college, $\chi^2 = 67.70$, df = 4, P<.001; between those who attended but did not graduate from college, $\chi^2 = 72.59$, df = 3, P<.001; between those who obtained a college degree, $\chi^2 = 375.16$, df = 4, P<.001; between those who did not engage in postgraduate or professional study, $\chi^2 = 166.11$, df = 4, P<.001; between those who had some postgraduate education, $\chi^2 = 97.24$, df = 4, P<.001; between those who obtained an advanced degree, $\chi^2 = 250.32$, df = 4, P<.001.

[140] For the scores of the Mobilizables who reported no, some, and a full college experience, $\chi^2 = 74.27$, df = 10, P<.001; for those who reported no, some, and full postgraduate study, $\chi^2 = 33.25$, df = 10, P<.001. For

TABLE 7–14

MEAN SCORES RECORDED ON THE INDEX OF
ORGANIZATIONAL ACTIVITY BY THE MOBILIZABLES
AND ATTENTIVES AT VARIOUS EDUCATIONAL
LEVELS

Level of Educational Attainment	The Mobilizables	The Attentives
	(n =)	
Item #37		
Did not attend college	42	34
	(213)	(237)
Some college (attended for less than four years)	48	41
	(229)	(228)
Graduated from college	52	43
	(1219)	(1156)
Item #38		
Did not attend graduate or professional school	47	39
	(509)	(586)
Some postgraduate study (attended but did not obtain an advanced degree)	52	46
	(326)	(267)
Obtained a postgraduate or professional degree	52	42
	(781)	(738)

ucation, however, did not entirely erase the differences between
the two groups, so that at four of the six educational levels the
tendency of the Mobilizables to engage in more activity than the
Attentives still prevailed.[141]

An explanation of why education had a greater effect on
organizational than on letter-writing activity cannot be derived
from these data. We can only speculate that it reflects the facil-

---

the scores of the Attentives who reported no, some, and a full college
experience, $\chi^2 = 60.90$, df $= 10$, P$<.001$; for those who reported no,
some, and full postgraduate study, $\chi^2 = 41.68$, df $= 10$, P$<.001$.

[141] For the difference between those in each group who never attended
college, $\chi^2 = 22.77$, df $= 5$, P$<.001$; between those who graduated from
college, $\chi^2 = 92.37$, df $= 5$, P$<.001$; between those who did not pursue
graduate study, $\chi^2 = 33.13$, df $= 5$, P$<.001$; and between those who
obtained an advanced degree, $\chi^2 = 70.59$, df $= 5$, P$<.001$.

itating predispositions fostered by education. The more schooling
one has, the more likely one is to want to use his intellectual skills
and to seek out others in order to exchange ideas. Voluntary
associations provide such an outlet, whereas interaction through
letter-writing is not nearly as rewarding in this respect. Whatever
the reasons for this finding, however, it is clear that the effects of
education are not spurious. An examination of the relationship
between education and organizational activity holding other background variables constant yielded thirteen out of twenty-six cases
in which it remained. With the Mobilizables and Attentives clustered together for statistical purposes, the relationships fully persisted among men,[142] women,[143] whites,[144] persons between 51 and
65 years old,[145] Far Westerners,[146] married respondents,[147] Democrats,[148] Protestants,[149] and persons with an annual income of
between $5,000 and $10,000,[150] and persisted partially among those
older than 65,[151] Northeasterners,[152] Midwesterners,[153] and single

[142] At the college level, $\chi^2 = 85.37$, df $= 10$, P$<.001$; at the postgraduate
level, $\chi^2 = 54.47$, df $= 10$, P$<.001$.

[143] At the college level, $\chi^2 = 41.44$, df $= 10$, P$<.001$; at the postgraduate
level, $\chi^2 = 33.31$, df $= 10$, P$<.001$.

[144] At the college level, $\chi^2 = 108.11$, df $= 10$, P$<.001$; at the postgraduate
level, $\chi^2 = 66.98$, df $= 10$, P$<.001$.

[145] At the college level, $\chi^2 = 36.18$, df $= 10$, P$<.001$; at the postgraduate
level, $\chi^2 = 30.22$, df $= 10$, P$<.001$.

[146] At the college level, $\chi^2 = 62.02$, df $= 10$, P$<.001$; at the postgraduate
level, $\chi^2 = 29.68$, df $= 10$, P$<.001$.

[147] At the college level, $\chi^2 = 84.72$, df $= 10$, P$<.001$; at the postgraduate
level, $\chi^2 = 49.24$, df $= 10$, P$<.001$.

[148] At the college level, $\chi^2 = 97.41$, df $= 10$, P$<.001$; at the postgraduate
level, $\chi^2 = 41.62$, df $= 10$, P$<.001$.

[149] At the college level, $\chi^2 = 86.92$, df $= 10$, P$<.001$; at the postgraduate
level, $\chi^2 = 47.27$, df $= 10$, P$<.001$.

[150] At the college level, $\chi^2 = 35.21$, df $= 10$, P$<.001$; at the postgraduate
level, $\chi^2 = 36.16$, df $= 10$, P$<.001$.

[151] At the college level, $\chi^2 = 40.70$, df $= 10$, P$<.001$; not significant at the
postgraduate level.

[152] At the college level, $\chi^2 = 53.14$, df $= 10$, P$<.001$; not significant at the
postgraduate level.

[153] At the college level, $\chi^2 = 29.84$, df $= 10$, P$<.001$; not significant at the
postgraduate level.

respondents.[154] It is perhaps noteworthy that most of the groups in which the effects of educational experience were erased—blacks, persons under 35 years old and those between 36 and 53, Southerners, Independents, Catholics, Jews, those with no religious affiliations, and five of the six income groups—represent minority segments of the general population.

INCOME

Money would seem to be a facilitating resource in politics as in everything else. Although closely related to other background variables, especially education and occupation, income has also been found to be independently associated with political behavior. A variety of inquiries have shown that more prosperous citizens establish wider contacts with public affairs than those who are less well off.[155] Although the effect does not occur uniformly with each step up the income ladder, the difference between the top and bottom rungs has appeared consistently.[156] Presumably this is because the time as well as the wherewithal to establish first-hand contacts with the course of events is more available to those with high incomes. In addition, financial resources at least partly determine one's stake in the welfare of the community and thus serve as either facilitating or interfering predispositions.

Although the effects of income can be traced in our data, the

---

[154] At the college level, $\chi^2 = 38.61$, df $= 8$, P$<.001$; not significant at the postgraduate level.

[155] Cf. Lane, *Political Life*, pp. 326–27; Milbrath, *Political Participation*, pp. 120–21; Woodward and Roper, "Political Activity of American Citizens," p. 877; Hausknecht, *The Joiners*, pp. 24–25; and Erbe, "Social Involvement and Political Activity," p. 203.

[156] One interesting exception to this pattern is the finding that the income variable did not prove to be a predictor of the size of donations to a campaign on behalf of peace research. Indeed, it did not even differentiate contributors from noncontributors (Laulicht and Alcock, "The Support of Peace Research," p. 205). Since this finding is closer to our own (below) and since it was uncovered in the context of an explicit effort to mobilize support (i.e., money for peace research), it is of more than passing interest.

patterns involved are somewhat startling in that they are quite contrary to the overall finding just cited. The positive relationship between income and political activity was found only in a comparison between the ADA sample and the general public. As can be seen in Table 7–15, both the Mobilizables and the Attentives reported annual family incomes [#39] that greatly exceed the equivalent figures for two samples of the electorate, even allowing for the several years of prosperity and inflation that intervened between the surveys. Otherwise, however, the composition and behavior of the Mobilizables and Attentives deviate surprisingly from both the findings of other studies and our expectations. Most notably, not only did the distribution of the Mobilizables and Attentives along the income scale differ significantly[157] (and

TABLE 7–15
INCOME OF THE MOBILIZABLES, THE ATTENTIVES, AND THE GENERAL POPULATION (in percentages)

Income Level (in $)	The Mobilizables	The Attentives	Michigan Survey Research Center Sample of 1956 Electorate*	McClosky National General Population Sample (January, 1958)*
Under 5,000	14	10	53	54
5,000–10,000	32	28	36	36
Over 10,000	52	60	8	6
10,000–15,000	23	24		
15,000–20,000	12	14		
20,000–25,000	7	9		
Over 25,000	10	13		
Codable answer not given	2	2	3	4
Total	100	100	100	100
(n =)	(1,704)	(1,658)	(1,762)	(1,484)

* As reproduced in Herbert McClosky, "Consensus and Ideology in American Politics," *American Political Science Review*, Vol. LVIII (June 1964), p. 382.

[157] $\chi^2 = 25.13$, df $= 5$, P$<.001$.

thereby negate the prediction in Hypothesis IVg that income would be irrelevant to the propensity to be mobilizable), but it also indicates that mobilizability is greater the worse off active citizens are financially. Inspection of Table 7–15 reveals that the proportion of Mobilizables at the two lowest rungs of the income ladder (under $5,000 and $10,000) exceeded the proportion of Attentives, while the opposite was the case for each of the four higher income levels.

Two lines of reasoning, both highly speculative, suggest themselves to explain why mobilizability diminishes as income increases among members of the Attentive Public. One concerns time as a resource provided by income. It is conceivable that annual incomes over $10,000, rather than freeing their recipients from other cares and allowing them to be responsive to mobilizers, involve extensive responsibilities that leave little time for participation in support-building efforts. In other words, such incomes may actually be an interfering resource insofar as mobilizability is concerned. Secondly, it could be argued that incomes under $10,000 operate as facilitating predispositions if we assume that mobilizability to some extent reflects submissiveness which, in turn, is associated with an unfavorable self-image. If persons who are financially well off tend to think more highly of themselves than those who are not, then the latter would be more likely than the former to express their attentiveness through co-operation with mobilizers. Stated differently, the high income person with a more favorable self-image is more likely than his low income counterpart to be more self-sustaining in his political activities and is consequently less likely to be dependent on a mobilizer's stimulus in order to establish first-hand contacts with public affairs.[158]

Some evidence supporting both of these interpretations is provided by the data on the organizational activities of those at

---

[158] For evidence that a favorable self-image is more likely to foster a self-sustaining orientation toward public affairs than an unfavorable one, see Morris Rosenberg, *Society and the Adolescent Self-Image* (Princeton: Princeton University Press, 1965), Chap. 11.

various levels. At four of the six levels the Mobilizables conformed to expectations (Hypothesis VI) and reported more extensive involvement in organizations than the comparable Attentives,[159] but at the "under $5,000" and "$20–25,000" levels the scores of the two groups were not significantly different. This finding can be interpreted as indicating that a less positive self-image among those on the bottom rungs of the income ladder and less time among those at the top account for the unexpected difference in the incomes of the Mobilizables and Attentives. Such an interpretation is supported further by the fact that, while the organizational activity scores of the Attentives did not differ across the income levels, those of the Mobilizables did.[160] Moving from the bottom to the top rung of the income ladder, the mean scores of the Mobilizables at each level were 44, 49, 52, 54, and 51. In other words, organizational activity among the Mobilizables tends to peak at the middle of the income scale, again suggesting that a less favorable self-image at the lower end of the scale and less time at the top end may account for the decline on either side of the $15–20,000 bracket.

Given the different kinds of resources required to establish first-hand contacts through letter-writing, it is consistent with this interpretation that the impact of income was not traceable in the letter-writing activities reported by both groups. As expected (Hypothesis VI and VII), the Mobilizables recorded significantly higher letter-writing scores than the Attentives at every level[161] and within both groups those with different incomes did not differ significantly in their letter-writing activities.

[159] At the "$5–10,000" level, $\chi^2 = 33.33$, df $= 5$, P$<.001$; at the "$10–15,000" level, $\chi^2 = 25.63$, df $= 5$, P$<.001$; at the "$15–20,000" level, $\chi^2 = 32.36$, df $= 5$, P$<.001$; and at the "over $25,000" level, $\chi^2 = 20.63$, df $= 5$, P$<.001$.

[160] $\chi^2 = 45.33$, df $= 20$, P$<.001$.

[161] For the difference at the "under $5,000" level, $\chi^2 = 90.75$, df $= 3$, P$<.001$; at the "$5–10,000" level, $\chi^2 = 150.94$, df $= 4$, P$<.001$; at the "$10–15,000" level, $\chi^2 = 138.90$, df $= 4$, P$<.001$; at the "$15–20,000" level, $\chi^2 = 60.26$, df $= 4$, P$<.001$; at the "$20–25,000" level, $\chi^2 = 39.16$, df $= 3$, P$<.001$; and at the "over $25,000" level, $\chi^2 = 42.58$, df $= 3$, P$<.001$.

Whatever the validity of these interpretations, the general finding that income is systematically linked to citizenship between elections would seem to have a number of implications. Most importantly, if income is a measure of socio-economic status, the finding that lower status members of the Attentive Public are more mobilizable than those with higher status seems to have considerable importance. If the Attentive Public grows to the extent anticipated in Chapter 2, this growth is likely to result from an influx of persons who are in or just emerging from lower income groups. Hence, if the pattern of our ADA sample represents a general tendency, the mobilizable segment of the Attentive Public seems likely to grow at an even faster rate than its attentive segment, a conclusion that may be disturbing to analysts who fear that greater involvement of the mass public in the political process adds to its instability and thus poses a threat to the democratic polity.[162] At the same time the implications of our data should be encouraging for those whose mobilization efforts are directed at large organizations with mass memberships and discouraging for those who rely on small groups of specialists in the upper or intellectual classes to provide support when it is needed. In evaluating the implications of the foregoing data, however, it must be remembered that we are highlighting relative tendencies, and that in fact a major portion of the Mobilizables reported incomes in excess of $10,000.

OCCUPATION

There have been many inquiries into the resources and predispositions associated with different occupations. With respect to resources, occupations are conceived to vary in the skills and time they provide for participation in public affairs. Some lines of work are presumed to develop the capacity to formulate, an-

---

[162] For the pros and cons of this question, see the debate between Jack L. Walker ("A Critique of the Elitist Theory of Democracy") and Robert A. Dahl ("Further Reflections on 'The Elitist Theory of Democracy'") in the *American Political Science Review*, Vol. LX (June 1966), pp. 285–305.

alyze, and express ideas and the ability to interact effectively with other people, skills which facilitate the establishment of both first- and second-hand contacts. Others are presumed not to develop these talents and thus to interfere with political activity. Those jobs that provide facilitating skills also tend to afford time to participate in the public arena, whereas those that contribute interfering skills tend to involve a fixed work schedule and restrict activity to non-working hours. With respect to predispositions, occupations are conceived to vary in their proximity to public affairs and in the social roles they require their practitioners to perform. Some jobs are highly affected by events in the public arena and others are not, producing different predispositions among their occupants to establish contact with these events. Like- wise, jobs differ in the status accorded to them, and those with high status are presumed to foster stronger feelings of obligation to engage in citizenship activities than those with low status. In general, lines of work whose proximity and status constitute facil- itating predispositions also tend to be those that maximize the facilitating resources of time and intellectual skill, with the result that wide differences in political behavior can be expected from those in different occupations.[163]

This conceptualization is amply supported by empirical data. Large occupational differences in citizenship activity have been observed, with professional and managerial persons tending to be among the most active and laborers among the least active cit- izens.[164] Indeed, occupation has been found to be "the most satis- factory index of status[165] and persons in high status occupations have been shown to be more active letter-writers[166] and organiza- tional members,[167] as well as to manifest a greater sense of "citizen

---

163 For formulations that differentiate occupational resources and predis- positions along these lines, see Lane, *Political Life*, p. 331, and Milbrath, *Political Participation*, p. 125.

164 For example, see Woodward and Roper, "Political Activity of American Citizens," p. 877.

165 Key, *Public Opinion and American Democracy*, p. 122.

166 Lane, *Political Life*, p. 68.

167 *Ibid.*, p. 78; Hausknecht, *The Joiners*, p. 25; and Scott, "Membership and Participation in Voluntary Associations," p. 322.

duty" [168] and political involvement,[169] than those in low status occupations.

Notwithstanding the consistency of the findings, however, the classifications of occupations are anything but uniform. There are so many different lines of work that standardized categories have not evolved and each researcher tends to develop a classification scheme to suit his particular purposes. Some inquiries use generalized schemes that distinguish between professional and white collar persons and between skilled and unskilled workers, while others rely on more elaborate formulations and specify types of occupations within these broad categories. Since we are interested in the predispositions as well as in the resources provided by a particular line of work, a more elaborate formulation has been employed here. The occupational item of the questionnaire [#35] was open-ended and allowed the respondents to indicate both their primary and secondary occupations. The primary line of work was coded in terms of the appropriate subcategory of eleven broad occupational fields and the same was done for the secondary occupation if it involved another field.[170]

The results of this initial processing of the occupation data are presented in Table 7–16. Here it can be seen that, as in the case of other background variables, the occupational composition of the ADA sample deviated sharply from that of the population as a whole. This group of active citizens consisted of many more professional and managerial persons and many fewer skilled and unskilled workers than tend to be found in a random sample of the electorate.

While the categorization presented in Table 7–16 gives an overall picture of the varied lines of work pursued by the respondents, it must be further refined in order to pursue the conse-

---

[168] Campbell, et al., *The Voter Decides*, p. 197.

[169] Key, *Public Opinion and American Democracy*, p. 328.

[170] In other words, respondents who cited primary and secondary occupations in the same broad field were not coded twice. A teacher who also reported being a part-time student, for example, was coded only once in the educational field even though teacher and student are separate subcategories of this field.

TABLE 7–16
PRIMARY AND SECONDARY OCCUPATIONS OF THE ADA SAMPLE

BUSINESS AND INDUSTRY   714
    Merchants (92); Corporation executives (96); Engineers (119);
    Advertising (40); Finance (100); Agriculture (49); Others (218)

POLITICS AND GOVERNMENT   215
    Civil servants (43); Elected or appointed officials (24); Non-
    governmental politicians (2); Interest group officials (18);
    Volunteer political work (19); Volunteer interest group work (97);
    Others (12)

HEALERS   404
    Physicians (114); Psychoanalysts (6); Psychiatrists (20); Clinical
    Psychologists (12); Social Workers (157); Dentists (17); Others (78)

INTELLECTUAL ENDEAVOR AND EDUCATION   1161
    University teaching and research (452); University administration
    (24); Pre-college teaching (432); Pre-college administration (40);
    Librarians (42); Students (137); Others (34)

ARTISTIC EXPRESSION   228
    Writers, playwrights, and poets (112); Painters (40); Musicians (24);
    Producers and directors (6); Actors (9); Architects (10); Others (27)

COMMUNICATIONS   82
    Journalists (19); Editors (38); Publishers (9); Radio and television (9);
    Others (7)

LABOR, WAGE EARNERS, AND SALARIED WORKERS   286
    Labor union officials (21); White collar workers (118); Blue collar
    workers (122); Nurses (21); Others (4)

LAW   115
    Lawyers (104); Judges (4); Others (7)

RELIGION   170
    Clergy (142); Others (28)

MISCELLANEOUS   1139
    Housewives (533); Retired (480); Housewives and retired (36);
    Unemployed (21); Others (69)

OCCUPATION UNKNOWN   57
    Item #35 not answered (57)

quences of present responsibilities. The double coding of a sizable proportion of the respondents[171] makes statistical analysis difficult, and some of the eleven fields comprise positions that may vary considerably in the responsibilities they impose on their occupants. To overcome these limitations, the analysis of the occupation variable in this and subsequent chapters relies on contrasts among those subcategories in the various fields that contained at least 28 Mobilizables and 28 Attentives who listed them as their primary occupations. This procedure excludes those respondents in the least populated lines of work,[172] but it avoids the difficulties due to double coding and the loss of meaning from excessively broad categories. At the same time there are enough Mobilizables and Attentives in each subcategory to permit statistical analysis. This more specific categorization, with the number and the percentage of Mobilizables and Attentives whose primary occupations were so classified, is presented in Table 7–17.

The distribution of these data do not clearly uphold our expectation (Hypothesis Vc) that occupationally derived resources and predispositions would prove to be sufficiently varied to differentiate the Mobilizables and Attentives. On the one hand, the difference between the distribution of the Mobilizables and Attentives among the sixteen occupations fell short of significance.[173] On the other hand, an interesting pattern is suggested by the data in Table 7–17, namely, that the occupations of the Mobilizables

---

[171] Thirty-eight percent of the Mobilizables and 33 percent of the Attentives were coded in two different fields.

[172] However, in order to minimize the number who had to be omitted, certain of the subcategories that seemed to involve essentially similar resources and predispositions were combined (see the parenthetic notations in Table 7–17). The most notable omissions that remain are the communications and politics-government fields. The former had to be omitted because there were not enough Mobilizables and Attentives whose primary occupations were in the communications field, whereas the politics-government field could be preserved only by combining civil servants and elected officials into a single category, a combination that did not seem warranted on substantive grounds.

[173] $\chi^2 = 56.76$, df = 31, $.01 > P < .001$.

are more likely to involve the development of human talent than the production of nonhuman materials. Although the differences are small, there are a greater number of merchants, corporation executives, financiers, and engineers among the Attentives than

TABLE 7–17
PRIMARY OCCUPATIONS OF THE MOBILIZABLES AND ATTENTIVES

	Mobilizables		Attentives	
	No.	%	No.	%
Merchants	31	2	45	3
Corporation executives	28	1	56	3
Financiers (includes bankers, brokers, etc.)	30	2	44	3
Engineers	39	2	61	4
Physicians (includes dentists)	58	3	63	4
Social workers	65	4	28	2
College teachers (includes university teachers and researchers)	183	11	195	12
Pre-college teachers	144	8	122	7
Students	61	4	37	2
Artists (includes writers, painters, musicians, and actors)	28	1	36	2
White collar workers (includes clerks, secretaries, nurses, etc.)	47	3	34	2
Blue collar workers (includes printers, bus drivers, policemen, electricians, etc.)	34	2	51	3
Lawyers (includes judges)	45	3	46	3
Clergymen (includes others with primary occupation in field of religion)	77	5	52	3
Housewives	220	13	202	12
Retired persons	264	16	230	14
Others*	321	19	328	20
Occupation unknown (Item #35 not answered)	29	1	28	1
Total	1,704	100	1,658	100

* Being a composite of many occupations, this category is not included in subsequent analyses of the occupation variable.

among the Mobilizables, while the opposite is true of social workers, students, and clergymen. This pattern must be interpreted cautiously, but it suggests that predispositions toward mobilizability are inherent in occupations dedicated to the improvement of human talent. It is probably true that such occupations attract people who are especially responsive to social stimuli, but they may also make their practitioners more sensitive to human problems and thus more ready to respond to calls for action aimed to resolve them.

Turning to the relationship between occupation and first-hand contacts, the data are again somewhat ambiguous. On the one hand, contrary to expectations (Hypothesis VII), among neither the Mobilizables nor the Attentives did the sixteen occupations differ significantly from each other with respect to letter-writing and organizational activity. On the other hand, in comparisons within occupational groups, occupation did, as predicted (Hypothesis VI), narrow the overall differences between the letter-writing and organizational activities of the Mobilizables and Attentives. As can be seen in Table 7–18, the Mobilizables recorded a significantly higher degree of organization activity than the Attentives in only two of the sixteen occupations. The data on letter-writing reveal the same pattern to a lesser extent, with no significant differences between the two groups in nine of the occupational clusters. To be sure, the Mobilizables reported significantly greater letter-writing activity than their Attentive counterparts in seven occupational clusters; and inspection of Table 7–18 reveals that, in absolute terms, the Mobilizables registered higher mean scores than the Attentives in thirty-one cases. The central finding, however, suggests that the tendency of Mobilizables to engage in more letter-writing and organizational activity than Attentives may be narrowed or eliminated by the resources or predispositions embedded in many occupational fields. This finding is most conspicuous with respect to clergymen. Not only did the Mobilizables and Attentives in this occupational category register the highest mean letter-writing score, and not only did the clergymen among the Attentives compile the highest mean organizational activity score; but the attentive clergymen

TABLE 7–18
MEAN SCORES RECORDED ON THE INDICES OF LETTER-WRITING AND ORGANIZATIONAL ACTIVITY BY OCCUPATIONAL GROUPINGS AMONG THE MOBILIZABLES AND ATTENTIVES

| Occupational group | INDEX OF LETTER-WRITING ACTIVITY | | | | | INDEX OF ORGANIZATIONAL ACTIVITY | | | | |
| | Mean scores of the | | χ^2 test for significance of the difference | | | Mean scores of the | | χ^2 test for significance of the difference | | |
	Mobilizables	Attentives	χ^2	df	P	Mobilizables	Attentives	χ^2	df	P
Merchants	29	18	9.82	3	ns*	42	39	1.43	3	ns*
Corporation executives	30	18	11.76	3	ns	46	38	7.75	3	ns
Financiers	31	18	13.10	3	ns	46	36	6.34	3	ns
Engineers	32	20	13.39	3	ns	48	40	7.75	3	ns
Physicians	30	18	16.46	3	.001	46	34	12.34	3	ns
Social workers	36	29	11.98	2	ns	59	54	.73	2	ns
College teachers	31	20	64.73	3	.001	51	40	24.69	5	.001
Pre-college teachers	33	21	44.02	3	.001	54	46	11.60	4	ns
Students	32	15	23.23	3	.001	51	42	7.24	3	ns
Artists	39	16	14.54	1	.001	48	45	.01	2	ns
White-collar workers	35	20	7.69	1	ns	45	37	3.05	4	ns
Blue-collar workers	25	21	3.39	3	ns	40	39	1.13	3	ns
Lawyers	38	24	7.28	2	ns	55	43	6.02	3	ns
Clergymen	39	35	6.95	2	ns	57	57	1.43	4	ns
Housewives	36	22	54.83	2	.001	56	49	9.25	5	ns
Retired persons	34	20	87.30	3	.001	46	35	23.01	5	.001

* ns = not significant.

actually reported engaging in as much organizational activity as their Mobilizable counterparts. Apparently the almost daily need of clergymen to devote effort to coordinating the interests and foci of their congregations equip them with both the skills and motivation to establish extensive first-hand contacts with public affairs once they enter the Attentive Public. The fact that social workers and lawyers also registered high mean scores on both indices suggests that any occupation that requires constant experience in helping individuals cope with their environments is especially conducive to active citizenship between elections. Contrariwise, occupations that do not provide such experience would appear to serve as interfering factors. Such a conclusion would seem to follow from the finding that blue-collar workers among the Mobilizables recorded lower mean scores in both letter-writing and organizational activity than any other occupational cluster.

In sum, whatever resources and predispositions are associated with particular lines of work, the data suggest that occupations do vary in this regard. Those who seek to mobilize support would be well advised to consider whether the time, energy, and commitment required to give the support are consistent with the occupational obligations of those whom they are trying to activate.

FOREIGN TRAVEL

Little work has been done on the relationship between foreign travel experience and citizenship behavior. The few data that exist suggest that foreign travel has "a profound effect" on attitudes toward public issues[174] and that it is positively associated with political activity.[175] But these findings are based only on businessmen and they do not indicate whether travel abroad actually produces awareness of and involvement in public affairs

---

[174] Bauer, Pool, and Dexter, *American Business and Public Policy*, p. 155.

[175] Ithiel de Sola Pool, Suzanne Keller, and Raymond A. Bauer, "The Influence of Foreign Travel on Political Attitudes of American Businessmen," *Public Opinion Quarterly*, Vol. XX (Spring, 1956), p. 172.

or whether it is a reflection itself of a pre-existing concern about such matters. The proposition that travel serves as a broadening and involving experience may seem logical, but it is too simple and too little explored to be accepted at face value.

The data provided by the ADA sample yielded a positive association between foreign travel and political activity, except that the relationship does not extend to mobilizability. The positive association is most evident in a comparison of the foreign travel reported by the respondents [Item #54] and by members of the Mass Public. As can be seen in Table 7–19, members of the Attentive Public go abroad more frequently than the population as a whole. In contrast to "the man on the street," who is estimated to be "still above average if he has one trip [abroad] in his lifetime," [176] the Mobilizables reported an average of 2.0 trips "since World War II" and the mean figure for the Attentives was 2.1. Even if those who did not provide an answer are assumed never to have been abroad, half of both groups indicated that they had taken at least one trip outside the country. This is not comparable to the foreign travel experience of national leaders, who reported an average of 6.1 trips abroad over a shorter span of time,[177] but it is consistent with the presumption that curiosity and initiative are necessary conditions for both foreign travel and attentiveness.

Foreign travel, however, would appear to have little relevance to the dynamics of mobilizability. As can be seen in Table 7–19, the Mobilizables and Attentives did not differ significantly in the number of trips they reported. Such an outcome had been expected (Hypothesis IVh) on the grounds that while travel may provide unique resources and predispositions, these would not

---

[176] *Ibid.,* p. 161. Indeed, the physical mobility of the general public is so minimal that "one out of three Americans have never traveled more than two hundred miles from their birthplaces, and a majority are still living in the states in which they were born" (Peter H. Rossi, "Community Social Indicators," in Angus Campbell and Philip E. Converse, eds., *The Human Meaning of Social Change* [New York: Russell Sage Foundation, 1972], p. 87).

[177] Rosenau, *National Leadership and Foreign Policy,* p. 187.

TABLE 7–19

PREVIOUS FOREIGN TRAVEL EXPERIENCE OF THE
MOBILIZABLES, THE ATTENTIVES AND NATIONAL
LEADERS (in percentages)

[#54] About how many times have you been abroad since World War II?

	The Mobilizables	The Attentives	National Leaders*
No trips	42	42	18
One trip	20	19	16
Two trips	12	13	13
Three to five trips	13	12	21
Six to ten trips	4	4	14
Eleven or more trips	2	2	14
Question not answered	7	8	4
Total	100	100	100
(n =)	(1,704)	(1,658)	(647)

* As adapted from James N. Rosenau, *National Leadership and Foreign Policy: A Case Study in the Mobilization of Public Support* (Princeton: Princeton University Press, 1963), p. 187.

seem to be related to the propensity to respond to appeals for support.

The minimal impact of foreign travel is further demonstrated by an analysis of its interaction with the measures of first-hand contact. As had been expected (Hypothesis VII), the more traveled Mobilizables and Attentives did not differ significantly from their less traveled counterparts in either the letter-writing or organizational activities they reported. Foreign travel may affect attitudes toward public issues, but it appears to have little consequence for the inclination to establish first-hand contact with them.

Such a conclusion is further supported by comparisons between the letter-writing and organizational activities of Mobilizables and Attentives who had similar degrees of foreign travel experience. As anticipated in Hypothesis VI, the tendency of the Mobilizables to establish wider first-hand contacts than the Attentives persisted for both types of activity among those who never traveled abroad,[178] those who reported only one trip,[179] and those who reported two trips,[180] and the difference in letter-writing held among those who specified three to five trips.[181] The differences between the Mobilizables and Attentives who cited six to ten trips and those who reported eleven or more were not significant for either form of activity. It is not immediately obvious why the gap between the behavioral orientations of mobilizable and attentive citizens narrows somewhat among the most widely traveled. Perhaps other factors, such as occupational requirements, become sufficiently important at this extreme to diminish some of the differences between the two form of citizenship. As noted elsewhere, occupationally derived travel is associated with first-hand forms of citizenship activity[182] and some of those who made six or more trips abroad probably did so for business as well as pleasure.

SUMMARY AND CONCLUSIONS

The central findings of this chapter can be discerned in Table 7–20, which summarizes virtually all the data that have been examined.[183] The first row of the table shows that the ADA data are fully consistent with other findings that indicate that the social backgrounds of active citizens deviate substantially from those of the general public. Both the Mobilizables and the Atten-

[178] For letter-writing, $\chi^2 = 250.62$, df $= 4$, P$<$.001; for organizational activity, $\chi^2 = 55.68$, df$= 5$, P$<$.001.

[179] For letter-writing, $\chi^2 = 123.31$, df $= 4$, P$<$.001; for organizational activity, $\chi^2 = 22.49$, df $= 5$, P$<$.001.

[180] For letter-writing, $\chi^2 = 48.99$, df $= 4$, P$<$.001; for organizational activity, $\chi^2 = 24.49$, df $= 5$, P$<$.001.

[181] $\chi^2 = 68.45$, df $= 4$, P$<$.001.

[182] See pp. 395–97.

[183] Not summarized in the table are two peripheral findings pertaining to the age variable. In one case it was found that men tend to leave the Mobilizable and Attentive Publics as they age, while women tend to enter them. Equally interesting, in contrast to the population as a whole, both the Mobilizables and Attentives were found to be more inclined to regard themselves as Independents, rather than identifying with a political party, as they move through the life cycle.

TABLE 7–20
SUMMARY OF THE IMPACT OF ELEVEN BACKGROUND VARIABLES

	Age	Sex	Family Status	Race	Religion	Region	Party Identification	Education	Income	Occupation	Foreign Travel
Did the Mobilizables and Attentives clearly deviate from the general population along this dimension?	Yes	Yes	No	Yes	Yes	Yes	No	Yes	Yes	Yes	Yes
Did the Mobilizables and Attentives differ significantly from each other in this regard?	No	*	No	No**	Yes	*	Yes	No	Yes	No	No
Did the letter-writing activities of the various groups of Mobilizables comprising this dimension differ significantly?	No	No	No	No**	No	No	No	No	No	No	No
Did the letter-writing activities of the various groups of Attentives comprising this dimension differ significantly?	No	No	No	No**	Yes	No	No	No	No	No	No

Question											
How many, if any, of the Mobilizables groups comprising this dimension reported significantly greater letter-writing activities than their Attentive counterparts?	4 of 4	2 of 2	4 of 4	2 of 2	4 of 4	4 of 4	2 of 2	6 of 6	6 of 6	7 of 16	4 of 6
Did the organizational activities of the various groups of Mobilizables comprising this dimension differ significantly?	No	No	No	No**	No	No	No	Yes	Yes	No	No
Did the organizational activities of the various groups of Attentives comprising this dimension differ significantly?	Yes	Yes	No	No**	Yes	No	No	Yes	Yes	No	No
How many, if any, of the Mobilizables groups comprising this dimension reported significantly greater organizational activities than their Attentive counterparts?	4 of 4	2 of 2	4 of 4	2 of 2**	3 of 4	2 of 4	2 of 2	4 of 6	4 of 6	2 of 16	3 of 6

* For methodological reasons (p. 193), this comparison could not be made.

** Due to an insufficient number of Blacks, this conclusion is based on inspection of the data rather than a statistical test.

tives were found to be older, better educated, wealthier, more widely traveled, and composed of more men, whites, Jews, Northeasterners, Far Westerners, and professional and managerial persons than is the population as a whole. The two groups resemble the larger electorate only with respect to family status and the tendency to identify with a political party. No background characteristic proved to be a prerequisite to the practice of citizenship between elections, but some characteristics seem to provide more facilitating resources and predispositions than others. A comparison among the columns in Table 7–20 indicates that religion had the most potent impact upon the Mobilizables and Attentives, followed closely by education and income, whereas family status was the least potent.

The second row of the table depicts another major finding: that the data confirm, with three notable exceptions, the expectation (Hypothesis IV) that background variables are not major determinants of whether a member of the Attentive Public also becomes mobilizable. The Mobilizables and Attentives differed significantly only with respect to religion, party identification, and income. The first of these differences, which was due to the greater mobilizability of Protestants and the lesser mobilizability of Jews, had been anticipated (Hypothesis Vb) on grounds other than those that produced it. The differences in party identification and income negated our predictions, with party identifiers and persons with low incomes proving more mobilizable than Independents and those with high incomes.

Still another set of findings confirm the prediction (Hypotheses VI and VII) that the greater tendency of the Mobilizables than the Attentives to establish first-hand contacts with public affairs would persist within most social background categories. As summarized in the fifth and eighth rows of Table 7–20, in 77 of 112 background groups the first-hand activities of the Mobilizables were significantly greater than those of the Attentives. Consequently, as indicated in the third and sixth rows, of 22 comparisons of the various groups of Mobilizables within a background category, 20 did not yield differences in their first-hand contacts. The fourth and seventh rows reveal that the same finding obtained in 17 of 22 comparisons among the Attentives. Once a person enters the Mobilizable or Attentive Public, in short, his social background is not likely to affect how much he relates himself to public affairs.

Some qualifications of this conclusion are also noteworthy. A comparison between the fifth and eighth rows in Table 7–20 reveals that social background was more relevant to the organizational activities of the Mobilizables and Attentives than to their letter-writing activities. Twenty-four of the 35 cases in which the Mobilizables did not exceed the Attentives in first-hand contacts involved organizational activity, whereas the differences in the letter-writing activities of the two groups were erased in all but nine of the occupation and two of the foreign travel categories. An obvious interpretation of this finding would seem to be that, since the original distinction between the Mobilizables and Attentives was drawn on the basis of their responses to an appeal to write letters, it is hardly surprising that our hypotheses about first-hand contacts were most accurate with respect to letter-writing. It is nonetheless surprising that social background did make a difference for organizational activities. Earlier we found that the two forms of first-hand contact are highly correlated,[184] but the data presented in this chapter suggest that letter-writing and organizational activity are not identical and that past experiences conducive to the establishment of one do not automatically foster a readiness toward the other.

Another pattern that can be discerned in the disconfirmed hypotheses is that social background had a greater effect on the behavior of the Attentives than of the Mobilizables. As noted above, only one-eleventh of the comparisons among the Mobilizables yielded significant differences, whereas between one-fifth and one-fourth of those among the Attentives did so. This apparent immunity of the Mobilizables to the systematic influence of social background suggests that perhaps personality variables are a major source of their readiness to respond to appeals for support. Our data do not permit further exploration of this in-

[184] See above, p. 226.

ference, but the literature on the subject is sufficiently suggestive to lead us to explore several personality factors that may be relevant to mobilizability after all the data have been examined.[185]

The finding that the first-hand contacts of the Mobilizables were less affected by social background variables than were those of the Attentives is consistent with our view of mobilizability as a basic propensity. If, as suggested in Chapter 3, the habit of attentiveness is less complex than the tendency to be mobilizable, then the resources and predispositions inherent in past experience should have a more direct impact on the behavior of Attentives.

However, the greater sensitivity of attentiveness to background influences must be seen in perspective, since it represents a deviation from the main finding of the chapter that neither the Mobilizables nor the Attentives are easily characterized in terms of the conventional categories of social analysis. Social background appears to have a systematic impact on those who engage in citizenship activities between elections only when they are compared to the population as a whole.

[185] See pp. 477–82.

CHAPTER 8

THE BALANCING OF ATTITUDES

Among the most consistent findings of social science are those that indicate a tendency for people to achieve and maintain harmony among their beliefs about, their perceptions of, and their actions toward salient objects in their environment, including themselves. Explored in a variety of contexts, man's need to impose evaluative and cognitive structure on the world around him has been demonstrated repeatedly.[1] An individual will tend to have difficulty, for example, with favorable feelings towards another person whom his best friend intensely dislikes. Eventu-

---

[1] For summary evaluations of these findings, see J. W. Brehm and A. R. Cohen, *Explorations in Cognitive Dissonance* (New York: Wiley, 1962); and Charles Insko, *Theories of Attitude Change* (New York: Appleton-Century-Crofts, 1968).

ally such discrepancies tend to be reduced, either by liking one individual more and the other less or by bringing into play still other attitudes that can serve to explain and justify the continued existence of the discrepant circumstances.

Presumably these findings are just as relevant to the practices of citizenship between elections as they are to any other type of activity.[2] Presumably Mobilizables and Attentives are made just as uncomfortable by attitudinal inconsistencies as are other types of actors. Indeed, they may have a special need to achieve and maintain attitudinal balance for two reasons.[3] One is that the tendency to seek balance among attitudes toward public issues appears to be greater the more formal education a citizen has experienced.[4] Since the educational attainments of the ADA sample were considerable,[5] it seems reasonable to look for evidence of attitudinal balance in their responses. Secondly, for citizens to respond to the appeals of mobilizers or sustain autonomous attentiveness to public issues, presumably they must have strong views

[2] For data demonstrating that the need to maintain attitudinal balance underlies the practice of citizenship during elections, see Angus Campbell, et al., *The American Voter* (New York: Wiley, 1960), pp. 176–79; Angus Campbell, et al., *The Voter Decides* (Evanston: Row, Peterson, 1954), pp. 120–23; Robert E. Lane and David O. Sears, *Public Opinion* (Englewood Cliffs, N.J.: Prentice-Hall, 1964), p. 59; William A. Gamson and Andre Modigliani, "Knowledge and Foreign Policy Opinions: Some Models for Consideration," *Public Opinion Quarterly*, Vol. XXX (Summer, 1966), pp. 187–99; and Donald R. Matthews and James W. Prothro, *Negroes and the New Southern Politics* (New York: Harcourt, Brace and World, 1966), p. 322.

[3] An interesting discussion—with some evidence—bearing on the likelihood that active citizens have more coherent and integrated sets of attitudes than their inactive counterparts can be found in Philip E. Converse, "The Nature of Belief Systems in Mass Publics," in David E. Apter, ed., *Ideology and Discontent* (New York: Free Press, 1964), pp. 206–61. Similar findings are developed in V. O. Key, Jr., *Public Opinion and American Democracy* (New York: Alfred A. Knopf, 1961), Chap. 8.

[4] Cf. John Robinson, "Balance Theory and Vietnam-Related Attitudes," *Social Science Quarterly*, Vol. 51 (December 1970), pp. 610–16.

[5] See pp. 293–96.

about some of the issues and regard their resolution as important. Attitudes toward the contents of issues are not the only factors that account for mobilizability and attentiveness, but it is difficult to imagine an individual establishing first- and second-hand contacts with public affairs on a regular basis without holding attitudes that justify the nature and extent of such contacts. As one observer put it, "From our daily impression of politics we feel that persons who have opinions of high intensity are likely to seek energetically to achieve the ends in which they believe." [6]

This is not to suggest that the attitudes of Mobilizables and Attentives are derived from a coherent ideology. Attitudinal balance does not necessarily mean consistency among the beliefs toward the contents of various issues. There is evidence that Americans do not share a well-defined ideology and, instead, tend "to view each issue independently of the others." [7] Rather, in this context attitudinal balance refers to consistency among all of a citizen's attitudes relevant to a single issue—such as his attitudes toward active citizenship and toward the effectiveness of political action, as well as the importance he attaches to an issue and the kind of solution he favors for it. His attitudes may combine in different ways for different issues—with the result that his orientations toward the contents of several issues may be inconsistent—

---

[6] Key, *Public Opinion and American Democracy.* p. 229. For additional evidence on this point, see Sidney Verba and Richard Brody, "Participation, Policy Preferences, and the War in Vietnam," *Public Opinion Quarterly*, Vol. XXXIV (Fall, 1970), pp. 325–32.

[7] Robert Axelrod, "The Structure of Public Opinion on Policy Issues," *Public Opinion Quarterly*, Vol. XXXI (Spring, 1967), pp. 51–60. It should be noted, however, that Axelrod's findings as well as those cited earlier by Converse ("The Nature of Belief Systems in Mass Publics") may no longer hold for the Mass Public, that since 1964 there is mounting evidence of ideological inconsistency at the the mass level (Sidney Verba, personal communication, June 21, 1973). But even if such a trend continues, it does not necessarily undermine the theme developed here (see also pp. 60–61) that technological advance has led to the replacement of ideological with issue-area orientations. Here we are concerned with attentive citizens, to whom the recent trend uncovered in the mass public may not apply.

but his combination of the various attitudinal dimensions for a single issue is likely to be balanced.

Attitudinal balance also does not imply that attitudes necessarily give rise to action in a simple causal sequence. Beliefs about an issue and actions toward it may both be the product of still other variables, including other seemingly unrelated attitudes. There is considerable evidence indicating that attitudes are most likely to predict to behavior in specific and routinized situations, whereas their links to action becomes increasingly tenuous under more undefined and unusual circumstances.[8] However, to conclude that the cause and effect relationships among attitudinal and behavioral factors are extraordinarily complex does not negate the existence of a tendency to maintain balance among such factors. It may well be that action cannot occur until attitudinal balance is achieved. A multitude of attitudes may be involved, but unless a modicum of balance among them, and between them and behavior, is maintained the practice of citizenship between elections may be impossible. It is the purpose of this chapter to explore this reasoning and to test several hypotheses (VIII–XII) which have been derived from it.

THE IMPORTANCE AND EXTREMITY VARIABLES

To hold an attitude toward an object is to be ready to respond to it in a characteristic way. Any attitude can be conceived to consist of a number of dimensions and here we have identified two basic dimensions of attitudes toward any issue of public affairs, each of which would seem central to the characteristic way in which a person is ready to respond to that issue. One

---

[8] See, for example, Irving Crespi, "What Kinds of Attitude Measures Are Predictive of Behavior?" *Public Opinion Quarterly*, Vol. XXXV (Fall, 1971), pp. 327–34; and Alan G. Weinstein, "Predicting Behavior from Attitudes," *Public Opinion Quarterly*, Vol. XXXVI (Fall, 1972), pp. 355–60. For a concrete example of the complex link between attitudes and action, see Robert A. Devine, "The Silent Majority: Neither Simple Nor Simple-Minded," *Public Opinion Quarterly*, Vol. XXXV (1971), pp. 571–77.

is the degree of importance that the citizen attaches to the issue, and the other is the extremity of the citizen's evaluation of how the issue should be resolved, i.e., whether a proposed solution is viewed favorably, neutrally, or unfavorably. We shall refer to these dimensions as the "importance" and the "extremity" variables.

Viewed in these terms, it seems clear that when a person's attitudes move toward the favorable or unfavorable extremes, corresponding increases along the importance dimension must occur if attitudinal balance is to be achieved and the chances of action maximized. It is difficult to imagine a person evaluating an issue at one or the other judgmental extreme but not attaching importance to it. In order to probe this relationship and to test the other attitude hypotheses derived from our model, the questionnaire contained two sets of items designed to operationalize the importance and extremity variables. Item #47 assessed importance by asking the respondents "how strongly" they felt "that a solution to each of the problems listed at the left is essential to the welfare of the country?" The problems were the same eleven issues used throughout the questionnaire and in each case the respondent had to choose among five points on the importance scale (see Table 8–1). The extremity variable was operationalized through ten items [#19, 20, 21, 22, 43, 44, 45, 46, 51, and 52] that required the respondents to judge ten of the issues[9] and proposed policies to resolve them on five-point scales that ranged from high to low extremity in both positive and negative directions (see Table 8–2).

The distributions of responses along the importance and extremity scales for both the Mobilizables and Attentives are presented in the tables below and were used to test Hypothesis VIII, which predicted that both groups would attribute high importance to and evidence extreme beliefs about at least one of the issues. This prediction was based on the assumption that a cap-

---

[9] It proved impossible to develop appropriate wording for one of the issues, balance of payments, so that there were extremity items for only ten of the eleven issues.

TABLE 8–1

DISTRIBUTION OF THE RESPONSES OF THE 1,704 MOBILIZABLES (Ms) AND THE 1,658 ATTENTIVES (As) TO ITEM #47 (in percentages)

[#47] How strongly do you feel that a solution to each of the problems listed at the left is essential to the welfare of the country? (Place one check in *each* row)

Issue		Extremely strongly	Very strongly	Quite strongly	Weakly	Not at all	Un-codable and no answer	Total
Agricultural	Ms	15	24	38	17	1	5	100
surpluses	As	12	23	39	19	2	5	100
Balance of	Ms	9	19	38	22	3	9	100
payments	As	9	18	39	23	3	3	100
Berlin	Ms	26	28	29	11	2	4	100
	As	22	28	30	13	2	5	100
Civil rights	Ms	85	11	2	0	0	2	100
	As	73	18	4	1	0	4	100
The Congo	Ms	12	19	37	24	2	6	100
	As	9	18	36	26	5	6	100
Federal tax	Ms	19	23	31	17	4	6	100
reduction	As	14	21	33	22	4	6	100
Foreign aid	Ms	35	35	21	4	1	4	100
	As	29	35	25	6	1	4	100
Nuclear testing	Ms	76	16	4	1	0	3	100
	As	65	21	8	2	0	4	100
Tariff reduction	Ms	16	29	36	12	1	6	100
	As	12	28	38	14	2	6	100
Vietnam	Ms	25	25	28	14	3	5	100
	As	21	27	27	17	3	5	100
Western unity	Ms	20	22	32	17	3	6	100
	As	20	23	32	18	2	5	100

acity for strong conviction is surely one of the factors that underlies membership in the Mobilizable or Attentive Public and that
therefore the respondents would be unlikely to express moderate
views toward all the issues that were included. The data in Tables
8–1 and 8–2 would seem to fully confirm the hypothesis, even
though the latter did not specify exact criteria of importance and
extremity. Civil rights and nuclear testing stand out as issues with
respect to which both the Mobilizables and Attentives held strong
convictions. In the case of importance (Table 8–1), more than
four-fifths of the Mobilizables and nearly three-fourths of the
Attentives felt "extremely strongly" about civil rights and these
proportions approach unanimity if those who responded "very
strongly" are included. The proportions of both groups who
indicated they attached considerable importance to the nuclear
testing issue were only slightly lower. Similarly, with respect to
extremity (Table 8–2), more than four-fifths of both groups
described their attitude toward the nuclear test ban treaty as
"very favorable." If the "very unfavorable" response is also considered to reflect "extreme belief," the proportions exceed
nine-tenths among the Mobilizables and five-sixths among the
Attentives. For the civil rights issue, the equivalent proportions
combining the two most extreme alternatives, also reached or exceeded nine-tenths of both groups. In addition, roughly two-thirds
of both groups indicated extreme or very strong feeling with
respect to the issue of foreign aid.

The validity of this confirmation of Hypothesis VIII might
be questioned on the grounds that the nuclear testing and civil
rights issues were predominant aspects of public affairs during the
period when the questionnaire was completed. But predominant
issues do not necessarily evoke strong attitudes and it seems doubtful that a random sample of citizens would almost unanimously
select the most extreme of five alternative attitudes toward the
importance and content of a salient issue. It is only after a citizen
becomes attentive to public affairs and inclined to establish contact with them that the issue of the day seems crucial and the
need for a thoroughgoing solution of it seems mandatory. Any

TABLE 8–2
DISTRIBUTION OF THE RESPONSES OF THE
MOBILIZABLES AND ATTENTIVES TO TEN ATTITUDE
EXTREMITY ITEMS (in percentages)

	Mobilizables *(1,704)*	Attentives *(1,658)*
[#19] If the Russians should attempt to block access to West Berlin, how justified would the United States be in resisting with force?		
Completely justified	19	22
Very justified	20	21
Somewhat justified	26	26
Hardly justified	13	13
Not at all justified	16	13
Uncodable and no answer	6	5
[#20] In your opinion, how much of an extension of civil rights should Congress approve?		
An unlimited extension	54	47
A great extension	40	43
Somewhat of an extension	3	6
A very small extension	0	1
No extension	1	1
Uncodable and no answer	2	3
[#21] In your opinion, to what extent should the amount of governmental subsidies designed to reduce agricultural surpluses be altered?		
Increased greatly	4	2
Increased somewhat	12	10
Kept as they are	20	20
Decreased somewhat	30	35
Decreased greatly	17	19
Uncodable and no answer	17	14
[#22] What do you think should be done to tariffs on goods imported into the U.S.?		
Reduced greatly	33	31
Reduced somewhat	45	47
Kept as they are	12	12
Increased somewhat	1	3
Increased greatly	1	0
Uncodable and no answer	8	7

[#43] If the U.N. proves unable to continue its peace-keeping efforts in the Congo without additional financing, how justified do you feel the United States would be in supplying most of the money?

Completely justified	24	22
Very justified	38	35
Somewhat justified	22	26
Hardly justified	9	10
Not at all justified	3	4
Uncodable and no answer	4	3

[#44] The president has asked Congress for a $10 billion tax reduction. How much of a reduction do you think Congress should approve?

No reduction at all	6	7
$5 billion	7	9
$10 billion	66	66
$12 billion	4	4
$15 billion	7	6
Uncodable and no answer	10	8

[#45] What is your opinion of the Nuclear Test Ban Treaty?

Very unfavorable	5	4
Somewhat unfavorable	0	1
Neither for nor against	1	1
Somewhat favorable	6	10
Very favorable	86	81
Uncodable and no answer	2	3

[#46] With how much enthusiasm do you think the United States should continue to speak of Western Unity as a major foreign policy goal?

Unqualified enthusiasm	18	17
Great enthusiasm	32	35
Moderate enthusiasm	33	32
Little enthusiasm	8	8
No enthusiasm	5	4
Uncodable and no answer	4	4

[#51] If the guerrilla war in Vietnam continues un-abated, how should the United States respond in terms of the number of men and the amount

(continued)

TABLE 8–2 *(continued)*

	Mobilizables (1,704)	Attentives (1,658)
of material it commits to the situation?		
Increase them greatly	8	11
Increase them somewhat	22	23
Maintain them as they are	18	19
Decrease them somewhat	8	6
Decrease them greatly	30	30
Uncodable and no answer	14	11
[#52] What do you think Congress should do with respect to the President's annual request for about $4 billion in foreign aid appropriations?		
Increase it greatly	13	9
Increase it a little	12	10
Approve it as is	57	59
Decrease it a little	10	11
Decrease it greatly	4	7
Uncodable and no answer	4	4

other set of attitudes would make the active citizen's readiness to be active incongruent with his view of the situations toward which his action might be directed.

THE INTERACTION OF ATTITUDINAL DIMENSIONS

The correlation between the importance and extremity variables further demonstrates that Mobilizables and Attentives tend to maintain balance among their attitudes toward public issues. It had been anticipated that active citizens could hardly regard the solution of an issue as essential to the national welfare without feeling correspondingly strong about its contents (Hypothesis IX) and that therefore the more importance Mobilizables and Attentives attribute to an issue, the more extreme will be their beliefs about it. Table 8–3 reveals that this expectation was affirmed: in both groups there was a significant positive association

TABLE 8–3
CORRELATION (Pearson product moment [r]) OF THE
RESPONSES OF THE MOBILIZABLES AND
ATTENTIVES TO THE ATTITUDINAL IMPORTANCE
AND EXTREMITY ITEMS FOR FIVE ISSUES

Issue	Mobilizables		Attentives	
	Pearson r	Number	Pearson r	Number
Berlin	.203*	1543	.210*	1533
Civil rights	.272*	1630	.427*	1571
The Congo	.325*	1580	.331*	1553
Federal tax reduction	.359*	1484	.384*	1492
Western unity	.732*	1586	.690*	1561
* P < .001.				

between the importance and extremity scales for each of the five issues for which a product moment correlation could be calculated.[10]

This is not to say that either attitudinal dimension is a major determinant of the other. The significance of all the correlations indicates only that the probability of their occurring by chance is less than one in a thousand. The square of each correlation gives the percentage of the variance in one variable that can be attributed to the other and on this basis it is clear that, except for the issue of Western unity, the need to maintain attitudinal balance is far from the prime source of the interaction between the importance and extremity variables. Western unity was the only issue with respect to which one of the attitudes accounted for more than fifteen percent of the variance of the other for both the Mobilizables and Attentives. Moreover, Western unity is not necessarily as discrepant from this finding as it seems. The wording of the extremity item [#46] for this issue is so similar to the

---

[10] Such a correlation could not be calculated for the agricultural surpluses, foreign aid, nuclear testing, tariff reduction, and Vietnam issues because the five alternatives comprising the extremity item for these five issues posited two extremes rather than a decreasing degree of extremity.

wording of the stem of the importance item [#47] that the high correlations may mean that the same attitude was reflected in the two dimensions rather than that there was an interaction between them.[11]

There is no inconsistency between the original model and the finding that the balance among issue-related attitudes is not a major determinant of the attitudes themselves. The model posits attitudinal balance as only one of many variables that, interactively, give rise to citizenship between elections. Nothing in the model implies that the balancing process is an especially powerful variable. The fact that it accounts for but a small portion of mobilizability and attentiveness does not diminish the finding that it is necessary to these forms of citizenship.

ATTITUDES AND ACTION

It is conceivable that those who practice citizenship between elections could achieve balance among their relevant attitudes without attaining a corresponding balance between the strength of these attitudes toward public issues and the extent of the activities they direct at the issues. One may attribute great importance to a public question and favor an extreme solution for it, but a number of real and imagined circumstances can prevent one from establishing first- or second-hand contacts with it. Writing letters takes time, participating in organizational activities takes energy, discussing issues with friends and acquaintances takes confidence, and these resources do not necessarily become

[11] That is, just as the importance item required the respondents to assess the issues in terms of a highly abstract dimension (importance), so did the extremity item for Western unity require them to consider committing a highly abstract resource (enthusiasm), whereas the resources required for an extreme commitment on the other four issues were quite specific (money, men, and rights). For other evidence that "the specificity with which [an] issue is formulated does play some role in responses," see Campbell, et al., *The American Voter*, pp. 172–75.

available to attentive and mobilizable citizens simply because they feel strongly about public affairs.[12]

The complexity of the relationship between attitudes and behavior is apparent in the correlations between the two attitudinal variables and the measures of first- and second-hand contact among the Attentives and Mobilizables. The data confirm the expectation (Hypotheses X and XI) that second-hand contacts would be congruent with attitudes, but the predictions were not upheld for first-hand contacts. That is, as the importance that the Attentives and Mobilizables attached to an issue and the extremity of the solution to it they deemed desirable increased, so did the likelihood that they would discuss it with friends and acquaintances; but the likelihood that they would write letters about it or engage in organizational activity with respect to it was mostly unaffected. Let us look first at the correlations between importance and the two forms of behavior, presented in Table 8–4. All twenty-two of the correlations involving the measure of second-hand contact [#49] were significant, but less than half of the correlations involving the two measures of first-hand contact were significant (and those that were significant were noticeably lower). The responses of the Mobilizables to the importance item were significantly related to their letter-writing scores on only two of the eleven issues and to their organizational activity scores on only three issues. Moreover, in the case of the Western unity issue the significant correlations were negative. Similarly, the correlations involving the extremity variable show the same pattern (Table 8–5), with many more of those with the measure of second-hand contacts being significant than those with the two measures of first-hand contacts. Again the significant correlations

---

[12] An indication that the opportunity to express attitudes through action may depend on the channels available for action is provided by the finding that working-class voters were much more opposed to U.S. participation in the Vietnam war in local referenda on the issue than in public opinion polls. See Harlan Hahn, "Correlates of Public Sentiments about War: Local Referenda on the Vietnam Issue," *American Political Science Review,* Vol. 64 (1970), p. 1197.

TABLE 8-4

CORRELATIONS (Pearson product moment [r]) OF THE RESPONSES OF AT LEAST 1,526 MOBILIZABLES AND 1,492 ATTENTIVES TO THE ATTITUDINAL IMPORTANCE ITEM [#47] ON THE ONE HAND AND THE MEASURES OF FIRST- AND SECOND-HAND CONTACT WITH ELEVEN ISSUES ON THE OTHER

Issue	FIRST-HAND CONTACT MEASURES				SECOND-HAND CONTACT MEASURE Frequency of conversations with friends and acquaintances in regard to the issues listed at the left [#49]	
	Index of letter-writing activity		Index of organizational activity			
	Mobilizables	Attentives	Mobilizables	Attentives	Mobilizables	Attentives
Agricultural surpluses	.093*	.070	−.014	.034	.313*	.346*
Balance of payments	.037	.016	−.036	−.039	.306*	.346*
Berlin	.031	.065	−.026	.070	.272*	.296*
Civil rights	.055	.065	.104*	.135*	.177*	.336*
The Congo	.094*	.138*	.016	.136*	.312*	.314*
Federal tax reduction	.045	.006	−.024	−.041	.374*	.344*
Foreign aid	.056	.109*	.110*	.198*	.212*	.219*
Nuclear testing	.066	.139*	.047	.194*	.248*	.329*
Tariff reduction	.076	.078	.034	.062	.295*	.275*
Vietnam	.070	.120*	.067	.143*	.266*	.284*
Western unity	−.069	−.107*	−.128*	−.080	.373*	.380*

* P < .001.

TABLE 8-5

CORRELATIONS (Pearson product moment [r]) OF THE RESPONSES OF AT LEAST 1,491 MOBILIZABLES AND 1,488 ATTENTIVES TO THE ATTITUDINAL EXTREMITY ITEMS [#19, 20, 43, 44, 46] ON THE ONE HAND AND THE MEASURES OF FIRST- AND SECOND-HAND CONTACT WITH FIVE ISSUES ON THE OTHER

| | FIRST-HAND CONTACT MEASURES | | | | SECOND-HAND CONTACT MEASURE Frequency of conversations with friends and acquaintances in regard to the issues listed at the left [#49] | |
| | Index of letter-writing activity | | Index of organizational activity | | | |
Issue	Mobilizables	Attentives	Mobilizables	Attentives	Mobilizables	Attentives
Berlin	−.098*	−.138*	−.095*	−.141*	−.007	.056
Civil rights	.064	.039	.098*	.106*	.105*	.236*
The Congo	.027	.101*	.043	.139*	.087*	.103*
Federal tax reduction	.031	−.018	.026	.019	.146*	.144*
Western unity	−.118*	−.110*	−.135*	−.094*	.307*	.287*

* P < .001.

involving Western unity were negative and, in this case, so were those involving the Berlin issue.

Despite the ambiguity of these findings, a plausible interpretation of them can be developed in terms of the joint effect of attitude strength and interfering resources and predispositions. The data uphold the expectation that the strength of the Mobilizables' and Attentives' attitudes would be associated with the extent of their citizenship activities, but this association is strongest with respect to the activities that required the least time or talent. It seems clear that both groups find it easier to act on their convictions through discussions with friends and acquaintances than by writing letters to public officials or participating in the activities of an organization. In the case of the first-hand contacts, the contrary attitudes, commitments, and demands of life in a family and job are apparently enough of an interference to reduce the amount of behavior that would follow from the strength of attitudes toward public issues.[13]

ATTITUDES AND MOBILIZABILITY

Our original reasoning had led us to expect (Hypothesis XII) that the Mobilizables would evidence stronger attitudes toward the various issues than the Attentives because presumably mobilizability requires a greater readiness to attach importance to and register extreme beliefs about public issues than does attentiveness. The conclusion derived from the findings presented in the previous section, however, that attitudes are more readily translated

---

[13] Additional evidence for this interpretation is provided by the responses of a national sample whose attitudes toward the Vietnam war were surveyed at the height of that conflict. Comparing the attitudes of those in the sample who reported writing letters to officials or newspapers with those who did not engage in such a practice, the investigators found that "letter writers are *not* more likely to take extreme positions" than their nonwriting counterparts. See Sidney Verba, Richard A. Brody, Edwin B. Parker, Norman H. Nie, Nelson W. Polsby, Paul Ekman, and Gordon S. Black, "Public Opinion and the War in Vietnam," *American Political Science Review*, Vol. LXI (June 1967), p. 329.

into second-hand than first-hand contacts, suggests that the data might not uphold this reasoning.

The distribution of the relevant data have already been presented in Tables 8–1 and 8–2. The first of these presents the responses of the Mobilizables and Attentives to the importance item [#47] and they provide some confirmation of both the original hypothesis and our subsequent doubts. Statistical comparison of the responses of the two groups confirmed the hypothesis on four issues (foreign aid, nuclear testing, tax reduction, and civil rights),[14] but not on the other seven. A similar pattern resulted from a comparison of the responses to the extremity items presented in Table 8–2: The Mobilizables recorded more extreme attitudes than the Attentives on the foreign aid, nuclear testing, agricultural surpluses, and civil rights issues,[15] but not on the other issues.

These findings may be interpreted as indicating that although mobilizability and attitudes are related, not all of a mobilizable citizen's attitudes toward the issues that constitute public affairs at a moment in time are involved. The establishment of first-hand contacts does lead mobilizable citizens to develop stronger attitudes than attentive citizens, but apparently only with respect to those issues toward which they have been mobilized. On both of the issues (civil rights and nuclear testing) toward which the Mobilizables are known to have been mobilized, they recorded higher scores than the Attentives on both attitudinal dimensions, but there were not even traces of such differences on most of the issues mentioned in the questionnaire.

The fact that the two groups differed on both attitudinal dimensions on the foreign aid issue is not necessarily inconsistent with this interpretation. As will be seen, this is but one of many

[14] For the foreign aid issue, $\chi^2 = 23.28$, df $= 4$, P$<.001$; for nuclear testing, $\chi^2 = 62.54$, df $= 3$, P$<.001$; for federal tax reduction, $\chi^2 = 22.65$, df $= 4$, P$<.001$; for civil rights, $\chi^2 = 68.70$, df $= 3$, P$<.001$.

[15] For foreign aid, $\chi^2 = 23.13$, df $= 4$, P$<.001$; for nuclear testing, $\chi^2 = 22.74$, df $= 4$, P$<.001$; for agricultural surpluses, $\chi^2 = 19.56$, df $= 4$, P$<.001$; for civil rights, $\chi^2 = 25.68$, df $= 3$, P$<.001$.

instances in which the responses on this issue resembled those on nuclear testing and civil rights. This suggests that the respondents may have been exposed to mobilization attempts with respect to foreign aid, and certainly the 1963–1964 period was one in which many groups sought to generate support for the foreign aid program. We cannot account in any simple manner for the significant differences on the importance variable for tax reduction or on the extremity variable for agricultural surpluses, but these deviations do not seem sufficient to negate the central pattern of selective association between mobilizability and attitudinal intensity.

Although unanticipated, the finding that the interaction between mobilizability and attitudes is selective should not be surprising. A citizen does not have the time, energy, or skill to become deeply involved in all the conflicts that mark world affairs at a moment in time. Just as newspapers do not have the resources to give adequate coverage to more than a few issues at a time, an individual's span of attention is limited. Students of voting behavior have found that, in general, there is a "widespread lack of familiarity with issues of public policy" [16] among the citizenry. It is true that concern about public affairs distinguishes the Attentive Public from the general population, but this does not mean that attentive citizens have an undifferentiated and unlimited concern for every issue that arises. They may be aware of and informed about the full spectrum of issues that arise between elections, but to be knowledgeable does not necessitate deep involvement. Choices have to be made, often implicitly, as to how limited time and resources are to be allocated, and thus the solutions of only a few of the issues clamoring for public support at any moment can assume extreme importance. Thus it is clear in retrospect that our model erred in anticipating that the attitudes of Mobilizables and Attentives would differ on all the issues on which their responses were evoked. The process by which an issue becomes the focus of involvement and mobilizability is, of course, a crucial question which the findings of this chapter do not elucidate and to which we shall return in Chapter 12.

[16] Campbell, et al., *The American Voter*, p. 188.

SUMMARY

The responses of the Mobilizables and Attentives along two attitudinal dimensions, importance and extremity, confirmed the expectation (Hypothesis VIII) that those who engage in citizenship between elections would hold strong attitudes toward at least one of the issues that constitute public affairs at a given moment in time. Our prediction (Hypothesis IX) that the attitudes of active citizens would be internally consistent was confirmed by the significant correlations between the importance and extremity attitude variables among both the Mobilizables and Attentives. The more importance they attributed to an issue, in other words, the more extreme were their beliefs about it.

With respect to the relationship between attitudes and behavior the data were ambiguous. It had been expected (Hypotheses X and XI) that the Mobilizables and Attentives would be more likely to establish contact with public affairs the more strongly they felt toward the outstanding issues of the day, but this proved to be the case primarily with respect to second-hand forms of contact. This was interpreted as demonstrating the importance of the differences in the amount of time and resources necessary to establish the two types of contact. It would seem to be easier, even for an active citizen, to express attitudes through discussions of public affairs with friends and acquaintances than through letters to public officials or organizational activity.

Our prediction (Hypothesis XII) that the Mobilizables would attach more importance to and register more extreme beliefs about public issues than the Attentives was upheld on four issues, but the two groups did not differ significantly on most of the issues. The identity of the issues on which the responses of the two groups differed suggested that being mobilized to establish first-hand contacts does lead citizens to develop stronger attitudes, but only toward those issues with respect to which they were mobilized.

CHAPTER 9

THE STRUCTURE OF PERCEPTIONS

The practices of citizenship are shaped not only by an individual's attitudes toward public issues, but also by his perceptions of where he fits in the structures and processes through which issues arise, persist, and terminate. It may be that attentiveness and mobilizability are more directly related to the evaluative than to the cognitive dimension, but it seems reasonable to presume that a citizen's actions are at least somewhat influenced by his conception of the sources and consequences of public affairs.

Cognitions of the political process and one's role in it are as susceptible to becoming imbalanced as are evaluations of its contents, and as responsive to the subsequent pressures toward restoring balance. Reality may be discrepant with what one wishes it to be and perceptions can thus be said to always be the outcome of a contest between wish and reality. The more clear-cut the reality, the less will perceptions of it be distorted by wishes; and the more potent the wish, the less accurately will perceptions reflect reality.[1] Within the limits set by needs and reality, however, perceptions will tend to be consistent with each other. In addition, people cannot tolerate inconsistency between their perceptions and attitudes or between their perceptions and their behavior and the interplay among these is a constant and complex one. We do not perceive without evaluating or evaluate without perceiving, so that the distinction is valid only for analytic purposes. Furthermore, since one has attitudes toward and perceptions of ones' own behavior, one tailors what one does to make it consistent with what one feels and thinks and one shapes one's attitudes and perceptions to agree with what one has done.

The fact that the data on attitudes and perceptions have been analyzed separately should thus not be construed as suggesting the existence of two independent balancing processes. Our concern in this chapter is with the balancing of perceptions, but it is part and parcel of the same process explored in the previous chapter. At several points below we shall consider the interaction between the perceptual and attitudinal data as well as between the former and the various forms of behavior in which the Mobilizables and Attentives engaged.

The perceptions that underlie citizenship between elections, being the outcome of a contest between wish and reality, may not be accurate. It seems probable, moreover, that perceptual inaccuracy will be much greater between than during elections. Elections involve the competition of a few identifiable candidates whose activities are purposefully visible. Issues contested between elections, however, encompass the competition of many groups

---

[1] This formulation was suggested by a reading of William J. McGuire, "A Syllogistic Analysis of Cognitive Relationships," in Milton J. Rosenberg, et al., *Attitude Organization and Change: An Analysis of Consistency among Attitude Components* (New Haven: Yale University Press, 1960), pp. 65–111.

and persons whose activities are more varied and less subject to scrutiny. So much is going on in such situations that perceptual accuracy and detail may be sacrificed as citizens attempt to achieve and maintain balance among all their perceptual inputs.

Perceptions of the political process can have as many aspects as there are actors, groups, norms, and institutions who comprise it, but our model singles out two general clusters—perceptions of information possessed and perceptions of civic competence—as especially relevant to the attitudes and activities of attentive and mobilizable citizens. The information cluster embraces a person's perceptions of his own and the general population's degree of information about the issues being contested in the public arena —what we call, respectively, the "self-information" and "public-information" variables. The competence cluster encompasses a person's perceptions of the susceptibility of officials to public opinion, of the capacity of specific groups to influence them, and of his own capacity to influence both the officials and the groups —what we shall call, respectively, the "public-competence," "group-competence," and "individual-competence" variables. The two clusters are conceptually interdependent in that the degree to which one perceives oneself to be informed about public affairs is likely to have consequences for the extent to which one feels competent to influence them. In order to explore this interdependence empirically, however, it seems preferable in the ensuing analysis to maintain the distinction between the two clusters rather than treating all five variables as aspects of competence.

SELF-PERCEPTION OF INFORMATION POSSESSED

Citizens who are attentive to the course of events are, virtually by definition, better informed about them than those members of the mass public who are normally indifferent to national and international affairs. To be attentive to issues is to acquire information about them and to acquire information about issues is to be attentive to them. This interaction has been found to exist irrespective of the form of attentiveness involved. One analyst, for example, found that whether the activity is registering to vote, attending a meeting of a civil rights group, or participating in a riot, "political information has a significant effect on all three forms of political activity. In each case the higher the level of political information the greater the participation." [2]

This is not to imply a direct causal relationship between the two variables. Citizens are conceived to be better able to interpret the course of events, to feel more politically competent, and to have greater awareness of their stake in the political process as they acquire more information, and these factors are in turn regarded as stimuli to participation. The authors of a comparative investigation of the sources of active citizenship in five countries, including the United States, found that, "Information does not directly increase participation, but does act strongly and consistently through sense of governmental impact, political efficacy, and, especially, attentiveness to politics. Basic information . . . seems to be a fundamental prerequisite to the interest and awareness which stimulate participation." [3] Furthermore, it seems clear that increased information leads to a greater strain toward attitudinal balance and greater support for official public policies.[4]

To be sure, the information that active citizens acquire may be partial and it may be distorted in the direction of what is desired. While most active citizens are more knowledgeable than their inactive counterparts, this is not true of all of them. As one

[2] Jeffrey M. Paige, "Political Orientation and Riot Participation," *American Sociological Review*, Vol. 36 (October 1971), p. 818.

[3] Nie, Powell, Prewitt, "Social Structure and Political Participation," p. 816. For other data depicting the close association between levels of political information and participation, see Alfred O. Hero, *Americans in World Affairs* (Boston: World Peace Foundation, 1959), *passim*; V. O. Key, *Public Opinion and American Democracy*, p. 185; Matthews and Prothro, *Negroes and the New Southern Politics*, pp. 271–74; and William C. Rogers, Barbara Stuhler, and Donald Koenig, "A Comparison of Informed and General Public Opinion on U.S. Foreign Policy," *Public Opinion Quarterly*, Vol. 31 (Summer, 1967), pp. 242–52.

[4] William A. Gamson and Andre Modigliani, "Knowledge and Foreign Policy Opinions: Some Models for Consideration," *Public Opinion Quarterly*, Vol. XXX (Summer, 1966), p. 197.

investigation of two peace marches in two different countries found, in any survey of citizens active in a particular situation there will be at least some individuals in every cell of a 2 × 2 matrix that distingushes between low and high amounts of political activity and high and low degrees of information about public affairs. The low-low cell will be filled by "the raw recruit with little knowledge of practical politics ... [who is] activated by a deeply held but crudely formulated moral belief." Those in the high activity-low information cell will be the " 'professional demonstrator' or 'mindless militant' who has never got much beyond the slogan stage in his political thinking but simply believes in 'being active.' "[5]

Yet, whatever the sufficiency and accuracy of their information, as active citizens acquire more and more of it they become increasingly involved in one or another issue. The tendency to distort the situation may on occasion be so strong that new information about it is not perceived, but the active citizen is likely nonetheless to perceive himself as informed about it.[6] While many public issues are exceedingly complex and would seem to defy comprehension by anyone other than a specialist, it is doubtful whether attentive and mobilizable citizens would bow to complexity and perceive themselves as uninformed about the issues that interest them. The pressures to perceive themselves as adequately informed seem likely to come from several sources. One is simply the need to provide a basis for their attentiveness and mobilizability. In order to see their attitudes and actions toward an issue as justified, they must presumably see themselves as appropriately informed about it. Likewise, as their sense of being informed about the issue builds up, presumably they will feel more confident in holding attitudes and undertaking behavior

---

[5] Robin Jenkins, "Who Are These Marchers?" *Journal of Peace Research,* Vol. 1 (1967), p. 57.

[6] For evidence that citizens can be uninformed about public affairs even as they perceive themselves as informed, see Don D. Smith, " 'Dark Areas of Ignorance' Revisited: Current Knowledge About Asian Affairs," *Social Science Quarterly,* Vol. 51, No. 3 (December 1970), pp. 668–673.

with respect to it, and this confidence will in turn reinforce the self-perception of mounting information. In addition, the norms of American political culture seem likely to generate pressure toward perceptual balance. The culture equates good citizenship with involvement in public affairs, and thus attentive and mobilizable citizens are not only likely to see themselves as attentive and mobilizable, but are also likely to be proud of these traits and to have a stake in maintaining them as part of their self-images. If this is so, then they will also tend to want to see themselves as adequately informed about one or more of the issues of the day.

The conclusion that active citizens are under considerable pressure to perceive themselves as well-informed—at least about one current issue—was embodied in Hypothesis XIII and explored in Item #50 of the questionnaire. The latter operationalized the self-information variable in terms of a five-point scale that called on the respondents to rate "how much information" they felt they had "on the problems listed at the left." The five points ranged from an "enormous amount" to "none."

Table 9–1 presents the distribution of responses to the self-information item for both the Mobilizables and Attentives. It can be immediately seen that in the narrow sense of a single issue being the focus of high self-information perceptions, the foregoing reasoning was upheld. More than three-fourths of both groups did see themselves as possessing an "enormous" or "large" amount of information on one issue, civil rights. Hypothesis XIII did not specify how large the proportion of those who perceived themselves as well informed had to be to constitute confirmation, but surely the fact that 85 percent of the Mobilizables and 79 percent of the Attentives opted for one of the two highest points on the scale amounts to confirmation.

Perhaps no less striking than the proportion of Mobilizables and Attentives who perceived themselves as informed about civil rights is the finding that this was the only one of the eleven issues that substantial numbers of both groups plainly felt they comprehended. A bare majority of the Mobilizables selected the "enormous" and "large" alternatives on the nuclear testing issue,

TABLE 9–1
DISTRIBUTION OF THE RESPONSES OF THE 1,704 MOBILIZABLES (Ms) AND THE 1,658 ATTENTIVES (As) TO ITEM #50 (in percentages)

[#50] How much information do you feel you have on the problems listed at the left? (Place *one* check in each row)

Issue		An enormous amount	A large amount	A moderate amount	Very little	None	Un-codable and no answer	Total
Agricultural	Ms	1	9	42	40	5	3	100
surpluses	As	1	8	46	37	5	3	100
Balance of	Ms	0	5	33	44	14	4	100
payments	As	1	6	36	43	11	3	100
Berlin	Ms	5	31	52	8	1	3	100
	As	4	29	54	9	1	3	100
Civil rights	Ms	33	52	11	1	0	3	100
	As	26	53	16	1	1	3	100
The Congo	Ms	2	13	49	30	2	4	100
	As	1	12	47	33	3	4	100
Federal tax	Ms	3	20	47	24	2	4	100
reduction	As	4	18	51	21	2	4	100
Foreign aid	Ms	4	30	52	10	1	3	100
	As	5	26	52	13	1	3	100
Nuclear testing	Ms	11	45	37	4	0	3	100
	As	8	39	41	8	1	3	100
Tariff reduction	Ms	1	11	45	35	4	4	100
	As	2	9	44	36	5	4	100
Vietnam	Ms	4	21	45	24	2	4	100
	As	3	20	45	26	3	3	100
Western unity	Ms	3	22	53	17	1	4	100
	As	3	22	51	19	2	3	100

but otherwise neither group had a majority that perceived themselves as well informed on any of the other issues. Indeed, on one issue, balance of payments, a majority of both groups opted for the two alternatives at the low end of the scale and a similar tendency is evident in their responses on some of the other economic issues, particularly agricultural surpluses and tariff reduction.

This it would seem that the pressures toward perceptual balance operate within narrow bounds with respect to the self-information variable. Tendencies for active citizens to perceive themselves as well informed about more than one issue are difficult to discern in the data. Rather the findings suggest that the Mobilizables and Attentives appreciate the complexity of public affairs and are appropriately modest in their perceptions of themselves as informed citizens. Given the strength of their attitudes on some of the issues, it is striking that they were not inclined to see themselves as well informed about them and in several cases even saw themselves as uninformed. This appreciation of complexity is most evident in their temperate responses on the nuclear testing issue, an issue which was highly salient at the time of the survey, to which both the Mobilizables and Attentives attached considerable importance, and about which they expressed extreme attitudes.[7] The Mobilizables and Attentives did not bow to the complexity of the testing issue and perceive themselves as uninformed about it, but neither did they allow their involvement in it to exaggerate their comprehension of it.

The conclusion that active citizens perceive the information they possess modestly is not negated by the finding that the civil rights issue evoked self-perceptions of high information. This is the only status issue among the eleven listed[8] and the value conflicts it embraces are much more clear-cut and the technological complexities it subsumes much less crucial than was the case for the other ten issues. The development of a sense that one com-

[7] See Tables 8–1 and 8–2.
[8] For a discussion of the characteristics that differentiate status issues from other major types, see Rosenau, *The Scientific Study of Foreign Policy* (New York: The Free Press, 1970), pp. 142–47.

prehends the civil rights issue probably requires less information than for any other type of issue.

In sum, it appears that active citizens can feel confident about their understanding of status issues because such matters are in fact more comprehensible to the nonexpert. But their inability to grasp the other types of issues as thoroughly does not diminish their readiness to engage in the practices of active citizenship.

Although the Mobilizables and Attentives were moderate in their estimates of their own information about public affairs, the same can hardly be said about their assessment of the level of comprehension of the general population. Table 9–2 presents the data for the public-information variable, an item [#11] that asked for a rating on a five-point scale of "how well" the "American people understood the problems" inherent in the eleven issues. As can be seen, the respondents expressed little faith in the Mass Public's grasp of the current scene. There was no issue on which a majority of either group recorded an assessment in the two highest levels of understanding, while well over a majority of both groups perceived them as understanding six of the issues "poorly" or "not at all." Roughly four-fifths of both groups rated the Mass Public's understanding at the two lowest points on the Congo and balance of payments issues. In view of the events of the late 1960s, it is perhaps also interesting that 72 percent of both groups assessed the public's grasp of the Vietnam problem as either poor or nonexistent.

This low estimate of the public's level of information had been anticipated (Hypothesis XIV) for two interrelated reasons. In the first place, being themselves well-informed, members of the Attentive Public are likely to be aware of the well documented and widely known finding that most citizens are unconcerned and uninformed about public affairs. Secondly, the data presented in Table 9–2 are also consistent with the requirements of perceptual balance. In order to justify their own involvement in public affairs, attentive and mobilizable citizens are likely to see themselves as guardians of the public interest, as making up for the passivity of the population in general. To perceive all citizens as equally interested and informed would diminish the relevance of their actions for the course of events. The mean scores of both groups on the eleven self-information items were significantly

---

TABLE 9–2
DISTRIBUTION OF THE RESPONSES OF THE 1,704 MOBILIZABLES (Ms) AND THE 1,658 ATTENTIVES (As) TO ITEM #11 (in percentages)

[#11] How well would you say the American people understand the problems listed at the left? (Place *one* check in each row)

Issue		Extremely well	Quite well	Some-what	Poorly	Not at all	Un-codable and no answer	Total
Agricultural	Ms	0	5	33	49	10	3	100
surpluses	As	0	6	32	47	12	3	100
Balance of	Ms	0	1	11	49	35	4	100
payments	As	0	1	12	48	35	4	100
Berlin	Ms	1	20	48	25	3	3	100
	As	2	20	48	24	3	3	100
Civil rights	Ms	4	36	44	13	1	2	100
	As	4	33	45	15	1	2	100
The Congo	Ms	0	1	19	63	14	3	100
	As	0	1	18	63	15	3	100
Federal tax	Ms	2	15	47	29	4	3	100
reduction	As	2	15	47	29	4	3	100
Foreign aid	Ms	0	7	43	43	4	3	100
	As	0	7	43	43	4	3	100
Nuclear testing	Ms	2	23	45	26	1	3	100
	As	2	18	44	31	2	3	100
Tariff reduction	Ms	0	2	26	55	13	4	100
	As	0	2	27	53	14	4	100
Vietnam	Ms	0	3	22	56	16	3	100
	As	0	3	22	55	17	3	100
Western unity	Ms	1	15	48	29	4	3	100
	As	1	15	46	29	5	4	100

higher than their scores on the corresponding public-information items,[9] indicating that both the Mobilizables and the Attentives achieved perceptual balance in this respect.

INFORMATION AND ATTITUDES

Notwithstanding the above finding that the Mobilizables and Attentives had a modest view of themselves as informed citizens, in both groups there was a positive association between these self-perceptions and attitudes, as anticipated in Hypothesis XV. As can be seen in Tables 9-3 and 9-4, the more importance a member of either group attached to an issue and the more extremely he felt about it, the more informed about that issue was he likely to perceive himself. The correlations between the importance and self-information variables proved to be significant for both the

---

TABLE 9-3
CORRELATIONS (Pearson product moment [r]) OF THE RESPONSES OF AT LEAST 1,500 MOBILIZABLES AND 1,499 ATTENTIVES TO THE EXTREMITY [#19, 20, 43, 44, 46] AND SELF-INFORMATION [#50] ITEMS

Issue	Mobilizables	Attentives
Berlin	.016	.074
Civil rights	.184*	.221*
The Congo	.129*	.100*
Federal tax reduction	.170*	.159*
Western unity	.189*	.233*
* P < .001.		

---

[9] The *t* values resulting from a comparison of the scores on each of the eleven issues ranged from between 10.57 and 53.53 for at least 1,593 Mobilizables and between 9.52 and 46.67 for at least 1,542 Attentives. The two lowest values involved the tax reduction issue and the two highest involved the civil rights issue. The values for the Mobilizables exceeded 38.42 on five of the issues and the five highest for the Attentives were greater than 32.00. All of the values, including the lowest, are significant at the .001 level.

TABLE 9–4
CORRELATIONS (Pearson product moment [r]) OF THE
RESPONSES OF AT LEAST 1,535 MOBILIZABLES
AND 1,515 ATTENTIVES TO THE IMPORTANCE [#47]
AND SELF-INFORMATION [#50] ITEMS

Issue	Mobilizables	Attentives
Agricultural surpluses	.204*	.221*
Balance of payments	.275*	.310*
Berlin	.209*	.202*
Civil rights	.230*	.280*
Congo	.215*	.216*
Federal tax reduction	.329*	.298*
Foreign aid	.255*	.260*
Nuclear testing	.213*	.299*
Tariff reduction	.371*	.353*
Vietnam	.258*	.290*
Western unity	.246*	.268*
* P < .001.		

Mobilizables and Attentives on all eleven issues (Table 9–4) and
the same was true for four of the five issues on which correlations
between the extremity and self-information variables were possible (Table 9–3). The associations depicted in the tables are not
strong enough to permit the conclusion that the requirements
of cognitive and evaluative balance are major determinants of
the way in which active citizens perceive issues. It is clear, however, that a balancing process was operative. The modesty of their
self-information perceptions may have minimized the degree to
which they saw themselves as highly informed, but even a modest
person needs to balance the degree to which he perceives himself
as informed with the strength of his attitudes.[10]

[10] For additional data on the balance between information and attitudes,
see William A. Gamson and Andre Modigliani, "Knowledge and
Foreign Policy Opinions: Some Models for Consideration," *Public
Opinion Quarterly*, Vol. XXX (Summer, 1966), pp. 190–91. For findings
which run counter to those presented here and show "little relationship
between information and . . . the intensity of [a respondent's] attitudes;

PERCEIVED INFORMATION AND ACTION

The act of establishing contact with public affairs stems from a multitude of interacting attitudes and perceptions, some of which are likely to involve notions of how the behavior serves to relate the individual to the world around him. The data analyzed in the previous chapter have already demonstrated that these links between evaluation, cognition, and behavior are extraordinarily complex, but it seems reasonable to presume that the extent to which an individual engages in citizenship between elections will be at least partially influenced by the degree to which he perceives himself to be informed about the course of events. Hypothesis XVI reflected this reasoning, predicting that both the Attentives and Mobilizables would establish more first- and second-hand contacts with an issue the more they perceived themselves as informed about it.

As was the case with the relationship between attitudes and actions,[11] the association between perceptions and behavior proved to be less straightforward than had been anticipated. Once again the predicted relationship is much stronger for second-hand than for first-hand contact with public affairs. As can be seen in Table 9–5, all eleven correlations between the self-information and second-hand contact variables were significant for both the Mobilizables and Attentives. In the case of the two forms of first-hand contact, on the other hand, neither group recorded significant correlations for all the issues. Indeed, fewer than half (five of eleven) of the Mobilizables' correlations between the self-information and organizational activity variables proved to be significant and the corresponding results for the Attentives (six of eleven) are quite similar.

---

and, especially surprising, his own felt knowledge about the issue," see Stephen I. Fitzsimmons and Hobart G. Osburn, "The Impact of Social Issues and Public Affairs Documentaries," *Public Opinion Quarterly*, Vol. XXXII (Fall, 1968), p. 392. The latter findings, however, were derived from a sample of college sophomores rather than active citizens.

[11] See above, pp. 332–36.

TABLE 9-5

CORRELATIONS (Pearson product moment [r]) OF THE RESPONSES OF AT LEAST 1,598 MOBILIZABLES AND 1,558 ATTENTIVES TO THE SELF-INFORMATION ITEM [#50] ON THE ONE HAND AND THE MEASURES OF FIRST- AND SECOND-HAND CONTACT WITH ELEVEN ISSUES ON THE OTHER

| | FIRST-HAND CONTACT MEASURES | | | | SECOND-HAND CONTACT MEASURE Frequency of conversations with friends and acquaintances in regard to the issues at the left [#49] | |
| | Index of letter-writing activity | | Index of organizational activity | | | |
	Mobilizables	Attentives	Mobilizables	Attentives	Mobilizables	Attentives
Agricultural surpluses	.136*	.099*	.020	.016	.481*	.454*
Balance of payments	.081	.095*	.042	.047	.475*	.459*
Berlin	.119*	.143*	.061	.072	.354*	.334*
Civil rights	.211*	.219	.187*	.259*	.347*	.408*
The Congo	.175*	.169*	.139*	.154*	.370*	.381*
Federal tax reduction	.084	.088*	.040	.011	.459*	.398*
Foreign aid	.192*	.197*	.165*	.198*	.332*	.334*
Nuclear testing	.210*	.270*	.141*	.218*	.360*	.410*
Tariff reduction	.157*	.148*	.085	.106*	.453*	.392*
Vietnam	.157*	.185*	.117*	.094*	.422*	.402*
Western unity	.067	.048	.042	.040	.401*	.385*

* P < .001.

The close similarity between these findings and those involving the attitude variables suggests a similar, if not an identical, interpretation, that it is easier for active citizens to express their perceptions when all that is involved is discussing issues with friends and acquaintances. Less time and, indeed, less information is necessary to enter into such discussions than is required when letter-writing and organizational activity is the form of citizenship being practiced.

INFORMATION AND MOBILIZABILITY

Although it can be readily argued that a sense of being adequately informed about a public issue is as necessary to attentive as to mobilized contact, the logic of our model led to the expectation (Hypothesis XVII) that the Mobilizables would attribute higher levels of information to themselves than would the Attentives. Since perceived information was expected to be greater the more a citizen engaged in letter-writing and organizational activities, it followed that the readiness to respond to the appeals of mobilizers should be greater the more informed a person felt. Stated differently, since the first-hand forms of contact that result from mobilizability require more time and energy than the second-hand forms that are associated with attentiveness, mobilizable citizens can be expected to require a greater sense of being informed in order to be active than their attentive counterparts.

A comparison of the responses of the Attentives and Mobilizables to the self-information variable yields clear-cut support for this expectation. Already presented in Table 9–1, the responses of the two groups differed significantly on only two issues, civil rights and nuclear testing, and in both cases the Mobilizables reported perceiving themselves as more informed than did the Attentives.[12] Since these were also the only two issues on which the Mobilizables were in fact known to have been mobilized, the reasoning underlying Hypothesis XVII was upheld even more

---

[12] For the civil rights issue, $\chi^2 = 29.65$, df $= 3$, P$<.001$; for nuclear testing, $\chi^2 = 33.71$, df $= 4$, P$<.001$.

unambiguously than had been anticipated. The hypothesis allowed for the possibility that the Mobilizables would feel generally more informed than the Attentives, but the data show that the perception of greater information was confined to those issues on which mobilization had occurred.

SELF-PERCEPTION OF COMPETENCE

Perhaps the best evidence that perceptual variables are relevant to the practices of citizenship is provided by inquiries into citizens' perceptions of their competence to influence public affairs. A number of studies have shown a close association between individuals' self-perceptions of competence and their information about and involvement in public affairs. Key, for example, found that a person's subjective competence—what he and others call "the sense of political efficacy"—"taps an important political motivation" since it correlates with attitudes toward foreign affairs as well as with measures of issue familiarity and political participation.[13] Matthews and Prothro found that even if account is taken of such correlates, perceptions of competence are closely linked to the practices of citizenship: ". . . while sense of civic competence is related to both political information and interest, it has a discernible impact on Negro participation which is independent of these two important variables."[14] Students of voting behavior reached a similar conclusion when they found that 40 percentage points in the voting turnout rate separated those in their sample who felt highly efficacious and those whose sense of political efficacy was low.[15] Likewise, in a cross-national study of subjective competence in five different societies Almond and Verba interpreted their data as indicating that in comparison to

the citizen whose subjective competence is low, the self-confident citizen is likely to be the active citizen: to follow politics, to discuss politics, to be a more active partisan. He

[13] *Public Opinion and American Democracy*, pp. 192–94.
[14] *Negroes and the New Southern Politics*, p. 280.
[15] Campbell, et al., *The American Voter*, p. 105.

is also more likely to be satisfied with his role as a participant and ... to be more favorably disposed toward the performance of his political system and to have a generally more positive orientation toward it.[16]

Findings such as the foregoing led to the derivation of several hypotheses (XVIII–XXII) in which high absolute degrees of perceived civic competence were predicted for the Attentives and Mobilizables as well as significant correlations between their sense of competence and their self-information perceptions, their attitudes, and their activities. Perhaps more than any other citizens. it was reasoned, those who are attentive or mobilizable would be likely to perceive officialdom as susceptible to influence by the citizenry. It was presumed that one can only be ready to respond to the appeal of mobilizers if one perceives the political process as capable of being affected by such activities. Notwithstanding the logic of this reasoning, it is not fully upheld by the data presented below. The data suggest that the interaction between the perception of civic competence and the practices of citizenship is more complex than previous findings seem to indicate.

In order to probe this perceptual dimension, three clusters of variables involving different levels of competence—the individual's, the group's, and the general public's—were included in the questionnaire.[17] The individual-competence cluster consisted of only one variable, an item [#56] that asked the respondents to record on a five-point scale their assessments of the magnitude of

---

[16] *The Civic Culture*, p. 257. For additional evidence that high subjective competence tends to be associated with favorable attitudes toward the political system in which citizens participate, see John Fraser, "The Mistrustful-Efficacious Hypothesis and Political Participation," *Journal of Politics*, Vol. 32 (1970), pp. 444–49; and Brett W. Hawkins, Vincent L. Marando. George A. Taylor, "Efficacy, Mistrust, and Political Participation: Findings from Additional Data and Indicators," *Journal of Politics*, Vol. 33 (1971), pp. 1130–36.

[17] For a discussion of why it is conceptually important to distinguish among these different levels of competence, see Edward N. Muller, "Cross-National Dimensions of Political Competence," *American Political Science Review*. Vol. LXIV (September 1970), pp. 792–93.

"the opportunities for the individual citizen to influence governmental and public opinion on foreign policy questions." Table 9–6 presents the responses of the Mobilizables and Attentives to this item. Here it is evident that the expectation (Hypothesis XVIIIa) that both groups would perceive the individual citizen as highly competent to influence public affairs fell far short of confirmation. Less than one-third of both groups perceived the individual as possessing "enormous" or "large" opportunities to influence the handling of foreign policy issues. While it is difficult to specify what constitutes perceptions of high competence, surely the fact that the two highest points on the individual-competence scale were passed over by a substantial majority of both groups negates our expectations.

On the other hand, proportions much closer to what had been expected (Hypothesis XVIIIb and XVIIIc) resulted from the responses to the group- and public-competence variables. The latter, which called for an assessment of the responsiveness to public opinion of several types of officials [Item #58], failed to elicit impressively large proportions of responses at the high end

---

TABLE 9–6
DISTRIBUTION OF THE RESPONSES OF THE 1,704 MOBILIZABLES AND 1,658 ATTENTIVES TO ITEM #56 (in percentages)

[#56] As you see it, how great are the opportunities for the individual citizen to influence governmental and public opinion on foreign policy questions? (Check only one)

	Mobilizables	Attentives
Enormous	8	4
Large	24	18
Moderate	38	34
Small	26	37
Nonexistent	2	5
Uncodable and no answer	2	2
Total	100	100

of the competence scale (see Table 9–7), but in the case of several of the listed officials the two highest points of the scale were selected by substantially larger proportions of both the Attentives and the Mobilizables than occurred with the individual-competence variable. Roughly half of both groups perceived that it was "extremely" or "very" probable that three different types of officials "will act according to public opinion on questions of public policy." Admittedly these proportions do not reveal a pervasive sense of civic competence, but they do come closer to our expectations. Interestingly, this conclusion is especially applicable to

---

TABLE 9–7
DISTRIBUTION OF THE RESPONSES OF THE 1,704
MOBILIZABLES (Ms) AND 1,658 ATTENTIVES (As)
TO ITEM #58 (in percentages)

[#58] In general, how would you characterize the probability that the officials listed at the left will act according to public opinion on questions of public policy? (Place *one* check in *each* row)

		Extremely probable	Very probable	Some-what probable	Hardly probable	Not at all probable	Un-codable and no answer	Total
Local officials	Ms	20	37	29	8	2	4	100
	As	19	37	30	8	2	4	100
The Governor of your State	Ms	8	43	37	7	2	3	100
	As	7	40	42	6	2	3	100
Members of your State Legislature	Ms	7	31	40	15	3	4	100
	As	6	29	41	17	4	3	100
The President	Ms	13	42	36	4	1	4	100
	As	12	37	40	6	1	4	100
Members of Congress	Ms	9	37	42	8	1	3	100
	As	7	34	46	8	2	3	100
United Nations Officials or delegates	Ms	6	21	42	20	6	5	100
	As	6	20	40	24	5	5	100

officials on the executive side of government. Both the Attentives and Mobilizables perceived the three types of officials found in legislatures—at the state, national, and international levels—as being less responsive to public opinion than their executive counterparts.

The responses to the group-competence variables provide even greater evidence of a subjective sense of political efficacy. Table 9–8 presents the responses to the three items [#23, 40, 59] that called for assessments of the influence exerted by specific groups on specific pieces of major national legislation. Strong indications of high subjective civic competence are discernible in these data. Three-fifths of both the Attentives and Mobilizables perceived "peace groups" as having had "enormous" or "large" influence in "convincing the Senate to ratify the Nuclear Test Ban Treaty" and similar degrees of influence were accorded "church leaders," "leading educators," and "journalists and commentators" by more than half of both groups. Even more impressive, 92 percent of the Mobilizables and 86 percent of the Attentives perceived that "civil rights groups" exerted an "enormous" or "large" degree of influence "in convincing the Congress to pass the 1964 Civil Rights Act." More than three-fifths of the Attentives and nearly three-fourths of the Mobilizables also attributed similar amounts of influence to "church leaders."

How should we interpret the wide differences in the three sets of responses to the three sets of competence variables? Should we emphasize the low degree of individual competence or the high degree of group competence? Since the three parts of Hypothesis XVIII yielded seemingly contradictory results, can meaningful conclusions be reached from these data about whether or not active citizens are especially prone to perceive themselves as possessing high degrees of political competence? A closer inspection of the data presented in Tables 9–6, 9–7, and 9–8 suggests that these questions can be answered, that the different findings uncovered are not as contradictory as they seem at first glance, and that, indeed, they suggest important conclusions about the nature of the competence variables.

Stated most succinctly, the findings become coherent if they are interpreted as showing that active citizens are realistic about their role in public affairs but also confident that policy outcomes are susceptible to influence. Emphasis on the differences in the levels of competence probed by the three questionnaire items underlies this interpretation. In retrospect the original reasoning seems faulty because it did not allow for perceptions that differentiated among the levels of competence. A number of aspects of the data make it clear that greater influence was attributed to groups than to individuals because active citizens are not so naive about politics as to exaggerate and generalize the degree to which one person can have an impact on public affairs. Being knowledgeable about the political process, they are realistic about the limited likelihood that a single individual can affect the course of events, but they also perceive that joint action on the part of many individuals can tap a readiness to be responsive on the part of public officials. Accordingly, relatively few Attentives and Mobilizables fell at the high end of the individual-competence scale, while a large number fell at the high end of the public-competence scale and a preponderant majority selected the high alternatives on some of the group-competence measures.

Active citizens, in other words, are sustained by what can be accurately, if inelegantly, called a sense of "subjective collective competence." Whatever their objective competence, they feel subjectively competent primarily as members of groups. Further support for this interpretation is provided by several other aspects of the data.[18] Perhaps most conspicuous is the variability in the responses to the three group-competence variables. The perceptions by both the Attentives and Mobilizables that civil rights groups and church leaders were much more influential than business leaders in Congress's adoption of the 1964 Civil Rights

[18] It is also supported by the results of another inquiry in which the data upheld an "analytic distinction . . . between an individual's sense of confidence in his personal ability to influence government decisions, and his beliefs in the capacity of members of his political system in general to influence government. . . ." Cf. Edward N. Muller, "Cross-National Dimensions of Political Competence," *American Political Science Review*, Vol. 64 (1970), p. 807.

TABLE 9-8
DISTRIBUTION OF THE RESPONSES OF THE MOBILIZABLES AND ATTENTIVES TO ITEMS #23, 40, 59 (in percentages)

[#23] In your opinion, how much influence did the groups listed at the left exert in convincing the Congress to pass the 1962 Trade Expansion Act which permitted the President to negotiate substantial tariff reductions? (Place *one* check in *each* row)

		An enormous amount	A large amount	A moderate amount	Very little	None	Uncodable and no answer	Total
Business leaders	Ms*	11	31	20	14	3	21	100
	As**	12	32	19	14	4	19	100
Church leaders	Ms*	0	4	16	37	20	23	100
	As**	1	4	13	38	22	22	100
Journalists and commentators	Ms*	6	30	32	10	1	21	100
	As**	6	27	34	12	1	20	100
Labor leaders	Ms*	6	20	28	19	7	20	100
	As**	4	21	27	20	7	21	100
Leading educators	Ms*	4	17	29	23	5	22	100
	As**	4	18	27	24	6	21	100
World affairs groups	Ms*	14	37	23	7	1	18	100
	As**	13	34	23	10	1	19	100

[#40] In your opinion, how much influence did the groups listed at the left exert in convincing the Senate to ratify the Nuclear Test Ban Treaty? (Place *one* check in *each* row)

		An enormous amount	A large amount	A moderate amount	Very little	None	Uncodable and no answer	Total
Business leaders	Ms*	2	12	33	34	5	14	100
	As**	2	13	35	33	5	12	100
Church leaders	Ms*	16	39	27	9	1	8	100
	As**	16	34	28	12	2	8	100
Journalists and commentators	Ms*	12	43	30	6	1	8	100
	As**	10	40	32	7	1	10	100

								Total
Labor leaders	Ms*	6	29	36	16	2	11	100
	As**	6	27	36	17	2	12	100
Leading educators	Ms*	17	40	26	8	1	8	100
	As**	17	39	25	8	1	10	100
Peace groups	Ms*	32	31	23	7	0	7	100
	As**	29	30	22	10	1	8	100

[#59] In your opinion, how much influence did the groups listed at the left exert in convincing the Congress to pass the 1964 Civil Rights Act? (Place *one* check in *each* row)***

								Total
Business leaders	Ms****	2	12	39	38	4	5	100
	As*****	2	12	35	40	5	8	100
Church leaders	Ms****	33	40	21	4	0	2	100
	As*****	21	41	26	7	1	4	100
Civil rights groups	Ms****	58	34	6	1	0	1	100
	As*****	46	40	8	1	1	4	100
Journalists and commentators	Ms****	15	44	32	5	0	4	100
	As*****	9	43	36	6	1	5	100
Labor leaders	Ms****	9	37	36	14	1	3	100
	As*****	7	34	39	14	1	5	100
Leading educators	Ms****	8	36	42	11	1	2	100
	As*****	8	37	37	11	1	6	100

* Ms = 1,704 Mobilizables.

** As = 1,658 Attentives.

*** It should be noted that in the original questionnaire the order of the five points on the scale were reversed, with "none" being the alternative listed at the left and "an enormous amount" being the alternative listed at the right. In order to facilitate analysis, however, the order of the points on the scale for this item has been made consistent with that of the other two items.

**** Ms = 600 Mobilizables (since this item was added to the questionnaire for the second mailing and was thus not answered by all the Mobilizables).

***** As = 576 Attentives (since this item was added to the questionnaire for the second mailing and was thus not answered by all the Attentives).

Act seems realistic. In addition, such perceptions appear to reflect the respondents' own subjective collective competence, since their affiliations with the ADA and similar organizations probably led them to identify themselves as part of the civil rights groups to which they attributed so much relative influence.[19] Stated differently, since both the Attentives and Mobilizables attached high importance to the civil rights issue and since all of the Mobilizables are known to have established first-hand contacts with the issue, their perception that civil rights groups exerted extensive influence in the adoption of the legislation would seem to be a measure of their high sense of political efficacy.

The variability in the responses to the group-competence item that focused on the nuclear test ban treaty can be interpreted in a similar manner. In this case both the Attentives and the Mobilizables attributed much greater influence to peace groups, church leaders, and leading educators than to business or labor leaders, a view which is probably accurate and which probably also reflects the fact that their ADA-type affiliations led them to perceive themselves as members of a peace group. Following the same line of reasoning, and assuming that the respondents were much less active with respect to the 1962 Trade Expansion Act, it is hardly surprising that neither the Attentives nor the Mobilizables saw any group as having had extensive influence over Congress's adoption of the Act, but that nevertheless world affairs groups (with whom the respondents were most likely to identify) were seen by both the Attentives and Mobilizables to be considerably more influential than any of the others.

The responses to the public-competence items provide additional evidence that those who practice citizenship between elections approach the task realistically and perceive the political process as amenable to their collective influence. Both the Attentives and the Mobilizables recorded considerable variability in their perceptions of the extent to which different types of officials

---

[19] Some evidence for this interpretation is provided by the fact that a number of the respondents actually wrote in "the ADA" in response to the "others?" question of the group-competence items.

can be affected by public opinion, and they did so in a way that suggests both confidence and realism. It certainly seems realistic to perceive "United Nations officials or delegates" as much less receptive to public opinion than "local officials." The fact that nearly three-fifths of the Attentives and Mobilizables perceived it to be "extremely" or "very" probable that local officials "will act according to public opinion on questions of public policy," while only one-quarter of each group perceived U.N. officials in a comparable manner, indicates the absence of a naive view of the political process and a clear-cut appreciation that the opportunities for influencing it diminish as the issues become more remote. This interpretation is somewhat weakened by other data in Table 9–8 which show that both the Mobilizables and Attentives perceived the President as being almost as receptive to public opinion as local officials. However, as had already been seen[20] (and as will be seen even more strikingly in a later chapter[21]), a preoccupation with the chief executive is a pervasive characteristic of active citizens. Indeed, given the salience of the President for the Attentives and Mobilizables, it is remarkable that both groups nevertheless perceived local officials as more responsive to public opinion than the occupant of the White House.

COMPETENCE AND INFORMATION

It is perhaps another measure of the realism of active citizens that neither the Attentives nor the Mobilizables were inclined to link their self-perceptions of information possessed and influence possessed. We had reasoned (Hypothesis XIX) that to feel informed is to have the basis for feeling that influence can be effectively wielded, but the data do not clearly reveal such a pattern for either group. Both the Mobilizables and Attentives recorded only a few significant correlations between the information and competence variables and even these were in most instances so low as to account for less than two percent of the variance. The responses of the Attentives to the individual-competence item

[20] See pp. 210–15.
[21] See pp. 422–28.

were correlated with their responses to only five of the eleven issues comprising the self-information variable and there were only four such associations for the Mobilizables. The correlations between the self-information and public-competence variables provide even more clear-cut evidence that our original reasoning was faulty. Only 13 of 66 possible correlations between perceptions of information possessed on eleven issues and the responsiveness of six types of officials to public opinion were significant for the Attentives. The comparable figure for the Mobilizables was 5 of 66.

Nor was this pattern conspicuously reversed by the relationship between the self-information and group-competence variables. The correlations between the amount of information they perceived themselves as possessing on the nuclear test ban treaty and the amount of influence over the Senate's approval of the treaty they attributed to each of six groups was significant for only one group among the Attentives and for two groups among the Mobilizables. The comparable figures for the correlations between perceptions of self-possessed information and group competence relative to the 1964 Civil Rights Act was three groups for the Attentives and two groups for the Mobilizables. Some traces of the anticipated association between subjective competence and perceptions of possessed information can be discerned with respect to the 1962 Trade Expansion Act, where there were significant correlations in both groups between the influence they attributed to four of the six groups and the information they believed they possessed on the tariff issue.

In sum, whatever the combination of factors that sustain citizens who are active between elections, it does not appear to include a process of mutual reinforcement between a sense of being informed and subjective competence. Mobilizers who flood members of the Attentive Public with information on an issue will not necessarily be more successful in mobilizing support for their positions because active citizens may be too realistic about their ability to grasp the complexities of issues and their capacity to influence policy outcomes. It seems that to feel informed is to appreciate that influence is difficult to exercise, which suggests that a high sense of civic competence is nourished and sustained by sources other than knowledge about public affairs. Viewed in this way, it seems quite possible that gains in information about public affairs may in some ways dampen rather than foster the subjective competence of citizens.

The earlier conclusion that active citizens share a sense of collective rather than individual competence suggests another interpretation of the sources of self-perceptions of information and competence. Information is a personal possession and joining with others in coordinated action does not necessarily expand it. Competence, on the other hand, is cumulative. There is strength in numbers and the act of joining together may add to a sense of competence irrespective of the degree of information the individual may feel he possesses.[22]

COMPETENCE AND ATTITUDES

The anticipated close association between the competence and attitude variables (Hypothesis XX) was more evident than the one between competence and information. Most notably, as can be seen in Table 9–9, the responses to the individual competence and importance variables were significantly correlated on ten of the eleven issues among the attentives and on nine of the issues for the Mobilizables. Similarly, of the 66 possible correla-

---

[22] Viewed in this way, it is perhaps noteworthy that while the Mobilizables and Attentives did not register many significant correlations between the information and group-competence variables, the few that were significant included those groups in which their sense of collective competence was likely to be highest. World affairs groups, peace groups, and civil rights groups were the groups whose actions with respect to, respectively, the Trade Expansion Act, the Test Ban Treaty, and the Civil Rights Act both the Mobilizables and Attentives were most likely to identify, and in all three cases their perceptions of the influence wielded by these groups and their perceptions of the information they possessed on the issues correlated significantly.

TABLE 9-9
SIGNIFICANT (P < .001) PRODUCT MOMENT CORRELATIONS (*r*) BETWEEN THE PERCEPTIONS OF CITIZEN COMPETENCE AND THE TWO ATTITUDE MEASURES FOR THE MOBILIZABLES AND THE ATTENTIVES

Issues on which the perceptions of individual competence [#56] correlated significantly with the eleven importance [#47] and five extremity [#19, 20, 43, 44, 46] measures*	Agricultural surpluses (.110) Balance of payments (.108) Berlin (.126) The Congo (.173) Federal tax reduction (.135) Foreign aid (.169) Tariff reduction (.155) Vietnam (.101) Western unity (.146)	Berlin (.098) The Congo (.135) Western unity (.121)	Agricultural surpluses (.093) Berlin (.177) Civil rights (.098) The Congo (.233) Federal tax reduction (.112) Foreign aid (.208) Nuclear testing (.126) Tariff reduction (.165) Vietnam (.165) Western unity (.139)	The Congo (.132) Western unity (.141)
Issues on which the two attitude measures correlated significantly with perceptions [#58] of the responsiveness to public opinion of**				
Local officials	Berlin (.116) The Congo (.096) Foreign aid (.093) Vietnam (.099)	The Congo (.088)	Civil rights (.110)	Western unity (.111)

State Governor	Berlin (.141) The Congo (.144) Foreign aid (.110) Vietnam (.098) Western unity (.110)	Western unity (.095)	Berlin (.095) Western unity (.127)	Western unity (.111)
State Legislators	Agricultural surpluses (.103) Balance of payments (.085) Foreign aid (.111) Vietnam (.118) Western unity (.101)	Federal tax reduction (.097)	Western unity (.100)	None
The President	Balance of payments (.097) Berlin (.097) The Congo (.124) Federal tax reduction (.115) Foreign aid (.136) Tariff reduction (.108) Western unity (.125)	The Congo (.110) Western unity (.123)	Balance of payments (.125) Berlin (.115) The Congo (.114) Federal tax reduction (.150) Foreign aid (.119) Tariff reduction (.138) Vietnam (.088) Western unity (.154)	Western unity (.137)
Members of Congress	Balance of payments (.108) Berlin (.107) The Congo (.118) Foreign aid (.136) Tariff reduction (.102) Vietnam (.097) Western unity (.129)	Berlin (.105) Western unity (.132)	Berlin (.118) The Congo (.089) Foreign aid (.114) Tariff reduction (.102) Vietnam (.102) Western unity (.136)	Berlin (.129) Western unity (.149)

(continued)

TABLE 9-9 (continued)

	The Mobilizables		The Attentives	
	Attitudinal importance	Attitudinal extremity	Attitudinal importance	Attitudinal extremity
U.N. officials	Agricultural surpluses (.129) Balance of payments (.120) The Congo (.151) Federal tax reduction (.127) Western unity (.101)	The Congo (.091)	Agricultural surpluses (.093) Balance of payments (.092) The Congo (.149) Federal tax reduction (.127) Foreign aid (.102) Tariff reduction (.138) Vietnam (.100) Western unity (.166)	Western unity (.105)
Perceptions of groups influencing the adoption of the 1962 Trade Expansion Act [#23] that were significantly correlated with attitudes toward tariff reduction***	Church leaders (.161) Journalists and commentators (.184) Leading educators (.178) World affairs groups (.157)	None	Church leaders (.106) Labor leaders (.094) Journalists and commentators (.132) Leading educators (.147) World affairs groups (.199)	None

Perceptions of groups influencing the ratification of the 1963 Nuclear Test Ban Treaty [#40] that were significantly correlated with attitudes toward the nuclear testing issue****	Church leaders (.114) Labor Leaders (.103) Journalists and commentators (.092) Leading educators (.117) Peace groups (.144)	None	Church leaders (.092) Labor leaders (.086) Leading educators (.120) Peace groups (.188)	None
Perceptions of groups influencing the adoption of the 1964 Civil Rights Act [#59] that were significantly correlated with attitudes toward the civil rights issue******	Church leaders (.179) Civil rights groups (.189)	None	Leading educators (.190) Civil rights groups (.155)	Leading educators (.155)

* These correlations were based on at least 1,529 Mobilizables and 1,509 Attentives.
** These correlations were based on at least 1,482 Mobilizables and 1,486 Attentives.
*** These correlations were based on at least 1,268 Mobilizables and 1,247 Attentives.
**** These correlations were based on at least 1,486 Mobilizables and 1,426 Attentives.
***** These correlations were based on at least 580 Mobilizables and 538 Attentives.

tions between the importance attached to the eleven issues and the perceived responsiveness to public opinion of six types of officials, 26 proved to be significant for the Attentives and 34 for the Mobilizables. The association between the importance and group-competence variables was also consistent with expectations: the correlations between the importance attached to the tariff issue and the influence over the 1962 Trade Expansion Act ascribed to various groups was significant for four groups among the Attentives and for five of the six groups among the Mobilizables. The comparable figures for the nuclear testing and civil rights issues were, respectively, five and two significant correlations among the Mobilizables and four and two among the Attentives.

On the other hand, in the case of the extremity of their attitudes, Table 9–9 reveals that the patterns of association with the competence variables were much less pronounced. For the five issues on which correlations between individual-competence and extremity were possible, there were three significant associations among the Mobilizables and two among the Attentives. The pattern of association becomes even more tenuous between the public-competence and extremity variables. Only 8 of 30 possible correlations between the extremity of their attitudes and the responsiveness to public opinion of the several types of officials proved to be significant for the Mobilizables. The comparable figure for the Attentives was 6 out of 30. Likewise, although it was methodologically possible to correlate only one of the group-competence variables with the measures of attitudinal extremity, the results again fall short of the predicted pattern: the correlation between attitude toward the civil rights issue and influence over the Civil Rights Act ascribed to the six groups comprising Item #59 was significant with respect to only one group among the Attentives and none among the Mobilizables.

In sum, the evidence on the process of balance between attitudes and subjective competence is mixed. Some such process does appear to occur with respect to the importance dimension of attitudes, but not for the extremity dimension. Whatever the reasons why active citizens develop a sense of collective political competence, the intensity of their attitudes toward political issues would seem to be only a small part of the explanation and, in turn, their sense of competence is apparently only a minor influence on the strength of their attitudes.[23]

COMPETENCE AND ACTION

Although a pronounced pattern can be discerned in the data depicting the interaction between the competence variables and those pertaining to first- and second-hand forms of contact, it is not consistent either with our expectations (Hypothesis XXI) or with the above finding that active citizens tend to feel more collectively than individually competent. It had been expected that both the Mobilizables and Attentives would establish more contacts with public affairs the greater the competence they ascribed to the individual, the group, and the general public. Writing letters to officials and participating in the work of organizations, it was reasoned, constitute instrumental as well as expressive acts, so that a person is not likely to engage in such behavior unless he perceives the political process as amenable to influence by private individuals and groups. Similarly, while discussing public issues with family and friends may be more expressive than instrumental, such second-hand contacts were viewed as likely to reinforce, and be reinforced by, perceptions of the extent to which citizenship between elections can be effective.

This line of reasoning, however, was only partially supported by the data. The individual-competence variable was associated with both first- and second-hand forms of contact, among both the Mobilizables and Attentives, but the public-competence variable was not associated with either form of contact and the group-competence variable was associated only with second-hand contacts. These distinctions could hardly be more pronounced. As can be seen in Table 9–10, there were no significant correlations among the Mobilizables between their responses to any of the six

---

[23] For another study that turned up ambiguous findings on the interaction of the competence and attitude variables, see Stanley J. Morse and Stanton Peele, "A Study of the Participants in an Anti-Vietnam War Demonstration," *Journal of Social Issues*, Vol. 27 (1971), pp. 121–22.

TABLE 9-10
SIGNIFICANT (P < .001) PRODUCT MOMENT CORRELATIONS (r) BETWEEN THE PERCEPTIONS OF CITIZEN COMPETENCE AND THE MEASURES OF FIRST- AND SECOND-HAND CONTACT FOR THE MOBILIZABLES AND THE ATTENTIVES

Correlations involving perceptions of individual competence [#56]	.176 (n = 1,662)	.125 (n = 1,663)	.200 (n = 1,582) Agricultural surpluses (.102) Balance of payments (.116) Berlin (.110) Civil rights (.094) The Congo (.123) Federal tax reduction (.104) Foreign aid (.122) Tariff reduction (.136) Western unity (.119)*	.180 (n = 1,608) Civil rights (.119) The Congo (.130) Foreign aid (.106) Nuclear testing (.122) Tariff reduction (.124) Western unity (.107)**
Correlations involving perceptions of the responsiveness to public opinion [#58] of			

Local officials	ns			.103 (n = 1,561)	ns
State Governor	ns			ns	ns
State Legislators	ns			ns	ns
The President	ns		Western unity (.088; n = 1,582)	ns	ns
Members of Congress	ns		Western unity (.089; n = 1,590)	ns	ns
U.N. officials	ns		Agricultural surpluses (.113; n = 1,568) Tariff reduction (.087; n = 1,569)	ns	ns

Correlations involving perceptions of six groups influencing the adoption of the 1962 Trade Expansion Act [#23]	Church leaders (.088; n = 1,262)	Church leaders (.109; n = 1,295)	Church leaders (.134; n = 1,272) Labor leaders (.117; n = 1,306) Journalists and commentators (.117; n = 1,332) Leading educators (.191; n = 1,303) World affairs groups (.111; n = 1,350)	Church leaders (.088; n = 1,262)	Church leaders (.091; n = 1,277) Labor leaders (.101; n = 1,299)	The Congo (.094; n = 1,532) Western unity (.096; n = 1,527) Church leaders (.167; n = 1,254) Labor leaders (.133; n = 1,277) Journalists and commentators (.130; n = 1,302) Leading educators (.141; n = 1,281) World affairs groups (.128; n = 1,308)

(continued)

TABLE 9-10 *(continued)*

	The Mobilizables			The Attentives		
	Letter-writing activity scores	*Organizational activity scores*	*Face-to-face conversations about eleven issues* [#49]	*Letter-writing activity scores*	*Organizational activity scores*	*Face-to-face conversations about eleven issues* [#49]
Correlations involving perceptions of six groups influencing the adoption of the 1963 Nuclear Test Ban Treaty [#40]	None	None	Church leaders (.120; n = 1,536) Labor leaders (.120; n = 1,481) Leading educators (.158; n = 1,537) Peace groups (.155; n = 1,558)	Peace groups (.087; n = 1,484)	None	Church leaders (.137; n = 1,483) Labor leaders (.107; n = 1,433) Leading educators (.178; n = 1,472) Peace groups (.231; n = 1,492)
Correlations involving perceptions of six groups influencing the adoption of the 1964 Civil Rights Act [#59]	None	None	Church leaders (.162; n = 577) Labor leaders (.173; n = 564) Journalists and commentators (.165; n = 566) Civil rights groups (.222; n = 577)	None	None	Church leaders (.174; n = 542) Journalists and commentators (.144; n = 541) Civil rights groups (.259; n = 545)

* These nine correlations were based on at least 1,588 Mobilizables.

** These six correlations were based on at least 1,546 Attentives.

ns = not significant.

public-competence variables and their scores on either the letter-writing or organizational activity indices. Of the sixty-six correlations between their responses to the public-competence and second-hand contact variables, only four were significant. Similarly, there were no significant correlations between the six public-competence and organizational activity measures among the Attentives, while only one of the six involving the letter-writing index and two of the sixty-six involving the measures of second-hand contact were significant.

Table 9–10 also reveals that the many correlations between the two measures of first-hand contact and the group-competence variables were generally not significant. With respect to the influence wielded by six groups over the 1962 Trade Expansion Act, the 1963 Nuclear Test Ban Treaty, and the 1964 Civil Rights Act, the Mobilizables' perceptions of only one group in one of these situations was significantly correlated with their scores on the organizational activity scale, and exactly the same results were obtained when the eighteen group-competence variables were correlated with the letter-writing scores. The comparable figures for the Attentives were two significant correlations for both the organizational activity and letter-writing scores. Only with respect to the interactions between second-hand contact on the tariff, nuclear testing, and civil rights issues and the perceived influence of groups over the outcome of these issues can traces of the expected pattern involving the group-competence variables be discerned. The Mobilizables recorded, respectively, five, four, and four significant correlations and the equivalent figures for the Attentives were five, four, and three.

The association between the individual-competence and activity variables stand in sharp contrast to the overall lack of interaction involving the group- and public-competence variables. As can be seen in Table 9–10, the responses of both the Mobilizables and the Attentives to the individual-competence variable were significantly correlated with their scores on both the letter-writing and organizational activity scales. An elaboration of this close link between subjective individual competence and actual behavior is provided by Table 9–11, which presents the distribution of the Attentives' responses to the individual-competence item along the letter-writing scale. Here it can be seen that the relationship between the two variables was such that the data in three of the columns are perfectly arrayed. The interactions involving the measures of second-hand contact are not exceptions to this overall pattern. Nine of the eleven measures were significantly associated to the Mobilizables' responses to the individual-competence variable and the comparable figure for the Attentives was six significant associations.

The fact that the foregoing distributions are discrepant with earlier findings as well as with our original expectations is somewhat perplexing.[24] Earlier it was concluded that active citizens are realistic in their perception of their own political competence and ascribe much greater effectiveness to group actions than to those of individuals.[25] Yet, here we were correct in anticipating that actual citizenship behavior would be linked to perceptions of individual competence, but erroneous in predicting that the perceptions of group and public competence would also be associated with letter-writing and organizational activity. Does this mean that active citizens are realistic in their perceptions of the processes of political influence, but at the same time unrealistically allow their own subjective sense of competence to guide their actual practice of citizenship? A clear answer cannot be derived from the data, but one interpretation of the discrepancy does seem plausible. Letter-writing and organizational activities are the citizenship practices of individuals. A person may attribute greater influence to groups and publics than to himself, but it is he who writes the letters and joins the organizations. Hence, while his personal sense of political competence may be low, it is likely to underlie what-

---

[24] And perplexity is further heightened by the fact that the distributions are also discrepant with those of another study which found, contrary to both our initial reasoning and our empirical findings, that "a sense of efficacy is a more important resource for initiating government [i.e., first-hand] contacts than for less active [i.e., second-hand] forms of political involvement." See Nie, Powell, Prewitt, "Social Structure and Political Participation: Developmental Relationships, II," p. 817.

[25] See above, pp. 356–65.

TABLE 9–11

CROSS-TABULATION OF THE RESPONSES OF THE ATTENTIVES TO THE INDIVIDUAL COMPETENCE ITEM [#56] AND THEIR SCORES ON THE INDEX OF LETTER-WRITING ACTIVITY* (in percentages)

[#56] As you see it, how great are the opportunities for the individual citizen to influence governmental and public opinion on foreign policy questions?

Letter-writing groups (see p. 219)	(n =)	Enormous	Large	Moderate	Small	Non-existent	No answer, don't know	Total
Steady writers	(38)	13	34	24	21	3	5	100
Frequent writers	(210)	9	23	34	31	2	1	100
Occasional writers	(475)	5	19	36	33	3	4	100
Sporadic writers	(347)	4	16	37	38	4	1	100
Nonwriters	(541)	2	14	31	43	8	2	100

* The responses of the 47 Attentives who did not provide enough data to calculate a letter-writing score are omitted from the table.

ever citizenship practices he does undertake. On the other hand, viewing groups and the public as collectively competent does not necessarily have implications for individual behavior. Groups and publics are influential in a variety of ways, ranging from the demands voiced by spokesmen to the pressures inherent in opinion polls, and there is thus no necessary pressure toward consistency between an individual's perceptions of collective competence and his own political activities.

This interpretation admittedly fails to account for the finding that the group-competence variables were significantly associated with the measures of second-hand contact. Reasons for this exception to the overall pattern of the data cannot be readily derived, but the exception does not necessarily negate our interpretation of the overall pattern. This is not the first time we have uncovered distinctions between the first- and second-hand forms of contact, and the exception may well reflect the aforenoted link between perceptions and second-hand activities[26] rather than being a negation of the above interpretation. Certainly this interpretation does adequately explain the seemingly discrepant findings insofar as first-hand forms of contact are concerned.

COMPETENCE AND MOBILIZABILITY

The foregoing reasoning relative to the interaction of competence and first-hand forms of contact with public affairs would also seem to be applicable to the data on competence and mobilizability. For comparisons of the Mobilizables and Attentives again yielded sharp differences between perceptions of the individual's influence and those pertaining to the influence of private groups and the general public. Our expectation, based on the view that instrumental as well as expressive purposes underlie the practices of citizenship between elections, was that there would be no differences among the competence variables insofar as mobilizability was concerned. That is, it seemed reasonable to presume that active citizens who are predisposed to respond to appeals to establish first-hand contacts with the political process would perceive it as more susceptible to any external influence than do those less predisposed to be mobilizable. Thus we anticipated (Hypothesis XXII) that the individual, the group, and the general public would all be perceived as more competent by the Mobilizables than by the Attentives.

This reasoning held up for perceptions of the individual's influence, but not for perceptions of group and public influence. The data relevant to these findings have already been presented (Tables 9–6, 9–7, and 9–8). The differences between the Mobilizables and Attentives displayed in Table 9–6 clearly indicate that

[26] See above, pp. 353–55.

the former perceived the individual as more competent than did the latter, and they are statistically significant.[27] None of the six comparisons presented in Table 9–7, on the other hand, are significant. The Mobilizables did not perceive local officials, state governors, state legislators, the President, members of Congress, or U.N. officials as either more or less receptive to public opinion than did the Attentives. Likewise, only two of the eighteen comparisons contained in Table 9–8 were significant. The perceptions of the Mobilizables and Attentives did not differ with respect to any of the six groups whose influence was posited as possibly relevant to the passage of the 1962 Trade Expansion Act or the 1963 Nuclear Test Ban Treaty or with respect to the role played by four groups in the adoption of the 1964 Civil Rights Act. Only in the case of the perceived role of "church leaders" and "civil rights groups" in relation to the Civil Rights Act were the differences significant, the Mobilizables perceiving these two groups as wielding more influence over the legislation than did the Attentives.[28]

Given the foregoing interpretation of why subjective individual competence is more likely to be linked to first-hand forms of contact than are perceptions of collective competence, an explanation of these findings can be readily developed. Mobilizability is a personal propensity, not a group attribute, and consequently the difference between individuals who do and do not possess it is likely to be much greater with respect to perceptions of the individual's competence to influence the course of events than to perceptions of the group's or the public's influence. Two persons may both have a very low sense of individual competence; but if one is predisposed to be mobilized and the other is not, then the former's subjective assessment of his own influence will nevertheless be higher than the latter's. The mobilizable citizen may share his nonmobilizable counterpart's perceptions of

[27] $\chi^2 = 79.77$, df $= 4$, P$<.001$.

[28] For the difference involving church leaders, $\chi^2 = 27.96$; df $=3$; P$<.001$; for the difference involving civil rights groups, $\chi^2 = 15.62$; df $= 2$; P$<.001$.

collective competence, but he is likely to develop a greater sense of subjective competence in justifying his readiness to respond to the appeal of a mobilizer. In short, if this interpretation of the data presented in the previous paragraph is correct, our original reasoning was only partly confirmed because it did not allow for the possibility that perceptions of individual and collective competence would have different effects on mobilizability.

SUMMARY

While the perceptions which active citizens have of themselves as citizens were shown to be relevant to their practice of citizenship between elections, the central finding of this chapter is that the process by which a subjective sense of civic competence shapes posture toward and behavior in the public arena is complex. Even the consequences of the feeling of being informed about issues were shown to be more complex than anticipated. The prediction that the Mobilizables and Attentives would perceive themselves as well informed about at least one public issue was confirmed by the data, but both groups were conspicuously modest in their perceptions of how well they comprehended many issues. They saw themselves as highly informed about civil rights, but in the case of several issues they conceded that they were uninformed. Notwithstanding their modesty, both groups perceived themselves as considerably more informed about every issue than the general public, supporting our hypothesis that pressures toward perceptual balance make the active citizen see himself as better informed than his inactive counterpart. The presence of balancing process was also affirmed in the finding that the importance they attached to all eleven issues and the degree to which they saw themselves as informed about them, were significantly correlated among both the Mobilizables and the Attentives. The same was true for four of the five issues on which correlations with attitudinal extremity were possible.

Although the Mobilizables and Attentives managed to balance their self-perceptions of information possessed with their attitudes, they did so only partially in relation to actual behavior.

The data revealed that self-perceptions of information possessed were much more strongly related to second-hand than to first-hand forms of contact. This same discrepancy was uncovered in the interaction of attitudes and behavior, indicating again that more than appropriate self-perceptions are required to mobilize the energy and time needed to establish direct contacts with politics through letter-writing and organizational activity. It is much easier to translate the feeling of being informed about an issue into conversations with friends and acquaintances than into letter-writing and organizational initiative.

Yet a feeling of being informed is not irrelevant to action. The Mobilizables perceived themselves as more informed than the Attentives on only two of the eleven issues (civil rights and nuclear testing), but these were the two issues with respect to which the former were known to have been, and the latter not to have been, mobilized into action. This suggests that this dimension of subjective competence is a necessary even if not a sufficient condition for the actual practice of citizenship.

Perceptions of competence were also probed at the more general level of how the Mobilizables and Attentives perceived the individual's, the group's, and the general public's capacity to influence public affairs. In this case the analysis yielded the interesting finding that both the Mobilizables and the Attentives perceived the private group and the general public as considerably more capable of influencing the course of events than the individual citizen. This finding was interpreted as indicating an inclination to distinguish between subjective individual and collective competence and to view the active citizen as realistically giving more consequence to the latter than to the former. Just as the data revealed the Mobilizables and Attentives to be modest about the amount of information on public affairs they saw themselves as possessing, so do they appear to avoid exaggerating the amount of influence they can wield.

It had been anticipated that the necessities of perceptual balance would lead both the Mobilizables and the Attentives to link their perceptions of their information about public issues to their perceptions of their influence over them, but this was not the case. Relatively few of the eleven measures of self-perceptions of information possessed were significantly associated with the individual-competence measure, the eighteen group-competence measures, or the six public-competence measures. On the other hand, traces of the predicted pattern were evident for both groups in the case of the interaction between their competence perceptions and their attitudes. The pattern was readily discernible in the case of the importance dimension of attitudes, but was less pronounced with respect to the extremity dimension.

An even more complex set of findings was uncovered in the data that probed the interaction between the perceptions of competence and the actual practices of citizenship. The assumption that there would be pressures toward balance between these two variables led to two predictions, one that perceptions of competence and actions in the public arena would be related for both groups, and the other that the Mobilizables would ascribe greater competence to the individual, the group, and the public than would the Attentives. Both expectations proved to be sound insofar as the competence of the individual was concerned, but highly unreliable in the case of perceptions of group and public competence. Perceptions of the individual's influence were clearly associated with measures of first- and second-hand contacts with public affairs, but perceptions of the influence wielded by the private group and the general public did not correlate with the scores on the letter-writing and organizational activity indices. Some evidence of an interaction between perceptions of group competence and second-hand contacts was uncovered, but it was minimal in relation to the absence of interaction involving the measures of first-hand contact. Similarly, the Mobilizables did ascribe greater competence to the individual than did the Attentives, but the two groups did not differ in their perceptions of the competence of either the group or the public.

These complex findings relative to the interaction of perceptions of competence on the one hand and behavior and mobilizability on the other were interpreted as indicating the extent to which citizenship activity and mobilizability are attributes of individuals and not of collectivities. A citizen may attribute greater

competence to groups or publics than to individuals, but it is he
who writes letters and joins organizations. Consequently, whether
he does so on his own or in response to the appeals of a mobilizer,
it is his own contacts with public affairs that he experiences and
it is these which he must balance with his perceptions of competence. Groups and publics may be perceived as very influential
in a variety of ways that do not stem from the individual citizen's
action, and thus there is no reason for an active person to achieve
consistency between his perceptions of collective competence and
his own political activities. For essentially the same reason it is
not surprising that while the Mobilizables were more inclined to
perceive the individual as competent than were the Attentives,
the two groups did not differ in their perceptions of collective
competence.

CHAPTER 10

THE INFLUENCE OF
PRESENT RESPONSIBILITIES

Although the seeds of attentiveness and mobilizability are rooted in past experience and nourished by attitudes and perceptions, they flower and take concrete form in the objective circumstances of the present. And the objective conditions of the present, like those subjectively experienced in the past, are highly variable. Citizens who are oriented toward public affairs must occupy facilitating statuses and roles if their orientations are to be sustained. Present responsibilities may never offset the attitudes, perceptions, and habits derived from social background, but they can greatly influence both the extent and the form of citizenship between elections. Such, at least, is the underlying premise to which the analysis of this chapter is addressed. Our model presumes that the subjective attitudes and perceptions to which social background gives rise can only be expressed in the context of an objective situation, which may or may not make such expression possible. At any moment in time every citizen is seen as occupying statuses and roles that enlarge or curb his capacity to establish contact with public affairs. Some roles require their occupants to establish or maintain contacts and others do not. Some statuses involve responsibilities that encourage a felt obligation to be involved in public affairs and others do not. In short, objective responsibility is conceived to breed a subjective sense of responsibility.

It should be noted that some evidence has already been gathered in support of the premise that the greater the responsibilities attached to a person's statuses and roles, the more likely he is to feel obliged to engage in the practices of citizenship. An earlier inquiry into the contacts with public affairs established by a sample of 647 national leaders yielded the clear-cut finding that the greater the access to the communications system provided by a leadership position, the more likely it was that the attitudes and activities of its occupant would reflect an active orientation toward the political arena.[1] Findings about national leaders, however, may have little relevance for members of the Attentive Public. The objective responsibilities of the former are, by definition, so much greater than those of the latter that the association that occurs among leaders between possession of formal access to the communications system and involvement in public affairs may not be paralleled among the active but nonleader stratum of the citizenry. Our model presumes that the same association does exist, that even minimal objective responsibilities breed political involvement, and that therefore it matters to the practice of citizenship between elections whether the present responsibilities of an attentive or mobilizable citizen are large or small.

Probing the "responsibility breeds responsibility" hypothesis, however, is not without difficulty. The line dividing the effects of past experience and present responsibility is not as sharp as the

---

[1] Rosenau, *National Leadership and Foreign Policy*, esp. Ch. V.

foregoing would seem to suggest. Many statuses and roles occupied in the past continue to be occupied in the present, and while they may currently foster different facilitating or interfering resources and predispositions than they did in the past, a clear distinction is not always possible. This difficulty is especially pronounced in the case of occupation. On the one hand, many years in the same line of work can generate skills and orientations that would not be possessed if another line of work had been pursued. One researcher, for example, discovered that "in spite of . . . many changes, considerable stability was found in the characteristic interests of bankers over thirty years." [2] On the other hand, in most occupational fields new responsibilities are acquired with the passage of time and each level of responsibility can also generate resources and predispositions that would not be possessed if the advancement to it had not occurred. Thus it is not surprising that another researcher uncovered data which pointed to "the possibility that interests associated with occupational status are strong generators of a sense of political involvement." [3]

Our procedure for coping with this problem is simple. In order to make certain that resources and predispositions derived from present responsibilities are assessed apart from those that may have been previously acquired, our initial model includes three synthesizing variables that cumulate the requirements and responsibilities of all the statuses and roles a citizen presently occupies. Referred to as indicators of "objective proximity," "domestic travel," and "opinion-making potential," these variables focus, respectively, on perceptions of occupational requirements relevant to contact with public affairs, on actual behavior arising out of the occupational requirements, and on the use of the opportunities to circulate opinions that stem from both vocational and

[2] David P. Campbell, "Stability of Interests Within an Occupation over Thirty Years," *Journal of Applied Psychology*, Vol. 50 (1966), pp. 5–56.

[3] V. O. Key, Jr., *Public Opinion and American Democracy*, p. 328. For similar findings see Robert E. Lane, *Political Life*, p. 78; J. C. Scott, Jr., "Membership and Participation in Voluntary Associations," p. 322; Murray Hausknecht, *The Joiners*, p. 25; and Campbell, Gurin, Miller, *The Voter Decides*, p. 191.

avocational statuses and roles. Taken together, the three variables provide an elaborate measure with which to probe the degree to which objective circumstances of the present influenced the orientations and activities of the Attentives and Mobilizables.

THE THREE MEASURES OF PRESENT RESPONSIBILITY

That their day-to-day life does not place those who are not leaders in the society close to public affairs can be readily discerned in the responses to all three measures of present responsibility. Let us consider first the objective proximity variable, which assessed the degree to which the respondents' main occupations required them to relate themselves to issues in the political arena. In order to increase the chances that they would distinguish clearly between their private inclinations and their occupational responsibilities, the item [#36] was cast in terms of international affairs. It was reasoned that many lines of work link their practitioners to their community and that the difference between vocational and avocational interests is likely to be more clear-cut for foreign affairs than for domestic affairs. The measure of objective proximity thus consisted of a five-point scale on which the respondents had to estimate their occupational distance "from the course of events and developments abroad." The responses of the Attentives and Mobilizables to this item are presented in Table 10–1, where it is apparent that the occupational roles of concerned citizens do not bring them into close contact with world affairs. Clear-cut majorities of both groups reported that their jobs required little or no attention to developments abroad.[4] A breakdown of the responses

---

[4] A further check on this finding is provided by the responses to an item [#48] that inquired about the extent to which "your work bring[s] you into contact with foreigners, either in person or by mail." Again majorities in both groups did not indicate extensive contacts. Among the Mobilizables 22 percent replied "frequently," 37 percent said "occasionally," and 36 percent chose the "very rarely" alternative (the remaining 5 percent did not supply a codable answer). The equivalent figures for the Attentives were 24, 35, and 35 percent (with 6 percent uncodable).

TABLE 10–1
DISTRIBUTION OF THE RESPONSES OF THE 1,704
MOBILIZABLES AND 1,658 ATTENTIVES TO ITEM #36
(in percentages)

[#36] To what extent does your chief occupation, apart from your personal inclinations, require you to follow the course of events and developments
abroad? (Check only one)

	An enormous amount	A large amount	A moderate amount	Very little	Not at all	Un codable and no answer	Total
Mobilizables	5	13	19	24	33	6	100
Attentives	4	12	21	26	33	4	100

by occupational field, however, reveals that there are important differences among the requirements of different fields. As can be seen in Table 10–2, for example, three-fourths of the blue- and white-collar workers reported that the extent of their job requirements was "little" or none in this respect, whereas more than half of the clergymen reported that their occupational responsibility for following developments abroad was "enormous" or "large." [5]

It might be argued that the responses to the objective proximity measure convey a misleading impression because of the international focus in the wording of the item. The responses to the domestic travel item [#55], however, also support the conclusion that the occupational responsibilities of attentive citizens do not locate them close to public affairs. As can be seen in Table 10–

[5] An interesting sidelight of Table 10–2 is the large extent to which both Attentive and Mobilizable pre-college teachers exceeded college teachers in the amount of attention their jobs required them to pay to foreign affairs. The most logical interpretation of this finding is that only those pre-college teachers who teach in fields involving public affairs (e.g., social studies) are likely to be active citizens between elections, whereas college teachers are likely to be or not to be active as citizens irrespective of their professional specialization.

TABLE 10-2
DISTRIBUTION OF THE RESPONSES OF THE MOBILIZABLES AND ATTENTIVES TO ITEM #36 BY OCCUPATION (in percentages)

[#36] To what extent does your chief occupation, apart from your personal inclinations, require you to follow the course of events and developments abroad? (Check only one)

	Mobilizables								Attentives							
(n =)	(n =)	Enormous amount	Large amount	Moderate amount	Very little	Not at all	Un-codable	Total	(n =)	Enormous amount	Large amount	Moderate amount	Very little	Not at all	Un-codable	Total
Artists	(28)	18	7	25	25	25	0	100	(36)	6	22	14	17	39	2	100
Blue Collar Workers	(34)	0	3	12	12	65	8	100	(51)	2	4	10	18	63	3	100
Clergymen	(77)	13	39	32	10	5	0	100	(52)	19	35	35	8	2	1	100
College Teachers	(183)	7	16	27	28	22	0	100	(195)	5	14	23	35	23	1	100
Corporate Executives	(28)	0	11	14	50	25	0	100	(56)	2	16	29	32	21	0	100
Engineers	(39)	0	8	13	33	44	2	100	(61)	2	7	10	39	43	0	100
Financiers	(30)	3	13	23	23	41	0	100	(44)	2	7	43	25	23	0	100
Housewives	(220)	3	8	11	19	53	6	100	(202)	1	7	15	20	54	3	100
Lawyers	(45)	2	13	13	43	27	2	100	(46)	4	7	22	39	28	0	100
Merchants	(31)	0	0	16	26	58	0	100	(45)	4	4	16	38	38	0	100
Physicians	(58)	0	2	2	41	55	0	100	(63)	0	2	16	51	31	0	100
Pre-college Teachers	(144)	10	22	32	22	13	1	100	(122)	11	26	24	26	13	0	100
Retired Persons	(264)	4	14	11	13	39	19	100	(230)	3	12	17	15	40	13	100
Social Workers	(65)	6	8	30	38	18	0	100	(28)	0	14	39	43	11	0	100
Students	(61)	11	15	18	34	20	2	100	(37)	2	14	43	22	19	0	100
White Collar Workers	(47)	2	4	15	15	64	0	100	(34)	3	0	18	18	58	3	100

TABLE 10–3
DISTRIBUTION OF THE RESPONSES OF THE 1,704
MOBILIZABLES AND 1,658 ATTENTIVES TO ITEM #55
(in percentages)

[#55] On the average, and not counting vacations, how often do you go more than 100 miles away from home? (Check only one)

	Never	Once or twice a year	Every two or three months	Every month	once a week or more	Un-codable and no answer	Total
Mobilizables	15	45	26	11	2	1	100
Attentives	12	40	30	13	3	2	100

3, a majority of both the Attentives and the Mobilizables reported averaging, at the most, one or two trips a year that took them more than 100 miles from home, not including vacations. To be sure, a job can require attention to public affairs without also calling for extended travel; but as suggested by the finding that national leaders make frequent trips to Washington, D.C.,[6] it is reasonable to presume that the more one is obliged to extend one's involvement beyond local affairs, the more likely it is that one's occupational responsibilities will take one away from home.

Further evidence that the present responsibilities of attentive citizens do not bring them close to the arena of public affairs is provided by their scores on the index of opinion-making potential. As already indicated, this index consists of ten items that probed different forms of access, both vocational and avocational, to the society's channels of communication.[7] A comparison of the responses to the items and the composite score on the index of the 3,362 members of the ADA sample on the one hand and of a sample of 647 national leaders on the other revealed that occupants of leadership positions have considerably greater opportunities than do members of the Attentive Public to circulate their opin-

---

[6] Rosenau, *National Leadership and Foreign Policy*, pp. 101–102.
[7] See pp. 177–82.

ions to unknown others.[8] Not only were the scores of the ADA respondents strikingly lower than those of the leadership sample, but in absolute terms they also indicate clearly that their daily responsibilities do not extend far into the public arena. Table 10–4 presents the distribution of both the Attentives and Mobilizables among the five ranges comprising the index of opinion-making potential and makes evident the large extent to which both groups clustered toward the lower end of the scale. More than three-fifths of both groups scored in the lowest quintile and less than two percent scored in either of the two highest quintiles.

All three measures of present responsibility, in short, tell the same story: the concern and activities of the Attentive Public do not spring from formal obligations to follow the course of events. Yet such a conclusion does not in itself negate the responsibility-breeds-responsibility hypothesis because it is not based on distinctions within the Attentive Public itself. The hypothesis must be tested not through comparisons with leaders, but through comparisons of the behavior of those who responded differently to the three measures of responsibility. The objective circumstances of attentive citizens may not locate them close to public affairs, but the pertinent question is whether whatever responsibilities they do have, however slight, foster activity and concern. It is to this question that we now turn.

TABLE 10–4
DISTRIBUTION OF THE 1,704 MOBILIZABLES AND 1,658 ATTENTIVES AMONG THE FIVE RANGES OF THE OPINION-MAKING POTENTIAL INDEX (in percentages)

	Lower range	Lower middle range	Middle range	Upper middle range	Upper range	Index score not derivable	Total
Mobilizables	61	29	7	1	0	2	100
Attentives	65	27	6	1	0	1	100

[8] See Table 5–1 and Figure 5–1.

PRESENT RESPONSIBILITIES AND ACTION

The reasoning that responsibility breeds responsibility was operationalized in terms of nine hypotheses (XXIIIa, b, c, XXVa, b, c, and XXVIIa, b, c) which predicted that the first- and second-hand contacts of the Attentives and Mobilizables would be greater the greater their objective proximity, the more extensive their domestic travel, and the higher their opinion-making potential. All of these predictions were upheld by the data. The occupations of concerned citizens may not make strong demands on them to relate to the larger community, but the more they do experience such obligations the more likely they are to establish contact with public issues. In the case of their second-hand contacts, the responses of the Attentives and Mobilizables to the objective proximity item were significantly correlated with the frequency with which they discussed, respectively, nine and ten of the eleven issues comprising this form of behavior. The comparable figures for the domestic travel item were seven and eight significant correlations, and nine and eight for the opinion-making potential index. Table 10–5 lists these correlations.

Similarly, among both the Attentives and the Mobilizables the three measures of their present responsibilities were significantly correlated with the two indicators of their first-hand contacts. The index of opinion-making potential correlated noticeably higher than did the objective proximity and domestic travel items with the indices of letter-writing and organizational activity, but a significant association was found in all twelve instances. These correlations are also presented in Table 10–5.

PRESENT RESPONSIBILITIES AND PERCEPTIONS

Occupational responsibilities appear to underlie self-perceptions of information possessed as much as they do citizenship activity. As anticipated (Hypotheses XXIIIe, XXVe, XXVIIe), all three of the responsibility measures were found to be significantly related to self-perceptions of information for both the Attentives and the Mobilizables. Of the thirty-three correlations involved,

TABLE 10-5
SIGNIFICANT (P < .001) PRODUCT MOMENT CORRELATIONS (r) BETWEEN THE THREE MEASURES OF PRESENT RESPONSIBILITY AND THE MEASURES OF FIRST- AND SECOND-HAND CONTACT FOR THE MOBILIZABLES AND THE ATTENTIVES*

	Objective proximity [Item #36]	Domestic travel [Item #55]	Opinion-making potential
Were the scores of the *Attentives* on the index of letter-writing activity correlated with this measure of present responsibility?	Yes (.133)	Yes (.131)	Yes (.362)
Were the scores of the *Mobilizables* on the index of letter-writing activity correlated with this measure of present responsibility?	Yes (.109)	Yes (.090)	Yes (.264)
Were the scores of the *Attentives* on the index of organizational activity correlated with this measure of present responsibility?	Yes (.145)	Yes (.147)	Yes (.340)
Were the scores of the *Mobilizables* on the index of organizational activity correlated with this measure of present responsibility?	Yes (.154)	Yes (.162)	Yes (.316)
Were the second-hand contacts of the *Attentives* correlated on most issues with this measure of present responsibility?	Yes	Yes	Yes
With which of the eleven issues?	Balance of payments (.166) Berlin (.087)	Agricultural surpluses (.093) Balance of payments (.116)	Balance of payments (.103) Berlin (.093)

	Column 1	Column 2	Column 3	Column 4	Column 5	Column 6
Were the second-hand contacts of the *Mobilizables* correlated on most issues with this measure of present responsibility?	Yes	Yes	Yes		Yes	
With which of the eleven issues?	Civil rights (.133) The Congo (.152) Foreign aid (.168) Nuclear testing (.131) Tariff reduction (.120) Vietnam (.103) Western unity (.102)	Agricultural surpluses (.099) Balance of payments (.103) Civil rights (.121) The Congo (.172) Foreign aid (.138) Tariff reduction (.114) Vietnam (.101) Western unity (.105)	The Congo (.099) Federal tax reduction (.087) Foreign aid (.157) Tariff reduction (.131) Western unity (.120)	Agricultural surpluses (.112) Balance of payments (.139) Civil rights (.125) Federal tax reduction (.087) Foreign aid (.110) Nuclear testing (.094) Tariff reduction (.129) Vietnam (.093)	Civil rights (.090) The Congo (.154) Foreign aid (.169) Nuclear testing (.092) Tariff reduction (.155) Vietnam (.123) Western unity (.160)	Agricultural surpluses (.121) Balance of payments (.140) Berlin (.116) Civil rights (.101) The Congo (.150) Foreign aid (.166) Nuclear testing (.109) Tariff reduction (.168) Vietnam (.147) Western unity (.124)

* All the correlations for the Mobilizables involved between 1,539 and 1,674 respondents. The comparable figures for the Attentives are 1,529 and 1,618.

thirty-two were significant among the Attentives and twenty-eight among the Mobilizables. These data are presented in Table 10–6, which also contains the tests of the prediction that the responsibility measures would be associated with the perceptions of competence (Hypotheses XXIIIf, XXVf, and XXVIIf). The distributions of these data, however, fell far short of the expected patterns. While both the Mobilizables and Attentives registered significant correlations between the opinion-making potential index and the individual-competence variable, only one of them recorded such a pattern with respect to the objective proximity and domestic travel measures. In addition, neither the Attentives nor the Mobilizables compiled a persistent pattern of association between any of the measures of present responsibility and the public-competence and group-competence variables. Only seven of the seventy-two possible correlations (not shown in Table 10–6) were significant among the Attentives and twelve among the Mobilizables.

. The reasons why the original model proved highly accurate with respect to the link between present responsibilities and self-perceptions of information possessed and quite inaccurate in the case of perceived competence seem clear in retrospect. The more a person's occupation requires him to be in touch with the course of affairs, the more likely he is to acquire information on the issues of the day and thus the more likely he is to perceive himself as informed. On the other hand, such occupational requirements do not necessarily oblige him to perceive public affairs as readily influenced by individuals or groups. On the contrary, just as his occupation can provide the active citizen with a sense of the complexity of issues, it may also lead him to appreciate the many obstacles that limit the success of efforts to influence their outcomes. Such an interpretation is also consistent with the findings presented in the previous chapter that showed little interaction between the information and competence variables.

PRESENT RESPONSIBILITIES AND ATTITUDES

Although occupational responsibilities seem to foster citizenship activity and a sense of being informed about public affairs, their influence does not seem to extend into the realm of attitudes.

Contrary to the expectation that the inclination to maintain attitudinal balance would lead both the Attentives and the Mobilizables to attach more importance to and feel more strongly about public issues the closer to the political arena their present circumstances placed them (Hypotheses XXIIId, XXVd, and XXVIId), neither group evidenced such a tendency. Of the thirty-three correlations between the three measures of present responsibility and the eleven-part attitudinal importance variable, only five were significant among the Attentives and two among the Mobilizables. Similarly, of the fifteen correlations between the three measures of present responsibility and the five-part attitudinal extremity variable, the Attentives had only one that was significant and the Mobilizables none.

The sharpness of these negative findings is startling. Not only do they point to the absence of a relationship between present responsibilities and both attitude variables, but they contrast sharply with the close and pervasive association found between present responsibilities and both citizenship behavior and self-perceived level of information. Upon reflection, however, these discrepancies are not as confounding as they may appear. They can be viewed as simply another instance of the complexity of attitudes and the danger—noted several times in previous chapters—of assuming that they are direct determinants of behavior. A citizen's present circumstances may necessitate that he be informed and active, but they do not imply particular views about the importance of public issues or the extremity of the action necessary to resolve them. Indeed, an individual's responsibilities may be such as to encourage neutral attitudes toward issues even as they foster greater involvement in them. The weak and tenuous link previously noted (Table 8–4) between the attitude and behavior variables provides further support for this interpretation. On the other hand, the earlier finding (Tables 9–3 and 9–4) that the attitude and self-information variables are closely linked indicates again that attitudinal dynamics are not easily summarized.

Whatever the proper interpretation, it seems clear that the responsibility-breeds-responsibility hypothesis needs to be revised. Responsibility breeds citizenship behavior, but not necessarily corresponding attitudes.

TABLE 10–6

SIGNIFICANT (P < .001) PRODUCT MOMENT CORRELATIONS (r) BETWEEN THE THREE MEASURES OF PRESENT RESPONSIBILITY AND THE PERCEPTIONS OF INFORMATION POSSESSED AND CITIZEN COMPETENCE FOR THE ATTENTIVES AND MOBILIZABLES*

	Objective proximity [Item #36]	Domestic travel [Item #55]	Opinion-making potential
Were the *Attentives'* perceptions of the information they possessed [#50] correlated on most issues with this measure of present responsibility?	Yes	Yes	Yes
With which of the eleven issues?	Agricultural surpluses (.173)	Agricultural surpluses (.152)	Agricultural surpluses (.117)
	Balance of payments (.194)	Balance of payments (.174)	Balance of payments (.132)
	Berlin (.189)	Berlin (.090)	Berlin (.124)
	Civil rights (.131)	Civil rights (.121)	Civil rights (.204)
	The Congo (.150)	The Congo (.113)	The Congo (.173)
	Federal tax reduction (.177)	Federal tax reduction (.149)	Federal tax reduction (.105)
	Foreign aid (.249)	Foreign aid (.163)	Foreign aid (.222)
	Nuclear testing (.108)	Nuclear testing (.114)	Nuclear testing (.144)
	Tariff reduction (.182)	Tariff reduction (.161)	Tariff reduction (.175)
	Vietnam (.115)	Western unity (.100)	Vietnam (.104)
	Western unity (.200)		Western unity (.121)

Were the *Mobilizables'* perceptions of the information they possessed [#50] correlated on most issues with this measure of present responsibility?	Yes		
With which of the eleven issues?	Yes	Yes	Yes
	Agricultural surpluses (.118)	Agricultural surpluses (.139)	Agricultural surpluses (.087)
	Balance of payments (.108)	Balance of payments (.149)	Balance of payments (.095)
	Berlin (.132)	Berlin (.087)	Berlin (.127)
	Civil rights (.128)	Civil rights (.133)	Civil rights (.221)
	The Congo (.190)	Federal tax reduction (.107)	The Congo (.175)
	Foreign aid (.179)	Foreign aid (.101)	Foreign aid (.171)
	Nuclear testing (.102)	Nuclear testing (.086)	Nuclear testing (.123)
	Tariff reduction (.128)	Tariff reduction (.128)	Tariff reduction (.139)
	Vietnam (.090)		Vietnam (.093)
	Western unity (.138)		Western unity (.085)
Were the *Attentives'* perceptions of the competence of the individual citizen to influence public policy [#56] correlated with this measure of present responsibility?	No	Yes (.086)	Yes (.137)
Were the *Mobilizables'* perceptions of the competence of the individual citizen to influence public policy [#56] correlated with this measure of present responsibility?	Yes (.093)	No	Yes (.138)

* All the correlations for the Mobilizables involved between 1,293 and 1,653 respondents. The comparable figures for the Attentives are 1,253 and 1,598.

PRESENT RESPONSIBILITIES AND MOBILIZABILITY

A comparison of the Attentives and Mobilizables in terms of their response to the three responsibility measures makes further qualification of the responsibility-breeds-responsibility hypothesis necessary. We had reasoned that the more responsibilities a person shoulders, the more likely he is to engage in behavior consistent with the societal norm that values active citizenship. It had thus been anticipated that the Mobilizables would report greater objective proximity, higher opinion-making potentials, and more extensive domestic travel than the Attentives (Hypotheses XXIV, XXVI, and XXVIII). All three of these predictions proved erroneous. None of the differences between the two groups presented in Tables 10–1, 10–3, and 10–4 is significant.

This negative finding provides an important clarification of the dynamics of mobilizability. It indicates that the readiness to respond to appeals for support is not a function of a citizen's proximity to the political arena and suggests the importance of situational factors—perhaps as they interact with certain personality characteristics—as sources of mobilizability. The earlier finding that a citizen's past experiences and social background do not constitute a major source of his mobilizability[9] fits plausibly with this conclusion. If nothing in an active citizen's present circumstances predispose him to be mobilizable, there is no reason why his past statuses should do so. If this is so, situational factors loom large as determinants of which citizens can be mobilized among those in the Attentive Public. Whatever the role played by situational variables,[10] the reasoning underlying our initial model was sound in anticipating that present responsibilities foster greater first-hand contacts on the part of attentive citizens, but it exaggerated the extent to which they lead to the establishment of these contacts in response to mobilizers.

[9] See pp. 316–18.
[10] See Chapters 11 and 12 below.

SUMMARY

The findings uncovered in the preceding analysis are both clarifying and confounding. The fact that all three measures of present responsibility are unmistakably associated with citizenship activity and perceptions of information possessed on the one hand and unrelated to attitudes, perceived competence, and mobilizability on the other is clarifying, but it is also confounding inasmuch as only the positive associations had been anticipated. We hypothesized that the closer to public affairs a citizen's objective responsibilities place him, the more would his behavior, attitudes, and perceptions reflect involvement in them. Such a hypothesis had been confirmed with a leadership sample and it seemed reasonable to expect that the same relationship would hold for attentive citizens. Yet the findings reveal that, while the responsibility-breeds-responsibility hypothesis does obtain in the area of behavior, it does not operate for attitudes and operates only minimally for perceptions. These discrepancies were interpreted as indicating once again the complex nature of the processes whereby attitudes and perceptions are translated into behavior. The finding that greater responsibilities do not conduce to greater mobilizability was seen as pointing to the importance of situational factors as determinants of when attentive citizens respond to attempts to mobilize their support. The next two chapters are addressed to exploring the relevance of two major kinds of situational factors.

CHAPTER **11**

THE APPEAL OF MOBILIZERS

A great number and variety of situational factors can shape the readiness of citizens to become involved in politics between elections: the identity of the mobilizer who seeks their support, the nature of the support he seeks, the ease with which the support can be given or withheld, the case that is made for giving it, the time frame within which it must be given, the issue involved and the other issues competing for attention and support. These are but a few of the situational variables that may contribute to determining which members of the Attentive Public can be mobilized in specific situations. Due to the nature of the data about the ADA sample generated by the research instrument, here the analysis focuses mainly on two aspects of situations that can interact with the backgrounds, attitudes, perceptions, and responsibilities of citizens to produce their independent or mobilized behavior toward public affairs. One is the identity of the mobilizer and the other is the identity of the issue. The appeal of various mobilizers is subjected to analysis in this chapter, and the appeal of various issues is taken up in the next chapter.

Although the interaction of mobilizers and mobilizees lies at the heart of the political process, little is known about its dynamics between elections. The literature on political leadership focuses almost exclusively on the quality and behavior of leaders,[1] and analyses of citizen behavior tend to concentrate on the backgrounds and attitudes of various strata of the public.[2] To be sure, the role of candidates, parties, and issues in mobilizing people to vote has been investigated,[3] and some work has also been done on the role of the mass media and voluntary associations as molders of opinion and stimuli of action,[4] but comparisons of the effectiveness of different kinds of mobilizers in nonelection periods have been conspicuously lacking. Indeed, the data on the subject are so scarce that it is not even clear that the identity of the mobilizers does operate as an important determinant in the support-building process. One knows from everyday life that people do respond to political appeals for their support, but what is not known is whether any mobilizer could have produced the same result. The conclusion that the identity of the mobilizer matters is at the moment supported only by logic and common sense.[5]

[1] See, for example, Glenn D. Paige, ed., *Political Leadership: Readings for an Emerging Field* (New York: The Free Press, 1972).

[2] Cf. Sidney Verba and Norman H. Nie, *Participation in America: Political Democracy and Social Equality* (New York: Harper & Row, 1972).

[3] Illustrative of such inquiries are Angus Campbell, Philip E. Converse, Warren E. Miller, and Donald Stokes, *Elections and the Political Order* (New York: John Wiley, 1966); and Ithiel de Sola Pool, Robert P. Abelson, and Samuel L. Popkin, *Candidates, Issues, and Strategies: A Computer Simulation of the 1960 Presidential Election* (Cambridge: The M.I.T. Press, 1964).

[4] Cf. Joseph T. Klapper, *The Effects of Mass Communication* (New York: The Free Press, 1960).

[5] One possible exception to the dearth of research findings on the way in which the identity of the mobilizer serves as a determinant of be-

Given this theoretical and empirical wasteland, two broad considerations guided the way in which the identity of the mobilizer was built into the original model. One is the basic assumption that mobilizability is a relational phenomenon, that citizens respond to appeals for support because factors inherent in them interact with others in the situational contexts out of which the appeals emanate. Accordingly, two hypotheses (XXXIII and XXXIV) posited an interaction between the backgrounds, perceptions, attitudes, and responsibilities of citizens on the one hand and the identity and appeals of mobilizers on the other.

The second consideration underlying our analysis is a conception of politics as a specialized case of mobilized behavior. All kinds of actors—parents, advertisers, friends, strangers, teachers, employers—try to get others to respond to their efforts, and situations become increasingly political the wider the temporal, spatial, functional, and/or cultural distance spanned by the attempts to

---

havior is the series of experimental studies carried out by social psychologists at Yale during the 1950s on the role played by the identity of the "source" as a variable in the dynamics of attitude change. In general, these studies found that recipients of messages were more likely to be persuaded by sources held in high esteem than by those held in low esteem. Such findings, however, have only partial relevance to our concern here since they deal with "persuasibility" rather than mobilizability. To be mobilized a citizen is likely to be persuaded that he ought to respond to the appeal for his support, but the Yale studies focused on persuasibility that resulted in attitude change and were not concerned with situations in which actions specified by the mobilizers resulted. For some summary treatments of the Yale studies, see Carl I. Hovland, Irving L. Janis, and Harold H. Kelley, *Communication and Persuasion* (New Haven: Yale University Press, 1953); Carl I. Hovland and W. Weiss, "The Influence of Source Credibility on Communication Effectiveness," *Public Opinion Quarterly*, Vol. XV (1951), pp. 635–50; and Irving L. Janis, et al., *Personality and Persuasibility* (New Haven: Yale University Press, 1959). For a discussion of the relevance of persuasibility to political behavior, see Giuseppe Di Palma and Herbert McClosky, "Personality and Conformity: The Learning of Political Attitudes," *American Political Science Review*, Vol. 64 (1970), pp. 1054–73.

modify and mobilize behavior.[6] Viewed in this way, it is the remoteness of public affairs from the lives of citizens that makes them so complex and makes success at mobilizing support for public policies so difficult. If getting family and friends to make simple and clear responses is often a vexing and delicate task, getting unknown persons to give time, energy, or money on behalf of distant goals that may or may not be realized seems awesome. Such a contrast led to the general expectation that the more proximate mobilizers and mobilizees were to each other, the more likely it would be for the latter to respond to the appeals of the former. It was recognized that, virtually by definition, members of the Attentive Public—and especially its more mobilizable members—are familiar with the world of politics and therefore political mobilizers would not seem as remote to them as they might to members of the mass public. Nevertheless, it seemed reasonable to expect that even attentive citizens would be more responsive to friends and organizations who are proximate and with whom they interact frequently and directly than to distant political leaders with whom they have only occasional and peripheral contact (Hypotheses XXIX and XXX), although this might be less true for the Mobilizables than for the Attentives (Hypotheses XXXI and XXXII).

SELF-PERCEIVED MOBILIZABILITY

Several items in the questionnaire were designed to explore the foregoing considerations. One [#5] made no reference to distant political leaders as mobilizers, but simply sought to determine whether the respondents perceived themselves as the sole initiators of first-hand contacts with public affairs or whether they had some awareness that they were responsive to such relatively proximate mobilizers as friends and organizations. The responses to this item are presented in Table 11–1. Here it can be seen that both the

[6] For an elaboration of this conception, see Rosenau, *The Scientific Study of Foreign Policy* (New York: The Free Press, 1971), pp. 204–10.

TABLE 11–1
DISTRIBUTION OF THE RESPONSES OF THE 1,704
MOBILIZABLES AND 1,658 ATTENTIVES TO ITEM #5
(in percentages)

[#5] If and when you write letters to legislative or executive officials (at any level), where does the idea for them usually come from? (Check only one)*

	Mobilizables	Attentives
I usually develop the idea for such letters in discussions with friends	15	12
It is usually urged on me by an organization of which I am a member	48	29
It is usually the result of my own thinking and initiative.	53	43
I never write such letters	1	8
Other	6	5
Codable answer not given	1	15
Total	124	112

* As indicated by the fact that the totals exceed 100 percent, many of the respondents were unable to comply with this instruction and cited the source that "usually" stimulates their letters.

Mobilizables and Attentives saw themselves as initiators of "letters to legislative or executive officials," but that they also perceived that the stimuli for such contacts emanate from their external worlds. Roughly half of the Mobilizables and two-fifths of the Attentives cited themselves as "usually" the source of the letters they write, but even more of the former and the same proportion of the latter also perceived that friends and organizations stimulated them to write. The finding that many active citizens cite external mobilizers more than themselves as stimuli to their letter-writing activities is consistent with the interpretation developed in Chapter 9 that the political competence that members of the Attentive Public see themselves as possessing tends to be collective rather than individual.

Also of interest is the finding that substantially more respondents cited organizations than friends as mobilizers to whom they are responsive. Not more than 15 percent of either group specified friends as sources of their letter-writing activities, but nearly half of the Mobilizables and one-third of the Attentives identified organizations as playing this role. As will be seen, this is not the only finding that negates our expectation (Hypothesis XXIX) that active citizens are more mobilizable the closer the mobilizer is to their daily lives.

The data in Table 11–1 also reveal some important differences between the two groups. The Mobilizables saw themselves as more mobilizable by organizations than did the Attentives,[7] a difference that had been anticipated (Hypothesis XXXI) on the grounds that the more mobilizable a citizen is the more he will perceive himself as mobilizable. The Mobilizables also perceived themselves as more self-sustaining as letter-writers than the Attentives,[8] a difference which can be explained in terms of the earlier findings that the Mobilizables are more likely to establish first-hand contacts than the Attentives.[9] Somewhat in contrast, the difference between the two groups in their self-perceived responsiveness to friends was small. We had predicted (Hypothesis XXXII) that this difference between them would be less than that which obtained with respect to organizations, but the fact that the difference was not significant contradicts our reasoning. Perhaps it indicates again the fallacy of our original expectation that proximate mobilizers would be particularly salient in the world of active citizens. It seems that all members of the Attentive Public separate their personal worlds from the world of public affairs, which makes the Mobilizables and Attentives similar in their self-perceived responsiveness to proximate mobilizers. Other data presented below support this interpretation.

Three other items in the questionnaire dealt with the iden-

---

[7] $\chi^2 = 135.64$, df $= 1$, P$<$.001.

[8] $\chi^2 = 34.02$, df $= 1$, P$<$.001.

[9] The fact that significantly more of the Attentives said, "I never write such letters" ($\chi^2 = 111.69$, df $= 1$, P$<$.001) and that substantially more of them did not answer Item #5 is also consistent with this finding.

tity of the mobilizer. These were designed to make sharper contrasts between proximate and distant mobilizers possible and also
to examine mobilizability with respect to specific issues. Except for
the identity of the mobilizer, all three items were worded alike
and asked the respondents to estimate on five-point scales the likelihood that they would respond to a mobilizer who urged them to
write a member of Congress about each of eleven issues. The three
mobilizers used were "a close friend" [#14], "an organization to
which you belong" [#53], and "the President" [#42]. In order
to prevent rote responses to such similarly worded items, the orders
of the issues comprising the rows was different in each case and
the three items were widely scattered throughout the questionnaire. That the close similarity of the items was disguised and the
differences between them highlighted can be readily seen in the
pages that follow. Rote responses to the three items could not
have yielded either the variability or the systematic patterns that
are manifest in the data.

Tables 11–2, 11–3, and 11–4 present the responses of the
Attentives and the Mobilizables to the three items. A comparative
analysis of them yields several important patterns, perhaps the
most notable one being the differences between the two groups.
In all thirty-three comparisons between the Attentives and the
Mobilizables, the mean scores of the latter indicate greater self-
perceived mobilizability and thirty-two of these differences are
significant. Irrespective of the identity of either the issue or the
mobilizer, in other words, a mobilizable citizen is more likely than
one who is simply attentive to public affairs to perceive himself as
responsive to appeals for support. In view of the operational distinction between the Attentives and the Mobilizables, of course,
such perceptions are likely to be accurate. The Mobilizables did
respond to the ADA and the Attentives did not, and the data
presented in these three tables reflect this difference. Whatever
the factors are that produce mobilizability, they also appear to
result in self-awareness of this mobilizability. The expected association between mobilizability and self-perceptions of it (Hypothesis XXXI) could hardly have been upheld more strikingly by
the data.

The data also reveal that the Mobilizables did not see them-

TABLE 11–2
DISTRIBUTION OF THE RESPONSES OF THE 1,704 MOBILIZABLES (Ms) AND 1,658 ATTENTIVES (As) TO ITEM #14 (in percentages)

[#14] Quite apart from what you think you ought to do, what would you do, what would you be *likely* to do if, at different times, a close friend urged you to write Congressmen on behalf of his position on each of the problems listed at the left? That is (and assuming you did not differ greatly with his viewpoint on the matter), what would be the *likelihood* of your actually writing a representative or senator as a result of your friend's urging on each problem? (Place *one* check in *each* row)

		Extremely likely (5*)	Very likely (4*)	Somewhat likely (3*)	Hardly likely (2*)	Not at all likely (1*)	Codable answer not given	Total	Mean score	Statistical comparison of the responses of the Mobilizables and Attentives X^2	df	$P <$
Agricultural surpluses	Ms	8	16	25	25	20	6	100	2.65	24.69	4	.001
	As	6	13	23	28	26	4	100	2.44			
Balance of payments	Ms	5	10	20	32	27	6	100	2.31	12.10	4	ns**
	As	4	8	20	31	31	6	100	2.18			
Berlin	Ms	17	23	28	16	10	6	100	3.23	45.20	4	.001
	As	13	20	25	20	16	6	100	2.95			
Civil rights	Ms	62	23	7	3	3	2	100	4.41	131.53	4	.001
	As	45	26	14	5	7	3	100	3.99			
The Congo	Ms	11	20	30	21	13	5	100	2.94	48.26	4	.001
	As	9	18	24	24	20	5	100	2.69			

Federal tax reduction	Ms	13	19	24	21	18	5	100	2.86	34.04	4	.001
	As	8	16	23	25	23	5	100	2.60			
Foreign aid	Ms	37	30	19	6	5	3	100	3.90	96.57	4	.001
	As	25	28	22	11	10	4	100	3.48			
Nuclear testing	Ms	59	25	9	2	1	4	100	4.30	160.32	4	.001
	As	39	24	16	8	10	3	100	3.77			
Tariff reduction	Ms	9	20	28	22	17	4	100	2.83	35.79	4	.001
	As	7	18	23	24	23	5	100	2.59			
Vietnam	Ms	16	22	28	18	12	4	100	3.11	46.11	4	.001
	As	11	20	24	23	18	6	100	2.83			
Western unity	Ms	11	18	29	21	16	5	100	2.87	23.89	4	.001
	As	9	16	26	25	20	4	100	2.67			

* This value was given to responses recorded here in order to calculate mean scores for all the Mobilizables and Attentives.
** Not significant.

TABLE 11-3
DISTRIBUTION OF THE RESPONSES OF THE 1,704 MOBILIZABLES (Ms) AND 1,658 ATTENTIVES (As) TO ITEM #53 (in percentages)

[#53] Quite apart from what you think you ought to do, what would you be *likely* to do if, at different times, an organization to which you belong urged its members to write Congressmen on behalf of its position on each of the problems listed at the left? That is (and assuming you did not differ greatly with its viewpoint on the matter), what would be the *likelihood* of your actually writing a representative or senator as a result of the organization's urging on each problem? (Place *one* check in *each* row)

		Extremely likely (5*)	Very likely (4*)	Some- what likely (3*)	Hardly likely (2*)	Not at all likely (1*)	Codable answer not given	Total	Mean score	Statistical comparison of the responses of the Mobilizables and Attentives		
										X^2	df	P <
Agricultural surpluses	Ms	9	18	30	28	11	4	100	2.84	61.62	4	.001
	As	6	14	24	32	19	5	100	2.55			
Balance of payments	Ms	6	10	29	34	16	5	100	2.53	41.71	4	.001
	As	4	8	23	37	22	6	100	2.31			
Berlin	Ms	14	23	35	19	5	4	100	3.22	90.72	4	.001
	As	10	16	32	25	12	5	100	2.87			
Civil rights	Ms	64	23	8	1	1	3	100	4.51	238.96	4	.001
	As	41	27	17	7	4	4	100	3.97			
The Congo	Ms	10	18	35	26	7	4	100	2.97	87.23	4	.001
	As	6	13	29	32	15	5	100	2.62			

Federal tax reduction	Ms	17	21	31	20	7	4	100	3.21	78.57	4	.001
	As	10	16	29	26	13	6	100	2.85			
Foreign aid	Ms	28	33	26	8	3	2	100	3.78	152.90	4	.001
	As	16	27	28	17	7	5	100	3.30			
Nuclear testing	Ms	59	25	9	2	1	4	100	4.43	243.25	4	.001
	As	38	27	17	9	5	4	100	3.85			
Tariff reduction	Ms	11	20	32	23	9	5	100	3.01	74.10	4	.001
	As	6	15	30	28	16	5	100	2.66			
Vietnam	Ms	17	22	31	19	6	5	100	3.25	92.68	4	.001
	As	11	18	27	28	12	4	100	2.87			
Western unity	Ms	12	19	33	22	9	5	100	3.03	58.13	4	.001
	As	9	15	28	29	15	4	100	2.73			

* This value was given to responses recorded here in order to calculate mean scores for all the Mobilizables and Attentives.

TABLE 11–4
DISTRIBUTION OF THE RESPONSES OF THE 1,704 MOBILIZABLES (Ms) AND 1,658 ATTENTIVES (As) TO ITEM #42 (in percentages)

[#42] Quite apart from what you think you ought to do, what would you be *likely* to do if, at different times, the President gave a television address in which he urged citizens to write Congressmen on behalf of his position on each of the problems listed at the left? That is (and assuming you do not differ greatly with his viewpoint on the matter), what would be the *likelihood* of your actually writing a representative or a senator as a result of the President's urging on each problem? (Place *one* check in *each row*)

		Extremely likely (5*)	Very likely (4*)	Some-what likely (3*)	Hardly likely (2*)	Not at all likely (1*)	Codable answer not given	Total	Mean score	Statistical comparison of the responses of the Mobilizables and Attentives		
										X^2	df	P<
Agricultural surpluses	Ms	17	19	27	23	10	4	100	3.12	55.17	4	.001
	As	10	16	26	26	15	7	100	2.80			
Balance of payments	Ms	11	14	25	27	16	7	100	2.76	35.47	4	.001
	As	7	13	22	29	22	7	100	2.51			
Berlin	Ms	26	25	25	13	5	6	100	3.58	81.15	4	.001
	As	18	22	25	19	10	6	100	3.19			
Civil rights	Ms	69	20	6	1	1	3	100	4.58	206.89	4	.001
	As	47	27	14	5	5	2	100	4.10			
The Congo	Ms	21	22	27	17	7	6	100	3.37	88.99	4	.001
	As	14	19	24	25	13	5	100	2.96			

Federal tax reduction	Ms	24	25	26	14	7	4	100	3.48	86.35	4	.001
	As	16	21	25	22	11	5	100	3.08			
Foreign aid	Ms	39	31	19	5	3	3	100	4.01	157.16	4	.001
	As	23	30	22	14	7	4	100	3.52			
Nuclear testing	Ms	68	20	6	2	2	2	100	4.56	237.83	4	.001
	As	45	26	14	7	5	3	100	4.02			
Tariff reduction	Ms	21	24	28	16	7	4	100	3.37	74.40	4	.001
	As	13	22	26	21	13	5	100	3.01			
Vietnam	Ms	26	22	26	14	6	6	100	3.51	74.08	4	.001
	As	18	20	25	20	12	5	100	3.13			
Western unity	Ms	23	24	24	17	7	5	100	3.39	64.61	4	.001
	As	15	20	24	23	12	6	100	3.04			

* This value was given to responses recorded here in order to calculate mean scores for all the Mobilizables and Attentives.

selves as readily galvanized by any mobilizer on any issue. They consistently perceived themselves as more mobilizable than the Attentives, but the degree of perceived mobilizability varied considerably across the eleven issues and the three mobilizers. This variability can be seen even more clearly in Table 11–5, which summarizes the responses into mean scores for all the issues and mobilizers. These data also tend to confirm the expectation (Hypothesis XXXII) that the differences between the self-perceived mobilizability of the Mobilizables and Attentives would be greater for distant mobilizers than proximate ones: the differences between their mean scores were .30 for a friend as mobilizer, .38 for an organization, and .39 for the President.

The fact that the greatest differences between the Mobilizables and Attentives were recorded on those issues, nuclear testing and civil rights, which were the focus of the ADA's mobilizing efforts is further evidence of both the variability and the accuracy of their self-perceptions. The chi square values for the differences on these two issues are considerably greater than for any of the others and so are those for the differences among their mean scores for the three types of mobilizers. It is interesting also to note in Table 11–5 that the mean scores of the Mobilizables and Attentives on these two issues were higher than on any other and also most different from each other. On other issues, where they had not all been exposed to an effort to procure their support and therefore had to conjecture about their responsiveness, both the differences between the mobilizable and attentive citizen and the degree of anticipated responsiveness diminish. The data uncovered for most of the issues therefore probably underestimate the differences between the Mobilizables and Attentives in their readiness to be mobilized. They also suggest a plausible explanation for why the responses on the foreign aid issue more closely resemble those on nuclear testing and civil rights than on the other eight issues: during the same period mobilizers other than ADA were probably more active on the foreign aid issue than any of the other eight,[10] thereby exposing the respondents to appeals for sup-

---

[10] For analyses indicating the considerable extent to which the foreign aid issue fostered mobilization efforts in the 1950s and 1960s, see H.

TABLE 11–5
COMPOSITE MEAN SELF-PERCEIVED MOBILIZABILITY
SCORES RECORDED BY THE 1,704 MOBILIZABLES
AND 1,658 ATTENTIVES IN TERMS OF THREE TYPES
OF MOBILIZERS AND ELEVEN ISSUES*

	Mobilizables	Attentives
Self-perceived mobilizability by issue		
Agricultural surpluses (n = 3)	3.31	3.04
Balance of payments (n = 3)	2.54	2.33
Berlin (n = 3)	3.34	3.00
Civil rights (n = 3)	4.50	4.00
The Congo (n = 3)	3.09	2.75
Federal tax reduction (n = 3)	3.18	2.84
Foreign aid (n = 3)	3.89	3.42
Nuclear testing (n = 3)	4.32	3.86
Tariff reduction (n = 3)	3.07	2.75
Vietnam (n = 3)	3.29	2.93
Western unity (n = 3)	3.10	2.88
Self-perceived mobilizability by identity of the mobilizer		
Friend (n = 11)	3.25	2.95
Organization (n = 11)	3.36	2.98
President (n = 11)	3.63	3.24
Self-perceived mobilizability by both issue and mobilizer (n = 33)	3.31	3.04

* In calculating the mean scores, values of 5, 4, 3, 2, and 1 were given, respectively, to "extremely likely," "very likely," "somewhat likely," "hardly likely," and "not at all likely" responses to Items #14, 42, and 53.

port on this question which, in turn, underlies the finding that both the mean scores of the Attentives and Mobilizables on foreign aid and the chi square values for the differences between them were the third highest among the issues.

Field Haviland, Jr., "Foreign Aid and the Policy Process: 1957," *American Political Science Review*, Vol. LII (September 1958), pp. 689–724; Michael Kent O'Leary, *The Politics of American Foreign Aid* (New York: Atherton, 1967); and James N. Rosenau, *National Leadership and Foreign Policy: A Case Study in the Mobilization of Public Support* (Princeton: Princeton University Press, 1963).

The correlations among the responses to the three items, presented in Table 11–6, provide additional insight into active citizens' perceptions of their own mobilizability. These correlations are the highest uncovered in the study and they indicate that both the Attentives and the Mobilizables were sufficiently aware of their manner of relating to public affairs to give interdependent as well as varied answers to the three items. For some this meant a view of themselves as possessing source-oriented mobilizability—as equally susceptible or unsusceptible to being mobilized on any issue by the same mobilizer. Others contributed to the high correlations by perceiving their mobilizability as issue-oriented—as equally likely in response to any mobilizer on the same issue. Such source- and issue-oriented patterns describe fundamentally different forms of mobilizability,[11] but they also indicate that active citizens have in common a self-awareness of their responses to political stimuli.

Two other patterns in Table 11–6 are worthy of note. One is that the Mobilizables recorded substantially lower correlations among the three items on those issues, civil rights and nuclear testing (and particularly the former), with respect to which they are known to have been mobilized, whereas this was not the case for the Attentives, who did not respond to the ADA as a mobilizer. Such a finding must be interpreted with extreme caution, but it may be seen as suggesting that the experience of being mobilized feeds back into self-perceptions of mobilizability. Having been mobilized on these two issues, the Mobilizables had more differentiated perceptions of the particular stimuli to their behavior than did those for whom the identity of the mobilizer was hypothetical.

The other interesting pattern in Table 11–6 is that in all forty-four instances the organization-President correlations are larger than the friend-organization and friend-President correlations and that nineteen of the twenty-two friend-organization correlations exceed the friend-President correlations. This finding supports our expectation that the mobilizability of active citizens

[11]For data on these source- and issue-oriented differences, see below, pp. 460–66.

TABLE 11–6
PRODUCT MOMENT CORRELATIONS (r) RECORDED
BY THE 1,704 MOBILIZABLES AND THE 1,658
ATTENTIVES BETWEEN THEIR RESPONSES TO THE
THREE MEASURES (#14, 42, 53) OF SELF-
PERCEIVED MOBILIZABILITY (all the correlations are
significant at the .001 level*)

Issue	MOBILIZABLES Correlations between self-perceived mobilizability by			ATTENTIVES Correlations between self-perceived mobilizability by		
	the President and a friend	an organization and a friend	an organization and the President	the President and a friend	an organization and a friend	an organization and the President
Agricultural surpluses	.559	.596	.646	.553	.590	.673
Balance of payments	.542	.577	.606	.515	.569	.633
Berlin	.580	.599	.616	.608	.607	.660
Civil rights	.483	.488	.596	.555	.562	.684
The Congo	.546	.560	.607	.601	.597	.641
Federal tax reduction	.559	.611	.652	.555	.565	.669
Foreign aid	.551	.553	.621	.578	.600	.665
Nuclear testing	.497	.537	.612	.582	.610	.694
Tariff reduction	.523	.568	.610	.559	.575	.650
Vietnam	.593	.630	.650	.621	.645	.678
Western unity	.579	.587	.639	.659	.565	.649

* All the correlations involve an *n* of no less than 1,522 for the Mobilizables and no
less than 1,489 for the Attentives.

is partly a function of the spatial, geographic, functional, and temporal distance between them and the mobilizer. An organization and the President are both more distant than a friend and thus are sufficiently more alike in the perceptual world of mobilizees to foster higher correlations. Likewise, a friend and an organization are both closer than the President and thus are sufficiently more alike to give rise to higher correlations. As noted in the next section, however, the direction of these relationships was quite contrary to the one that had been anticipated.

THE IDENTITY OF THE MOBILIZER

To the extent that perceptions of mobilizability accurately represent reality, our expectation (Hypotheses XXIX and XXX) that attentive and mobilizable citizens are more responsive to close-at-hand mobilizers than to distant ones could hardly have been more erroneous. Both the Mobilizables and the Attentives indicated a greater receptivity to an appeal from the President than to one from a friend or an organization. The mean scores for their perceived mobilizability by the President were higher than the comparable figures for mobilizability by organizations or friends on all eleven issues. As can be seen in Tables 11–7 and 11–8, moreover, the differences in all but two of the twenty-two comparisons involving the President were significant for the Mobilizables and the same pattern also describes the responses of the Attentives. Only the President-friend difference on foreign aid and the President-organization difference on civil rights for the Mobilizables and the President-friend differences on the same two issues for the Attentives were not significant.

Nor does the negation of our original reasoning end here. Both groups also tended to perceive themselves as more responsive to the appeals of organizations than those of friends, thus further contradicting the expected link between mobilizability and closeness of the mobilizer. The Mobilizables indicated significantly greater responsiveness to organizations than to friends on nine of the issues, and the Attentives did so on seven.

The identity of the mobilizer thus appears to be relevant as a source of mobilizability, but the relationship may not be as simple as it seems. It could be argued that the unmistakable clarity of the data point to a simple relationship in a direction opposite to the one anticipated. Such an argument could add that the clear-cut pattern merely affirms the earlier finding in which the President emerged as the most salient figure in the attentive citizen's world.[12] In questioning this line of reasoning, it must be

---

[12] See pp. 210–15.

stressed that the data depict self-perceived mobilizability, which is different from actual mobilized behavior in concrete situations. It is noteworthy that all four of the nonsignificant differences among the forty-four comparisons presented in Tables 11–7 and 11–8 involved the President, two as the mobilizer with respect to an issue (civil rights) on which the respondents are known to have been subjected to mobilization efforts and two on an issue (foreign aid) that it seems reasonable to assume was also the focus of similar efforts (see the preceding section). In other words, it may be that the importance attached to the chief of state is primarily symbolic and is actually less relevant as a determinant of behavior. If this is the case, close-at-hand mobilizers may be more effective than the contrary data outlined here suggest.[13]

On the other hand, if these perceptual data are good indicators of behavior—and we have already presented some findings that suggest that attentive citizens do have a realistic sense of the role they play in public affairs[14]—it is not difficult to construct an explanation for them. With the advantage of hindsight it can be reasoned that, unlike members of the mass public, attentive citizens are sufficiently politicized to differentiate between the personal and political worlds and to assess that the support they give in response to the appeals of public officials or nongovernmental leaders is much more likely to be aggregated effectively and thereby to affect the political process than that which they provide in response to friends. To be mobilized by a friend is to engage in an act which may or may not be politically instrumental. To respond to a distant leader is at least to promote the possibility

---

[13] I am indebted to Sidney Verba for another possible explanation of why close-at-hand mobilizers may be more effective than the data indicate. The respondents knew the identity of the President (although he was not actually mentioned in the question), whereas the identity of the "close friend" was less certain, a difference in specificity that may have affected the way in which they responded to the two items (personal communication, June 21, 1973).

[14] See pp. 363–65.

TABLE 11–7
COMPARISONS OF THE RESPONSES OF THE 1,704 MOBILIZABLES TO THE THREE SELF-PERCEIVED MOBILIZABILITY ITEMS IN TERMS OF ELEVEN ISSUES*

Issue and mobilizer	Mean scores	X^2 of the differences between their responses to the President and a friend as mobilizers			an organization and a friend as mobilizers			an organization and the President as mobilizers		
		X^2	df	P	X^2	df	P	X^2	df	P
Agricultural surpluses										
friend	2.65	125.88	4	.001	54.68	4	.001	56.73	4	.001
organization	2.84									
President	3.12									
Balance of payments										
friend	2.31	110.11	4	.001	74.94	4	.001	57.47	4	.001
organization	2.53									
President	2.76									
Berlin										
friend	3.23	70.31	4	.001	51.86	4	.001	114.60	4	.001
organization	3.22									
President	3.58									
Civil rights										
friend	4.41	34.03	4	.001	29.88	4	.001	13.42	4	ns**
organization	4.51									
President	4.58									
The Congo										
friend	2.94	106.39	4	.001	42.93	4	.001	129.60	4	.001
organization	2.97									
President	3.37									

Issue	Source	Mean	X^2	df	sig	X^2	df	sig	X^2	df	sig
Federal tax reduction	friend	2.86	189.51	4	.001	108.81	4	.001	55.42	4	.001
	organization	3.21									
	President	3.48									
Foreign aid	friend	3.90	13.03	4	ns**	59.52	4	.001	57.68	4	.001
	organization	3.78									
	President	4.01									
Nuclear testing	friend	4.30	63.86	4	.001	39.54	4	.001	37.74	4	.001
	organization	4.43									
	President	4.56									
Tariff reduction	friend	2.83	162.28	4	.001	42.14	4	.001	84.05	4	.001
	organization	3.01									
	President	3.37									
Vietnam	friend	3.11	90.07	4	.001	45.27	4	.001	56.31	4	.001
	organization	3.25									
	President	3.51									
Western unity	friend	2.87	145.47	4	.001	37.31	4	.001	99.60	4	.001
	organization	3.03									
	President	3.39									

* See Tables 11-2, 11-3, and 11-4 for the distributions from which the mean scores and the X^2 comparisons presented here were derived.

** Not significant.

TABLE 11-8
COMPARISONS OF THE RESPONSES OF THE 1,658 ATTENTIVES TO THE THREE
SELF-PERCEIVED MOBILIZABILITY ITEMS IN TERMS OF ELEVEN ISSUES*

Issue and mobilizer	Mean scores	X^2 OF THE DIFFERENCES BETWEEN THEIR RESPONSES TO								
		the President and a friend as mobilizers			an organization and a friend as mobilizers			an organization and the President as mobilizers		
		X^2	df	P	X^2	df	P	X^2	df	P
Agricultural surpluses										
friend	2.44	69.90	4	.001	25.92	4	.001	39.34	4	.001
organization	2.55									
President	2.80									
Balance of payments										
friend	2.18	60.71	4	.001	37.90	4	.001	50.48	4	.001
organization	2.31									
President	2.51									
Berlin										
friend	2.95	34.01	4	.001	45.44	4	.001	79.78	4	.001
organization	2.87									
President	3.19									
Civil rights										
friend	3.99	11.15	4	ns**	27.10	4	.001	19.02	4	.001
organization	3.97									
President	4.10									
The Congo										
friend	2.69	48.37	4	.001	61.17	4	.001	91.99	4	.001
organization	2.62									
President	2.96									

	Mean	X^2	df	p	X^2	df	p	X^2	df	p
Federal tax reduction										
friend	2.60									
organization	2.85	118.30	4	.001	63.82	4	.001	40.47	4	.001
President	3.08									
Foreign aid										
friend	3.48									
organization	3.30	17.85	4	ns**	73.32	4	.001	76.10	4	.001
President	3.52									
Nuclear testing										
friend	3.77									
organization	3.85	36.29	4	.001	23.61	4	.001	22.10	4	.001.
President	4.02									
Tariff reduction										
friend	2.59									
organization	2.66	95.39	4	.001	43.53	4	.001	79.80	4	.001
President	3.01									
Vietnam										
friend	2.83									
organization	2.87	49.13	4	.001	34.61	4	.001	52.37	4	.001
President	3.13									
Western unity										
friend	2.67									
organization	2.73	73.35	4	.001	24.17	4	.001	62.04	4	.001
President	3.04									

* See Tables 11-2, 11-3, and 11-4 for the distributions from which the mean scores and the X^2 comparisons presented here were derived.

** Not significant.

that one's action will be put to use by that leader. If the distant leader happens to be the chief of state, one can be especially confident that the mobilized support will serve some larger purpose.

THE CORRELATES OF SELF-PERCEIVED MOBILIZABILITY

An analysis of the interaction of the self-perceived mobilizability variables and those examined in previous chapters helps very little in choosing between these two contradictory interpretations of the data on the identity of the mobilizer. Indeed, the correlational patterns provide little evidence that the identity of the mobilizer is relevant to the interaction between self-perceptions of mobilizability and the other factors that give rise to citizenship orientations and activities. Table 11–9 summarizes the correlations for both the Mobilizables and Attentives. Here it is clear that the central tendency is one of no differences among the three types of mobilizers. The number of issues significantly correlated with the friend, organization, and President items was essentially the same for most variables. The fact that the significant correlations involving perceived mobilizability by an organization or the President were higher than those involving perceived mobilizability by a friend lends some support to the interpretation that citizens differentiate between the personal and political worlds. Yet this finding seems slight in comparison to the similarity in the number of significant correlations registered for all three mobilizers. Only the public-competence variables (especially those involving the President and the United Nations) are an exception in this regard, one that also suggests differentiation between the personal and political worlds: for the Mobilizables, and especially for the Attentives, the perceptions of mobilizability by a friend were much less related than perceptions of mobilizability by an organization or the President to perceptions of the susceptibility of officials to public opinion. A similar pattern can also be discerned in the letter-writing activities of both groups, but again this finding seems slight compared to the extent to which uniformity marks the columns of Table 11–9.

A more important feature of the correlational patterns is the large degree of interdependence between self-perceived mobilizability and the attitudes, perceptions, and activities of attentive and mobilizable citizens. The three self-perceived mobilizability variables were thoroughly and pervasively associated, for both the Mobilizables and the Attentives, with the two attitudinal variables, the perceptual measures of information possessed and of individual and group competence, and the behavioral indicators of first- and second-hand contacts. Only the measures of present responsibility and the public-competence variables (especially for the Mobilizables) were not a part of this network of association, although the correlations involving these variables were substantially higher than any presented in previous chapters.

The strength of the self-perceived mobilizability variables cannot be seen as an artifact of the attitudinal, perceptual, or behavioral variables, as many of the associations involving them persisted when other variables were held constant. In the case of the interaction among the importance, second-hand contact, and self-perceived mobilizability-by-friend variables, for example, with second-hand contact held constant, 34 of the 55 correlations between the mobilizability-by-friend and importance variables were significant for the Mobilizables and 33 for the Attentives. With importance held constant, there were 31 and 26 significant associations for the Mobilizables and Attentives, respectively, between the same mobilizability variable and the measure of second-hand contact. At the same time the self-perceived mobilizability variables were not so powerful as to erase the significant associations among the others. With mobilizability-by-friend held constant, 34 of the Mobilizables' 55 correlations and 36 of the Attentives' between the measures of attitudinal importance and second-hand contact were significant. Similar analyses of the patterns of association among the other two self-perceived mobilizability variables and the other attitudinal, perceptual and behavioral variables yielded roughly the same results.

In short, the basic premise of our original model—that the sources of active citizenship are interdependent—is confirmed by the self-perceived mobilizability variables even though limits to its applicability were uncovered in previous chapters. Stated dif-

TABLE 11-9
FREQUENCY OF SIGNIFICANT CORRELATIONS RECORDED BY THE 1,704 MOBILIZABLES AND 1,658 ATTENTIVES BETWEEN THEIR RESPONSES TO THE THREE SELF-PERCEIVED MOBILIZABILITY VARIABLES ON THE ONE HAND AND THE ATTITUDINAL, PERCEPTUAL, BEHAVIORAL, AND PRESENT RESPONSIBILITY MEASURES ON THE OTHER (with the range between the highest and lowest significant correlations indicated parenthetically)

	THE MOBILIZABLES Self-perceived mobilizability by			THE ATTENTIVES Self-perceived mobilizability by		
Correlations between	a friend [#14]	an organization [#53]	the President [#42]	a friend [#14]	an organization [#53]	the President [#42]
Attitude Variables						
Importance* [#47]	11 of 11 (.403–.267)	11 of 11 (.547–.329)	11 of 11 (.514–.315)	11 of 11 (.392–.285)	11 of 11 (.497–.392)	11 of 11 (.457–.384)
Extremity* [#19, 20, 43, 44, 46]	4 of 5 (.343–.120)	4 of 5 (.442–.146)	4 of 5 (.179–.398)	4 of 5 (.322–.110)	4 of 5 (.376–.144)	4 of 5 (.347–.159)
Perceptual Variables						
Information Possessed* [#50]	11 of 11 (.395–.244)	11 of 11 (.471–.295)	11 of 11 (.382–.254)	11 of 11 (.368–.234)	11 of 11 (.417–.282)	11 of 11 (.358–.236)
Individual Competence* [#56]	8 of 11 (.172–.088)	10 of 11 (.201–.097)	8 of 11 (.197–.090)	11 of 11 (.220–.109)	11 of 11 (.257–.155)	11 of 11 (.244–.161)
Group Competence—re tariff reduction** [#23]	4 of 6 (.182–.114)	4 of 6 (.178–.132)	2 of 6 (.138–.118)	4 of 6 (.175–.118)	4 of 6 (.203–.163)	4 of 6 (.188–.132)
nuclear testing** [#40]	3 of 6 (.167–.094)	4 of 6 (.178–.088)	3 of 6 (.136–.099)	4 of 6 (.215–.100)	5 of 6 (.295–.087)	4 of 6 (.239–.097)
civil rights** [#59]	2 of 6 (.198–.191)	4 of 6 (.208–.149)	3 of 6 (.190–.158)	2 of 6 (.201–.144)	1 of 6 (.190)	4 of 6 (.238–.154)

	6	5	4	3	2	1
Public Competence—re						
local officials* [#58]	0 of 11	1 of 11 (.090)	0 of 11	3 of 11 (.131–.106)	5 of 11 (.140–.091)	8 of 11 (.143–.092)
state governor* [#58]	1 of 11 (.136)	1 of 11 (.102)	1 of 11 (.091)	11 of 11 (.142–.090)	2 of 11 (.101–.100)	9 of 11 (.118–.095)
state legislature* [#58]	0 of 11	1 of 11 (.099)	0 of 11	5 of 11 (.117–.096)	8 of 11 (.123–.088)	6 of 11 (.111–.088)
the President* [#58]	1 of 11 (.118)	4 of 11 (.125–.091)	4 of 11 (.118–.089)	5 of 11 (.127–.087)	10 of 11 (.160–.098)	11 of 11 (.190–.109)
Members of Congress* [#58]	1 of 11 (.115)	6 of 11 (.145–.094)	1 of 11 (.102)	3 of 11 (.118–.091)	6 of 11 (.145–.094)	3 of 11 (.134–.090)
U.N. officials* [#58]	3 of 11 (.156–.111)	7 of 11 (.145–.095)	5 of 11 (.143–.089)	4 of 11 (.100–.088)	9 of 11 (.153–.094)	9 of 11 (.147–.090)
Behavioral Variables						
2nd-hand contacts* [#49]	11 of 11 (.366–.189)	11 of 11 (.444–.269)	11 of 11 (.349–.245)	11 of 11 (.400–.237)	11 of 11 (.444–.323)	11 of 11 (.375–.244)
letter-writing*	8 of 11 (.153–.093)	11 of 11 (.221–.118)	9 of 11 (.165–.106)	8 of 11 (.270–.111)	11 of 11 (.360–.180)	11 of 11 (.318–.170)
organizational activity*	4 of 11 (.125–.104)	6 of 11 (.157–.093)	4 of 11 (.118–.088)	7 of 11 (.196–.111)	7 of 11 (.233–.127)	7 of 11 (.186–.118)
Present Responsibilities						
opinion-making potential*	1 of 11 (.092)	2 of 11 (.138–.107)	1 of 11 (.109)	6 of 11 (.141–.088)	9 of 11 (.180–.096)	6 of 11 (.135–.096)
objective proximity* [#36]	0 of 11	1 of 11 (.096)	0 of 11	0 of 11	1 of 11 (.090)	1 of 11 (.099)
domestic travel* [#55]	0 of 11	0 of 11	0 of 11	0 of 11	0 of 11	0 of 11

* These variables consist of eleven types of issues.   ** These variables consist of six types of groups.

ferently, the hypothesis (XXXIII) that self-perceived mobilizability would interact with attitudes, perceptions, and behaviors was upheld more unambiguously than any of the others that anticipated interactive effects.

It does not detract from this clear-cut conclusion to note some curious and unexpected differences between the correlational patterns for the Mobilizables and Attentives. The Mobilizables consistently perceived themselves as more mobilizable than did the Attentives, but the relationships between self-perceived mobilizability and some of the other variables of our original model were stronger among the Attentives than the Mobilizables. As can be seen in Table 11–9, there were many more significant correlations between the mobilizability items and the public-competence and opinion-making potential variables among the Attentives than the Mobilizables and, to a lesser extent, the same is true of the correlations involving the individual-competence and organizational activity variables. The reasons for this pattern are difficult to fathom, but perhaps it suggests that the Attentives integrate a more accurate picture of their mobilizability into their views of themselves as political actors than do the Mobilizables. Since this is the first finding that suggests that the original model may be more applicable to the Attentives than to the Mobilizables, it seems best to interpret it cautiously and even skeptically.

Although the research instrument does not permit investigation of the personality factors that sustain active citizenship, the self-perceived mobilizability items do allow us to explore the relevance of one such factor. For want of a better term we will refer to it as submissiveness, meaning the tendency to yield to authority and comply with requests. We reasoned that, whatever its situational and intellectual sources, mobilizability consists of followership behavior and that it is thus likely to be especially characteristic of those who occupy roles which routinely involve compliance with leadership. Certain occupational roles require that one adhere to the decisions of superiors, while others do not. Likewise, some social roles, such as those related to age and sex, are partly founded on differentiation as to who should make and who should comply with decisions. It was thus anticipated (Hypothesis XXXIV) that women would be more likely to see themselves as responsive to mobilizers than men, and that the same would be true for young persons as compared to old persons, white collar workers as compared to corporation executives, blue collar workers as compared to artists, pre-college as compared to university educators, and engineers as compared to students.

Table 11–10 presents the mean scores on the mobilizability items for each of these groupings. These data support our expectation that occupants of different social or occupational roles would differ in their self-perceived mobilizability, but the evidence indicating that submissiveness is a source of mobilizability is less clear-cut. In all six of the comparisons embraced by Hypothesis XXXIV, the two groupings differed in their responsiveness to mobilizers, but only four of these differences were in the predicted direction. Women perceived themselves as more mobilizable than men (13 of their 15 mean scores were higher), engineers more than students (11 of 15), pre-college educators more than university educators (15 of 15), and white collar workers more than corporation executives (10 of 15, with 3 ties). On the other hand, respondents over 65 recorded substantially higher mean scores (12 of 15) than those under 30 and artists did the same (14 of 15) compared to blue collar workers. These results suggest that while submissiveness may be a part of mobilizability, social roles cannot be classified in terms of submissiveness in any simple manner and there may be cases where this dimension is overwhelmed by others. Either we exaggerated the submissiveness of the young and the blue collar workers[15] or we ignored the extent to which older persons and artists possess more of the attitudinal requisites and behavioral skills necessary to political involvement than do those with whom they were compared.

---

[15] The possibility of exaggeration in the case of blue collar workers is underscored by Inkeles' finding, which he regards as the "distinctive contribution'" of his elaborate cross-national inquiry into the behavior of citizens, that factory work is especially "effective in preparing men for more active participation in their roles as citizens" ("Participant Citizenship in Six Developing Countries," p. 1139).

TABLE 11–10
COMPOSITE SELF-PERCEIVED MOBILIZABILITY SCORES RECORDED BY DIFFERENT SOCIAL AND OCCUPATIONAL GROUPINGS IN TERMS OF THREE TYPES OF MOBILIZERS AND ELEVEN ISSUES*

	Women (n = 1,225)	Men (n = 2,073)	Under 30 (n = 295)	Over 65 (n = 725)	White-collar workers (n = 81)	Corporation executives (n = 84)	Blue-collar workers (n = 85)	Artists (n = 64)	Pre-college educators (n = 266)	University educators (n = 378)	Engineers (n = 100)	Students (n = 98)
Self-perceived mobilizability by issue												
agricultural surpluses (n = 3)	2.80	2.70	2.52	3.00	2.74	2.79	2.55	2.74	2.70	2.52	2.64	2.36
balance of payments (n = 3)	2.41	2.45	2.29	2.65	2.57	2.57	2.36	2.40	2.40	2.28	2.33	2.14
Berlin (n = 3)	3.28	3.12	3.00	3.26	3.24	3.24	2.94	3.37	3.21	2.98	3.05	2.88
civil rights (n = 3)	4.39	4.18	4.42	4.11	4.42	4.21	4.04	4.24	4.37	4.04	4.11	4.41
the Congo (n = 3)	3.02	2.87	2.82	3.02	3.08	2.92	2.80	2.99	2.93	2.75	2.79	2.76
federal tax reduction (n = 3)	3.01	3.02	3.06	3.14	3.28	3.14	3.17	2.88	2.93	2.76	2.81	2.80
foreign aid (n = 3)	3.88	3.54	3.71	3.78	3.71	3.65	3.23	3.77	3.74	3.56	3.40	3.63
nuclear testing (n = 3)	4.28	4.08	4.33	4.05	4.12	4.12	4.01	4.21	4.30	3.97	3.99	4.24
tariff reduction (n = 3)	3.03	2.84	2.76	3.06	3.00	2.91	2.50	2.93	2.94	2.74	2.81	2.74
Vietnam (n = 3)	3.18	3.08	3.18	3.10	3.23	3.13	2.97	3.28	3.15	2.97	3.12	3.09
Western unity (n = 3)	3.10	2.87	2.66	3.16	3.25	3.10	2.70	3.13	2.99	2.67	2.68	2.51
Self-perceived mobilizability by identity of the mobilizer												
friend (n = 11)	3.17	3.07	3.13	3.19	3.28	3.19	2.89	3.09	3.10	2.92	3.06	3.05
organization (n = 11)	3.31	3.09	3.13	3.41	3.25	3.13	3.07	3.14	3.21	2.94	2.91	2.96
President (n = 11)	3.57	3.36	3.25	3.62	3.57	3.45	3.30	3.59	3.47	3.21	3.23	3.13
Self-perceived mobilizability by both issue and mobilizer (n = 33)	3.34	3.17	3.15	3.29	3.34	3.26	3.08	3.26	3.26	3.02	3.07	3.05

* In calculating the mean score values of 5, 4, 3, 2, and 1 were given, respectively, to "extremely likely," "very likely," "somewhat likely," "hardly likely," and "not at all likely" responses to Items #14, 42, and 53.

SUMMARY

A series of clear-cut, if not entirely expected, findings emerged from the preceding effort to assess the extent to which the identity of the mobilizer is a source of mobilizability. It was found that members of the Mobilizable Public do not see themselves as autonomous, self-motivated actors and are aware of themselves as responsive to the appeals of mobilizers, but they see themselves as more responsive to distant than to proximate mobilizers. Contrary to expectations, both the Attentives and the Mobilizables perceived themselves as more mobilizable by organizations to which they belonged than by friends and more mobilizable by the President than by organizations. Both groups perceived themselves as more mobilizable on those issues, nuclear testing and civil rights, where they are known to have been exposed to attempts to mobilize their support. Their self-perceived mobilizability on foreign aid more closely resembled their responses to the nuclear test and civil rights issues than to the other eight, suggesting that they had also been exposed to mobilization efforts on this issue.

The differences between the Mobilizables and Attentives supported the expectation that the former would see themselves as more mobilizable than would the latter. On virtually every issue and with respect to virtually every type of mobilizer, the self-perceived mobilizability scores of the Mobilizables were significantly higher than those of the Attentives. These differences were greatest on those issues for which their support had been sought and with respect to those mobilizers (organizations and the President) who were more distant from their daily lives.

These data also affirm the underlying premise of the model that the sources of active citizenship between elections are interdependent. All the measures of self-perceived mobilizability were found to correlate, for both the Mobilizables and the Attentives, with the attitudinal, perceptual, and activity variables. Only the present responsibility and public-competence variables were not linked to the respondents' perceptions of their own mobilizability.

A separate analysis of the self-perceived mobilizability of

respondents in selected occupations revealed that persons in different lines of work have different conceptions of their own mobilizability. It was suggested that differences in the degree of "submissiveness" inherent in different occupations may underlie this finding.

CHAPTER 12

THE APPEAL OF ISSUES

Of the many situational factors that can condition citizenship between elections, a central one may be the nature and interplay of the public issues clamoring for attention and support. Public issues consist of the prevailing conflicts over the ends and means used to distribute or redistribute resources and statuses within a community. The core of a public issue is the debate about the priorities attached to values and their allocation, and the processes through which the debate is conducted and the values allocated may be crucial determinants of attentive and mobilized behavior. Different kinds of issues can appeal in differing degrees to different kinds of people for different reasons, and it is all of these differences, and the interaction between them and the other variables in our model, that constitute the focus of this chapter. The main concern thus far have been the interdependence of background, attitudinal, perceptual, and behavioral variables and the differences between the Mobilizables and the Attentives, irrespective of the issue at stake. To be sure, the analysis has touched on some issue differences, but the data have not been systematically explored for the purpose of estimating the effect of the appeal of issues on the extent and direction of active citizenship. Here the effects of four issue dimensions, content, scope, complexity, and salience, are explored and contrasted with the effects of mobilizers.

Although there are many findings indicating that issues do operate as independent variables—as sources of different attitudinal, perceptual, and behavioral responses—there has not been much investigation of the particular aspects of issues that foster the different consequences. The finding, for example, that more information on foreign policy issues increases support for official government policy[1] does not tell us whether such a tendency results from the greater salience of foreign policy issues, from their greater complexity, or from the kinds of values they embrace. Do issues precipitate certain kinds of behavior because of their salience or because of the values they encompass? Or are issues always salient when they involve certain values? If so, what kinds of values lead to the greatest salience? Or is salience due to other factors that are unrelated to the values at stake? Is it partly a function of the process through which an issue is considered, so that, for example, an issue that requires legislative action is more likely to be salient than an issue that can be resolved through executive action? Or is salience determined by the relative importance of the other issues clamoring for attention, so that the same issue may lose or gain in salience as other issues enter and leave the public arena? Or does salience arise out of the simplicity or complexity of an issue? What makes an issue more or less complex? Does complexity stem from the degree of technical knowledge an issue

[1] David O. Sears, "Political Behavior," in Gardner Lindzey and Elliot Aronson, eds., *The Handbook of Social Psychology* (Reading, Mass.: Addison-Wesley, 1969), Second Edition, Vol. Five, pp. 351–52.

embraces or from the prolonged social processes required for its solution? Can a highly complex issue also be highly salient? Or are complex issues bound to be dull insofar as citizen involvement is concerned? Are all foreign policy issues likely to be more complex than domestic ones? Can a salient mobilizer render a dull issue salient through efforts to mobilize support for or against it? Indeed, if some active citizens are more likely to be responsive to mobilizers than to issues, and others to issues than to mobilizers, are the two types likely to differ along other attitudinal, perceptual, and behavioral dimensions? Are those oriented toward a number of issues likely to differ from those whose scope is confined to a single issue?

In the absence of prior findings relative to such questions, we did not derive many hypotheses pertaining to the interaction between the dynamics of issues and other key variables in our original model. Only the consequences of the relative appeal of issues and mobilizers were specifically anticipated (Hypotheses XXXV and XXXVI). At the same time, however, the questionnaire items were designed so that the foregoing questions could be explored and a determination made as to whether the data affirmed the interdependence of the various components of the model.

THE SALIENCE OF ISSUES

Two aspects of the questionnaire were designed to probe issue salience as a source of attentive and mobilized citizenship. One was an item [#57] that directly confronted the respondents with the question of salience, asking them to compare the extent of their attention to the legislative handling of six different issues. The responses of the Attentives and Mobilizables are presented in Table 12–1[2] and here it is immediately evident that neither type

[2] Since Item #57 was replaced by #59 in the second mailing of the questionnaire, the data in Table 12–1 do not consist of responses from all 1,704 Mobilizables and 1,658 Attentives.

TABLE 12–1

DISTRIBUTION OF THE RESPONSES OF 1,104
MOBILIZABLES (Ms) AND 1,082 ATTENTIVES (As) TO
ITEM #57 (in percentages)

[#57] When the issues listed at the left are under consideration by Congress, with how much attention do you follow the various legislative stages through which each passes?

Issue		Great atten- tion	Con- siderable atten- tion	Some atten- tion	Little atten- tion	No atten- tion	Codable answer not given	Total	Statistical comparison of the responses of the Ms and As χ^2	df	P
Agricultural	Ms	7	19	38	25	8	3	100	11.87	4	ns*
surpluses	As	6	16	36	32	8	2	100			
Civil rights	Ms	69	23	5	1	0	2	100	27.03	3	.001
	As	58	29	8	2	1	2	100			
Federal tax	Ms	19	35	32	11	2	1	100	11.83	4	ns*
reduction	As	17	29	36	13	2	3	100			
Foreign aid	Ms	23	44	25	5	1	2	100	18.33	4	.001
	As	19	39	31	7	1	3	100			
Nuclear	Ms	56	30	10	2	0	2	100	78.56	3	.001
testing	As	40	34	20	4	1	1	100			
Tariff	Ms	8	24	40	21	5	2	100	7.49	4	ns*
reduction	As	8	20	40	24	6	2	100			

* Not significant.

of citizen is so fully caught up in the world of public affairs as to feel equally concerned about all the events transpiring within it. Confirming some earlier indications, the responses of both groups reveal that the salience of issues varied over a wide range even during the most public (i.e., the legislative) phase of the debate over them. For example, 62 and 52 percentage points separated the degree to which the Mobilizables and Attentives, respectively, perceived themselves as paying "great" attention to Congressional consideration of civil rights and agricultural surpluses. Table 12–1 also reveals that the Mobilizables significantly exceeded the Attentives in the degree of attention they saw themselves as paying to three of the issues, but this does not negate the essential finding that for both groups there was substantial variation in the salience they attached to the issues of the day.

Another interesting dimension of the data presented in Table 12–1 is the finding that the differences between the Mobilizables and Attentives were greatest on the most salient issues, civil rights, nuclear testing, and foreign aid. Indeed, the differences between them on the three issues to which they were least attentive did not prove to be significant. Also consistent with earlier indications, this finding suggests the considerable degree to which mobilizability may be self-reinforcing. Having been mobilized on at least two (and probably three) of the issues which were significantly more salient for them than the Attentives, the Mobilizables also followed the legislative passage of the three issues more closely than they did the other issues. Such an interpretation treats salience as a dependent variable. As noted below, it may also operate as an independent variable and contribute to the extent and nature of citizenship behavior. Viewed that way, the significant differences in Table 12–1 can be seen as demonstrating that the greater salience of the civil rights, nuclear testing, and foreign aid issues underlay the Mobilizables' greater predisposition to respond to appeals for support.

Neither interpretation, however, explains why some issues are more salient than others. Another aspect of the questionnaire was addressed to this question. This consisted of several items embracing eleven different issues. The eleven issues were selected not only in terms of the criterion that they had been in or had entered the public arena during the time of the survey, but also in terms of more theoretical criteria related to their scope, complexity, and content. That is, the eleven issues were chosen in such a way that at least one of them could reasonably be classified in each cell of two 2×3 matrices that differentiated among foreign, mixed, and domestic issues on the one hand and complex and simple or self-interest and public-interest issues on the other.

Since the complex-simple and self-public distinctions refer to different aspects of an issue, the eleven were clustered differently in the two matrices (see Tables 12–2 and 12–3). These two cluster patterns were then compared with the way in which the issues clustered in terms of their salience for the respondents in the hope of thereby clarifying the dynamics that underlie the appeal of different issues. As will be seen, this procedure did yield useful insights into the sources of issue saliency.

It will be recalled that the basis for classifying an issue in the foreign-mixed-domestic categories is a simple one, consisting of whether the officials and agencies active with respect to the issue are those responsible for the society's external affairs, for aspects of its internal life, or for both.[3] The application of this formulation to the eleven issues included in the questionnaire has already been indicated[4] and is set forth again in the matrices. Ten of the classifications were readily made, as the identity of those officials in the 1963–1964 period who were most fully involved in each issue was clear-cut. Although a wide variety of officials were momentarily or peripherally involved in the balance of payments, Berlin, Congo, and Western unity issues, those from the State and Defense Departments, along with those on the international side of the Treasury Department, were the central figures continuously responsible for handling them before and during the nine months that intervened between the two mailings of the questionnaire. Hence it seemed clear that these four issues fell in the foreign area, just as the involvement of members of Congress and officials from the domestic side of the Treasury, Agriculture, and Justice Departments made it seem appropriate to classify the tax reduction, agricultural surpluses, and civil rights issues in the domestic area. The substantial and sustained involvement of Congressmen and Senators, as well as of the executive officers responsible for the conduct of foreign policy also made it easy to classify the foreign aid, nuclear testing, and tariff reduction issues in the mixed area.

[3] See pp. 120–22.
[4] See pp. 163–64.

Only the issue of Vietnam, in short, posed a classification problem. At the time of the first mailing in January 1964, it had not yet become a major and sustained preoccupation of both foreign and domestic policy officials, but by the time of the second mailing in early September of 1964 the Congress, and particularly the Senate, had become heavily involved through consideration and passage of the Tonkin Gulf Resolution. Thus, in effect, the Vietnam issue began to shift from the foreign to the mixed area between the mailings and its location in the matrices is thus somewhat arbitrary. As will be seen, a special analysis of the responses on this issue evoked by the two mailings reveals shifts consistent with its relocation as a mixed issue.

The classification of the eleven issues in terms of the complex-simple distinction was based on the somewhat more impressionistic criterion of how the actors involved perceived the issue. An issue was classified as simple if the goals articulated by the key actors seemed relatively specific and their conceptions of the process used to achieve the goals relatively clear-cut. If the actors were viewed as operating in terms of abstract goals that were to be achieved through unspecified or vague channels, then the issue was classified as complex. Indeed, if either the ends or means were estimated to be not clearly envisioned by the actors, then the issue was assigned to the complex category. Berlin, for example, was classified as a simple issue because all concerned knew that the maintenance of free surface and air access to the city from the West was at stake and that this goal was to be realized through a constant monitoring of the extent to which East German border guards interfered with transportation and, if the interference was unduly extensive, getting it reduced through official protests, shows of force, and so on. Western unity, on the other hand, was classified as a complex issue because discussions of it rarely rested on clear notions of how movement toward unity would occur or what unity might look like if it ever came to pass. Similarly, while all concerned had clear conceptions of what constituted an appropriate balance of payments, confusion and argumentation prevailed with respect to the proper means of achieving the balance and the issue was thus coded as complex. The classifications that resulted from the application of these criteria to the other eight issues can be seen in the rows of Table 12–2.

Estimates of whether members of the society would be affected equally by the resolution of an issue or whether some would benefit more than others—were used as the criteria for classifying the issues along the public-self dimension.[5] Generally speaking, for example, the benefits (or costs) from an amelioration (or intensification) of the Berlin conflict would be the same for all citizens, whereas the reduction of a tariff on one or more commodities would have different consequences for domestic pro-

---

TABLE 12–2
DISTRIBUTION OF FOUR FOREIGN, FOUR MIXED, AND THREE DOMESTIC POLICY ISSUES IN TERMS OF THEIR THEORETICAL CLASSIFICATION ALONG A SIMPLE-COMPLEX DIMENSION

	Foreign policy issues	Mixed policy issues	Domestic policy issues
Complex issues	Western unity The Congo Balance of payments	Foreign aid	Agricultural surpluses
Simple issues	Berlin	Tariff reduction Nuclear testing Vietnam	Civil rights Federal tax reduction

---

[5] Although my nomenclature is different, this distinction between public- and self-interest issues corresponds to the oft-used delineation between collective and private goods, wherein the former are those shared by the entire community and the latter those enjoyed only by segments of it. For elaborate analyses along this line, see Mancur Olson, Jr., *The Logic of Collective Action: Public Goods and the Theory of Groups* (Cambridge: Harvard University Press, 1965), Chap. I; and Norman Frohlich, Joe A. Oppenheimer, and Oran R. Young, *Political Leadership and Collective Goods* (Princeton: Princeton University Press, 1971), Chap. One.

TABLE 12–3
DISTRIBUTION OF FOUR FOREIGN, FOUR MIXED,
AND THREE DOMESTIC POLICY ISSUES IN TERMS
OF THEIR THEORETICAL CLASSIFICATION ALONG
A SELF-PUBLIC DIMENSION

	Foreign policy issues	Mixed policy issues	Domestic policy issues
Self-interest issues	Balance of payments	Tariff reduction	Agricultural surpluses Federal tax reduction
Public-interest issues	Berlin The Congo Western unity	Foreign aid Nuclear testing Vietnam	Civil rights

ducers and for consumers. The rows of Table 12–3 contain the estimates that resulted when this distinction was applied to all the issues.

A number of differences in the clustering of the eleven issues are evident in the two matrices. In the case of the four foreign policy issues, Berlin is alone in a separate category in the complex-simple matrix, while the balance of payments issue stands apart in the self-public matrix. Similarly, all but foreign aid of the four mixed issues are clustered together in the complex-simple matrix, whereas the tariff reduction issue is separated out in the self-public formulation. As for the three domestic issues, the agricultural surpluses question stands apart in the simple-complex matrix, but clusters with the tax reduction issue to leave civil rights alone in the self-public matrix.

In order to determine whether it is the complexity or the content of an issue that underlies its saliency to attentive citizens, the clusterings of the issues in these two theoretically derived classifications were compared with their empirical distribution in a third matrix that substituted a high-low saliency dimension for the simple-complex and self-public dimensions and used the responses of the Mobilizables and Attentives as the basis for classifying the issues. A mean saliency score for each issue was derived from the mean scores recorded by both groups on six of the eleven-part questions.[6] The issues were then ranked in terms of their mean saliency scores and the five highest ranked issues were classified in the high saliency category and the six lowest ranked issues were assigned to the low saliency category.[7] Table 12–4 presents the mean saliency scores, the six means from which they were derived, and their rankings for both groups. The rankings make it clear that the five high saliency issues consisted of one in the domestic policy area (civil rights), one in the foreign policy area (Berlin), and three in the mixed policy area (foreign aid, nuclear testing, and Vietnam), while three of the low saliency issues were in the foreign policy area (balance of payments, the Congo, and Western unity), two in the domestic area (agricultural surpluses and federal tax reduction), and one in the mixed area (tariff reduction).

Table 12–5 compares the eleven issues distributed empirically in terms of salience with the two theoretically derived distributions in Tables 12–2 and 12–3. Several rather clear-cut conclusions about the salience of issues emerge, perhaps the main one being that the clustering of issues in the empirical distribution corresponds much more closely to the theoretical clustering based on the self-public distinction than to the clustering derived from the simple-complex dimension. More accurately, all the highly salient issues fell in the public interest category, whereas all those that had been classified as self-interest issues also proved to be low

---

[6] Items #14, 42, 47, 49, 50, and 53 were used to construct the mean saliency scores. The other eleven-part issue items were omitted either because they were couched in bi-modal terms or because they seemed inappropriate as measures of saliency.

[7] The issues were dichotomized in terms of five high and six low issues rather than six high and five low issues in order to keep the concept of high saliency stringent. This was facilitated by the fact that all five of the highest ranked issues were similarly ranked for the Mobilizables and Attentives, whereas only the two with the lowest scores were similarly ranked among the six classified in the low saliency category (see Table 12–4).

in salience. In both the domestic and mixed policy area, moreover, the distinction between low and high salience corresponded exactly with the distinction between self- and public-interest issues, irrespective of how they were classified in the simple and complex categories. The simple-complex distinction appears to have been relevant only with respect to foreign policy issues, the one issue classified as simple being highly salient and the three classified as complex being of low salience.

These indications as to the sources of issue salience seem important, and even startling. They violate the notion that citizens are moved to engage in political action by self-interest alone. At least they suggest that citizens who sustain a continued interest in public affairs, such as those affiliated with an organization like the ADA, are moved by problems that have implications for the larger society. Indeed, it might be hypothesized that maintaining active citizenship between elections requires a capacity to conceive of the political process as benefiting larger entities than one's self or one's group, whereas sporadic involvement between elections depends on a conception of public affairs as consisting only of narrowly defined self-interest issues.

The finding that most foreign policy issues are not likely to be highly salient, particularly those marked by complexity, suggests that there are limits to the larger entities whose welfare concerns active citizens and sustains their involvement. Except for the Berlin issue, it would seem that members of the Attentive Public do not become aroused by an issue until it becomes a part of the domestic political process, thus becoming relevant to their own national entity. The fact, for example, that the Congo proved to be a low-salient issue, even though it was clear that the plight of the Congolese people at the time was a dire one, suggests that the public regardingness of active citizens has national limits. This can be seen even more clearly in the fact that the three most salient issues, civil rights, nuclear testing, and foreign aid, were either of a mixed or domestic kind. The scores of both the Mobilizables and Attentives on these three issues were so much higher than on the other two highly salient issues as to indicate that foreign policy issues are unlikely to dominate public life unless

TABLE 12–4
MEAN ITEM AND COMBINED ITEM SCORES OF 1,704 MOBILIZABLES (Ms) AND 1,658 ATTENTIVES (As) WHO ANSWERED SIX 11-PART ISSUE ITEMS AND RANKINGS OF ISSUES BY MEAN SALIENCY SCORES

Issue		MEAN SCORES ON SIX ISSUE ITEMS*						SALIENCY SCORES (mean of six mean scores)	RANK OF THE ISSUES BY MEAN SALIENCY SCORES**
		Friend [#14]	President [#42]	Organization [#53]	Information possessed [#50]	Attitudinal importance [#47]	Conversations with friends, etc. [#49]		
Agricultural surpluses	Ms	2.65	3.12	2.84	2.61	3.36	2.31	2.82	10th
	As	2.44	2.80	2.55	2.63	3.26	2.36	2.67	10th
Balance of payments	Ms	2.31	2.76	2.53	2.31	3.10	1.95	2.49	11th
	As	2.18	2.51	2.31	2.42	3.08	2.04	2.42	11th
Berlin	Ms	3.23	3.58	3.22	3.32	3.69	2.85	3.32	4th
	As	2.95	3.19	2.87	3.28	3.57	2.85	3.12	4th
Civil rights	Ms	4.41	4.58	4.51	4.20	4.84	4.11	4.44	1st
	As	3.99	4.10	3.97	4.07	4.68	3.99	4.13	1st
The Congo	Ms	2.94	3.37	2.97	2.81	3.15	2.49	2.96	7.5th
	As	2.69	2.96	2.62	2.75	3.02	2.44	2.75	9th
Federal tax reduction	Ms	2.86	3.48	3.21	2.99	3.39	2.83	2.96	7.5th
	As	2.60	3.08	2.85	3.01	3.21	2.83	2.93	6th

Foreign aid	Ms	3.90	4.01	3.78	3.29	4.04	2.94	3.66	3rd
	As	3.48	3.52	3.30	3.22	3.88	2.91	3.39	3rd
Nuclear test ban	Ms	4.30	4.56	4.43	3.62	4.72	3.57	4.20	2nd
	As	3.77	4.02	3.85	3.47	4.53	3.40	3.84	2nd
Tariff reduction	Ms	2.83	3.37	3.01	2.69	3.51	2.18	2.93	9th
	As	2.59	3.01	2.66	2.66	3.38	2.26	2.76	8th
Vietnam	Ms	3.11	3.51	3.25	3.02	3.58	2.85	3.22	5th
	As	2.83	3.13	2.87	2.94	3.48	2.81	3.01	5th
Western unity	Ms	2.87	3.39	3.03	3.08	3.42	2.53	3.05	6th
	As	2.67	3.04	2.73	3.06	3.44	2.53	2.91	7th

* A response at the highest point on each 5-point scale was scored 5, the next highest as 4, the third highest as 3, the fourth highest as 2, and the lowest as 1.

** The issue with the highest saliency score was ranked 1st, the next highest as 2nd, and so on through all eleven issues.

TABLE 12–5
DISTRIBUTION OF FOUR FOREIGN, FOUR MIXED, AND THREE DOMESTIC POLICY ISSUES IN TERMS OF THEIR THEORETICAL CLASSIFICATION ALONG SIMPLE-COMPLEX AND PUBLIC-SELF INTEREST DIMENSIONS AND THEIR EMPIRICAL CLASSIFICATION ALONG A HIGH–LOW SALIENCY DIMENSION (with low salient issues listed in lower case and high salient issues listed in CAPITAL letters)

		Foreign policy issues	Mixed policy issues	Domestic policy issues
Self-interest issues	Complex issues	Balance of payments		Agricultural surpluses
	Simple issues		Tariff reduction	Federal tax reduction
Public-interest issues	Complex issues	The Congo Western unity	FOREIGN AID	
	Simple issues	BERLIN	NUCLEAR TESTING VIETNAM	CIVIL RIGHTS

and until they are introduced into the domestic side of the policy-making process. The domestication of an issue signifies not only that the society's interests have become more deeply involved, but also that the mass media are likely to pay considerably more attention to it, thus further heightening its salience.[8]

A comparison of the mean saliency scores of the first and second mailings of the questionnaire provides additional insight into the dynamics of issue salience. Table 12–6 presents the scores

---

[8] This interpretation suggests that the original classification of Berlin as a foreign policy issue may have been erroneous. Had it been classified as a mixed issue on the grounds that the mobilization of reserve units and the dispatch of troops to that beleaguered city in the summer of 1961 domesticated the issue by involving a number of previously uninvolved legislative and executive officials, the distribution of issues in Table 12–5 would not be marked by any exceptions to the foregoing analysis.

recorded by the Test Ban Mobilizables and Attentives (the first mailing) and the Civil Rights Mobilizables and Attentives (the second mailing) as well as the ranking of the issues by each of the four groups. That issues become more salient as they become domesticated is readily seen in the scores recorded with respect to Vietnam. While the Mobilizables and Attentives of the first mailing recorded scores of 3.14 and 2.94, respectively, nine months later—after the Senate had been drawn into the issue through the Gulf of Tonkin Resolution—their counterparts in the second mailing registered scores of 3.38 and 3.14. Table 12–6 reveals that Vietnam is the only issue whose saliency increased among both the Mobilizables and the Attentives. For eight of the other issues the saliency scores of both groups declined, and for the other two issues (civil rights and the Congo) only the scores of the Mobilizables increased.

Another interesting feature of the scores on issue saliency is that the scores of the Mobilizables and Attentives differed most on the three issues with the highest saliency. Close inspection of Tables 12–4 and 12–6 yields the finding that the two groups were much less similar with respect to civil rights, nuclear testing, and foreign aid than with respect to any other issue and that, in addition, their scores on these three issues were conspicuously higher than on any of the others. Issue saliency would thus seem to be an important source of mobilizability. Whatever other factors underlie the readiness of some citizens to be mobilized, they would appear to be most likely to come together—to produce behavior— when an issue is especially salient in the domestic political process. Short of this, the differences between mobilizable and attentive citizens diminish, although they do not disappear entirely.

THE CONTENTS OF ISSUES: DOMESTIC VERSUS MIXED VERSUS FOREIGN POLICY ISSUES

But what about issue content? Are not the different values inherent in foreign, mixed, and domestic issues also a source of differences in behavior? Or is the interest dimension the prime source of an issue's saliency and thus the only one of its aspects that contributes to the dynamics of mobilizability? If two public-interest

TABLE 12–6
MEAN ITEM AND COMBINED ITEM SCORES OF 1,104 NUCLEAR TEST MOBILIZABLES (NTMs), 1,082 NUCLEAR TEST ATTENTIVES (NTAs), 600 CIVIL RIGHTS MOBILIZABLES (CRMs), AND 576 CIVIL RIGHTS ATTENTIVES (CRAs) WHO ANSWERED SIX 11-PART ISSUE ITEMS AND RANKINGS OF ISSUES BY MEAN SALIENCY SCORES

Issue		MEAN SCORES ON SIX ISSUE ITEMS*						SALIENCY SCORES (mean of six mean scores)	RANK OF THE ISSUES BY MEAN SALIENCY SCORES**
		Friend [#14]	President [#42]	Organization [#53]	Information possessed [#50]	Attitudinal importance [#47]	Conversations with friends, etc. [#49]		
Agricultural surpluses	NTMs	2.73	3.20	2.93	2.67	3.44	2.39	2.89	10th
	NTAs	2.51	2.85	2.58	2.63	3.31	2.38	2.71	10th
	CRMs	2.50	2.95	2.69	2.49	3.21	2.17	2.67	10th
	CRAs	2.31	2.69	2.47	2.62	3.18	2.31	2.60	10th
Balance of payments	NTMs	2.37	2.86	2.60	2.35	3.18	2.00	2.56	11th
	NTAs	2.21	2.55	2.32	2.41	3.13	2.09	2.45	11th
	CRMs	2.21	2.57	2.42	2.26	2.97	1.97	2.38	11th
	CRAs	2.13	2.43	2.28	2.42	2.99	1.86	2.37	11th
Berlin	NTMs	3.29	3.64	3.26	3.35	3.76	2.92	3.37	4th
	NTAs	3.00	3.23	2.90	3.30	3.65	2.92	3.17	4th
	CRMs	3.13	3.48	3.15	3.27	3.55	2.72	3.22	5th
	CRAs	2.85	3.13	2.80	3.25	3.43	2.72	3.03	5th
Civil rights	NTMs	4.38	4.57	4.46	4.17	4.83	4.04	4.41	1st
	NTAs	4.01	4.13	3.98	4.07	4.71	3.94	4.14	1st
	CRMs	4.47	4.59	4.59	4.27	4.85	4.22	4.50	1st
	CRAs	3.94	4.04	3.93	4.08	4.63	4.02	4.11	1st
The Congo	NTMs	2.92	3.39	2.95	2.80	3.18	2.61	2.94	9th
	NTAs	2.69	2.98	2.80	2.75	3.04	2.49	2.75	9th
	CRMs	3.00	3.32	3.00	2.83	3.09	2.42	2.98	6th
	CRAs	2.69	2.94	2.66	2.76	2.97	2.42	2.75	8th

Federal tax reduction	NTMs	2.99	3.61	3.06	3.57	2.95	3.26	5th
	NTAs	2.97	3.17	3.02	3.37	2.90	3.06	5th
	CRMs	2.60	3.23	2.87	3.06	2.61	2.89	8th
	CRAs	2.40	2.91	2.98	2.91	2.71	2.77	7th
Foreign aid	NTMs	3.92	4.02	3.31	4.07	2.97	3.68	3rd
	NTAs	3.53	3.55	3.21	3.94	2.94	3.42	3rd
	CRMs	3.87	3.99	3.25	3.99	2.88	3.62	3rd
	CRAs	3.39	3.46	3.24	3.79	2.85	3.33	3rd
Nuclear test ban	NTMs	4.35	4.62	3.68	4.76	3.67	4.26	2nd
	NTAs	3.78	4.03	3.47	4.54	3.46	3.86	2nd
	CRMs	4.20	4.45	3.52	4.65	3.40	4.09	2nd
	CRAs	3.75	4.01	3.47	4.51	3.30	3.81	2nd
Tariff reduction	NTMs	2.88	3.45	2.71	3.56	2.25	2.99	8th
	NTAs	2.61	3.04	2.63	3.41	2.28	2.78	8th
	CRMs	2.73	3.24	2.64	3.41	2.06	2.83	9th
	CRAs	2.54	2.94	2.70	3.33	2.21	2.73	9th
Vietnam	NTMs	3.02	3.45	2.96	3.48	2.78	3.14	6th
	NTAs	2.79	3.08	2.90	3.42	2.67	2.94	6.5th
	CRMs	3.27	3.60	3.13	3.77	3.08	3.38	4th
	CRAs	2.90	3.22	3.09	3.58	3.05	3.14	4th
Western unity	NTMs	2.90	3.47	3.11	3.46	2.58	3.10	7th
	NTAs	2.71	3.06	3.06	3.48	2.58	2.94	6.5th
	CRMs	2.82	3.26	3.02	3.36	2.42	2.97	7th
	CRAs	2.59	3.00	3.06	3.35	2.44	2.86	6th

* A response at the highest point on each 5-point scale was scored 5, the next highest as 4, the third highest as 3, the fourth highest as 2, and the lowest as 1.

** The issue with the highest saliency score was ranked 1st, the next highest as 2nd, and so on through all eleven issues.

issues are highly salient but dissimilar in the kinds of values they encompass, will they evoke similar or different responses? Will a salient domestic policy issue give rise to the same attitudinal, perceptual, and behavioral tendencies as a salient mixed issue?

Our data permit a systematic analysis of these questions. By comparing the differences between the Civil Rights and Nuclear Test Mobilizables with the differences between their respective control groups (i.e., the Civil Rights and Nuclear Test Attentives), it is possible to ascertain whether the public-interest orientations of active citizens are sensitive to the different values embedded in various issues. A difference between the two mobilizable groups along any dimension, which differs significantly from the difference between the attentive groups on the same dimension, can be attributed to the values embraced by the issues on which support was mobilized rather than to the altered circumstances stemming from the passage of time.

The results of this analysis are clear. The Critical Ratios (C.R.) for the difference between the differences of the mean scores of the two mobilizable and the two attentive groups were calculated for all the variables examined in the previous chapters except those which could not be transformed into mean scores. Of the 152 so analyzed, only two proved to be significant at the .001 level. The Nuclear Test Mobilizables were older than the Civil Rights Mobilizables (C.R. $= 14.36$), while the latter exceeded the former in their scores on the opinion-making potential index (C.R. $= -4.31$). The first of these findings suggests that publics for war-peace issues are likely to be somewhat older than those for domestic ones,[9] perhaps because those who have lived longer have had more direct or indirect exposure to military conflict and thus more likely to be concerned about any issues which bear upon the conduct of war and the maintenance of international peace. An explanation of the second significant difference—between the mean opinion-making potential scores of 20.1 for the Civil Rights Mobilizables and 18.3 for their Nuclear

---

[9] The average age of the Nuclear Test Mobilizables was 51 and that of their Civil Rights counterparts 48.

Test counterparts—cannot be developed so readily. Perhaps it indicates that domestic issues, being of more immediate concern, create more opportunities for the circulation of ideas through the channels of communication than do mixed or foreign policy issues. It is of course possible that the difference between the opinion-making scores of the two mobilizable groups is due to chance, since it was one of 152 differences assessed in this way.

Whatever the proper explanation, however, the important finding is not that two differences were significant, but that 150 were not. It suggests that the values encompassed by a salient issue are essentially irrelevant to the mobilizability of active citizens. More accurately, for those whose involvement in public affairs is broad and springs from other than narrowly defined self-interests, it is the salience of an issue that matters and not its contents. It would seem that once an issue becomes salient, those predisposed to respond to the appeals of mobilizers will do so irrespective of the values on which the appeal is founded. Such individuals would seem to be ready to be mobilized and to provide their support on behalf of the public's most pressing problems, whatever these may be in any given era.

Such an interpretation is consistent with the patterns of continuous growth in the ranks of the Attentive Public depicted in Chapter 2. If the content of issues were more powerful sources of mobilizability than their salience, then the size of the Attentive Public would fluctuate unsystematically as different issues evoked the concern of different segments of the citizenry. The pattern of continuous growth, however, suggests that multi-area membership in the Attentive Public is permanent once it is established, and that a basic core of public-minded citizens will be responsive to any salient issue. To be sure, some citizens are essentially self-interested and are responsive only to those problems that impinge directly on their interests, but these "issue publics" do not appear to be primarily represented in the membership of a multi-purpose association like the ADA.

There is another possible interpretation of the absence of differences between the Nuclear Test Mobilizables and the Civil Rights Mobilizables. It could be argued that essentially the same values were embraced by the test ban and civil rights issues in the 1963–1964 period and that therefore the data do not measure the degree to which mobilizability is sensitive to the appeal of issues. Such an argument might stress that both issues focused on man's welfare and thus evoked similar attitudes, perceptions, and activities. The difficulty with this reasoning is that it requires a conception of welfare that is so all-encompassing as to be virtually meaningless. Test ban and civil rights issues involve very different aspects of man's welfare, pertaining to physical well-being in the former instance and to considerations of status and respect in the latter, and it seems unproductive to reject the implications of the data suggested above on the grounds that both sets of values are subsumed by human welfare.

THE SCOPE OF ATTENTIVENESS: SINGLE-AREA VERSUS MULTI-AREA ORIENTATIONS

To conclude that the content of issues is less relevant than their salience to the mobilization of active citizens is not necessarily to imply that citizens with multi-area orientations will not differ in any way from those whose concerns are limited to a single area. Both types of citizens may react only to salient issues, but more issues may be salient for those with the capability and inclination to respond to more than one issue. That is, they may perceive the political process as simultaneously coping with more problems than do those with single-area orientations. In turn, the wider scope of multi-area as compared to single-area attentiveness may reflect other distinguishing characteristics, such as more extensive activities, stronger attitudes, and greater subjective competence.

In order to explore some of the consequences of differences in the scope of attentiveness to public affairs, an operational definition of Item #49 was developed that distinguished multi- and single-area respondents in terms of the frequency with which they reported face-to-face communications about more than two issues.[10] All told, 56 percent of the Mobilizables and 51 percent of

[10] For the details of this definition, see footnote 60 on p. 238.

the Attentives were classified as having multi-area orientations, while 44 and 49 percent of the two groups, respectively, were defined as having single-area orientations. Since this difference between the Mobilizables and Attentives was not significant,[11] the ensuing analysis is confined mainly to the distinction between multi- and single-area respondents.

The data reveal clear-cut behavioral, attitudinal, and perceptual differences between citizens who differed in the scope of their attentiveness. The multi-area respondents reported significantly higher frequencies of first- and second-hand activities than did their single-area counterparts.[12] Similarly, on 10 of the 11 importance variables and 8 of the 10 extremity variables they reported significantly stronger attitudes.[13] As for the perceptual dimension, the same pattern held for 32 of the 33 self-perceived mobilizability variables and 10 of the 11 self-perceived information variables.[14] In addition, the multi-area respondents significantly exceeded the single-area ones on all three measures of present responsibility—the index of opinion-making potential, the objective proximity variable, and the domestic travel variable.[15] Although somewhat fewer, the differences for the competence variables were generally of the same order, with multi-area

[11] See p. 238.

[12] For the difference on the letter-writing index, $\chi^2 = 109.50$, df $= 4$, P$<$.001; for the difference in the organizational activity scores, $\chi^2 = 86.60$, df $= 5$, P$<$.001; and for the differences on all nine foci of face-to-face communications [#41], the χ^2 values ranged from 67.98 to 354.34, df $= 3$ or 4, P$<$.001.

[13] For the ten significant differences involving the importance variables, the χ^2 values ranged from 19.67 to 142.17, df $= 3$ or 4, P$<$.001; for the eight significant differences involving the extremity variables, the χ^2 values ranged from 21.77 to 51.04, df $= 4$, P$<$.001.

[14] For the thirty-two significant differences involving the self-perceived mobilizability variables, the χ^2 values ranged from 19.00 to 301.00, df $= 4$, P$<$.001; for the ten significant differences involving the self-perceived information variables, the χ^2 values ranged from 27.82 to 286.18, df $= 3$ or 4, P$<$.001.

[15] The χ^2 values for these three differences are, respectively, 64.50, df $= 3$, P$<$.001; 48.78, df $= 4$, P$<$.001; and 43.71, df $= 4$, P$<$.001.

exceeding single-area citizens on the individual competence variable, on 13 of the 18 group-competence variables, and on one of the 6 public-competence variables.[16] Only with respect to the background, mass media, and public-information variables were there no significant differences between the multi- and single-area respondents.[17]

To a large extent, in short, the multi- and single-area respondents are as distinct from each other as are the Mobilizables and Attentives, and in very similar ways. In some instances, in fact, the differences between the multi-area and single-area respondents were substantially larger than the parallel differences between the Mobilizables and Attentives. Furthermore, a crude analysis of the multi-area respondents yielded the impression that the effects of scope may be linear, that for many of the variables the wider the scope, the greater the extent of behavior, the stronger the attitudes, and the more pronounced the perceptions of information and competence. Such a linear pattern was evident up to a scope of four issues in many cases, but broke down for those whose scope exceeded four issues (their responses tended to resemble the responses of those whose scope extended to four issues).

The similarity between the potency of issue-scope and of mobilizability raises the question of whether one factor is a function of the other. If this were the case, either the differences between the Mobilizables and Attentives should disappear when those of each group with similar issue-scope are compared or the difference between the multi- and single-area respondents should

---

[16] For the difference on the individual-competence variable, $\chi^2 = 26.68$, $df = 4$, $P < .001$; for the thirteen significant differences involving the group-competence variables, the χ^2 values ranged from 18.85 to 68.68, $df = 2, 3,$ or 4, $P < .001$; for the one public-competence variable to yield a significant difference, $\chi^2 = 355.61$, $df = 4$, $P < .001$.

[17] The absence of differentiation was uncovered for 10 of the 11 background variables, 13 of 19 media variables, and all 11 public-information variables.

disappear when the Mobilizables and Attentives in each group are compared separately? Anticipating the results of these comparisons, issue-scope and mobilizability turn out to be largely independent sources of active citizenship, with the former somewhat more potent than the latter.

When the relative strengths of the two dimensions are compared on 104 variables, the differences between the multi- and single-area Mobilizables persist at the .001 level of significance in 51 cases, and the differences between the Mobilizables and Attentives among the multi-area respondents persist in 32 cases. Issue-scope and mobilizability were even more powerful among the Attentives and the single-area respondents: 77 of the differences between the multi- and single-area respondents persisted among the Attentives and 44 of those between the Mobilizables and Attentives persisted among the single-area respondents. A further breakdown of these figures reveals even more clearly that the effects of issue-scope and mobilizability are essentially independent of each other. That is, in the case of such key dimensions as letter-writing, organizational activity, individual competence, a majority of the 33 self-perceived mobilizability variables, and attitudes toward the civil rights and nuclear testing issues, the differences between the Mobilizables and Attentives persisted among both the multi- and single-area respondents and the differences between the multi- and single-area respondents persisted among both the Mobilizables and Attentives. Only with respect to self-perceived mobilizability and attitudes toward the less salient issues was one or another set of differences erased.

The data do not permit an inference as to the dynamics of the independent operation of issue-scope and mobilizability. We can only speculate that the sources of mobilizability are narrower and less political than the determinants of issue scope. Presumably the issue scope of a citizen's activity depends on the degree of his involvement in politics in general, whereas responsiveness to the appeals of a mobilizer stems from other, more personal factors. Conceivably, of course, issue-scope and mobilizability are mutually reinforcing, making the mobilizable, multi-area citizen the most energetic to be found in the political arena. Such a conclusion, however, also cannot be inferred from the data. But it is clear that, whatever the interaction between mobilizability and issue-scope, the breadth of a citizen's activities in politics is an important determinant of the nature and intensity of his participation. Whether or not greater scope leads to greater mobilizability, it does seem to foster greater involvement.

THE APPEAL OF ISSUES VERSUS THE APPEAL OF MOBILIZERS

Just as the activities of citizens can be shaped by the identity and number of issues that are salient for them, so does it seem likely that they will be affected by the relative importance they attach to issues and mobilizers. Some citizens will tend to be responsive only to issues, irrespective of the mobilizers who appeal to them, whereas others will be responsive to certain mobilizers, irrespective of the issues around which their appeals are cast. Examples of the latter type of citizen are activists known as the party or organizational "faithful," those rank-and-file members whose attitudes and behaviors are set by cues from the leadership. Similarly, given the symbolic power that our data have shown accrues to the President, there may be some citizens who respond to presidential appeals for support on any issue but who are unresponsive to other mobilizers on the same issue.

These are, of course, extreme examples. Most active citizens probably fall somewhere between the mobilizer-oriented and the issue-oriented extremes. Yet distinctions along this continuum may be crucial for understanding the dynamics of mobilizability and thus the responses to the three measures of self-perceived mobilizability [#14, 42, 53] were analyzed to determine whether there were any differences between those who estimated their mobilizability to be unwavering across issues and those who perceived themselves to be differentially responsive. Respondents who perceived themselves as similarly (and at least minimally) responsive to the same mobilizer on all eleven issues were classified as

TABLE 12–7

DISTRIBUTION OF RESPONSES TO THE THREE
SELF-PERCEIVED MOBILIZABILITY ITEMS IN TERMS
OF THE NUMBER OF THE ELEVEN ISSUES
SIMILARLY ANSWERED (in percentages, n = 3,362)

	Friend [#14]	President [#42]	Organization [#53]
Proportion of the respondents who answered all eleven parts and responded similarly on			
All eleven issues	8.6	11.3	7.9
Ten issues	1.6	2.1	1.7
Nine issues	3.5	3.8	3.5
Eight issues	5.1	6.5	6.8
Seven issues	8.7	10.1	9.7
Six issues	13.0	15.9	17.8
Five issues	19.8	18.2	20.5
Three or four issues	25.8	18.9	22.2
Proportion who did not answer all eleven parts of the question or who responded "not at all likely" to all eleven parts	13.9	13.2	9.9
	100.0	1.000	100.0

"mobilizer-oriented," [18] while those who selected the same alternative on the five-point scale for no more than four of the issues were classified as "issue-oriented."[19] Table 12–7 presents the dis-

[18] That is, those whose identical responses on all eleven issues were located on one of the first four points on the self-perceived mobilizability scale were classified as source oriented. Those who perceived themselves as "not at all likely" to respond to the mobilizer on any of the eleven issues—the fifth point on the scale—were not so classified because the uniformity of their answers obviously reflected a lack of a minimal degree of mobilizability rather than an orientation toward the mobilizer.

[19] Those who selected the same alternative for only three issues were so few in number that the cut-off point of four issues was employed in order to facilitate the ensuing comparisons between the two groups.

tribution of the respondents in terms of the number of issues
with respect to which they perceived themselves as similarly responsive to each mobilizer. Here it can be seen that issue-oriented
respondents were considerably more numerous than mobilizer-
oriented ones in the ADA sample, a finding that had been anticipated (Hypothesis XXVIb) on the grounds that citizens active
between elections are likely to be especially sensitive to issues (in
contrast to those active only during elections, for whom the
identity of the candidate or other campaign mobilizers seems
likely to be central). Indeed, Table 12–7 reveals that a preponderance of the respondents tended toward issue variability rather
than source uniformity: except for the mobilizer-oriented respondents in the first row, the proportion of respondents increases as
the number of issues to which they responded similarly decreases,
for all three mobilizers.

Interestingly, Table 12–7 also demonstrates once again the
symbolic power of the President as a mobilizer. The proportions
in the first three rows of the President column are higher than
the corresponding figures for the friend or organization columns.
This can be seen even more clearly in Table 12–8, which breaks
down the proportions of mobilizer-oriented respondents in the
first row of Table 12–7 by their degree of self-perceived mobili-

TABLE 12–8
SELF-PERCEIVED MOBILIZABILITY OF MOBILIZER-
ORIENTED RESPONDENTS (in percentages)

Perceived likelihood of responsiveness to appeals for support from the source	A friend [#14]	The President [#42]	An organization [#53]
Extremely likely	30	55	35
Very likely	26	22	19
Somewhat likely	16	10	19
Hardly likely	28	13	27
Not at all likely	0	0	0
Total	100	100	100
(n =)	(288)	(380)	(265)

zability. It is striking that the proportion of those who perceived themselves as "extremely likely" to respond to the President on all eleven issues was noticeably larger than the equivalent proportions for friend or organization.

An analysis of the relative proportions of Mobilizables and Attentives who were mobilizer-oriented and issue-oriented respondents yielded unexpected results. We had anticipated (Hypothesis XXXVIa) that the Mobilizables would be more mobilizer- and less issue-oriented than the Attentives, but the data suggest a contrary pattern. Table 12–9 reveals that the Attentives were located in greater proportions than the Mobilizables toward the end of the scale representing source uniformity with respect to all three mobilizers, and that the reverse pattern prevailed toward the end of the continuum representing issue variability. Stated differently, the mean number of similar responses to the eleven parts of the friend, President, and organization items recorded were 6.17, 6.52, and 6.34, respectively, for the Attentives and 5.89, 6.41, and 5.93, respectively, for the Mobilizables. These differences between the Attentives and Mobilizables were significant in the case of the organization as mobilizer.[20]

The data do not reveal why the Mobilizables were somewhat less mobilizer-oriented in their self-perceived mobilizability than the Attentives, since it had been reasoned that their greater responsiveness to the ADA would be reflected in responses indicating less issue variability. It may be that the explanation for this lack of confirmation lies in the relative meaningfulness of the mobilizability items to the Mobilizables and the Attentives. It is possible that the latter's relative lack of mobilizability resulted in less involvement on their part in dealing with these items and thus to responses that were relatively undifferentiated among the eleven parts. In any event, whether the findings presented in Table 12–9 were due to such artifacts or to more substantive factors, it is clear that more intensive inquiry is needed into the relative strength of issues and mobilizers as sources of citizenship between elections.

That our initial comprehension of the dynamics of these

[20] $\chi^2 = 36.68$, df = 8, P<.001.

TABLE 12–9
DISTRIBUTION OF THE 1,704 MOBILIZABLES AND 1,658
ATTENTIVES IN TERMS OF THE NUMBER OF ISSUES ON
WHICH THEY PERCEIVED THEMSELVES AS SIMILARLY
MOBILIZABLE BY A FRIEND, THE PRESIDENT, OR AN
ORGANIZATION (in percentages)

				Number of Issues					Proportion who did not answer all eleven parts of the item or who responded "not at all likely" to all eleven parts
Mobilizer	11	10	9	8	7	6	5	4 or 3	
[#14] Friend									
Mobilizables	7.2	1.1	3.1	4.5	8.6	13.3	21.1	27.7	13.5
Attentives	8.8	2.1	4.0	5.7	8.7	12.7	18.5	23.8	15.5
[#42] The President									
Mobilizables	11.4	1.8	3.8	6.5	9.5	15.7	19.2	19.5	12.5
Attentives	11.2	2.4	3.9	6.5	10.8	16.2	17.2	18.1	13.8
[#53] Organization									
Mobilizables	7.1	1.3	2.7	5.3	9.3	18.5	22.3	24.4	9.1
Attentives	8.6	2.1	4.4	8.3	10.2	17.1	18.7	19.9	10.7

variables was wanting is also evident in the outcome of the test
of Hypothesis XXXV, which predicted that issue-oriented Mobilizables and Attentives, being more sensitive to the values at
stake in public issues, would be more likely than their mobilizer-
oriented counterparts (a) to attach importance to an issue, (b) to
hold extreme attitudes toward it, and (c) to feel they are informed
about it. All three parts of the hypothesis were essentially negated,
and in the case of part (a) there are even traces of a reversal. As
can be seen in Table 12–10, neither among the Mobilizables nor
the Attentives did the mobilizer- and issue-oriented respondents
differ significantly from each other on more than two of either the
eleven information-possessed items or the ten additional extremity

items. Only with respect to the attitudinal importance variable was the prediction of differences at least partially confirmed (with 34 of the 66 differences proving to be significant), but even here the results are confounding. Thirty-one of the 34 significant differences indicated that the mobilizer-oriented respondents attached greater importance to the issues involved than did their issue-oriented counterparts.

It is difficult to derive a logically consistent interpretation of these findings. It might be argued that the tendency of the mobilizer-oriented respondents to treat both mobilizers and issues as important springs from their greater readiness to be involved in public affairs, but if this were the case they should have also recorded significantly more extreme attitudes than their issue-oriented counterparts. Yet, only 6 of these 60 differences proved to be significant and in three of these six cases the issue-oriented respondents recorded higher mean extremity scores than did the

TABLE 12–10
DISTRIBUTION OF THE SIGNIFICANT DIFFERENCES BETWEEN THE ISSUE- AND MOBILIZER-ORIENTED MOBILIZABLES AND ATTENTIVES DERIVED FROM THE THREE SELF-PERCEIVED MOBILIZABILITY ITEMS IN THEIR RESPONSES TO THE SIXTY-SIX PARTS OF THE ATTITUDE AND INFORMATION-POSSESSED VARIABLES

	Number of significant differences for the		
	friend [#14]	President [#42]	organization [#53]
Mobilizables			
Attitudinal importance variable	7	8	5
Attitudinal extremity variable	0	2	2
Information-possessed variable	1	2	0
Attentives			
Attitudinal importance variable	2	6	6
Attitudinal extremity variable	0	0	2
Information-possessed variable	2	2	3

mobilizer-oriented group. Similarly, even as we concede that our initial reasoning was faulty and that a readiness to respond more to mobilizers than to issues does not necessarily diminish knowledge of and involvement in issues, the reasons why the scores of the issue-oriented respondents did not exceed those located at the source end of the scale remain elusive. Such ambiguities merely underscore the need for further investigation of the dynamics of issue-bounded variables.

SUMMARY

The preceding analysis of how the salience, complexity, contents, and scope of a public issue shape the behavior of active citizens yielded both clear-cut and confounding findings. With respect to salience, the data showed clearly that different issues are not equally salient for attentive citizens. Both the Mobilizables and Attentives reported devoting widely disparate degrees of attention to the legislative treatment of six different issues. Interestingly, the Mobilizables and Attentives reported significantly different degrees of attention on the three issues that they followed most closely. Furthermore, two of these three issues were also the ones on which the Mobilizables are known to have been mobilized, suggesting that mobilizability feeds on itself, that an issue becomes especially salient once a citizen has been mobilized to do something with regard to it.

With respect to what aspects of an issue tend to make it salient, different aspects were found to be relevant to domestic and mixed (domestic and foreign) policy issues than to foreign policy issues. For the latter, whether the issue was simple or complex was more important as a source of salience than whether self or public interests were at stake, whereas the opposite pattern emerged for domestic and mixed issues. The less complex a foreign policy issue, the more likely it is to be salient, irrespective of whether the values it encompasses are general public interests or selected self-interests. In contrast, the more a domestic or mixed issue taps public- rather than self-interest values, the more salient it is likely to be, irrespective of the degree to which it is marked by complexity. In short, the data appear to negate the notion that citizens are moved by self-interest to engage in political action. Or at least it would seem that citizens who sustain a continued interest in public affairs between elections—such as those affiliated with an association like the ADA—do not fit this standard conception.

Although the salience of an issue was also found to be closely linked to mobilizability, there was virtually no evidence that the different contents of two highly salient issues led to different attitudes, perceptions, or behaviors. A special comparison of the Civil Rights and Nuclear Test Mobilizables yielded only two significant differences (age and opinion-making potential) attributable to issue content. It would appear that for all practical purposes the values and foci encompassed by an issue are essentially irrelevant to the identity, orientations, and actions of citizens who are active with respect to it.

On the other hand, the number of issues to which a citizen is responsive at any given time was highly correlated with attitudes, perceptions, and behaviors. Multi-issue citizens engage in considerably more first- and second-hand activities, hold stronger attitudes, and perceive themselves as more mobilizable, informed, and competent than do single-issue citizens. To a large extent, in fact, the pattern of differences between multi- and single-issue respondents was not only as pervasive as that between the Mobilizables and Attentives, but also very similar. Despite this close resemblance, however, issue scope and mobilizability were found to be largely independent of each other.

Finally, a comparison of the relative strength of issues and mobilizers as sources of mobilizability yielded some surprising findings. It had been expected that the Mobilizables would be more mobilizer-oriented and less issue-oriented than the Attentives, but the hypothesis (XXXVIa) was not upheld and an opposite pattern was even discernible. The expectation (Hypothesis XXXVI) that mobilizer-oriented citizens would have stronger attitudes and perceive themselves as more informed than their issue-oriented counterparts was essentially negated, although attitudinal importance was somewhat relevant to the distinction between issue- and mobilizer-oriented respondents.

In sum, the analysis of this chapter makes clear that a full understanding of the dynamics of active citizenship requires that public issues be treated as independent as well as dependent variables. At the same time it is even more clear that a great deal of work is needed if such understanding is to be attained.

CHAPTER 13

SUMMARY AND CONCLUSIONS: THE MODEL RECONSIDERED

It is easier to summarize the preceding chapters than to derive conclusions from them. The empirical analysis of the 36 hypotheses comprising our original model has raised more questions than it has answered. Stating the problem—and thus the theme of this chapter—most succinctly, we have affirmed the existence of mobilizability as a characteristic of some active citizens, but we have failed to uncover its main sources. This discrepancy suggests a number of areas for future research, but it also means that this lengthy analysis must end on a cautious and tentative note.

Only two general conclusions can be asserted with confidence. One is that the phenomenon we have designated as mobilizability exists and is distinguishable from attentiveness as a characteristic of citizenship between elections. All the data point to persistent and significant behavioral, attitudinal, and perceptual differences between those attentive citizens who can and those who cannot be mobilized into specific acts of support-giving. Furthermore, it seems clear that mobilizability is a generalized characteristic and is not rooted in a particular experience or value system. Just as persuasibility has been described as a general predisposition "reflecting an individual's susceptibility to influence from many different sources, on a wide variety of topics, and irrespective of the media employed,"[1] so can multi-area mobilizability be described as a general orientation to respond to the appeals of mobilizers seeking support on salient issues, irrespective of the identity of the mobilizer or the nature of the salient issue.

The second main conclusion to emerge from the analysis is that the basic premise of our original model, that citizenship between elections springs from a multiplicity of interdependent sources rather than from a single factor, was well founded. No single source, or even a few main ones, emerged as dominant and pervasive for either the Mobilizables or the Attentives. While some revisions of the original model are necessitated by the data, these do not include narrowing the extent to which interdependence is conceived to mark the dynamics of attentive and mobilized citizenship.

THE CORRELATES OF MOBILIZABILITY

The bases for these conclusions are perhaps best set forth by summarizing the empirical findings reported in the previous chapters. The data on the two forms of direct or first-hand contact with public affairs, writing of letters to public officials and activity in voluntary associations, reveal clear-cut behavioral differences

---

[1] Carl I. Hovland and Irving L. Janis, "Summary and Implications for Future Research," in Carl I. Hovland and Irving L. Janis, eds., *Personality and Persuasibility* (New Haven: Yale University Press, 1959), p. 225.

between active citizens who are mobilizable and those who are not. In both cases the Mobilizables were found to be considerably more active than the Attentives. With respect to letter-writing, the Mobilizables reported a significantly greater volume of mail than the Attentives to seven different types of officials at all levels of government. Both groups wrote to members of Congress more often than to any other officials, but the Mobilizables also evidenced a strong tendency to write to the President. The striking salience of the White House for the Mobilizables was interpreted as due to more than simply a concern with politics at the national level. The more frequent letter-writing of the Mobilizables was not confined to a single issue, but held for six of the eleven issues.

The findings pertaining to organizational activities were equally clear. Although multiple membership characterized both groups, the Mobilizables belonged to more organizations, attended organizational meetings more frequently, and participated in the deliberations of more organizations than the Attentives. Not surprisingly, letter-writing and organizational activity were positively correlated in both groups.

Two forms of indirect or "second-hand" contact with public affairs were examined, mass media consumption and face-to-face communication. In the case of contacts with the mass media the hypothesis that there would be no difference between the Mobilizables and Attentives was unmistakably affirmed. In addition. both groups resembled leadership groups in their preference for printed over electronic media.

The data on face-to-face communication were less clear. Although the Mobilizables and Attentives did not differ in the extent to which they reported discussing nine of the eleven issues with friends and acquaintances, the Mobilizables exceeded the Attentives in their discussions of civil rights and nuclear testing. Since these were the two issues on which the former were known to have been mobilized, this difference was interpreted as reflecting feedback from current behavior. The Mobilizables reported discussing public affairs in general with family, close friends, clergymen, politicians, and journalists more frequently than did the Attentives. The two groups did not differ in the frequency of their discussions with professional associates, educators, merchants, and business executives.

A comparison of the two groups in terms of eleven social background categories yielded no differences between them in eight cases—age, sex, family status, race, region, education, occupation, and foreign travel—and significant differences in three cases—religion, party identification, and income. The first of these differences was due to the greater mobilizability of Protestants and the lesser mobilizability of Jews. The second and third differences reflect the fact that party identifiers and persons with low incomes were more mobilizable than Independents and individuals with high incomes.

Comparison of the Mobilizables and Attentives in terms of the strength of their attitudes toward eleven public issues revealed that the Mobilizables attach greater importance to and hold more extreme beliefs about those issues with respect to which they were mobilized. In contrast, the attitudes of the two groups did not differ in strength on those issues on which neither of them had been subjected to mobilization attempts. Both groups indicated a clear-cut tendency toward attitudinal balance in that the more importance they attached to an issue, the more extreme were their beliefs about it.

The findings were somewhat similar with respect to the respondents' perceptions of the information they possessed on public issues and of their competence to affect the course of events. In the case of information, the Mobilizables perceived themselves as more informed than the Attentives on only two of the eleven public issues, but again these were issues with respect to which the former were known to have been, and the latter not to have been, mobilized. The tendency toward balance was also reflected in the significant positive correlations between attitudes toward issues and self-perceptions of information possessed about them, for virtually every issue and for both groups. Balance was much less conspicuous with respect to actual behavior. Thus, self-perceptions of information held were much more strongly related to second-hand forms of contact with public affairs than to first-hand forms of contact. This difference was also evident in the relationship between attitudes and contact, suggesting that the establishment of direct contacts with politics through letter-writing and organizational activity requires energy and time, the availability of which cannot be predicted on the basis of attitudes and perceptions alone.

Both the Mobilizables and the Attentives reported a sense of being well-informed about only one issue (civil rights) and in the case of several issues conceded that they were uninformed. Both groups, however, perceived themselves as considerably more informed about all the issues than the general public.

Perceptions of three levels of competence were probed: how the Mobilizables and Attentives perceived the individual's, the group's, and the general public's capacity to influence public affairs. The analysis yielded the interesting finding that both the Mobilizables and the Attentives perceived the private group and the general public (in that order) as considerably more capable of influencing the course of events than the individual citizen. This finding was interpreted as indicating that active citizens are inclined to distinguish between subjective individual competence and subjective collective competence and to consider the latter more important than the former. The data thus reveal the Mobilizables and Attentives to be as modest in their self-perceptions of the amount of influence they can wield as of the extent of their information on public affairs.

Such realism notwithstanding, neither the Mobilizables nor the Attentives tended to link their self-perceptions of information about public issues and of influence over them. It had been anticipated that pressures toward perceptual balance would foster such a link, but this proved not to be so in most cases. Both groups did show some evidence of a balance pattern in the relationship between their perceptions of competence and their attitudes toward issues.

The data bearing on the interaction between perceptions of competence and the practices of citizenship were even more complex. The assumption that there would be a tendency for these two variables to be balanced led to two predictions: that perceptions of competence and their actions in the public arena would be closely associated for both the Mobilizables and the Attentives and that the Mobilizables would ascribe greater competence to the individual, the group, and the public than would the Attentives. Both of these predictions were confirmed in the case of individual competence, but negated with respect to perceptions of group and public competence. These findings were interpreted as indicating the large extent to which citizenship activity and mobilizability are attributes of individuals and not of collectivities. A person may see groups or publics as more competent than individuals, but he can only write letters and join organizations as an individual. Consequently, whether he does so on his own or in response to the appeals of a mobilizer, it is his own contacts with public affairs that he experiences and it is these which he must balance with his perceptions of competence. The influence attributed to groups and publics can be independent of the individual citizen's actions, and thus the active person is unlikely to experience pressures to make his perceptions of collective competence consistent with his own political activities. For essentially the same reason it is not surprising that while the Mobilizables were more inclined than the Attentives to perceive the individual as competent, the two groups did not differ in their perceptions of collective competence.

The way in which the identity of the mobilizer affects the mobilizability of active citizens was assessed through several questions and some clear-cut, if not entirely expected, findings resulted. Neither the Mobilizables nor the Attentives saw themselves as autonomous, self-motivated actors, but they both were aware of themselves as responsive to the appeals of mobilizers, particularly of distant mobilizers. Contrary to expectations, both the Attentives and the Mobilizables perceived themselves as more mobilizable by organizations to which they belonged than by friends and more by the President than by organizations. In addition, both groups perceived themselves as more mobilizable on those issues where they are known to have been actually exposed to attempts to mobilize their support, and the Mobilizables perceived themselves as more mobilizable than did the Attentives on virtually every issue and with respect to virtually every type of mobilizer. These differences between the two groups were greatest on those issues for which their support had been sought and with respect to those mobilizers (organizations and the President) who were more distant from their daily lives.

A special analysis of respondents in selected occupations revealed that persons in different lines of work have different perceptions of the extent to which their support can be mobilized by others. This finding was attributed to differences in the degree of "submissiveness" inherent in the several occupations.

The data were also probed for clues as to the aspects of issues that render them salient for concerned citizens. Several conclusions emerged from this analysis: (1) Active citizens regard only two or three issues as salient at any given time. (2) The responses of Mobilizables and the Attentives are more likely to differ on salient than on nonsalient issues. (3) Domestic or mixed (domestic and foreign) policy issues are more likely to be salient if they appeal to public- rather than to self-interest values, regardless of where they fall on a simple-complex continuum. In contrast, foreign policy issues are more likely to be salient if they are simple, regardless of the kinds of interests they involve.

Although the salience of an issue was also found to be closely linked to mobilizability, there was virtually no evidence that the different contents of two highly salient issues led to different attitudes, perceptions, or behaviors. A special comparison of the Civil Rights and Nuclear Test Mobilizables yielded only two significant differences attributable to issue content. It would seem that the values and foci encompassed by an issue are essentially irrelevant to the identity, orientations, and actions of citizens who are active with respect to it.

On the other hand, the number of issues to which a citizen is responsive at any given time was correlated with attitudes, perceptions, and behaviors. Multi-issue citizens engage in considerably more first- and second-hand activities, hold stronger attitudes, and perceive themselves as more mobilizable, informed, and competent than single-issue citizens. Indeed, the pattern of differences responsibilities. While the responsibility-breeds-responsibility hy- as pervasive as that between the Mobilizables and Attentives, but it was also very similar. Despite this close resemblance, however, the issue scope and mobilizability variables were found to be largely independent of each other.

Finally, a comparison of the relative strength of issues and mobilizers as sources of mobilizability yielded the surprising finding that the Mobilizables were not more mobilizer-oriented and less issue-oriented than the Attentives. Likewise, the expectation that mobilizer-oriented citizens would have stronger attitudes and perceive themselves as more informed than their issue-oriented counterparts was essentially negated.

THE MODEL REVISED

Although the foregoing findings are essentially consistent with the basic premise of our original model that a multiplicity of interdependent factors underlie active citizenship between elections, one main feature of the model proved to be so much less important than expected that a major revision is necessary. The model did not confirm the expectation that a citizen's mobilizability is directly related to his occupational and community responsibilities. While the responsibility-breeds-responsibility hypothesis had been previously supported among national leaders,[2] the same measuring instrument did not yield a similar pattern in the ADA sample of active citizens. In addition, among both the Mobilizables and the Attentives, present responsibilities were not correlated with their attitudes or their perceptions of competence. In both groups, however, letter-writing and organizational activities were significantly related to all three responsibility measures, a finding which suggests that we cannot simply eliminate the present responsibility variable from the model. Rather a more delicate revision is indicated: the notion that greater responsibility fosters greater activity must be preserved, but the expectation that it also leads to greater mobilizability must be deleted.

Another necessary revision concerns the background variables. The finding that the Mobilizables and Attentives differed on only three of eleven background variables suggests that a care-

[2] Rosenau, *National Leadership and Foreign Policy,* Chap. 5.

ful distinction must be made between the operation of back-ground factors as a source of the differences between inactive and active citizens on the one hand and their role in differentiating mobilizable from attentive citizens on the other. The relevance of social background is substantial for the former difference, but minimal for the latter. Thus the predisposition to be mobilized does not stem from past experience any more than it does from present responsibilities.

If the responsibility-breeds-responsibility hypothesis of our model is the main casualty of our empirical findings, the major acquisition is the concept of subjective collective competence. The original model did not even recognize such a phenomenon, despite the considerable importance it attributed to subjective individual competence. The data suggest that to the extent that active citizens feel politically competent, they do so because of the effectiveness they attribute to the activities of large aggregates. This finding implies that a citizen does not have to experience individual success in the political arena to sustain or increase his sense of civic competence, and it thus constitutes a major addition to our model.

PERSONALITY AS A VARIABLE

Ironically, the validation of the basic premise that mobilizability springs from a multiplicity of interdependent sources poses more questions than it answers. If a single background, attitude, or perceptual variable had accounted for a preponderance of the data, the dynamics of mobilizability would seem much clearer than they do. To be sure, if this was the case, history would probably be full of instances of demagogues who capitalized on the single factor that predisposes people to respond to appeals for support. The fact that mobilizability emerges as extraordinarily complex is thus satisfying in a value sense, since it bespeaks societal stability and a degree of immunity to irrational appeals. Empirically, however, the possibility that a more parsimonious explanation of mobilizability may not be attainable is anything but satisfying. Even acknowledging that it cannot be explained in terms of one or two major variables, the complexity of the findings nonetheless leaves uneasiness as to whether our analysis somehow missed the central dynamics of mobilizability. To have identified a number of correlates of mobilizability is not to have uncovered its dynamics. To know that mobilizable citizens are inclined to establish more first-hand contacts, to have stronger attitudes, to perceive themselves as more informed and more mobilizable on salient issues, and to feel more politically competent than their attentive counterparts is not to understand the circumstances under which these characteristics converge to result in a mobilized response. We have presumed that mobilizability is a habit, but under what conditions is the habit acquired and evoked? Does it reflect a predisposition toward conformity? Does it imply a tendency to engage in rational calculation? Is it a form of cooperativeness, reflecting an appreciation that nothing happens in the political arena unless people rally to requests for support? Is it fostered by certain kinds of personality traits?

Having failed to achieve a satisfactory explanation of mobilizability in terms of behavioral, attitudinal, and perceptual variables, it is tempting to attribute the differences between the Mobilizables and Attentives to personality. Perhaps, for example, Mobilizables share with professional politicians what Dahl has described as "an inordinate capacity for multiplying human relationships without ever becoming deeply involved emotionally." [3] Such a capacity would facilitate mobilizability by enabling a citizen to respond to appeals for support from persons whom he does not know and has not met.

Unfortunately the questionnaire did not contain items that probed the operation of personality variables and the data provide no basis for speculating that they are central to the dynamics of mobilizability. In addition, the findings of other studies are not encouraging in this respect. At best, investigations of the role of personality factors in politics have yielded ambiguous results and have yet to provide satisfying evidence that such factors are capable of putting all the pieces of the puzzle together. As McClosky

[3] *Who Governs*, p. 298.

notes, "the 'distance' between a basic personality trait and a specific manifestation of political activity is too great and the route between them too circuitous for the one to be directly engaged by the other." [4]

A measure of the ambiguity of the findings on the role of personality is provided by three discordant conclusions McClosky derived from the literature on the subject. On the one hand, he notes that the "available evidence suggests that a number of the more basic or genotypic personality traits—rigidity, guilt neurasthenia, intolerance of ambiguity, manic-depressive tendencies, manifest anxiety—do not correlate highly with political participation." [5] On the other hand, one paragraph later McClosky modifies this observation by concluding that "although basic personality dimensions such as guilt and rigidity do not adequately distinguish participants from nonparticipants, they do differentiate somewhat the less active from the more active, the inactives exhibiting these traits in greater measure." [6] And shortly thereafter he returns to a more confident note by asserting that "although the correlations between psychological traits and participation are modest, their direction largely refutes much of the folklore about political practitioners as highly ambitious, exhibitionistic, 'folksy,' narcissistic, driven, enthusiastic, materialistic, authoritarian, and power-hungry. Research in the United States (very little has been conducted elsewhere) indicates that politicians and other active participants do not possess these traits in greater measure than do nonparticipants or members of other professions." [7]

Addressing the somewhat more manageable question of why two individuals with identical backgrounds might vary greatly in the extent of their political activities, Milbrath administered a number of personality tests to a sample of citizens and found that a "sociability" measure he derived from Gough's *California Psy-*

[4] "Political Participation," p. 258.
[5] *Ibid.*
[6] *Ibid.*
[7] *Ibid.*

chological Inventory "was the only scale which proved to have a high relationship to becoming" an active citizen. Milbrath describes the sociability scale as measuring "what might be called a predisposition toward social interaction. It implies a feeling of ease, graciousness, and confidence in social situations, and a willingness to accept the responsibilities that attended effective social relations." [8] He finds that,

> When political participation in general is broken down into several specific types of participation, sociability correlates more highly with certain types than with others. For the most part those types of participation that require interaction with other people are more highly correlated with sociability than those that do not necessarily require interaction. It was discovered that activities like contacting a politician, campaigning, soliciting political funds, and being consulted by a political leader related significantly to sociability despite the effect of SES; whereas merely holding a public or party office, being active in a party, attending meetings or caucuses, and contributing political funds did not relate significantly to sociability when SES was controlled.[9]

Accordingly, Milbrath concludes that active citizens are "more dominating, secure and confident, astute, self-expressive, optimistic, responsible, self-accepting, and likely to perceive political action as efficacious" than are those who are passive toward public affairs.[10]

Several other researchers reasoned along these lines in attempting to interpret their data. Inkeles, for example, concluded that "it appears that certain personal qualities perhaps appropriately defined as personality traits, such as intelligence and a

---

[8] Lester W. Milbrath, "Predispositions Toward Political Contention," *Western Political Quarterly*, Vol. 13 (1960), p. 9.

[9] *Ibid.*, p. 11.

[10] *Ibid.*, p. 17.

subjectively high estimate of one's skill and social standing, are also characteristic of those who manifest the syndrome of active citizenship." [11] Similarly, Erbe observes that his "findings as well as those showing that social participation is cumulative, suggest that further research should investigate the personality character- istics of the high participator. Perhaps the research dealing with extroversion could provide some clues." [12] In a like manner Troldahl and Van Dam found that the active citizens in their sample scored higher than the "inactives . . . on four of the five gregariousness indices." [13]

Nor does this exhaust the other types of variables that have been explored as possible sources of active citizenship. One re- searcher, for example, suggests that an orientation toward political action may not stem from complex personality factors but may instead be directly transmitted from parents to children, a con- clusion that is consistent with his finding that student activists were simply carrying into practice the ideals that their parents had preached (but not acted upon themselves).[14] Other inves- tigators found that a "sense of effectiveness in public affairs" was "moderately but consistently related to a feeling of competence in a variety of areas in the more immediate environment of per- sonal affairs," a finding that led them to conclude that an "attitude [of effectiveness] toward one's role in public affairs is in many people a reflection of a more general orientation toward the world." [15] Still other investigators probed what they called the

---

[11] "Participant Citizenship in Six Developing Countries," p. 1139.

[12] "Social Involvement and Political Activity," p. 215. However, for one study that found little difference between active and inactive citizens along an extroversion dimension, see Bernard Hennessy, "Politicals and Apoliticals: Some Measurements of Personality Traits," *Midwest Journal of Political Science*, Vol. 3 (1959), pp. 336–55.

[13] "Face-to-Face Communication about Major Topics in the News," p. 633.

[14] Richard Flacks, "Liberated Generation: An Exploration of the Roots of Student Protest," *Journal of Social Issues*, Vol. 23 (1967), pp. 52–75.

[15] Elizabeth Douvan and Alan M. Walker, "The Sense of Effectiveness in Public Affairs," *Psychological Monographs*, Vol. 70 (1956), p. 18.

"traditional socially responsible personality" and found that many of his political actions and beliefs are "influenced considerably by the culture in which he is embedded." [16]

None of these findings or formulations, however, are directly pertinent to mobilizability. They are as applicable to attentive as to mobilizable citizens and thus do not advance us much closer to an appreciation of why the latter are responsive to distant appeals for support and the former are not. Although the interaction between mobilizability and personality needs to be understood, the preceding discussion of past efforts to link personality and political variables suggests that such inquiry is not likely to add more than small increments to our comprehension of the predisposition to respond to mobilizers.

SUGGESTIONS FOR FURTHER RESEARCH

Given the prospect that personality variables are unlikely to explain the dynamics of mobilizability, a variety of other possible factors need to be explored. As implied above, it might be fruitful to pursue the possibility that conformity is an important source of responsiveness to mobilizers. DiPalma and McClosky found that U.S. citizens who subscribe to prevailing national norms—i.e., those they designated as conformers—evidence characteristics not unlike those associated with the Mobilizables in our data: conformers proved to be "more intellectually oriented, more politically aware, . . . more accessible to interaction, less withdrawn or socially isolated, and more strongly motivated to receive and respond to information on public questions [than] . . . deviants." [17] It is thus conceivable that the propensity to respond to appeals for support is rooted in a readiness to do as directed, to be dutiful,

---

[16] Leonard Berkowitz and Kenneth G. Lutterman, "The Traditional Socially Responsible Personality," *Public Opinion Quarterly*, Vol. 32 (1968), p. 173.

[17] Giuseppe DiPalma and Herbert McClosky, "Personality and Conformity: The Learning of Political Attitudes," *American Political Science Review*, Vol. 64 (December 1970), pp. 1068–69.

and thus to conform to all the requirements of the citizen role as it is idealized in the value system of the society. Sufficient evidence of such a tendency emerged from our comparisons of the self-perceived mobilizability of different occupational groups to suggest that further investigation along these lines might be fruitful. Some skepticism is again useful, however. As DiPalma and McClosky define conformity, it means agreement with the majority, which makes most citizens conformists. Yet most citizens are not mobilizable, so that the explanatory power of conformity variables in relation to mobilizability is not likely to be very great. Furthermore, some of the most dedicated and mobilizable citizens are members of minority groups who often deviate from the prevailing norms, adding further doubts to the likelihood that the explanation of mobilizability lies in this direction.

Another possibility, as noted earlier, is that mobilizability stems from rational calculation, from self-conscious estimates that goals are more likely to be realized by responding to appeals from leaders who are aggregating support on behalf of them. It is possible that active citizens who can be mobilized are more inclined to be instrumental in the political arena than their attentive counterparts. Such an inclination is certainly relevant to the behavior of single-area mobilizables who limit their responsiveness to only those matters that are closest to their concerns and who presumably engage in some kind of rational calculation when they resist mobilization attempts on other issues. In contrast, it is difficult to conceive of such calculations as guiding the behavior of multi-area mobilizables, given our data showing them to be responsive to any salient issue, whatever the values it embraces. Indeed, the distinction between single- and multi-area mobilizables suggests that future research should allow for the possibility that the dynamics of mobilizability may not be constant but may shift along a single-area/multi-area continuum, with rational calculation as a major determinant at the single-area extreme and an unconsidered propensity derived from a composite of personality, conformity, situational, and other variables as a dominant source at the multi-area extreme.

Whether or not single-area mobilizability proves to be rooted in rational calculation, further investigation of its dynamics would also seem to command a high place on an agenda for future research. Single-area mobilizability might easily be dismissed as too self-evident to warrant additional inquiry. The dynamics of self-interest on which it is founded seem clear-cut and the bases for action stemming from rational calculation seem readily discernible. Yet not all—or even most—persons whose self-interests are at stake in a situation can be mobilized to act to protect them (as any interest group leader can attest), so that the bases of such behavior—and the obstacles to it—are not as simple as they might seem. Furthermore, we know little about the long-range consequences of being mobilized on behalf of one's self-interest. As is true of all behavior, political activity is an occasion for learning, and it would be useful to examine the learning consequences of single-issue attentiveness and mobilizability. An attentive or mobilized single-issue citizen can retreat to passivity when the issue that moves him wanes, or the experience of being mobilized can lead to involvement in other issues and thus, in effect, to an expansion of mobilizability. Under what conditions does retreat occur? Under what conditions does expansion occur? Do some types of single-issue concerns lend themselves more readily to expansion than others? Are there circumstances under which learning can cumulate so that single-issue mobilizability gets transformed into a thoroughgoing multi-issue propensity? Insights into such questions would have an immediate payoff by shedding light on the dynamics of attentiveness and mobilizability in general even as they also provided guidance to those who seek to enlarge the support base for causes that are not readily defined in narrow, self-interest terms.

Still another possibility worth exploring is that mobilizability may be located in social roles rather than in individuals. The potential value of such an approach is that it would go a long way toward explaining parsimoniously why the various sources of mobilizability converge to produce responsiveness under certain circumstances and not under others. People move in and out of roles, whereas their behavioral and personality attributes are always with them, and their entrances into and exits from the mobilizee role might explain what appear as inconsistencies in their citizenship behavior. Although concerned with a more general phenomenon, Alford and Scoble interpreted their survey data as pointing to the utility of such a perspective:

> Political involvement may thus be usefully conceived as a social role, with attached normative expectations for self and others, varying with group and community membership, containing the possibility of role conflict, role sets, and role change. Involvement is thus connected with social and political structures through processes of role definition and learning. (One asks, how do people come to see themselves as related to politics? How and when is a political role fixed? How does it change? How is it related to other roles?) Viewing involvement thus, we attempt to avoid reifying a classification of individuals, something hard to do when analyzing survey data from one point in time. High involvement is not assumed to be a *permanent* characteristic of an individual, but only partial, segmentary, subject to pressures for change either for intensification or abandonment. When a political role becomes permanent and central, we normally refer to the "professional politician"—but this is not the entire role for most persons and, therefore, the structural conditions under which political roles are played become important.[18]

Such a point of view has the problem of identifying what constitute the expectations of the mobilizee role and then accounting for the conditions under which citizens enter and leave the role. In other words, even if the existence of such a role could be demonstrated, and even if the mobilized behavior in it would then be explicable, there would still remain the important question of why the individual did or did not assume the role in the first place.

Another possible line of future inquiry follows from the hypothesis that the dynamics of mobilizability are idiosyncratic, that different people are mobilizable for different reasons, and

---

[18] Robert R. Alford and Harry M. Scoble, "Sources of Local Political Involvement," *American Political Science Review*, Vol. 62 (1968), p. 1206.

that therefore a coherent model that will serve to explain it cannot be developed. Our findings suggest that this is unlikely, but different groups operating under different conditions and in response to different mobilization stimuli need to be investigated before the idiosyncratic alternative can be confidently rejected.

Finally, it may be that our original hypothesis—that the sources of mobilizability are multiple, interdependent, and cumulative—has far greater explanatory power than our analysis suggests. Responsiveness to a mobilizer may be the product of all the variables we have examined or suggested, plus a great many more, which supplement each other so as to result in mobilized action. Our original model may be less insufficient in conception as it is lacking in elaboration. If this is so—and perhaps even if it is not—then further research on the behavioral, attitudinal, and perceptual variables explored here clearly needs to be undertaken. It would seem, for example, that we need to probe more extensively how the frequency, extent, scope, and intensity of mobilized behavior vary in relation to variations in the identity of the mobilizer, the nature of the support he seeks (e.g., funds, votes, energy, attendance), the ease with which the support can be given or withheld (e.g., letter-writing, organizational activities, attending rallies, etc.), the case that is made for giving support (e.g., eloquent, succinct, rational, emotional, etc.), the time frame within which it must be given (e.g., immediately, in the near future, over the long term, etc.), the issue involved (e.g., local, international, economic, cultural, etc.), and the other issues competing for attention and support (e.g., an overriding national emergency, a few major issues, many minor conflicts, etc.).

Whatever the dynamics of mobilizability may be, and however parsimoniously it may be possible to comprehend them, our lengthy analysis has only scratched the surface. Notwithstanding the many problems that further inquiry entails, however, it seems well worth undertaking. Mobilizability—responding to appeals for support—lies at the heart of the political process. Thus, in a society as delicately balanced as ours, the Mobilizable American may hold the key to its future direction and evolution.

THE QUESTIONNAIRE

[The questionnaire is presented unchanged from the way it was mailed (except for Item #59, which replaced Item #57 in the second mailing). The bracketed numbers on the left constitute the numbering system used to identify the item throughout the book. The pages in the book where the overall responses to the item can be found are indicated at the end of each question.]

Center of International Studies   [January 1964—1st mailing]
Princeton University   September 1964 [2nd mailing]
                                     Project V857

Please answer every question on every page,
even those which may seem uninteresting to you

[1] DO YOU BELONG TO ANY ORGANIZATIONS WHICH PUBLICLY EXPRESS THEIR VIEWPOINTS ON NATIONAL OR INTERNATIONAL PROBLEMS ＿＿＿Yes ＿＿＿No

If yes, to about how many organizations? ＿＿＿＿＿

[see p. 222]

[2] ON THE AVERAGE, HOW OFTEN DO YOU ATTEND ORGANIZATIONAL MEETINGS WHERE NATIONAL OR INTERNATIONAL PROBLEMS ARE DISCUSSED?
(check only one)

□	□	□	□	□	□
every week	once a month	six times a year	three times a year	once a year	never

[see p. 222]

[3] IN THE LAST THREE YEARS HAVE YOU WRITTEN A LETTER TO

a United Nations official or delegate? Yes＿＿＿ No＿＿＿
a member of the U.S. House of Representatives? Yes＿＿＿ No＿＿＿
a member of the U.S. Senate? Yes＿＿＿ No＿＿＿
other Federal Executive officials (specify) Yes＿＿＿ No＿＿＿
a member of your State Legislature? Yes＿＿＿ No＿＿＿
the Governor of your State? Yes＿＿＿ No＿＿＿
other State Executive officials? (specify) Yes＿＿＿ No＿＿＿

[4] IF YOU CHECKED AT LEAST ONE "YES" IN THE PREVIOUS QUESTION, WHICH OF THE FOLLOWING PROBLEMS WERE MENTIONED IN YOUR LETTER (OR LETTERS)? (check as many as are appropriate)

＿＿＿Berlin   ＿＿＿foreign aid
＿＿＿Vietnam   ＿＿＿civil rights
＿＿＿nuclear testing   ＿＿＿tariff reduction
＿＿＿federal tax reduction ＿＿＿the Congo
＿＿＿agricultural surpluses ＿＿＿Western unity
＿＿＿balance of payments

[see p. 218]

[5] IF AND WHEN YOU WRITE LETTERS TO LEGISLATIVE OR EXECUTIVE OFFICIALS (AT ANY LEVEL), WHERE DOES THE IDEA FOR THEM USUALLY COME FROM? (check only one)

_____I usually develop the idea for such letters in discussion with friends.

_____It is usually urged on me by an organization of which I am a member.

_____It is usually the result of my own thinking and initiative.

_____I never write such letters.

_____other (specify)

[see p. 409]

[6] ARE YOU IN ANY WAY RESPONSIBLE FOR THE WRITING OF PRESS RELEASES? _____Yes _____No

[see p. 180]

[7] DO YOU HAVE SOME VOICE IN DETERMINING THE CONTENTS OF ANY PUBLICATION? _____Yes _____No. If yes, of approximately what circulation? _____

[see p. 180]

[8] HAVE YOU EVER WRITTEN A BOOK? _____Yes _____No If yes, how many? _____

[see p. 180]

[9] HAVE YOU EVER WRITTEN AN ARTICLE PUBLISHED IN A MAGAZINE CIRCULATED NATIONALLY AND SOLD AT NEWSTANDS? _____Yes _____No If yes, about how many articles? _____

[see p. 180]

[10] ALL TOLD, ABOUT HOW MANY LETTERS A *YEAR* DO YOU WRITE TO THE TYPES OF PERSONS LISTED AT THE LEFT (place *one* check in *each* row)

	none	1–3	4–6	7–9	10 or more
United Nations officials or delegates	☐	☐	☐	☐	☐
Members of Congress	☐	☐	☐	☐	☐

	none	1–3	4–6	7–9	10 or more
The President	☐	☐	☐	☐	☐
Other Federal Executive officials	☐	☐	☐	☐	☐
State officials (executive or legislative)	☐	☐	☐	☐	☐
Local officials	☐	☐	☐	☐	☐
Newspaper editors	☐	☐	☐	☐	☐
others (specify)	☐	☐	☐	☐	☐

[see p. 210]

[11] HOW WELL WOULD YOU SAY THE AMERICAN PEOPLE UNDERSTAND THE PROBLEMS LISTED AT THE LEFT? (place *one* check in *each* row)

	extremely well	quite well	somewhat	poorly	not at all
nuclear testing	☐	☐	☐	☐	☐
the Congo	☐	☐	☐	☐	☐
tariff reduction	☐	☐	☐	☐	☐
Berlin	☐	☐	☐	☐	☐
federal tax reduction	☐	☐	☐	☐	☐
foreign aid	☐	☐	☐	☐	☐
civil rights	☐	☐	☐	☐	☐
Vietnam	☐	☐	☐	☐	☐
balance of payments	☐	☐	☐	☐	☐
agricultural surpluses	☐	☐	☐	☐	☐
Western unity	☐	☐	☐	☐	☐

[see p. 350]

[12] DO ITEMS APPEAR IN THE NEWSPAPERS IN WHICH QUOTATIONS ARE ATTRIBUTED TO YOU?
(check only one)

_____quite often   _____occasionally   _____very rarely

[see p. 180]

[13] DO THE REQUESTS YOU RECEIVE TO GIVE LECTURES OR TALKS ON ANY SUBJECT AVERAGE ABOUT
(check only one)

☐	☐	☐	☐	☐	☐
20 or more a month	10 a month	5 a month	1 a month	less than 1 a month	other (specify)_____

[see p. 181]

[14] QUITE APART FROM WHAT YOU THINK YOU OUGHT TO DO, WHAT WOULD YOU BE *LIKELY* TO DO IF, AT DIFFERENT TIMES, A CLOSE FRIEND URGED YOU TO WRITE CONGRESSMEN ON BEHALF OF HIS POSITION ON EACH OF THE PROBLEMS LISTED AT THE LEFT? THAT IS (AND ASSUMING YOU DID NOT DIFFER GREATLY WITH HIS VIEWPOINT ON THE MATTER), WHAT WOULD BE THE *LIKELIHOOD* OF YOUR ACTUALLY WRITING A REPRESENTATIVE OR SENATOR AS A RESULT OF YOUR FRIEND'S URGING ON EACH PROBLEM?   (place *one* check in *each* row)

	extremely likely	very likely	somewhat likely	hardly likely	not at all likely
federal tax reduction	☐	☐	☐	☐	☐
agricultural surpluses	☐	☐	☐	☐	☐
Western unity	☐	☐	☐	☐	☐
balance of payments	☐	☐	☐	☐	☐
tariff reduction	☐	☐	☐	☐	☐
Vietnam	☐	☐	☐	☐	☐

	extremely likely	very likely	somewhat likely	hardly likely	not at all likely
the Congo	☐	☐	☐	☐	☐
civil rights	☐	☐	☐	☐	☐
nuclear testing	☐	☐	☐	☐	☐
foreign aid	☐	☐	☐	☐	☐
Berlin	☐	☐	☐	☐	☐

[see pp. 412–13]

[15] ON WHAT SOURCES DO YOU RELY FOR INFORMATION ABOUT FOREIGN AFFAIRS?
(check as many as are appropriate)

_____word of mouth   _____radio or television

_____newspapers   _____columnists or commentators

_____magazines   _____other (specify)

[see p. 227]

[16] MORE SPECIFICALLY, ON WHICH OF THESE SOURCES DO YOU RELY FOR INFORMATION ABOUT FOREIGN AFFAIRS?   (check as many as are appropriate)

_____Life   _____Newsweek

_____Harper's   _____The Reporter

_____Foreign Affairs   _____Time

_____New Republic   _____London Economist

_____US News and World Report _____Atlantic

_____Saturday Evening Post   _____Reader's Digest

[see p. 227]

[17] HOW OFTEN DO YOU READ THE *NEW YORK TIMES?*
(check only one)

_____every day   _____once in a great while

_____Sundays only   _____never

[see p. 228]

[18] HAVE YOU EVER APPEARED ON A TELEVISION OR RADIO PROGRAM? _____Yes_____No
If yes, about how many times a YEAR do you appear? _____

[see p. 181]

[19] IF THE RUSSIANS SHOULD ATTEMPT TO BLOCK ACCESS TO WEST BERLIN, HOW JUSTIFIED WOULD THE UNITED STATES BE IN RESISTING WITH FORCE?
(check only one)

☐	☐	☐	☐	☐
completely justified	very justified	somewhat justified	hardly justified	not at all justified

[see p. 328]

[20] IN YOUR OPINION, HOW MUCH OF AN EXTENSION OF CIVIL RIGHTS SHOULD CONGRESS HAVE APPROVED?
(check only one)

☐	☐	☐	☐	☐
an unlimited extension	a great extension	somewhat of an extension	a very small extension	no extension

[see p. 328]

[21] IN YOUR OPINION, TO WHAT EXTENT SHOULD THE AMOUNT OF GOVERNMENTAL SUBSIDIES DESIGNED TO REDUCE AGRICULTURAL SURPLUSES BE ALTERED?
(check only one)

☐	☐	☐	☐	☐
increased greatly	increased somewhat	kept as they are	decreased somewhat	decreased greatly

[see p. 328]

[22] WHAT DO YOU THINK SHOULD BE DONE TO TARIFFS ON GOODS IMPORTED INTO THE U.S.?   (check only one)

☐	☐	☐	☐	☐
reduced greatly	reduced somewhat	kept as they are	increased somewhat	increased greatly

[see p. 328]

[23] IN YOUR OPINION, HOW MUCH INFLUENCE DID THE GROUPS LISTED AT THE LEFT EXERT IN CONVINCING THE CONGRESS TO PASS THE 1962 TRADE EXPANSION ACT WHICH PERMITTED THE PRESIDENT TO NEGOTIATE SUBSTANTIAL TARIFF REDUCTIONS?
(place *one* check in *each* row)

	an enormous amount	a large amount	a moderate amount	very little	none
business leaders	☐	☐	☐	☐	☐
church leaders	☐	☐	☐	☐	☐
leading educators	☐	☐	☐	☐	☐
labor leaders	☐	☐	☐	☐	☐
world affairs groups	☐	☐	☐	☐	☐
journalists and commentators	☐	☐	☐	☐	☐
others (specify)	☐	☐	☐	☐	☐

[see p. 361]

[24] DO YOU PARTICIPATE IN THE DELIBERATIONS OF ANY ORGANIZATIONS WHICH TAKE STANDS ON PUBLIC ISSUES?

_____Yes _____No   If yes, about how many organizations?_____
[see pp. 181, 222]

[25] IF YOU WANTED TO DISSEMINATE A NEW IDEA, ABOUT HOW MANY PEOPLE COULD YOU REACH WITH IT?
(check only one)

☐	☐	☐	☐	☐	☐
one thousand or less	ten thousand	fifty thousand	one hundred thousand	a million or more	other (specify)___

[see p. 181]

[26] ARE YOU EVER ASKED TO LEND YOUR NAME TO AD-
VANCE WORTHY CAUSES?   (check only one)

_____quite often   _____occasionally   _____very rarely

[see p. 182]

BIOGRAPHICAL INFORMATION:

[27] (a) _____male _____female

[see p. 262]

[28] (b) _____Negro _____White

[see p. 271]

[29] (c) _____age

[see p. 253]

[30] (d) In what State do you work? _____

In what State do you vote? _____

[see p. 280]

[31] (e) _____single _____married _____widowed or divorced

[see p. 267]

[32] (f) number of children _____ number of other dependents _____

[see p. 269]

[33] (g) DO YOU CONSIDER YOURSELF

_____a Republican   _____an Independent

_____a Democrat   _____other (specify)

[see p. 285]

[34] (h) RELIGION:

_____Catholic   _____Protestant

_____Jewish   _____other (specify)

[see p. 275]

[35] (i) WHAT IS YOUR CHIEF OCCUPATION? _____

(j) WHAT IS YOUR SECONDARY OCCUPATION (IF ANY)?

_____

[see pp. 307, 309]

[36] (k) TO WHAT EXTENT DOES YOUR CHIEF OCCUPA-TION, APART FROM YOUR PERSONAL INCLINA-TIONS, REQUIRE YOU TO FOLLOW THE COURSE OF EVENTS AND DEVELOPMENTS ABROAD?
(check only one)

☐	☐	☐	☐	☐
an enormous amount	a large amount	a moderate amount	very little	not at all

[see p. 391]

[37] (l) DID YOU ATTEND COLLEGE?

____Yes ____No   If yes, how many years?____

DID YOU GRADUATE FROM COLLEGE?

____Yes ____No

[see p. 294]

[38] (m) DID YOU ATTEND GRADUATE OR PROFESSIONAL SCHOOL? ____Yes ____No

DID YOU OBTAIN AN ADVANCED DEGREE?

____Yes ____No   Which one(s)? _____

[see p. 295]

[39] (n) ON THE AVERAGE, WHAT IS YOUR TOTAL ANNUAL FAMILY INCOME?   (check only one)

☐	☐	☐	☐	☐	☐
under $5,000	$5,000– $10,000	$10,000– $15,000	$15,000– $20,000	$20,000– $25,000	over $25,000

[see p. 301]

[40] IN YOUR OPINION, HOW MUCH INFLUENCE DID THE GROUPS LISTED AT THE LEFT EXERT IN CONVINCING THE SENATE TO RATIFY THE NUCLEAR TEST BAN TREATY? (place *one* check in *each* row)

	an enormous amount	a large amount	a moderate amount	very little	none
church leaders	☐	☐	☐	☐	☐
labor leaders	☐	☐	☐	☐	☐
journalists and commentators	☐	☐	☐	☐	☐
leading educators	☐	☐	☐	☐	☐
business leaders	☐	☐	☐	☐	☐
peace groups	☐	☐	☐	☐	☐
others (specify)	☐	☐	☐	☐	☐

[see pp. 361–62]

[41] HOW FREQUENTLY DO YOU DISCUSS (IN PERSON, BY PHONE, OR BY MAIL) PUBLIC AFFAIRS WITH MEMBERS OF THE GROUPS LISTED AT THE LEFT? (place *one* check in *each* row)

	never	hardly ever	some-times	often	invari-ably
family	☐	☐	☐	☐	☐
close friends	☐	☐	☐	☐	☐
professional associates	☐	☐	☐	☐	☐
clergymen	☐	☐	☐	☐	☐
educators	☐	☐	☐	☐	☐
politicians	☐	☐	☐	☐	☐
journalists	☐	☐	☐	☐	☐

	never	hardly ever	some-times	often	invari-ably
merchants	☐	☐	☐	☐	☐
business executives	☐	☐	☐	☐	☐
others (specify)	☐	☐	☐	☐	☐

[see pp. 240–41]

[42] QUITE APART FROM WHAT YOU THINK YOU OUGHT TO DO, WHAT WOULD YOU BE *LIKELY* TO DO IF, AT DIFFERENT TIMES, THE PRESIDENT GAVE A TELE-VISION ADDRESS IN WHICH HE URGED CITIZENS TO WRITE CONGRESSMEN ON BEHALF OF HIS POSITION ON EACH OF THE PROBLEMS LISTED AT THE LEFT? THAT IS (AND ASSUMING YOU DO NOT DIFFER GREATLY WITH HIS VIEWPOINT ON THE MATTER), WHAT WOULD BE THE *LIKELIHOOD* OF YOUR ACTU-ALLY WRITING A REPRESENTATIVE OR A SENATOR AS A RESULT OF THE PRESIDENT'S URGING ON EACH PROBLEM?   (place *one* check in *each* row)

	extremely likely	very likely	some-what likely	hardly likely	not at all likely
balance of payments	☐	☐	☐	☐	☐
civil rights	☐	☐	☐	☐	☐
federal tax reduction	☐	☐	☐	☐	☐
tariff reduction	☐	☐	☐	☐	☐
nuclear testing	☐	☐	☐	☐	☐
agricultural surpluses	☐	☐	☐	☐	☐
Vietnam	☐	☐	☐	☐	☐
foreign aid	☐	☐	☐	☐	☐
Berlin	☐	☐	☐	☐	☐
the Congo	☐	☐	☐	☐	☐
Western unity	☐	☐	☐	☐	☐

[see pp. 416–17]

[43] IF THE U.N. SHOULD HAVE TO CONTINUE ITS PEACE-KEEPING EFFORTS IN THE CONGO WITHOUT ADDITIONAL FINANCING, HOW JUSTIFIED DO YOU FEEL THE UNITED STATES WOULD BE IN SUPPLYING MOST OF THE MONEY? (check only one)

☐	☐	☐	☐	☐
completely justified	very justified	somewhat justified	hardly justified	not at all justified

[see p. 329]

[44] WHEN THE PRESIDENT ASKED CONGRESS FOR A $10 BILLION TAX REDUCTION, HOW MUCH OF A REDUCTION DO YOU THINK CONGRESS SHOULD HAVE APPROVED? (check only one)

☐	☐	☐	☐	☐
no reduction at all	$5 billion	$10 billion	$12 billion	$15 billion

[see p. 329]

[45] WHAT IS YOUR OPINION OF THE NUCLEAR TEST BAN TREATY? (check only one)

☐	☐	☐	☐	☐
very unfavorable	somewhat unfavorable	neither for nor against	somewhat favorable	very favorable

[see p. 329]

[46] WITH HOW MUCH ENTHUSIASM DO YOU THINK THE UNITED STATES SHOULD CONTINUE TO SPEAK OF WESTERN UNITY AS A MAJOR FOREIGN POLICY GOAL? (check only one)

☐	☐	☐	☐	☐
unqualified enthusiasm	great enthusiasm	moderate enthusiasm	little enthusiasm	no enthusiasm

[see p. 329]

[47] HOW STRONGLY DO YOU FEEL THAT A SOLUTION TO EACH OF THE PROBLEMS LISTED AT THE LEFT IS ESSENTIAL TO THE WELFARE OF THE COUNTRY?
(place *one* check in *each* row)

	extremely strongly	very strongly	quite strongly	weakly	not at all
the Congo	☐	☐	☐	☐	☐
Berlin	☐	☐	☐	☐	☐
foreign aid	☐	☐	☐	☐	☐
Vietnam	☐	☐	☐	☐	☐
agricultural surpluses	☐	☐	☐	☐	☐
nuclear testing	☐	☐	☐	☐	☐
tariff reduction	☐	☐	☐	☐	☐
federal tax reduction	☐	☐	☐	☐	☐
civil rights	☐	☐	☐	☐	☐
balance of payments	☐	☐	☐	☐	☐
Western unity	☐	☐	☐	☐	☐

[see p. 326]

[48] DOES YOUR WORK BRING YOU INTO CONTACT WITH FOREIGNERS, EITHER IN PERSON OR BY MAIL?
(check only one)

———frequently　　———occasionally　　———very rarely

[see p. 390]

[49] HOW OFTEN DO YOUR CONVERSATIONS WITH FRIENDS AND ACQUAINTANCES TURN TO EACH OF THE PROBLEMS LISTED AT THE LEFT?　　(place *one* check in *each* row)

	never	hardly ever	some-times	usually	invari-ably
foreign aid	☐	☐	☐	☐	☐
Vietnam	☐	☐	☐	☐	☐

	never	hardly ever	some- times	usually	invari- ably
tariff reduction	☐	☐	☐	☐	☐
balance of payments	☐	☐	☐	☐	☐
Berlin	☐	☐	☐	☐	☐
agricultural surpluses	☐	☐	☐	☐	☐
federal tax reduction	☐	☐	☐	☐	☐
Western unity	☐	☐	☐	☐	☐
the Congo	☐	☐	☐	☐	☐
civil rights	☐	☐	☐	☐	☐
nuclear testing	☐	☐	☐	☐	☐

[see pp. 236–37]

[50] HOW MUCH INFORMATION DO YOU FEEL YOU HAVE ON THE PROBLEMS LISTED AT THE LEFT?
(place *one* check in *each* row)

	an enor- mous amount	a large amount	a mod- erate amount	very little	none
agricultural surpluses	☐	☐	☐	☐	☐
balance of payments	☐	☐	☐	☐	☐
nuclear testing	☐	☐	☐	☐	☐
Berlin	☐	☐	☐	☐	☐
civil rights	☐	☐	☐	☐	☐
tariff reduction	☐	☐	☐	☐	☐
foreign aid	☐	☐	☐	☐	☐
the Congo	☐	☐	☐	☐	☐
federal tax reduction	☐	☐	☐	☐	☐
Vietnam	☐	☐	☐	☐	☐
Western unity	☐	☐	☐	☐	☐

[see. p. 347]

[51] IF THE GUERILLA WAR IN VIETNAM CONTINUES UN-ABATED, HOW SHOULD THE UNITED STATES RESPOND IN TERMS OF THE NUMBER OF MEN AND THE AMOUNT OF MATERIAL IT COMMITS TO THE SITUATION? (check only one)

☐	☐	☐	☐	☐
increase them greatly	increase them somewhat	maintain them as they are	decrease them somewhat	decrease them greatly

[see pp. 329–30]

[52] WHAT DO YOU THINK CONGRESS SHOULD DO WITH RESPECT TO THE PRESIDENT'S 1963 REQUEST FOR $4.2 BILLION IN FOREIGN AID APPROPRIATIONS? (check only one)

☐	☐	☐	☐	☐
increase it greatly	increase it a little	approve it as is	decrease it a little	decrease it greatly

[see p. 330]

[53] QUITE APART FROM WHAT YOU THINK YOU OUGHT TO DO, WHAT WOULD YOU BE *LIKELY* TO DO IF, AT DIFFERENT TIMES, AN ORGANIZATION TO WHICH YOU BELONG URGED ITS MEMBERS TO WRITE CONGRESS-MEN ON BEHALF OF ITS POSITION ON EACH OF THE PROBLEMS LISTED AT THE LEFT? THAT IS (AND ASSUM-ING YOU DID NOT DIFFER GREATLY WITH ITS VIEW-POINT ON THE MATTER), WHAT WOULD BE THE *LIKELIHOOD* OF YOUR ACTUALLY WRITING A REPRE-SENTATIVE OR SENATOR AS A RESULT OF THE ORGA-NIZATION'S URGING ON EACH PROBLEM? (place *one* check in *each* row)

	extremely likely	very likely	somewhat likely	hardly likely	not at all likely
civil rights	☐	☐	☐	☐	☐
Western unity	☐	☐	☐	☐	☐

	extremely likely	very likely	somewhat likely	hardly likely	not at all likely
Berlin	☐	☐	☐	☐	☐
Vietnam	☐	☐	☐	☐	☐
nuclear testing	☐	☐	☐	☐	☐
federal tax reduction	☐	☐	☐	☐	☐
balance of payments	☐	☐	☐	☐	☐
the Congo	☐	☐	☐	☐	☐
foreign aid	☐	☐	☐	☐	☐
agricultural surpluses	☐	☐	☐	☐	☐
tariff reduction	☐	☐	☐	☐	☐

[see pp. 414–15]

[54] ABOUT HOW MANY TIMES HAVE YOU BEEN ABROAD SINCE WORLD WAR II? _____

[see p. 314]

[55] ON THE AVERAGE, AND NOT COUNTING VACATIONS, HOW OFTEN DO YOU GO MORE THAN 100 MILES AWAY FROM HOME? (check only one)

☐	☐	☐	☐	☐
never	once or twice a year	every two or three months	every month	once a week or more

[see p. 393]

[56] AS YOU SEE IT, HOW GREAT ARE THE OPPORTUNITIES FOR THE INDIVIDUAL CITIZEN TO INFLUENCE GOVERNMENTAL AND PUBLIC OPINION ON FOREIGN POLICY QUESTIONS? (check only one)

☐	☐	☐	☐	☐
enormous	large	moderate	small	nonexistent

[see p. 358]

[57] WHEN THE ISSUES LISTED AT THE LEFT ARE UNDER CONSIDERATION BY CONGRESS, WITH HOW MUCH ATTENTION DO YOU FOLLOW THE VARIOUS LEGISLATIVE STAGES THROUGH WHICH EACH PASSES?
(place *one* check in *each* row)

	great attention	considerable attention	some attention	little attention	no attention
nuclear testing	☐	☐	☐	☐	☐
federal tax reduction	☐	☐	☐	☐	☐
foreign aid	☐	☐	☐	☐	☐
tariff reduction	☐	☐	☐	☐	☐
civil rights	☐	☐	☐	☐	☐
agricultural surpluses	☐	☐	☐	☐	☐

[see p. 440]

[58] IN GENERAL, HOW WOULD YOU CHARACTERIZE THE PROBABILITY THAT THE OFFICIALS LISTED AT THE LEFT WILL ACT ACCORDING TO PUBLIC OPINION ON QUESTIONS OF PUBLIC POLICY?
(place *one* check in *each* row)

	extremely probable	very probable	somewhat probable	hardly probable	not at all probable
Local officials	☐	☐	☐	☐	☐
the Governor of your State	☐	☐	☐	☐	☐
Members of your State Legislature	☐	☐	☐	☐	☐
the President	☐	☐	☐	☐	☐

	extremely probable	very probable	somewhat probable	hardly probable	not at all probable
Members of Congress	☐	☐	☐	☐	☐
United Nations officials or delegates	☐	☐	☐	☐	☐

[see p. 359]

[59] IN YOUR OPINION, HOW MUCH INFLUENCE DID THE GROUPS LISTED AT THE LEFT EXERT IN CONVINCING THE CONGRESS TO PASS THE 1964 CIVIL RIGHTS ACT? (place *one* check in *each* row)

	none	very little	a moderate amount	a large amount	an enormous amount
leading educators	☐	☐	☐	☐	☐
civil rights groups	☐	☐	☐	☐	☐
business leaders	☐	☐	☐	☐	☐
journalists and commentators	☐	☐	☐	☐	☐
labor leaders	☐	☐	☐	☐	☐
church leaders	☐	☐	☐	☐	☐
others (specify)	☐	☐	☐	☐	☐

[see p. 362]

DERIVATION OF THE INDEX SCORES

I. THE INDEX OF LETTER-WRITING ACTIVITIES

a. Weights attached to the designated categories

(1) In Item #3 the components were scored as follows:

    0   "No" to all seven parts of the item

  +25   "No" to six of the parts

  +50   "No" to four or five of the parts

  +75   "No" to two or three of the parts

 +100   "No" to none or only one of the parts

(2) In Item #10 the components were scored as follows for each of the seven specified types of letter recipients:

    0   none
   50 1–3
   75 4–6
   90 7–9
  100 10 or more

b. Rules governing construction of the index

  (1) Each respondent's index score was compiled by summing his weighted answers to Item #3 and each of the seven main parts of Item #10 to which responses were made; this sum was then divided by the number of weighted answers.

  (2) If the number of weighted answers was less than three, either because Item #3 was not answered and no more than two parts of Item #10 were answered or because Item #3 was answered but no more than one part of Item #10 was answered, no score was calculated and the degree of the respondent's letter-writing activities was considered "undeterminable."

II. THE INDEX OF ORGANIZATIONAL ACTIVITIES

a. Weights attached to the designated categories

  (1) In Item #1 the components were scored as follows:

    0   "No"
   20 "Yes," in one organization or number of organizations not indicated
   40 "Yes," in two organizations
   60 "Yes," in three organizations
   70 "Yes," in four organizations
   80 "Yes," in five organizations
   90 "Yes," in six to ten organizations
  100 "Yes," in eleven or more organizations

  (2) In Item #2 the components were scored as follows:

    0   never
   20 once a year
   40 three times a year
   60 six times a year
   80 once a month
  100 every week

b. Rules governing construction of the index

    (1) Each respondent's index score was compiled by summing his weighted answers and dividing the sum by the number of weighted answers.

    (2) If neither Item #1 nor #2 was answered, no score was calculated and the degree of the respondent's organizational activities was considered "undeterminable."

THE MOBILIZING STIMULI

[The following are reproductions of the cards that the ADA sent out in an effort to mobilize support for the Nuclear Test Ban Treaty of 1963 and the Civil Rights Act of 1964. As indicated in Chapter 5, these served as the stimuli to the behavior that is subjected to empirical analysis in Chapters 6–12.]

YOU MUST ACT NOW . . . .
August, 1963
for the TEST BAN TREATY

Washington Report:

A treaty banning all nuclear explosions except those underground has been signed by the UK, USA, and USSR. Efforts by both Republican and Democratic Administrations have finally succeeded.

The treaty is before the Senate awaiting ratification. A two-thirds vote is required. 67 of 100 Senators must vote "yea". This is always a tough majority to obtain; remember Senate rejection of the League of Nations. The test ban vote will be equally crucial.

Most Senators are taking a "wait and see" position. They are waiting to see how their constituents feel. Extremists and Cold Warriors are doing battle with their pens. Their letters have tilted mail 9 to 1 *against* the treaty in some states. Only a deluge of letters supporting the treaty and urging a "yea" vote can win the overwhelming approval needed for this crucial forward step.

The Test Ban Treaty Will:

• Be a first step away from nuclear catastrophe and toward a reduction of tensions.

• Increase US security far more than would any benefits derived from continued uncontrolled testing.

• Open the way to further East-West exchanges making possible progress toward world law.

• Greatly reduce the dangers of radioactive fallout and contamination of food and bodies.

• Limit substantially the proliferation of nuclear weapons among more and more nations.

Urgent Action: Write short letters to the four persons below stating your strong support for this vital step toward peace. Urge them to declare publicly their support. Tell them you and your neighbors want this treaty. Raise your voice as if the treaty depends on you alone. Tomorrow will be too late to wish you had.

BOTH U.S. Senators
Senate Office Building
Washington 25, D.C.

Your U.S. Representative
House Office Building
Washington 25, D.C.

President John F. Kennedy
The White House
Washington, D.C.

Return Please:

CONFIRMATION OF ACTION ON THE TEST BAN TREATY

I wrote Senator . . . .

I wrote Senator . . . .

I wrote Representative . . . .
and I wrote the President too!　　☐

(Please Print)

Name . . . .

Street . . . .

City . . . .

<u>You</u> must act now . . .
for civil rights legislation

Washington Report:

Half the job is finished. The House of Representatives has passed the best piece of civil rights legislation in history. It isn't perfect—but it is a good bill. When passed it will be of enormous assistance in winning full equality for all Americans.

As you know, in many parts of our country hundreds of people are being jailed, beaten, punished for trying to exercise their constitutional rights. This must stop. The legislation before the U.S. Senate can help correct this terrible, tragic situation, but to win its passage we need your participation.

Not Everyone Can Be a Leader, But There Is a Way You Can Help

The bill has to overcome a Senate filibuster. Just as majority rule succeeded in the House, so WITH YOUR HELP majority rule can succeed in the Senate.

The U.S. Senate is now the battleground for civil rights legislation. Democracy is a government of the people, responsive to the expressed will of the people. If you are for civil rights, if you believe democracy means full equality under law, it is not only your opportunity but your responsibility to work for effective civil rights legislation. Only in this way can we attack discrimination in the land. Only in this way can we challenge the police dogs, the billy clubs, the fire hoses, and the electric cattle prods.

Write, Visit, or Wire Your U.S. Senators

Urge them to support the bill approved by the House of Representatives (H.R. 7152). This bill, enacted into law, will aid the achievement of full equality for all and will make possible the use of law by the Federal government to protect the right of everyone to full equality in voting, employment, public accommodations, Federal funds, and education. The road ahead is long and arduous but this law will help!

YOU CAN HELP! Visit, write, or wire your Senators immediately. Let them know how strongly you feel that civil rights legislation must pass the Congress in 1964. (Get your friends to do the same.)

Write the President

Urge him to use the power of his office to support H.R. 7152 intact. (Get your friends to do the same.)

(Tear Off)

....

CONFIRMATION OF ACTION ON CIVIL RIGHTS

I contacted Senators . . . . :

I wrote the President too . . . .

I want more information on civil rights legislative action . . . .

(Please Print)   Name . . . .

Street . . . .

City . . . .

INDEX